THE RELIGIOUS HISTOI

THE RELIGIOUS HISTORY OF WALES

Religious Life and Practice in Wales
From the Seventeenth Century
to the Present Day

Edited by Richard C. Allen and David Ceri Jones
with Trystan O. Hughes

Welsh Academic Press

Published in Wales by Welsh Academic Press, an imprint of

Ashley Drake Publishing Ltd
PO Box 733
Cardiff
CF14 7ZY

www.welsh-academic-press.com

First Impression – 2014

ISBN
978 1 86057 079 7

British Library Cataloguing-in-Publication Data.
A CIP catalogue for this book is available from the British Library.

Typeset by White Lotus Infotech Pvt. Ltd, Puducherry, India
Printed and bound by CPI Group (UK) Ltd, Croydon, CR0 4YY

CONTENTS

ACKNOWLEDGEMENTS

The editors would like to thank the contributors to this volume for their dedication, and for responding thoughtfully and with notable patience to our editorial queries and suggestions. We trust that they are pleased with the published version of their chapters. The examination of these religious communities will, it is hoped, provide the foundations for future studies in the religious history of Wales.

We are grateful to Ashley Drake and the Welsh Academic Press for agreeing to publish the collection. Finally, we would like to thank our wives and families as well as our friends and colleagues for their support and encouragement.

INTRODUCTION

Richard C. Allen and David Ceri Jones

A study of the history of religious identities in Wales needs to be carefully situated within wider developments in the British Isles as a whole and pay due attention to the still wider international scene. Cultural commentators and critics loudly proclaim the death of Christian Britain. The churches, having largely failed to offer any resistance to the inexorable march of modernity and its concomitant secularization,[1] have contributed as much as anyone to the dawning of a post-Christian era.[2] Yet, while organized Christianity in Britain, as in much of Western Europe, has been in terminal decline for much of the twentieth century, there is ample evidence to suggest that a significant proportion of the British population might actually attach much greater importance to religious belonging than appears on the surface to be the case. The 2001 Census perplexed many when it revealed that 77 per cent of the population of Britain reported themselves as having a religious affiliation, and that 71.6 per cent actually registered as being Christian. In Wales, a mere 19 per cent of the population claimed to have no religious belief whatsoever.[3] While interpreting these figures is fraught with difficulties, they do reveal a highly resilient residual attachment to religious belief, and to Christianity in particular, despite the obvious discrepancy they reveal between religious belief and religious practice.

This picture is complicated still further when one looks at the outpouring of emotion that followed the death of Diana, Princess of Wales, in August 1997, a grief that was eventually channelled into a state funeral according to the time-honoured rites of the Church of England.[4] On a slightly less dramatic scale in Britain at least, the death of Pope John Paul II in 2005 once again revealed the existence of powerful deep-seated religious emotions.[5] In the world of the early twenty-first century, far from quietly retreating to the margins of society, religion has once again returned to the centre of public discourse. The rise of religious fundamentalism, often in an aggressive and belligerent form, seen most powerfully in the terrorist attacks on the twin towers of the World Trade Centre in New York in September 2001, has alerted many in the West to the power and challenge of radically politicised, mainly Islamic, religious groups. The advent of the 'new atheism' in Britain and North America has similarly made questions about the role of religion in the public sphere a hot topic. And, of course, globalisation has had a significant impact. This has shifted the balance of power within world Christianity away from Western Europe towards what is now termed the Global South, a region that takes in sub-Saharan Africa, much of the Far East and China in particular,[6] a shift which can be seen most starkly perhaps in recent debates over human sexuality within the global Anglican communion.[7]

The contemporary situation in Wales mirrors, to a greater or lesser degree, the picture in the rest of the British Isles. While the traditional Christian denominations have effectively been marginalised in contemporary Wales, there are signs that some Christian communities are experiencing growth, however moderate. Evangelical groups, which usually combine theological conservatism with a progressive, even innovative, attitude towards their host culture, have appeared better equipped to put up at least some resistance to the downward trend in religious adherence. There has also been a diversification in the religious landscape of modern Wales. Although the 2001 Census indicated that only two per cent of the Welsh population belonged to an ethnic minority, Wales does nevertheless possess a multi-ethnic and a multi-faith structure. Grahame Davies has argued that this

> percentage is growing, and dualistic views of identity are becoming more and more inadequate, especially as a newly-devolved Wales develops a civic, as opposed to an ethnically-based, identity. And a binary vision, although conveniently simple, has never really been true of the reality in Wales, a country which has hosted significant minorities for very many years.[8]

In response to some of these developments, and as a means of reaching out to the diverse range of Christian religious groups, Cytûn: Eglwysi Ynghyd yng Nghymru (Churches Together in Wales) was launched in 1990 with the aim of encouraging understanding among some of the traditional Christian Churches and Denominations. At present it comprises as full-members: the Baptist Union of Wales, the Church in Wales, the Congregational Federation, the Covenanted Baptist Churches (BUGB), the German Speaking Lutheran Church in South Wales, the Methodist Church, the Presbyterian Church of Wales, the Religious Society of Friends, the Roman Catholic Church, the Salvation Army, the Union of Welsh Independents and the United Reformed Church. There are a number of other interested bodies who act as observers, and these include: the Black Majority Churches in Wales, Churches Together in Britain and Ireland, the Free Church Council of Wales, the Lutheran Council of Great Britain, the Orthodox Churches and the Seventh Day Adventists. By bringing people together from different religions and traditions it is hoped that an exchange of ideas and, more significantly, an appreciation of the different belief systems will encourage a better understanding of the rich diversity of religious worship in Wales.[9] In conjunction with Cytûn, ENFYS (The Commission of the Covenanted Churches) was established in 1975 and other inter-church organisations, both in Wales and elsewhere, have provided forums for churches and religious denominations to cultivate reciprocal understanding. In July 2000 Canolfan Astudiaethau Ecwmenaidd Genedlaethol Cymru (The National Centre for Ecumenical Studies) was launched at Trinity College, Carmarthen, the first academic institution in Wales to provide a centre for ecumenical studies. It encourages an 'appreciation and study of ecumenism', and proposes 'inter-church dialogue and joint Christian action for justice and reconciliation'.[10] Yet, much of this activity has been carried on without the support and active participation of the majority of evangelical Christians who, by any reckoning, must be both the most numerous and most highly motivated group of religious believers in contemporary Wales. Suspicious of the reductionism inherent in the ecumenical project, they have often preferred to stand apart in order to maintain their doctrinal purity and conservative stance.

The purpose of this collection of essays is to offer an insight into the contemporary religious diversity of Wales. It does this by adopting a largely, though not exclusively historical approach, charting the gradual proliferation of religious communities in Wales since the sixteenth-century Reformation. There are a number of good general studies on the history of religion in the British Isles, some of which touch on developments in Wales at relevant points.[11] Similarly, series such as the Oxford History of the Christian Church,[12] and the Religion, Politics and Society in Britain series, published by Longman,[13] contain much on Welsh developments. There have also been a plethora of detailed academic studies on individual religious communities in Wales, indeed this has been one of the traditional strengths of Welsh historiography.[14] What there has not been hitherto is a collection which attempts to explore the religious multiplicity of Wales. The essays offered here are by no means intended to be definitive studies, and many will be surpassed by more detailed and comprehensive analyses no doubt, but they do offer the reader a broad-brushed picture of the history of religious change from the sixteenth century to the present day. Regrettably this volume has been unable to provide modern studies of Buddhism and Hinduism despite making every attempt to do so.

It is, of course, a truism to say that Christianity has played an enormously important role in the history and development of Wales and the Welsh. One need not necessarily have to agree entirely with R. Tudur Jones' assertion that by 1890 Wales was a Christian country[15] to appreciate the extent to which the Christian faith, especially in the guise of Protestant nonconformity, became gradually interwoven into the Welsh national consciousness from the sixteenth century onwards. Yet that has often occurred hand-in-hand with a splintering of Welsh Christian identity. For the first fifteen hundred years or so of its existence the Christian Church in Wales was a unified entity. The Welsh Church, initially Celtic, but then Roman Catholic, held a virtual monopoly over religious life and belief in the country, there was simply no such thing as religious diversity. The teachings of Jesus Christ were in all likelihood first brought to Wales by Roman traders and soldiers, probably before 'Wales' actually existed as a distinct national or cultural entity.[16] The subsequent development of a distinctly Celtic Church owed much to the itinerant evangelism of the 'Celtic Saints' who, in the three hundred years from the fifth to the eighth centuries, won the Welsh over to a much deeper commitment to the Christian faith. But the 'Celtic Saints' propagated an extremely ascetic form of Christianity which owed much to Eastern expressions of the faith, and their introduction and encouragement of the monastic way of life ensured that the monastery came to play a far more prominent role in the Welsh Church than it tended to do elsewhere.[17] This is not to say that the Welsh Church did not develop some of the other elements of ecclesiastical administration; bishops emerged relatively early, for example, but the pre-Norman Welsh Church developed along more *ad hoc* lines and lacked an efficient parochial and diocesan system. The popular spirituality of the Welsh Church at this time was characterised by the adoration of the saints, especially devotion to their native saints, David, Bueno and Cadog.

It was the coming of the Normans that ended the quasi-independence of the Welsh Church. When Bishop Urban of Llandaff swore obedience to the Archbishop of Canterbury in 1107, the Welsh Church effectively came under the control of the English state, and a more efficient diocesan and parochial system was established.[18] The Welsh Church was now firmly plugged into the main currents of the wider continental Catholic Church. New Latin-style monastic groups, such as the Cistercians, struck a chord with the Welsh, as did the Franciscans and Benedictines later in the thirteenth century.[19] While the fortunes of Welsh Christianity ebbed and flowed throughout the Middle Ages, it is hard to escape the conclusion that this was a period suffused by Christianity at every level, one in which it became ever more closely intertwined with Welsh identity.[20] The conquest of Wales in 1282 merely integrated the Welsh Church more fully into the English ecclesiastical hierarchy, but this did not preclude a remarkable flowering of Welsh-language scholarship, much of which was based in and around the Welsh monastic communities. Owain Glyndŵr's attempts to secure both political and ecclesiastical independence for Wales in the early fifteenth century proved only temporarily attractive,[21] but the Welsh Church had been decimated by the Black Death and in all likelihood lacked the resources to stand apart from Canterbury. In the wake of the Glyndŵr rebellion in the early fifteenth century, far from suffering further decline the Welsh Church actually experienced a measure of renewal. There is ample evidence to suggest that on the eve of the Reformation there had been a revival of lay piety in Wales as elsewhere, based on the traditional Welsh dedication to the veneration of the saints and the rhythms of regular pilgrimage to the shrines of the saints and the many holy wells dotted around the Welsh countryside.[22]

It was the Protestant Reformation, crystallised in the British Isles by Henry VIII's split from the Roman Catholic Church in 1533 and the creation of the Church of England by Elizabeth I in 1559, which effectively introduced an element of diversity into the religious life of the Welsh for the first time. More out of a sense of loyalty to the Tudors than anything else, the Welsh transferred their allegiance to the new Church of England, becoming Protestants at least on paper. It was only as the early generations of Welsh Protestants valiantly endeavoured to translate the Bible and the Book of Common Prayer into the Welsh language, and convince the Welsh that the new Church of England actually represented a return to the uncorrupted pre-Catholic Celtic church, that Protestantism began to make sense to the inhabitants of Wales, and a more thoroughgoing acceptance of the new faith was secured.[23] The Church in Wales, as John Morgan-Guy's chapter demonstrates, has remained at the heart of Welsh Christianity since the Reformation, although its fortunes have fluctuated, often in direct response to the strength and confidence of the nonconformist denominations. While the nonconformists remained of marginal importance, throughout much of the sixteenth, seventeenth and the majority of the eighteenth centuries, the Anglican Church gained the respect and allegiance of most people in Wales by default and was able to maintain its position with relatively little effort. The growth of nonconformity, particularly in the nineteenth century, eventually brought about the disestablishment of the Church of England in Wales in 1922 and pushed it into a more peripheral role. It is surely no coincidence that the decline of nonconformity in twentieth century Wales has allowed the Church in Wales to once more regain its place at the heart of Christian practice in Wales.

It was not until the seventeenth century that realistic alternatives to the Church of England began to gain a foothold in Wales. Guto ap Gwynfor's chapter shows how the Independent congregation at Llanfaches in Monmouthshire, founded by William Wroth in 1629, became the inspiration for other dissenting groups. While it proved to be short-lived, in its wake other groups also attempted to establish themselves in Wales. The Baptists and Quakers, dealt with here in detail in the chapters by Hugh Matthews and Richard C. Allen, emerged during the tumultuous years of the Interregnum and its aftermath.[24] Together these three groups represented the older dissenting tradition in Wales, the Independents and Baptists eventually becoming the backbone of nonconformist Wales. The seventeenth century also witnessed the dogged survival of Roman Catholicism in Wales; although as Trystan Hughes' chapter shows anti-Catholic recusancy legislation kept numbers pretty low, limited largely to those who came within the orbit of a number of prominent traditionally Catholic families. The 'old faith' was far from an insignificant feature of the Welsh religious landscape. The toleration of Catholicism in 1828–9, and the large influx of Irish immigrants into south Wales from the 1840s onwards made Catholicism a much more visible presence in Wales, something abundantly clear by the upsurge of anti-Catholic agitation by the end of the nineteenth century.[25]

For much of the sixteenth and seventeenth centuries, the Welsh had found the pace of religious change bewildering, perhaps even slightly underwhelming. While they were won over to at least a tacit acceptance of the Anglican Church, more by default than anything else, they proved deeply resistant to those more demanding forms of Protestantism represented by the puritans. In the eighteenth century, overtly evangelical groups, in a number of forms, began to win the Welsh over to a much more enthusiastic and participatory form of Protestantism. While historians debate whether eighteenth-century Wales witnessed what amounted to a religious great awakening,[26] by the end of the century the religious complexion of the country had genuinely been transformed. The spiritual energy unleashed by the evangelical revival resulted, among other things, in the establishment of the first Protestant religious movement that was indigenous to Wales. Calvinistic Methodism, as Eryn M. White shows in her chapter, despite beginning life within the Church of England, was to become Wales' largest and most influential nonconformist denomination, following secession from the established church in 1811.

The evangelical revival also gave birth to a number of other groups that enjoyed a presence in eighteenth-century Wales. Methodism in its Wesleyan form struggled to get off the ground at least during the lifetime of its founder, and it was not until the early years of the nineteenth century, as David Ceri Jones shows, that Wesleyan Methodism began to become more established in some parts of Wales. Yet its growth was never as spectacular as its Calvinist counterpart, the many divisions within Wesleyan ranks undoubtedly contributing to this, but it also suffered from an image problem, the Welsh branch of Wesleyan Methodism often appearing more like an extension of the English Wesleyanism than a properly and thoroughly indigenised denomination. The fortunes of Wesleyan Methodism illustrate the reasons why some religious groups fared better in Wales than others; it was to be those denominational groups that proved themselves most adaptable to some of the distinguishing features of Welsh society and culture that would succeed in putting down the deepest roots in Welsh soil.

There was also room around the outer edges of the Welsh religious landscape for smaller groups to negotiate some space in which to operate. John Morgan-Guy's chapter on the Moravians looks at some of the reasons why this missionary-minded pietist denomination struggled to establish more than a toehold in Wales. Despite initially attracting some disgruntled Methodists to its Welsh congregations in Caernarfonshire and Haverfordwest in the 1750s, the Moravians proved unable to build on this initial foundation, largely as a consequence of the poor leadership offered by some of the Welsh Moravian pioneers. A number of preaching stations and Moravian chapels remained open in Wales but, as in England, Moravianism never really became a realistic alternative to Methodism, the last of its Welsh churches in Haverfordwest finally closed its doors in 1957. Of more indigenous growth Unitarianism, as Euros Lloyd shows, had a relatively limited appeal in Wales where Trinitarian evangelicalism enjoyed hegemonic dominance. Where that influence was weaker, as in the infamous *Smotyn Du* in Carmarthenshire, anti-trinitarian churches found enough space to exist with a measure of freedom.

Despite the spectacular growth of Protestant nonconformity in nineteenth century Wales, that saw its close coalescence with Welsh national identity,[27] there were actually relatively few new players on the Welsh religious scene. While the re-establishment of the Roman Catholic hierarchy in England in 1850 gave Welsh Catholics greater visibility, they were hardly a new religious movement! The exception was the Salvation Army which, as Jenny Fairbank shows, first appeared in Wales following a mission conducted by William Booth and his wife in Cardiff during 1863. Its aggressive evangelism in some of the most depressed neighbourhoods in the city was the backdrop for concerted attempts to extend its missionary activity to some of the other urban areas of Wales; the combination of a simple evangelical message and a commitment to practical help for those in need, undoubtedly stood in stark contrast to a nonconformity, with the notable exception of the Forward Movement of the Calvinistic Methodists,[28] that had become increasingly respectable and largely concerned with following a more politicised agenda.

At the margins of nineteenth-century Welsh religious life, there were small groups of slightly unorthodox religious believers. One of the unintended consequences of the American Second Great Awakening, which had begun in the closing years of the eighteenth century and lasted until the mid-nineteenth century, was the proliferation of less orthodox religious sects.[29] The first of these to appear on Welsh soil was the Church of the Latter-day Saints (Mormons) who, as Ronald Dennis' chapter outlines, founded their first assembly at Merthyr in 1842. Links with the United States remained strong and a significant proportion of Welsh Mormon converts made the journey across the Atlantic to re-settle in Utah throughout the twentieth century. Followers of Charles Taze Russell did not establish a presence in Wales until 1907. The Jehovah's Witnesses attracted some public antipathy during the twentieth century, but like the Mormons, they have been able to maintain a small, but often highly visible presence in Wales on account of their members long-standing commitment to street and door-to-door evangelism. Much less significant has been the Seventh-day Adventist Church which, despite opening its first congregation in Aberystwyth as a consequence of the preaching of the evangelist A. A. Johns in 1885, has struggled to establish a higher public profile for reasons outlined in detail in Brian Phillips' chapter.

These new religious movements anticipated the increased diversification, even polarisation, which took place in Welsh religious life, during the turbulent years of the twentieth century. The century, of course, was dominated by the decline of institutional Christianity in Wales. However, it is too easy to adopt a teleological approach to religious developments in twentieth-century Wales. For many of those caught up in the Welsh Revival of 1904–5, religion seemed to be in very robust health, while the suggestion that this was to be the last awakening of its kind for a century and more would have bewildered most of its participants. The 1904 Revival gave birth to a plethora of new religious groups in Wales and further afield, all united by their stress on the immediacy of the ministry of the third person of the Trinity, the Holy Spirit, evidenced by the regular use of ecstatic spiritual gifts. Some of these Pentecostal groups, as David Ceri Jones shows in his chapter, owed their origins to either a number of highly charismatic Welsh individuals or were actually first established in Wales. It has been the impressive global spread of Pentecostalism that has proven to be one of the most remarkable religious transformations of the twentieth century. There are now perhaps 500 million Pentecostals around the world and thus they comprise at least ten per cent of the global Christian population.[30] Recent statistical information also suggests that Pentecostal churches are the fastest growing churches in the British Isles,[31] and they remain among the few religious communities in contemporary Wales to be able to buck the downward trend.

For many in the traditional Christian churches the obvious answer to the marginalisation of Christianity during the second half of the twentieth century was to follow the ecumenical agenda. Noel Davies demonstrates that Wales has had a long tradition of engagement with the ecumenical project, right back to its birth in the world missionary conference in Edinburgh in 1910.[32] The first ecumenical body in Wales was formed in 1929, and along with its many successors much effort has been invested in facilitating a better understanding of the various religious denominations in Wales. Yet the kind of institutional unity that the ecumenical programme dreamed of in its more optimistic moments has been fraught with as many difficulties in Wales as elsewhere. The only success story, as Robert Pope reveals, has been the United Reformed Church, an amalgamation of the Presbyterian Church of England and the Congregational Church of England and Wales which was finally constituted in June 1972. Other attempts to facilitate more meaningful expressions of unity, at least on an institutional basis, have tended to founder even on into the twenty-first century.[33]

Not all Welsh Christians, however, have engaged enthusiastically with the ecumenical agenda. For some evangelical Christians, in particular, the ecumenical programme has been viewed with grave suspicion, charged with promoting a kind of lowest common denominator type of Christianity, where the emphasis has been on inclusivity rather than a clearly defined core of Christian belief. This has led some evangelicals, though not all it must be said, to withdraw from the traditional denominations and to establish and, with more difficulty, attempt to sustain doctrinally pure churches. As David Ceri Jones has observed, many of these evangelicals have formed their own associational networks, the largest being the Evangelical Movement of Wales, but the churches which it represents have often turned out to be fissiparous. As with most other groups of Welsh Christians they have been unable to resist decline or connect with modern generations of Welsh people.

The twentieth century witnessed the diversification of Welsh religious life in a further highly significant way, particularly the emergence of groups which did not belong to one or other of the major Christian religious traditions.[34] Their arrival has injected an element of religious diversity and plurality into Welsh society for the first time, but their enculturation has been more successful in some cases than others. Despite being present in Wales since the mid-eighteenth century, Wales has never had particularly large Jewish communities. Where they have existed they have been concentrated in some of the main urban communities of south Wales, Cardiff, Swansea and Merthyr Tydfil in particular. While there has been evidence of some anti-semitism, particularly in the early decades of the twentieth century, Lavinia Cohn-Sherbok's chapter argues that the small Jewish communities that have been sustained in Wales have enjoyed the toleration and respect of the Welsh people. The same may be said for the small communities of Muslims in Wales. Arriving first in the 1860s and then in successive waves throughout the second half of the twentieth century, firstly from Somalia and then the Indian sub-continent in the main, Muslims in Wales, as Muzafar Jilani shows, have experienced little hostility. The reason for this might be largely due to their smaller numbers and less conspicuous presence than in some of the larger English cities, but even in more recent times and in the wake of the terrorist attacks against America in September 2001 and London in July 2005, Welsh Muslim communities have not experienced significant levels of harassment or hostility. A similar story may be told of the smaller numbers of Sikhs in Wales who, as Shinder Thandi's chapter demonstrates, have made significant contributions to the economic, social, political and cultural life of those parts of Wales in which they have successfully settled.

The above contribution also holds true for other non-Christian communities in Wales. It is estimated that there are approximately 5,000 Buddhists and an additional 5,000 Hindus currently living in Wales.[35] Buddhism has had a presence in the country from the late-1970s when retreat centres were first established. While these have been limited in their impact, the establishment of smaller community-based groups throughout Wales have proven more successful in popularising aspects of their spirituality.[36] As with Buddhism, the establishment of Hindu communities in Wales is fairly recent and most Hindus settled in the country after World War Two. In 1991 the Hindu Cultural Association (HCA Wales) was founded in order to 'facilitate seamless integration of the Indian Community to the wider local community'. It encourages people of non-Indian backgrounds to become better acquainted with Hinduism and they provide classes which facilitate the learning of Indian languages, classical music, dance, yoga, Hindu philosophy, culture, tradition and mantras. Moreover, the HCA Wales provides 'help and support for [the] isolated, vulnerable and marginalised in the community by encouraging them to participate and to develop self confidence', and supports younger Hindus in the development of skills that will 'keep them engaged in a constructive way'.[37]

Followers of the Bahá'í Faith, as Vivian Bartlett shows, have been active in Wales since the late 1940s, and by the 1980s they had opened fourteen local spiritual Assemblies in different parts of Wales. Yet it is likely that the relatively small numbers of actual followers of these Eastern religions does not fully reflect the level of interest that exists in certain aspects of Eastern spirituality, for some the disciplines associated with meditation, for example, gives them the opportunity to reintegrate a spiritual dimension into their lives. The Welsh experience of other faiths has, therefore, been positive. As Paul Chambers argues, recognising the reality of religious pluralism and tolerating ethnic diversity is one thing, but it can occasionally falls short of the kind of unqualified acceptance of the right of minority groups to practice their faith that is surely the hallmark of a thoroughly tolerant society.[38] For too long the religious complexion of Wales has been locked into an earlier stereotype which emphasised the interchangeability of mine and chapel or a timeless Christian orthodoxy. Wales, as this volume demonstrates, is a land of greater religious plurality than some have registered. This speaks to the distinctive spirituality of Welsh culture and history, and the way that its people continue to reach out for something meaningful beyond the material world. In doing so, they have embraced a remarkably broad spectrum of faith and belief.

Notes

1. One need only read Richard Dawkins, *The God Delusion* (2nd edn. London, 2007) for confirmation of this popular perception.
2. See Paul Chambers, *Religion, Secularization and Social Change: Congregational Studies in a Post-Christian Society* (Cardiff, 2003).
3. Figures quoted in Keith Robbins, *England, Ireland, Scotland, Wales: The Christian Church 1900–2000* (Oxford, 2009), p. 471.
4. Willem Marie Speelman, 'The "Feast" of Diana's Death', in P. Post, G. Rouwhorst, L. van Tongeren and A. Scheer (eds), *Christian Feast and Festival: The Dynamics of Western Liturgy and Culture* (Leuven, 2001), pp. 775–801.
5. Grace Davie, 'A Papal Funeral and a Royal Wedding: reconfiguring religion in the twenty-first century', in Jane Garnett, Matthew Grimley, Alana Harris, William Whyte and Sarah Williams (eds), *Redefining Christian Britain: Post–1945 Perspectives* (London, 2007), pp. 110–12.
6. Philip Jenkins, *The Next Christianity: The Coming of Global Christianity* (New York, 2007).
7. Philip Jenkins, *The New Faces of Christianity: Believing the Bible in the Global South* (New York, 2006); Miranda K. Hassett, *Anglican Communion in Crisis: How Episcopal Dissidents and their African Allies are Re-Shaping Anglicanism* (Princeton, 2007).
8. Grahame Davies, 'Welsh and Jewish: Responses to Wales by Jewish Writers', in James Gifford and Gabrielle Zezulka-Mailloux (eds), *Culture and the State, Vol. III: Nationalisms* (4 vols. Edmonton, 2003), p. 211.
9. For details of Cytûn see http://www.cytun.org.uk/ (accessed March 2010).
10. See their website: http://www.trinity-cm.ac.uk/english/wnces/background.asp (accessed November 2009). Due to recent changes in Higher Education, particularly the merger of the University of Wales, Lampeter and the University of Wales, Trinity College, Carmarthen, the website is now redundant.
11. See, for example, Sheridan Gilley and W. J. Shiels (eds), *A History of Religion in Britain: Practice and Belief from Pre-Roman Times to the Present* (Oxford, 1994).

12. See Felicity Heal, *Reformation in Britain and Ireland* (Oxford, 2003); Keith Robbins, *England, Ireland, Scotland, Wales: The Christian Church, 1900–2000* (Oxford, 2008).
13. See Nigel Yates, *Eighteenth Century Britain: Religion and Politics, 1714–1815* (London, 2007); Callum Brown, *Religion and Society in Twentieth-Century Britain* (London, 2006).
14. R. Tudur Jones, *Congregationalism in Wales* (ed. Robert Pope) (Cardiff, 2004); T. M. Bassett, *The Welsh Baptists* (Swansea, 1977); Richard C. Allen, *Quaker Communities in Early Modern Wales: From Resistance to Respectability* (Cardiff, 2007); Trystan Owain Hughes, *Winds of Change: The Roman Catholic Church and Society in Wales, 1916–1962* (Cardiff, 1999); Glanmor Williams, William Jacob, Nigel Yates and Frances Knight, *The Welsh Church from Reformation to Disestablishment, 1603–1920* (Cardiff, 2007).
15. R. Tudur Jones, *Faith and the Crisis of a Nation: Wales 1890–1914* (ed. Robert Pope) (Cardiff, 2004), p. 1.
16. Christopher J. Arnold and Jeffrey L. Davies, *Roman and Early Medieval Wales* (Stroud, 2000), pp. 132, 180–1.
17. Glanmor Williams, 'Fire on Cambria's Altar: The Welsh and their Religion', in idem., *The Welsh and their Religion: Historical Essays by Glanmor Williams* (Cardiff, 1991), p. 4.
18. David A. Carpenter, *The Struggle for Mastery: Britain, 1066–1284* (London, 2003), p. 139.
19. David H. Williams, *The Welsh Cistercians* (Leominster, 2001).
20. Glanmor Williams, *Religion, Language and Nationality in Wales* (Cardiff, 1979), p. 7ff.
21. R. R. Davies, *The Revolt of Owain Glyndŵr* (Oxford, 1995), pp. 169–73; Glanmor Williams, *The Welsh Church from Conquest to Reformation* (Cardiff, 1976), ch. 7.
22. Williams, *Welsh Church from Conquest to Reformation*, part II. For examples of pilgrimages and the veneration of saints see Madeleine Gray, 'Women of Holiness and Power: The cults of St Radegund and St Mary Magdalene at Usk', *Monmouthshire Antiquary*, XVIII (2002), 3–11.
23. Eryn M. White, *The Welsh Bible* (Stroud, 2007), ch. 2.
24. Lloyd Bowen, 'Oliver Cromwell ('alias' Williams) and Wales', in Patrick Little (ed.), *Oliver Cromwell: New Perspectives* (Houndmills, 2008), pp. 168–94.
25. Paul O'Leary, 'When was anti-Catholicism?', *Journal of Ecclesiastical History*, 56 (April, 2005), 308–25.
26. For differing perspectives, see Geraint H. Jenkins, *Literature, Religion and Society in Wales, 1660–1730* (Cardiff, 1978), pp. 305–9; Derec Llwyd Morgan, *The Great Awakening in Wales* (London, 1988); David Ceri Jones, '"A Glorious Morn"?: Methodism and the Rise of Evangelicalism in Wales, 1735–1762', in Mark Smith (ed.), *British Evangelical Identities: Past and Present, Volume 1: Aspects of the History and Sociology of Evangelicalism in Britain and Ireland* (Milton Keynes, 2009), pp. 97–113.
27. David Hempton, *Religion and Political Culture in Britain and Ireland: From the Glorious Revolution to the Decline of Empire* (Cambridge, 1996), pp. 49–63; E. Wyn James, '"The New Birth of a People": Welsh language and identity and the Welsh Methodists, c.1740–1820', in Robert Pope (ed.), *Religion and National Identity: Wales and Scotland c.1700–2000* (Cardiff, 2001), pp. 14–42.
28. Geraint D. Fielder, *Grit, Grace and Gumption: The Exploits of Evangelists John Pugh, Frank and Seth Joshua* (Fearn and Bryntirion, 2000).
29. Daniel Walker Howe, *What God Hath Wrought: The Transformation of America, 1815–1848* (New York, 2007), chs. 5 and 8.
30. http://www.bbc.co.uk/religion/religions/christianity/subdivisions/pentecostal_1.shtml (accessed January 2010).
31. Ibid.
32. Brian Stanley, *The World Missionary Conference: Edinburgh 1910* (Grand Rapids, MH, 2009).
33. John A. Newton, 'Protestant Nonconformists and Ecumenism', in Alan P. F. Sell and Anthony R. Cross (eds), *Protestant Nonconformity in the Twentieth Century* (Milton Keynes, 2003), p. 376.
34. See Paul Badham, 'Religious Pluralism in Modern Britain', in Gilley and Shiels (eds), *History of Religion in Britain*, pp. 488–502.
35. This data has been extracted from the BBC: religious and belief – multicultural Wales. See http://www.bbc.co.uk/wales/religion/sites/timeline/pages/religion_in_wales_15.shtml (accessed July 2010).
36. For details of Buddhism in Britain see World Buddhist Foundation, *100 years of Buddhism in the UK: The Buddhist Legacy of United Kingdom* (London, 2008); The Buddhist Society, *The Buddhist*

Directory: A Directory of Buddhist Societies and Organisations in the United Kingdom and Elsewhere, 2004–2006 (9th edn. London, 2003); R. Gethin, 'Buddhism in Britain: A Brief Sketch of its History and Development', in Lakshman S. Perera (ed.), *Buddhism for the New Millennium* (London, 2000), pp. 26–41. For details of the various Buddhist retreats, the Fellowship of the Western Buddhist Order and meditation classes in Wales see http://www.westernchanfellowship.org/; http://www.lamrim.org.uk; http://www.samatha.org/trust/; http://www.fwbo.org/index.php (all accessed May 2010).

37. Information regarding the HCA Wales is available at: http://indiacentrewales.com/ (accessed July 2010). For examples of Hindu centres in Wales see http://www.hindupuja.co.uk/; http://www.skandavale.org/index.htm (accessed July 2010). For a wider study of Hinduism in the United Kingdom see Richard Burghart (ed.), *Hinduism in Great Britain: The Perpetuation of Religion in an Alien Cultural Milieu* (London, 1987).

38. Paul Chambers, 'Religious Diversity in Wales', in Charlotte Williams, Neil Evans and Paul O'Leary (eds), *A Tolerant Nation: Exploring Ethnic Diversity in Wales* (Cardiff, 2003), p. 136.

CHAPTER 1

THE CHURCH IN WALES

John Morgan-Guy

Even for those today who have little or no formal association with the institutional church, or contact with its worshipping life, the word 'parish', and its derivative, 'parochial', remain familiar. To be 'parochial' in one's concerns is to have a viewpoint which is restricted or confined; and when conversation is described as 'parish-pump', then it is likely to be local gossip. Thus the name of a defined territorial unit, designed to facilitate the ministry of a priest to the people committed to his care, has, over the centuries, achieved proverbial status – albeit with somewhat negative connotations. The essential meaning has not been, however, totally obscured. The parish is a localized community, a neighbourhood (the Greek word *paroikos* from which it ultimately derives means 'dwelling beside'); its parish church the *locus* for the public worship of its residents. At the latest from the twelfth or thirteenth centuries almost every inhabitant of England and Wales resided within a parish. As John Moorman wrote, 'by the thirteenth century the parish boundaries were all firmly drawn ... moreover, not only were they firmly drawn, they were also rigidly observed, so that each parish was a self-contained community'.[1]

England and Wales contained some 10,000 of such self-contained communities, and, as Bishop Moorman concluded,

> by far the majority of these were country parishes, covering a good many acres and often containing a number of villages or hamlets. The average population was about 300. It was, therefore, to a rural, agricultural community that the parochial system belonged.[2]

The parochial system in the four Welsh dioceses of Bangor, St Asaph, St Davids and Llandaff – themselves territorial units which achieved their fixed boundaries in the twelfth century – continued into the modern era to proclaim its relationship to the pattern of landownership and overlordship which had given it birth.[3] Only from the late-eighteenth century, with increasing internal and external population migrations into existing towns and new industrial centres, did the inherent weaknesses and inflexibilities of the parochial system become apparent. As Bishop Moorman observed, the parochial system 'has never been quite at home in large towns, where boundaries are always arbitrary and loyalties loose'.[4] By the mid-twentieth century the parochial system had become more fictive than real, and arguably no longer an effective unit wherein the church could undertake its primary mission. By the end of the twentieth century, with declining numbers of stipendiary clergy and the gathering together of (predominantly) rural parishes in increasingly large groups, it was fast becoming a nonsense.

The alarums and excursions of the English Reformations[5] left the institutional framework of *Ecclesia Anglicana* largely intact, and even the further alarums and excursions of the civil wars, the Commonwealth and Protectorate, Acts of Uniformity and Toleration, the Bartholemew Ejections and the Non-Juring Schism did little to shake it. The four Welsh dioceses remained until 1920 part of the province of Canterbury, their bishops owing canonical obedience to that province's metropolitan archbishop. All of the challenges which the established church faced in Wales, it had also to face elsewhere, and this included the problem of language.[6] The challenges facing the Church need to be examined at 'grass roots' level, at that level where each and every person came, to a greater or lesser degree, in contact with the established church; that is, in the parish. As Roger Brown has reminded us,

> The Church of England was a collection of corporations sole, each parish forming such a body. Its incumbent was vicar of a defined area, and had the legal right to the various tithes and fees allowed him by custom, as well as to the exclusive right of officiating at services and the occasional offices of baptism, marriage and burial in his parish.[7]

The ministry of the parish priest was under constant scrutiny, if not by his superiors, then certainly by his parishioners. Any breakdown in the relationship between priest and people would redound to the discredit of the Church at large. Eighteenth-century bishops were well aware of this danger. In 1716 William Fleetwood, after seven years as bishop of St Asaph, warned the clergy of the diocese of Ely to which he was newly translated, against imprudence, negligence, ignorance and ill-behaviour, wisely reminding them that there were many in society only too ready to point a finger of scorn or reprobation at them. The 'love, respect, esteem and honour' that were due to the 'holy calling' of the priesthood had to be earned, and could only be achieved by the prudent, discreet and diligent discharge of the duties and obligations inherent in the office. He suggested,

> Let us look for what we will, the world will still have more regard to our personal qualifications, than to the dignity of our calling; they will not reverence us for what we should be, but for what they see, and find in us.[8]

The clergy were 'Christ's immediate servants, stewards of his household, dispensers of his Word and Sacraments',[9] and these duties and obligations they discharged primarily in the parochial cures where they were delegated to serve. The life of the priest, his integrity, and his conscientious discharge of his functions as leader of worship were the yardsticks by which he, and the Church, would be judged. Did the eighteenth century Welsh clergy live up to their calling? The surviving evidence would point to the conclusion that, to a high degree, they did.

A detailed study of parochial life, and the ministry of the clergy, in eighteenth-century Wales still awaits the writing. Such research as has been undertaken does, however, reveal that views of it prevalent during the nineteenth and much of the twentieth centuries, that this was an age of religious torpor, neglect and indolence, stand in need of substantial revision.[10] The finger of accusation can be pointed at parochial clergy – a high percentage – who held more than one living (pluralism); at those who lived at a distance from their parishioners (non-residence); or who did not speak their language. These failings cannot be denied, but, at least in the first two instances, there are immensely complex histories which cannot be disentangled here.[11] But it needs to be borne in mind that a parochial benefice constituted a 'living' for its incumbent, and how could he 'live' if its income was insufficient to support him and his family? Debarred from secular employment, he was forced to seek an additional 'living' by way of augmentation of his income. And if his obligation was to reside among his parishioners, how could he do so if his benefice possessed no parsonage? He had no alternative but to purchase or rent the nearest suitable house, which may or may not have been within the parish boundaries. Only root-and-branch reform, possible only for the established church through the legislature of Parliament, could overcome the complex web of problems, structural and economic, which the eighteenth-century Church had inherited. And until Parliament was itself reformed in the nineteenth century, there was little realistic prospect of change. Eighteenth-century bishops were realists; they could regulate the system and endeavour to make it more efficient, but they were powerless to change it. The parochial clergy could only operate it, and there were always those (as there always will be) who manipulated it to their personal advantage and gain.

The important question is whether the 'abuses' in the system, and of the system, seriously affected the daily life of the parishes? The answer has to be, 'no'. Parishes were not bereft of ministry because the incumbent lived elsewhere, but he may have been little more than a name to his nominal parishioners. The ministry in the case of non-residents was discharged by assistant curates who often were resident, or resident in the immediate neighbourhood, sometimes themselves the incumbents of adjacent parishes. There is little evidence in the surviving Returns to the Visitation Queries of the four Welsh bishops that the performance of Sunday acts of worship and the due administration of the sacraments was any less frequent or regular in parishes served by curates than in those served by their incumbents. These things were dictated by local practice and custom, often of long standing, to a greater degree than they were by the residence or not of the clergyman.[12] There is evidence to show that, in the main, the parochial clergy were conscientious in providing for the cure of souls, even where and when they could not discharge it themselves. They also made efforts to provide suitably qualified deputies, and this meant, where necessary, a priest fluent in Welsh. Thus Hopton Williams Webb, rector of Welsh-speaking Goetre in Monmouthshire in 1774, who did not himself speak the vernacular, left his parish in the care of a bilingual curate. Sometimes, as in the case of Francis Pinkney, rector of Neath (1736–1768), a monoglot Englishman who nonetheless resided in his parish, they employed a Welsh-speaking curate to serve alongside them.[13] Of course, there is evidence of indifference and neglect, and even of moral turpitude[14] (as there is in every age of the Church's history) but this should not be allowed to obliterate or unduly distort a picture of a church at 'grass roots' level which was still very close to the centre, if not absolutely at the heart, of the life of local communities.[15]

Dissent does not seem to have been discerned as a major concern in most parishes, even where (as, for example, in north Monmouthshire) it took the form of Catholic recusancy.[16] Local communities were largely tolerant, and the only significant evidence of concern detectable in the Visitation Returns was where religious dissent had numerically reached a 'critical mass'. The Returns to Bishop Ewer's 1763 Visitation of Llandaff diocese illustrate the point. So far as can be judged, the clergy did not attempt either to conceal or 'play down' the strength of dissent in their parishes. As a result a fair picture can be obtained of its distribution, and it is immediately obvious that its strength was most apparent in the large upland parishes such as Merthyr Tydfil, Gelligaer and Llanwenarth, which, as a result of industrialization, were already being affected by population increase.[17] The inflexibility and lack of reality which characterized the parish structure in such areas was already hindering the clergy in making an adequate response. The outcome was to become all too apparent within the next one hundred years.[18]

Too much can be – has been, and in some cases, continues to be – made of the 'Great Awakening' in the Welsh Church in the mid-eighteenth century; that evangelical revival particularly associated with Daniel Rowland, Howel Harris and William Williams.[19] It is easy to forget that Rowland and Williams were both ordained ministers of the established church, and Harris, a frustrated ordinand. Their fundamental desire was to breathe new life into old traditions and an existing institution. They were, as Glyn Tegai Hughes has noted,

> all strongly heirs of the experiential tradition, stressing above all the individual relationship to the person of Christ ... Methodism, in England and Wales, was not just an outpouring of emotion; it was the revolt of high seriousness combined with rapture.[20]

The tragedy was that, ultimately, it proved impossible to contain, or retain, this seriousness and fervour within the established church, but it should not be lost sight of that the intent of the Wesleys, of George Whitefield and the leaders of the 'Great Awakening' in Wales was revival and not schism. That revival, particularly in rural, Welsh-speaking Wales, made a great impact is undeniable, but it should not be exaggerated. Arguably, the Circulating Schools, brainchild of the Rev. Griffith Jones of Llanddowror, which are associated with the Awakening, but were certainly not the fruit of it, did more to inculcate a sense of informed reverence and devotion the length and breadth of Wales. All too often the itinerant ministries and preaching tours of the Awakening's evangelists had the effect of 'sparks through stubble'; the fires died down as soon as the wind had passed over and was gone.[21] The weakness of the Church at parish level was not so much in Divine Worship or the provision of devotional literature, both of which were available in the vernacular, as in the preaching ministry. No small wonder, then, that fervour and enthusiasm should attract rather more than formal, and sometimes infrequent, discourses, however elegantly phrased.[22]

Little need be said for the eighteenth-century Church about either bishops or cathedrals in Wales. With few exceptions the former would have been little more than names to anyone in their dioceses but the clergy and the socially more prominent laity. By this period the spiritual duties of a bishop had become more and more limited to those inherent in his office, confirmation, ordination and visitation.[23] A few week's vigorous activity in the summer, when travel was easiest, usually sufficed for a bishop to discharge his obligations within his diocese.[24] The days of bishops ceaselessly perambulating from parish to parish to grace with their presence Flower Festivals or the blessing of church furniture were far in the future.[25] Even as late as 1827, when the bishop of Llandaff was the youthful Charles Sumner, his appearance in a small country parish could cause awe and uncertainty as to how he was to be approached (as at Trellech), or even, in the church of a sizeable town, chaos (as at Chepstow).[26] There is certainly little or no evidence to suggest that the bishops of the Welsh dioceses were any less conscientious in the discharge of such duties as befell them, either in person or by deputy, than their confreres in England, or their Roman Catholic counterparts in, for example, France, for that matter. Whether or not they could speak Welsh or were Welsh-born was an irrelevance. The circumscribed Episcopal ministry of the eighteenth century would not often have required it.[27]

As for the cathedrals, they were of no significance. All four of the Welsh cathedrals were sited in very small communities, in the case of St Davids and Llandaff at least, little more than villages. As the editors of a recent volume on the Elizabethan Church have remarked, 'it was not clear what protestant cathedrals were for. They were there because they were there ... and because, to be cynical, they provided relatively comfortable livings for their dignitaries.'[28] Even this last point is of minor importance, for, as the dignitaries' livings were related to income from rectorial tithe and capitular property, it mattered little whether the cathedral was in good or bad repair. Any pretence that the cathedrals were centres of corporate religious life, of learning, of exemplary liturgy, had been lost. That the cathedrals of south Wales at St Davids and Llandaff survived at all – and the latter nearly did not – is possibly due more to the fact that both (or parts of them) functioned also as the local parish church. Frank Bennett's *The Nature of a Cathedral*, written in 1925, with themes such as 'the cathedral and its diocesan family', encouraging parishes within a diocese to look upon the cathedral as its 'mother church'; 'the model church of the diocese'; and a place where visitors can be transformed into pilgrims, would have read strangely, if not incomprehensibly, in the eighteenth century.[29] That there *should* be a cathedral was little questioned. There was concern expressed in the early 1720s when it was rumoured that the see of Llandaff was to be removed to Cardiff, or even united with that of Bristol.[30] The concern engendered in some degree contributed to the initiative, taken from 1730 onwards, to rebuild on site. The result was John Wood's famous 'Italian Temple'.[31] A role for a cathedral was largely rediscovered, or invented, in the nineteenth and twentieth centuries, and the eighteenth-century Church should not be unduly criticized for being uncertain as to what exactly it was.

By the beginning of the nineteenth century, the patterns of parochial life were beginning to change, and in some places break down. The small-scale industry which had developed in some formerly deeply rural parishes such as Mounton (paper mills) and Chapel Hill (wire works) in Monmouthshire, with a concomitant rise in population, had by the mid-eighteenth century already brought with it, in embryo, the kind of problems the nineteenth-century Church would have to face, had anyone had eyes to see. This is revealed, for example, in the parish of Newchurch. In 1763 Rice Price, the curate, told his bishop that Newchurch contained about 150 families, 'and a great many dissenters'. So already there was a discernable dissenting presence here, in a growing artisan population, that turning away from the established church which the 1851 Census was to so cruelly expose.[32] Price was ill-placed to respond to a growing and changing need; the income of his parish was small, he served four other local churches, and Newchurch had only one fortnightly service. From his 150-plus families, there were only twelve communicants.[33]

The structures of the Church, and the mind-set of its leaders, were not equipped to cope with the kind of changes rapid industrialization, social and economic upheaval, were to bring in their wake.[34] The initiative passed to others; a rejuvenated nonconformity was quick to take advantage of the paralysis of the Church. Roger Brown has summarized the situation:

> Nonconformity was not bound by the legal restraints the Established Church faced when it desired to establish a new district or parish, or even build a church to cater for the needs of an emerging population. Buildings had to be obtained and licensed for worship. Curates had to be provided by the incumbent at his own expense, unless he could persuade his parishioners to assist him in such payments. A new district or parish required a parish church to be built in an acceptable style and with accommodation for a large proportion of the parishioners; the legal rights of the incumbent of the 'mother church' had to be respected; a stipend provided for the new incumbent and eventually a parsonage house; while existing rights of patrons, pewholders, even sextons, had to be protected. It took both time and money to establish new churches and parishes.[35]

Brown's own thorough researches, along with those of Ieuan Gwynedd Jones,[36] have clearly, almost mercilessly and certainly heartbreakingly, revealed the anguish, frustration and disillusionment felt by bishops and parochial clergy alike as they struggled with distant, often faceless, legal and ecclesiastical bureaucrats in their endeavours to provide adequately for the cure of souls. By contrast, as Brown states, 'nonconformity was able to start a 'cause' in a local house using a lay preacher'.[37] The established church was out-paced and out-manoeuvred. In the latter part of the nineteenth century, with reforms in place and (somewhat) streamlined administrative structures, there is considerable evidence to indicate that the Church was regaining the initiative and lost ground.[38] But it proved too little, too late. The storm clouds of disestablishment were fast gathering, and in the early twentieth century much optimism was drowned in Flanders' mud.[39]

Despite their Herculean task, the parochial clergy laboured with some success to stem the tides of infidelity and nonconformity. During the nineteenth (and well into the twentieth) century, Bishop Thomas Burgess of St Davids College at Lampeter (founded 1822) intended to provide university-standard education for ordinands who could not afford to matriculate at Oxford or Cambridge. This was greatly to assist in the provision of trained and dedicated clergy, particularly for work in the populous industrialized areas of his own diocese and that of neighbouring Llandaff.[40] As the century progressed, the leadership in parishes of clergy of two strands of theological opinion were to make a considerable impact, namely those associated with the Evangelical and Anglo-Catholic movements.[41] The Welsh evangelicals included men of the calibre of John Griffith of Aberdare and Merthyr Tydfil; David Howell of Cardiff and Wrexham;[42] John Powell Jones of Loughor and Llantrisant; and Evan Jenkins of Dowlais. When Bishop Sumner instituted Jenkins in 1827, he commented, 'I leave you as a missionary in the heart of Africa. God be with you.'[43] In a thirty-five year ministry, Jenkins gained the universal respect of his 'Africans' for his devotion and diligence.

In the latter part of the century, the dedication and self-sacrificial ministry of many of those clergy associated with the Anglo-Catholic Movement also made a great impression.[44] What distinguished these clergy from the Evangelicals was not just their different theological perspective, but the fact that many of them were English by birth and upbringing.[45] Welsh clergy and laity had been attracted by and were closely associated with the Oxford (Tractarian) Movement, with Isaac Williams among its leaders, but not so many were prominent in its second, more ritualist, phase.[46] Nonetheless, the impact of the Movement upon the parishes of Wales was to be both broad and deep. It also had its colourfully eccentric side. Two of the pioneering attempts to restore the 'Religious Life' to the Church were associated with Wales: the eclectic 'Benedictine' community at Llanthony under the erratic Father Ignatius,[47] and the more stable community established on Caldey Island by Aelred Carlyle.[48] Both were, unfortunately, in the diocese of St Davids, whose bishop, John Owen, was singularly ill-equipped by temperament and outlook to deal with such initiatives, certainly when they were associated with such egocentric and flamboyant figures as Ignatius and Carlyle.[49] The Llanthony community foundered, and that on Caldey seceded to Rome.

There is no room in so short an overview as this to deal with the long-drawn-out and often bitter disputes which characterized the relationship between the established church and dissent over the question of disestablishment and disendowment. It has, in any case, been discussed fully and analysed elsewhere.[50] Two points, however, should be stressed. First, that the picture should not be painted too starkly in black-and-white; that is, established church against disestablishment, nonconformity in favour. There were voices raised in the Church in favour of such a move, and there were nonconformists doubtful as to its wisdom.[51] It should not be forgotten that, however reluctantly, early in the nineteenth century men of the calibre of John Keble and William Van Mildert had reached the conclusion that under certain circumstances disestablishment might be inevitable, though admittedly they were not contemplating its piecemeal adoption, with the severing of the Church of Ireland and that in Wales from the

Church of England.[52] Second, the question of how much the disestablishment debates and arguments affected the daily life of the parishes is one that still needs answering. The conclusion, can, however, be drawn that the wearisomely long campaign, leading finally to the disestablishment of the Church in Wales in 1920, distracted the Christian denominations in the country from their true mission.[53]

This is not to say that Christianity itself was not important for many Welshmen, even after the 'double whammy' of the disestablishment campaigns and the First World War. However, R. Tudur Jones assertion that in 1890 'being a Welshman and being a Christian were virtually synonymous'[54] would certainly, only thirty years later, have stood in need of considerable modification. Adherents to the newly dis-established church were certainly in a minority, and the ebullient Christianity of Edwardian Wales was never to fulfil its promise. That newly disestablished church was compromised from the outset. The leadership of A. G. Edwards, the first arch-bishop of Wales, and his adjutant, John Owen, bishop of St Davids, was that of 'yesterday's men', of leopards who do not really change their spots.[55] Vociferous, vigorous and sometimes downright unscrupulous opponents of disestablishment, after 1920 they endeavoured to retain as much of the 'establishment' ethos and privi-lege of the Church as was possible. The result was, as Densil Morgan rightly pointed out, they 'did more than anyone to perpetuate the idea that the Episcopal Church ... was an alien institution'.[56] More than eighty-five years on from disestablishment, the Church in Wales is still a long way from coming out from under the shadow cast by Edwards and Owen. Until the 1960s, for example, the Church continued to use as its only authorized service book the 1662 Book of Common Prayer 'according to the use of the Church of England' (of which it was no longer a part), and therefrom pray for 'thy Servant Elizabeth, our most gracious Queen and Governor' (which was only partly true).[57] Congregations could be forgiven for thinking, or pretending, that 1920 had never happened.

The post-Second World War years, when the last leaders, and parochial clergy, who remembered and were influenced by pre-disestablishment times, were gradually pass-ing from the scene, did witness cautious and tentative movement, not the least in the fields of liturgical reform and ecumenism.[58] There are those, however, who consider that the fundamental mind-set of the Church, and its institutional structures, prevent it from ministering and witnessing effectively in a thoroughly secularized society. In 1995 D. P. Davies, a professor of theology at University of Wales, Lampeter, and himself an ordained priest of the Church in Wales, wrote:

> At this juncture in our national history and in the history of Christianity in our land what is required of Christians in Wales is the boldness and courage to be truly radical – to go back to our roots, not only to our roots in the Celtic Church, but to our original roots in the small communities of enthusiastic and committed Christians who first responded to the call of the gospel in countries around the Mediterranean Sea. If we can recover these roots and draw on the strength and inspiration they give we can face the new millennium not with despair but in hope, the hope that we shall be worthy servants of society in this dear land of Wales.[59]

Institutions are rarely repositories of boldness, courage and vision. There is in these early years of the twenty-first century little sign yet that the Church in Wales is either able or willing to listen to such a plea as this, or heed Davies' warning:

> It grieves me that the Church I love should be in decline, but it irritates and exasperates me to the point of despair that many in the Church refuse to read the signs of the times and are content, ostrich-like, to bury their heads in the comfortable sand of the status-quo, though such comfort as this affords is likely to be short-lived.[60]

Notes

1. John R. H. Moorman, *Church Life in England in the Thirteenth Century* (Cambridge, 1945), p. 4.
2. Ibid., p. 5.
3. A diocese was originally an administrative unit for civil government in the later Roman Empire – a territorial area over which supervision was exercised. The name was gradually adopted by the Christian Church from the fourth century onwards for a designated area under the pastoral oversight of a bishop. Undertones of 'administration' and 'governance', however, remained – and still do.
4. Moorman, *Church Life in England*, p. 5. In Wales, the parish of Merthyr Tydfil would be a good example of the increasing unreality of the parochial system in the face of urban growth. By 1839 the population of the former village had risen to 20,000 – with one church (and burial ground) to house them, and two clergy of the established church to minister to them. See Barrie Jones, 'The Reverend George Martin Maber, MA, Rector of Merthyr 1795–1844', *Merthyr Historian*, 9 (1997), 1–12.
5. Scholars today tend to refer to the turmoils of the sixteenth and seventeenth centuries in the plural rather than in the singular. For example, see Christopher Haigh, *English Reformations. Religion, Politics and Society Under the Tudors* (Oxford, 1993).
6. *The Book of Common Prayer* (1559) and the *New Testament* were translated into Welsh and authorised for use in the public worship of the Church in 1567. See Isaac Thomas, *William Salesbury and His Testament* (Cardiff, 1967); Glanmor Williams, *Welsh Reformation Essays* (Cardiff, 1967), especially chs. VII and VIII; and, more recently, Glanmor Williams, *Wales and the Reformation* (Cardiff, 1997), pp. 338–60. By contrast, the Book of Common Prayer was not translated into Irish until 1608. Before that date, although the Irish Parliament in 1560 had authorized the use of the 1559 (English language) prayerbook, as few of the clergy, and even fewer of the laity, understood English, it also sanctioned the use of 'all common and open prayer in the Latin tongue'. Presumably this was the Book of Common Prayer, published in Latin the same year as the petition of the English universities. This expedient does not seem to have been contemplated for Wales. Had it been, it might have delayed the production of a prayerbook in Welsh. On the other hand, it might have more swiftly reconciled the conservative Welsh to the Protestant Reformation. See Francis Procter and Walter Howard Frere, *A New History of the Book of Common Prayer* (3rd Imp. London, 1949), pp. 230, 108, 107.
7. Roger L. Brown, *Reclaiming the Wilderness* (Welshpool, 2001), pp. 14–15. In the nineteenth century all of these customs and rights came under scrutiny, and were the cause of sometimes acrimonious disputes between the clergy and their parishioners. For example, see Ronald Fletcher, *The Akenham Burial Case* (London, 1974). This centred upon the burial of an unbaptized child of nonconformist parents in the 1870s, and gained the proportions of a national scandal. At a more petty, local level, on one occasion cheese paid to the rector of Merthyr Tydfil as tithe came unsalted. It was placed in the church tower, and the resulting terrible stench permeated the whole building. See Jones, 'The Reverend George Martin Maber', 3.

8. William Fleetwood, *A Charge Delivered to the Clergy of the Diocese of Ely ... August the VIIth MDCCXVI ...* (2nd edn. Cambridge, 1716), pp. 8, 9.

9. Ibid., 10.

10. For a valuable historiographical survey, see William Gibson, *The Achievement of the Anglican Church 1689–1800* (Lewiston; Queenston; Lampeter, 1995), pp. 5–31. Although now over a decade old, Gibson's verdict on the current state of scholarship concerning the eighteenth-century Church still stands. See also Sir Glanmor Williams, William Jacob, Nigel Yates and Frances Knight, *The Welsh Church from Reformation to Disestablishment 1603–1920* (Cardiff, 2007), and particularly the chapters by William Jacob, for an important overview of church life in the seventeenth and eighteenth centuries. More specifically, see my chapter on religion and belief in Monmouthshire between 1660 and 1780 in Madeleine Gray and Prys Morgan (eds), *Gwent County History, Vol. 3: The Making of Monmouthshire 1536–1780* (Cardiff, 2009), pp. 146–73.

11. I attempted some disentangling in my doctoral dissertation. See John R. Guy, 'Patronage, Plurality and Non-Residence in the Diocese of Llandaff 1660–1816', unpublished University of Wales, Ph.D. thesis, 1983.

12. The surviving records of eighteenth-century Visitations of the four Welsh dioceses, which are voluminous, are available for consultation and study at the National Library of Wales, Aberystwyth.

13. I briefly discussed the subject of language in my edition of the 1763 Primary Visitation of Bishop John Ewer. See John R. Guy, *The Diocese of Llandaff in 1763* (Cardiff, 1991), especially p. 183. The question of language became more acute in the nineteenth century, when reforms were progressively enforcing residence upon parochial clergy. Witness Bishop Edward Copleston of Llandaff's 1848 speech in the House of Lords, and the response of leading laity and clergy printed in the *Cardiff and Merthyr Guardian* in November of that year.

14. There are sad examples of this recorded in Edward Tenison's 1710 Visitation of his Carmarthen archdeaconry. See my 'Riding against the Clock: The Visitations of Edward Tenison in Carmarthen and Ossory in the Early Eighteenth Century', in John R. Guy and W. G. Neely (eds), *Contrasts and Comparisons: Studies in Irish and Welsh Church History* (Llandysul, 1999), pp. 55–64. Isolation, loneliness and lack of support, sympathy and intellectual stimulation could all contribute to such lapses. They are precisely the kind of thing that Bishop Fleetwood was to warn his clergy about six years later.

15. A fascinating insight into parochial life can be gained from a series of six articles, which taken together form a monograph in themselves, published by Walter T. Morgan on the activities of the Consistory Courts in the diocese of St Davids during this period. See *Journal of the Historical Society of the Church in Wales*, VII (1957), 5–24; VIII (1958), 58–81; IX (1959), 70–90; X (1960), 17–42; XI (1961), 65–89; XII (1962), 28–54. The increasing 'professionalization' of the ordained ministry in the nineteenth century, ironically, contributed to a decline in the *local* influence of the established church. This is well brought out in Roger L. Brown, *Church and Clergy at Castle Caereinion* (Welshpool, 1997). At 'Castle' the ministry of David Williams (1872–1882), which was, on the surface, that of an energetic and reforming pastor, illustrates what happened. Indeed, he suggests that 'One has the impression ... that Williams made the parish a church parish, in other words, he enhanced church life and built it up, so that spiritual content was more important than numerical figures.' See Brown, *Church and Clergy at Castle Caereinion*, p. 37. There was a better identification of the priest with his Congregation (by 1872 a minority of the parishioners), and of that congregation with their (new) church building, than heretofore. By the late-nineteenth century it was more difficult for ordinary parishioners to 'own' the parish church as theirs; it was becoming more the preserve of those who were coming to see themselves as 'church members'. Frances Knight in her *The Nineteenth Century Church and English Society* (Cambridge, 1995) reached broadly similar conclusions.

16. See Guy, *Diocese of Llandaff in 1763*, especially pp. 175–77; John R. Guy, 'The Anglican Patronage of Monmouthshire Recusants in the Seventeenth and Eighteenth Centuries: Some Examples', *Recusant History*, 15 (1981), 452–4; John R. Guy, 'Eighteenth Century Gwent Catholics', *Recusant History*, 16 (1982), 78–88; John R. Guy, 'The Welsh Connection: Roman Catholicism in Somerset and South Wales in the Eighteenth and Early Nineteenth Centuries', *South Western Catholic History*, 9 (1991), 3–10.

17. Guy, *Diocese of Llandaff in 1763*, pp. 66–7; 56–8; 99–101.

18. This is an area of research which Roger L. Brown has made his own and provided the fruits of his labours in numerous papers and articles. There are too many to list here, but see Brown, *Reclaiming the Wilderness*.

19. The literature on this, in both Welsh and English, is vast. For useful introductions, see Derec Llwyd Morgan, *Y Diwygiad Mawr* (Llandysul, 1981); Eifion Evans, *Daniel Rowland and the Great Awakening in Wales* (Edinburgh, 1985); Geraint Tudur, *Howell Harris. From Conversion to Separation 1735–1750* (Cardiff, 2000); Glyn Tegai Hughes, *Williams Pantycelyn* (Cardiff, 1983). Both Tudur and Hughes have useful, and judiciously chosen, bibliographies.

20. Hughes, *Williams Pantycelyn*, pp. 7, 5. None of this was inimical to the tenets of the established church, and it was that Church, after all, which provided Methodism with its womb and gave it birth. Until the parting of the ways (after 1811) the established church continued to provide nurture and sustenance. For the debt owed by Ann Griffiths at the very end of the eighteenth century to the Church, see A. M. Allchin, 'Ann Griffiths, Mystic and Theologian', in A. M. Allchin, *The Kingdom of Love and Knowledge* (London, 1979), 54–70; A. M. Allchin, *Ann Griffiths. The Furnace and the Fountain* (Cardiff, 1987).

21. An up-to-date study of Griffith Jones and his schools is sorely needed. But see F. A. Cavenagh, *The Life and Work of Griffith Jones of Llanddowror* (Cardiff, 1930); W. Moses Williams, *Selections from the Welch Piety* (Cardiff, 1938); W. Moses Williams, *The Friends of Griffith Jones. A Study in Educational Philanthropy* (London, 1939); Thomas Kelly, *Griffith Jones, Llanddowror. Pioneer in Adult Education* (Cardiff, 1950). Although many of the luminaries of the 'Great Awakening' looked on Jones with reverence as kind of patriarch, he was careful, and shrewd enough, not to too closely identify himself and his schools with the revival. To have done so would have almost certainly alienated his wealthier benefactors, upon whom his work so much depended.

22. The best overview of the provision of Christian literature is Geraint H. Jenkins, *Literature, Religion and Society in Wales 1660–1730* (Cardiff, 1978). An enormous contribution to that provision was made by the Society for Promoting Christian Knowledge after its foundation (in which Welshmen played a prominent part) in 1699. See Mary Clement, *Correspondence and Minutes of the SPCK Relating to Wales 1699–1740* (Cardiff, 1952).

23. See John R. Guy, 'Richard Watson and the role of a bishop', in *Bibliotheque de la Revue D'Histoire Ecclesiastique*, fasc. 72. *Miscellanea Historiae Ecclesiastica*, VIII (1987), 390–7. How the eighteenth-century bishops themselves saw their role, and what their priorities were, would be an interesting field of study. Robert Clavering, Bishop of Llandaff 1725–1729, had something to say on this in *The Lord Bishop of Llandaff's Charge at His Primary Visitation ... in July 1726* (2nd edn. London, 1730).

24. Even as young and fit a bishop as Charles Richard Sumner (Llandaff 1826–27), despite only being able to spend a few months in the summer in his diocese, because of his other commitments (he was also Dean of St Paul's), still found time to devote most afternoons to country walks with his wife, and evenings to reading out loud to his family. See George Henry Sumner, *Life of Charles Richard Sumner, DD* (London, 1876), p. 118. For Sumner's brief episcopate at Llandaff, see pp. 114–32.

25. As long ago as 1925 F. S. M. Bennett, then Dean of Chester, warned that the ideal of a bishop as 'the Father in God of a knowable and manageable family [had been replaced] with something more like that of the old woman who lived in a shoe and had so many children that she didn't know what to do, or, worse still, with that of an overworked man who lives in a motor car'. See F. S. M. Bennett, *The Nature of a Cathedral* (Chester and London, 1925), p. 4. His warning has been totally ignored. Perhaps, as he wisely said, 'there still seem to be individual bishops who love to have it so'.

26. Sumner, *Life of Charles Richard Sumner*, pp. 116–18.

27. It was changing perceptions of the role of a bishop in the nineteenth century which made of this a vital and contentious issue. It became increasingly a preoccupation of the Welsh-speaking parochial clergy themselves, not the least among those serving outside of Wales. See Roger L. Brown, *'Welsh Patriotism' and 'Justice to Wales'. The Association of Welsh Clergy in the West Riding of Yorkshire* (Welshpool, 2001); William Gibson, 'Gladstone and the Llandaff Vacancy of 1882–3', *Transactions of the Honourable Society of Cymmrodorion* (1987), 105–11. There had been Welsh bishops of Welsh sees in the eighteenth century: John Wynne, St Asaph 1715–27; John Harris, Llandaff 1729–38, and of English ones for that matter: John Thomas, Peterborough 1747–57; Salisbury 1757–61 and Winchester

1761–81 who retained his canonry at Llandaff from 1733–57; and Richard Trevor, St Davids 1744–52 and Durham 1752–71. In the nineteenth century English-born bishops of the calibre of Connop Thirlwall of St Davids and Alfred Ollivant of Llandaff had learned Welsh, but the clamour for a Welsh-born, Welsh-speaking bishop for a Welsh see was becoming impossible to ignore. One reason for it, as Gibson hints, was that by the 1880s at the latest such an appointment was seen as an essential bulwark to shore up the established church in Wales, and muffle the cries for disestablishment. To re-assert the 'Welshness' of the Church required native-born and native-speaking Welsh bishops, so long as they were well-enough born and well-enough educated. That the appointment of native, Welsh-speaking bishops was a part of the political agenda of the time should not be lost sight of. Unfortunately, those men who *did* possess these required qualifications were not always best equipped in other respects for Episcopal office; would John Owen, Richard Lewis, Watkin Williams or Alfred George Edwards have made it to the bench if these criteria had not needed to be met?

28. Patrick Collinson, John Craig and Brett Usher (eds), *Conferences and Combination Lectures in the Elizabethan Church 1582–1590* (Woodbridge, 2003), p. xxii. The passionate, even vehement, defence of cathedral dignities mounted by Sydney Smith in the 1830s well illustrates the editors' remark. See Hesketh Pearson, *The Smith of Smiths* (London, 1934) especially ch. XII.

29. Bennett, *Nature of a Cathedral*, passim. The debate about the role, or roles, of cathedral churches in a secular age continues unabated.

30. In 1726 Thomas Davies, Chapter Clerk at Llandaff, had to deny the rumour, pointing out that Bishop John Tyler, who had been credited with the idea, had supported moves to restore the semi-ruinous cathedral church.

31. John Wood the elder (1705–1754) was a very young (25) and relatively untried architect when he surveyed Llandaff in 1730. He is closely associated with the development of Bath, where he had begun work in 1727. By 1730 he had the valuable patronage of the Duke of Chandos, who recommended him to the new bishop of Llandaff, John Harris. Wood's 'Temple' has received short shrift from its chroniclers, who do not seem to have had much sympathy with classical architecture, did not appreciate the underlying philosophy of his work, or fully appreciate the financial constraints upon it. See E. T. Davies, 'John Wood's Italianate Temple', *Journal of the Historical Society of the Church in Wales*, 6, 11 (1956), 70–81; Donald R. Buttress, 'Llandaff Cathedral in the Eighteenth and Nineteenth Centuries', *Journal of the Historical Society of the Church in Wales*, 16, 21 (1966), 61–76; John B. Hilling, *Llandaf: Past and Present* (Barry, 1978), pp. 37–41. It should not be forgotten that if Wood had not rebuilt the cathedral, the see would not have possessed one. Surviving illustrations (reproduced, for example in Hilling, *Llandaf*, pp. 38–9) show a distinguished building, arguably the most ambitious church built in Wales in the eighteenth century. What Wood could accomplish when funds *were* available can be seen in Bath (Queen Square and Grand Parade) and in Llandaff itself, at the Court (now part of the Cathedral School).

32. See I. G. Jones (ed.), *The Religious Census of 1851: A Calendar of the Returns Relating to Wales* (2 vols. Cardiff, 1976 [south Wales] and 1981 [north Wales]). The best recent discussion and analysis of the census is K. D. M. Snell and Paul S. Ell, *Rival Jerusalems. The Geography of Victorian Religion* (Cambridge, 2000), which also contains an extensive bibliography.

33. Guy, *Llandaff Diocese in 1763*, p. 117.

34. The best overall surveys remain E. T. Davies, *Religion and Society in the Nineteenth Century* (Llandybie, 1981); E. T. Davies, *Religion in the Industrial Revolution in South Wales* (Cardiff, 1965).

35. Brown, *Reclaiming the Wilderness*, p. 92. If the reference to pewholders seems hyperbolism, see Roger L. Brown, *Pews, Benches and Seats. Being a History of the Church Pew in Wales* (Welshpool, 1998).

36. In, for example, I. G. Jones, *Communities* (Llandysul, 1987).

37. Brown, *Reclaiming the Wilderness*, p. 92.

38. Ibid., 35–6.

39. For an important discussion of this latter point, see D. Densil Morgan, 'Christ and the War: Some Aspects of the Welsh Experience, 1914–1918', *Journal of Welsh Religious History*, 5 (1997), 73–91.

40. The history of the college has been thoroughly researched. In particular, see D. T. W. Price, *A History of St David's University College, Lampeter* (2 vols. Cardiff, 1977 and 1990). For a short introduction to Burgess, see D. T. W. Price, *Bishop Burgess and Lampeter College* (Cardiff, 1987).

The north Walian bishops were less enthusiastic about Lampeter, in the beginning favouring men trained at St Bees in the north-west of England, which had opened in 1816.

41. The impact of the nineteenth-century evangelicals, and in particular the invaluable work of the Church Pastoral-Aid Society in Wales, has been explored by Roger L. Brown, *The Welsh Evangelicals* (Tongwynlais, 1986). There is no equivalent published study of the Anglo-Catholic movement, though some leading figures, for example F. W. Puller, vicar of Roath, and Griffith Arthur Jones, Vicar of St Mary's, Cardiff, have been the subject of individual attention. See John V. Stewart, 'Puller of Roath as a Christian Apologist', *Journal of Welsh Ecclesiastical History*, 7 (1990), 55–67; J. H. Ward and H. A. Coe, *Father Jones of Cardiff* (London, 1907).

42. As with the clerical and lay leaders of the Anglo-Catholic Movement in Wales, many of the prominent Evangelicals await critical and contextual biographical studies. A notable exception is Roger L. Brown, *David Howell. A Pool of Spirituality* (Denbigh, 1998).

43. Sumner, *Life of Charles Richard Sumner*, pp. 122–3.

44. In 1897, at the funeral of the Rev. Harry North of St Martin's, Roath, who had died at the age of 37, his coffin was borne in procession from the church to the cemetery through streets lined with mourners, all the local shops being shut as a sign of respect.

45. F. W. Puller would be a good example. See n. 41. Notable exceptions would be Griffith Arthur Jones and J. D. Jenkins, Vicar of Aberdare. See Christopher B. Turner, 'Ritualism, Railwaymen and the Poor: The Ministry of Canon J. D. Jenkins, Vicar of Aberdare 1870–76', in Geraint H. Jenkins and J. Beverley Smith (eds), *Politics and Society in Wales 1840–1922: Essays in Honour of Ieuan Gwynedd Jones* (Cardiff, 1988), pp. 61–79; J. W. Ward and Hector A. Coe, *Father Jones of Cardiff. A Memoir of the Rev. Griffith Arthur Jones … Vicar of S. Mary's, Cardiff* (London, 1908).

46. O. W. Jones, *Isaac Williams and his Circle* (London, 1971). Among the laity, prominent was Robert Raikes. See O. W. Jones, 'The Mind of Robert Raikes', *Journal of the Historical Society of the Church in Wales*, 18, 23 (1968), 57–64.

47. It is difficult to obtain a clear picture of this unbalanced man. Ivor Davies, *Ignatius the Monk* (Brecon, nd *c*.1966) is a short, but fairly uncritical account of Ignatius and his community at Capel-y-Ffin. Peter F. Anson (the Rev. A. W. Campbell), *The Call of the Cloister* (London, 1964), pp. 51–72 is a useful corrective. A curiosity, which gives some insight into Ignatius' mind, is Ignatius, OSB, *Hymns and Tunes of Llanthony Monastery Suitable for Missions* (London, 1890; republished Westcliff-on-Sea, 1989).

48. Anson, *Call of the Cloister*, pp. 164–81; Peter F. Anson, *The Benedictines of Caldey* (London, 1940); Peter F. Anson, *Abbot Extraordinary* (London, 1958). Anson had himself at one time been a member of this community, and described Carlyle as 'monk and missionary, pioneer and adventurer'. See Anson, *Call of the Cloister*, 166 n. 2. See also Rene Kollar, 'Monks, Pilgrims, Tourists and the Attractions of Caldey Island in the time of Abbot Aelred Carlyle', *Journal of Welsh Ecclesiastical History*, 9 (1992), 52–63.

49. The relationship between Carlyle and Owen, something of a dialogue of the deaf, is touched upon in Rene Kollar, 'A Question of Monastic Independence: Caldey Island's status as an ecclesiastical peculiar in the early twentieth century', *Journal of Welsh Religious History*, 3 (1995), 54–65. Owen told Archbishop Davidson in 1911, 'I have avoided having any official relationship with the community as a community.' See Kollar, 'A Question of Monastic Independence', 57, a 'hands-off' approach which bordered on indifference. For Owen himself, see Eluned E. Owen, *The Early Life of Bishop Owen* (Llandysul, 1958); Eluned E. Owen, *The Later Life of Bishop Owen* (Llandysul, 1961). Although fully documented, the two volumes are the work of Owen's daughter, and to some extent an act of filial piety. A less hagiographical picture emerges from the bishop's papers, which are deposited at the National Library of Wales.

50. A bibliography of works on disestablishment, and of the literature, much of it polemical, produced during the long-protracted campaign, would fill a volume in itself. A succinct introduction to the principal issues is Kenneth O. Morgan, *Freedom or Sacrilege? A History of the Campaign for Welsh Disestablishment* (Penarth, 1966). Two very pertinent articles on the fiftieth anniversary of disestablishment were provided by R. Tudur Jones, 'The Origins of the Nonconformist Disestablishment Campaign' and W. B. George, 'Welsh Disestablishment and Welsh Nationalism', *Journal of the Historical Society of the Church in Wales*, 20, 25 (1970), 39–76, 77–91.

51. Roger L. Brown, 'Traitors and Compromisers: The Shadow Side of the Church's Fight against Disestablishment', *Journal of Welsh Religious History*, 3 (1995), 35–53.
52. Georgina Battiscombe, *John Keble. A Study in Limitations* (London, 1963), pp. 126, 301–2; E. A. Varley, *The Last of the Prince Bishops. William Van Mildert and the High Church Movement of the Early Nineteenth Century* (Cambridge, 1992), especially pp. 188–9.
53. Disestablishment was 'a hollow victory [for nonconformity]. Public concern had long moved away from narrowly ecclesiastical matters, and the mutual vilification in which the most zealous protagonists had indulged had served only to cause popular disenchantment with Christianity generally'. See D. Densil Morgan, 'Christianity and National Identity in Twentieth-century Wales', *Religion, State and Society*, 27, 3/4 (1999), 330; cf. 327–42.
54. Ibid., 327.
55. Brown, 'Traitors and Compromisers'; Brown, *David Howell*, was among the first scholars to dislodge the halo from Archbishop Edwards. For too long the picture painted in George Lerry, *Alfred George Edwards, Archbishop of Wales* (Oswestry, nd, *c.*1939) and by Edwards himself in *Memories* (London, 1927) remained uncriticised. A fresh study of this, sadly, rather unpleasant man is needed.
56. Morgan, 'Christianity and National Identity', 330.
57. The phrase is from a petition in The Litany.
58. The Church in Wales and its contributions to liturgical reform, and ecumenism, deserve separate treatment. For ecumenism, however, see Noel A. Davies, 'The Search for Christian Unity in Wales: The Beginnings', *Journal of Welsh Religious History*, 8 (2000), 63–76, and, more recently, his *A History of Ecumenism in Wales 1956–1990* (Cardiff, 2008) – an often rather sorry tale of unrealised, and perhaps unrealisable, hopes. The history of Christianity in Wales during the twentieth century is now receiving increasing attention. See, for example, D. Densil Morgan, *The Span of the Cross. Christian Religion and Society in Wales 1914–2000* (Cardiff, 1999). An illuminating study of the Church in Wales is Christopher Harris and Richard Startup, *The Church in Wales. The Sociology of a Traditional Institution* (Cardiff, 1999). Some leading figures, mainly bishops and archbishops, have been the subject of biographical studies, for example Bishop John Jones of Bangor, Archbishop Glyn Simon, Archbishop Charles Green, Archbishop Edwin Morris, Bishop John Poole-Hughes of Llandaff, and Bishop Watkin Williams of Bangor. Few other Welsh bishops of the twentieth century need, or warrant, separate biographies, with the possible exceptions of Archbishops John Morgan and G. O. Williams. However, a new study of Timothy Rees, CR, is urgently required. J. Lambert Rees, *Timothy Rees of Mirfield and Llandaff* (London, 1945) is little more than a brief memoir, and increasingly, thanks in part to the work of D. Densil Morgan, is his true significance for the Welsh church and society being recognized.
59. D. P. Davies, *Against the Tide. Christianity in Wales on the Threshold of a New Millennium* (Llandysul, 1995), p. 43.
60. Ibid., p. 60.

CHAPTER 2

INDEPENDENTS (CONGREGATIONALISTS)

Guto ap Gwynfor

'Jesus Christ is Lord'. This is the only creed or confession acknowledged by the Independents. To adhere to this basic principle implies that no synod nor bishop, committee nor denomination, and most certainly not the state, holds authority over a local community that has been gathered together in Jesus' name. Such a gathering, or congregation, is the Universal Church made visible in any given place. This is the meaning of 'Independent', a term guarded jealously by the Welsh Independents to the present day. It does not mean being apart from other churches, but it certainly does mean separation from any human religious or political establishment.[1]

Independency developed in Wales during a period of political, social and religious turmoil. During the sixteenth and seventeenth centuries new ideas flooded into the British Isles from the continent where the 'Radical Reformation'[2] had brought forth a variety of social and religious experiments that rejected any parochial controls.[3] The main advocates of these new ideas were the universities, but, as Wales had no such establishments, religious changes were introduced by English or English-trained clerics.[4] This made the people suspicious at first, and it took many generations for these ideas to take hold of the Welsh imagination. At the end of the sixteenth century, John Penri (1562/3–93)[5] had urged the Welsh people to take control of their own religious affairs. He was summarily executed as a traitor to Queen Elizabeth in 1593. His vision lay dormant for two generations until in 1639 William Wroth (1575/6–c.1641) gathered the first Independent church on Welsh soil at Llanfaches in Monmouthshire.[6] Wroth did not live to witness the tragic events that unfolded during the following decade, when the Civil Wars raged throughout the British Isles. The leaders of the Independents supported the Parliamentary cause in opposition to the majority Royalist forces in Wales, which ensured that the young church had to flee in 1642 to the Broadmead Church in Bristol and then in 1643 to London.[7] The end of the Second Civil War in Wales, with the fall of Pembroke castle to Oliver Cromwell in 1648, and the execution of the king the following January ushered in further religious changes.

During the Interregnum those who had been involved with the Llanfaches church now became significant preachers throughout Wales, propagating the gospel to the dark corners of the land.[8] To suggest that they were narrow-minded dull puritans would be a mistake as they were not quietist 'yes men', but rather lively and frequently controversial activists who were not afraid of debating new ideas. William Erbery (1604/5–54)[9] was the most original thinker amongst them, and he pleaded for social justice as well as a better deal for Wales:

> Ah pity pitty poor Wales! How are thy mighty fallen? But they are rising againe. England is yet too high, too stately, too proud, too full of pomp, and profit, and pleasure, to come down in the flesh, and to rise in the Spirit; though they can speak fine words: but Wales is a poor oppressed people, and despised also.[10]

Independency was not regarded as a denomination by these radicals, but was seen as an alternative way of constituting 'the Church'. These pioneers opposed 'denominationalism', but attempted to ensure that the Church in her local manifestation was a community of godly men and women. These 'Saints', as they were referred to, might differ upon many of the 'unimportant' matters such as baptism and church government, but were united in their love for Christ and guided by the Scriptures.[11] Walter Cradoc (1606–59)[12] appealed for

> more of the spirit of the Gospel, and of the Principles of the New Testament in us; and then for matter of Government of Churches, those things would follow: For to set up Government and Discipline before this comes into the soule, truly is to build Castles in the ayre [sic].[13]

He also claimed that the arguments concerning church government were but 'a little ruffling of the fringe',[14] and these issues should not divide the Saints.

Morgan Llwyd (1619–59), a preacher at Wrexham,[15] did the most to give the movement its Welsh identity. Heavily influenced by continental mysticism, particularly the work of Jacob Boehme,[16] Llwyd wrote mystical poems and many spiritual tracts in Welsh and in English. He emphasised the importance of the 'inner light', and it was no surprise that his close companion John ap John later became the main advocate of Quakerism in Wales. Llwyd emphasised the underlying principle of Independency that all those who loved the Lord were welcome in the local church:

> No honest soules [sic] kept out
> their presence we desire,
> no new engagement, no new bonds
> do we at all require.
> But welcome saincts [sic] as saincts,
> of all we make but one,
> exhorting one another more
> to live to Christ alone.[17]

Diversity, according to Llwyd, was to be welcomed rather than stifled:

> Know that Christs army hath two wings
> and diffring [sic] colours all

> his house hath divers sorted roomes [*sic*]
> his trees are short and tall.
>
> Mens faces, voices, differ much
> saincts are not all one size
> flowers in one garden vary too
> lett [*sic*] none monopolize.[18]

Vavasor Powell (1617–70)[19] was an 'antipaedobaptist' by conviction, yet he cooperated with the other Independents to evangelise Wales during the Interregnum. Having
been disillusioned by Cromwell's seizure of power in 1653 and the failure to provide
a Millenarian government that would, he hoped, lead to the second coming of Christ,
he vehemently protested against this military takeover.[20] Cradoc, on the other hand,
supported Cromwell, believing that both political and religious changes had to be
gradually introduced. Nevertheless both were a part of a 'revivalist' movement that
laid the foundations for a new Wales. Those foundations were more radical than
they were in England, and this, according to Pennar Davies, explains the difference
between Welsh and English nonconformity:

> It is often said that Welsh Puritanism came from England; but this is a confusing
> half-truth and needs to be qualified with the observations that Puritanism both
> in Wales and England is a part of the history of great European movements
> [i.e. the Radical Reformation or Anabaptism and Calvinism], and that
> Puritanism in Wales had its own ethos ... Welsh Puritanism had pro-
> portionately a greater measure of evangelicalism and radicalism in its
> composition ... The great Welsh leaders of the movement were Puritans
> of the left.[21]

After the restoration of the monarchy in 1660 circumstances rapidly changed. The
Church of England was reinstated as the state Church and by the Act of Uniformity
all those who refused to conform were to be punished. A series of draconian measures were introduced in order to curtail the activities of the dissenters. The result
of these measures was to ensure that the Independents and other dissenting communities, notably the Presbyterians, Baptists and Quakers, became underground
organisations. Even in the face of such hardships these communities increased in
number due to the tireless work of the second generation of dissenters. Men, such
as Stephen Hughes (1622? –1688),[22] 'the Apostle of Carmarthenshire', and Hugh
Owen (1639/40–1700), 'the Apostle of Meirionnydd',[23] succeeded in establishing a number of important churches which eventually became the parent institutions of a host of others. For example, congregations were established at Pencader,
Trelech, Carmarthen and Llanuwchllyn. Worshippers met in local houses, barns, or
in secluded areas near county borders,[24] which enabled them to escape the clutches
of the local sheriff by fleeing into the neighbouring county whenever the authorities
were sighted approaching their places of worship. Independents, Presbyterians and
Baptists cooperated and worshipped together without any animosity being shown.

In 1675 Henry Maurice (1647?–91)[25] explained that the church in Brecknockshire consisted 'mostly of independents in judgement and partly of baptists; their communion being founded upon union unto Christ, so far as may be, according to the rule of Gospel love'.[26]

There were a large number of these 'county' churches with their members congregating at different 'branches'. This was the situation in Brecknockshire when Rhys Prydderch (1620?–99) followed Maurice in ministering to the scattered membership from his home at Ystradwallter, near Llandovery. Prydderch had also established an Academy in c.1690 at Abercrychan, near his home, with the objective of training young men for the ministry as dissenters were barred from entering the official educational establishments.[27] This prohibition proved to be a blessing in disguise as, for the first time, Wales had institutions of higher education, even though they were illegal! Samuel Jones of Brynllywarch, near Maesteg (1628–1697), also established an Academy at his home.[28] These academies continued with their work over the centuries, but became peripatetic institutions as the tutors moved from one place to another. They were located at Wrexham, Newtown, Llanfyllin, Bala, Bangor, Abergavenny, Haverfordwest, Carmarthen, Llwynllwyd, near Talgarth, Brecon and Swansea, and their current successor is Coleg yr Annibynwyr Cymraeg presently situated at Aberystwyth.

Due to the difficult circumstances they encountered in the post-Restoration period the Independent churches became inward looking, abandoning their political radicalism and concentrating more on their own survival. Their political quietism needs best to be viewed in the context of their reputation as potential revolutionaries and regicides. Although greater freedom of worship was granted following the introduction of the Toleration Act in 1689 such groups were still regarded with some suspicion and therefore they continued their 'quietist' and pietistic way of life.[29] During the early decades of the eighteenth century the Independents unfortunately directed their energies towards internal squabbles and theological arguments with many congregations splitting into different groupings. New ideas from the continent influenced many of the leaders educated in the academies. Henllan, Amgoed and Wrexham churches were broken up by the dispute between High and Low Calvinists.[30] But it was in the 1730s that the most dangerous split occurred in the Teifi valley when Jenkin Jones (1700?–1742),[31] a member of Pantycreuddyn, Llandysul, left to form an Arminian Independent church at Llwynrhydowen. This was the first of many Independent churches that became Arminian throughout Wales, and by the end of the century many of these Arminian centres had become Arian and finally Unitarian. These internal arguments of the eighteenth century weakened the missionary work of the Independents and ensured that many left to evangelise through other religious communities. Among the secessionists was the hymn writer, William Williams, Pantycelyn, and Howel Harris who, after receiving their education at the Independent Academy while it was located at Llwynllwyd, near Talgarth, joined the Calvinistic Methodists.[32]

The Evangelical Revival was welcomed by many Independent ministers, and the momentum may not have survived had it not been for the cooperation of such preachers. For example, Edmund Jones of The Tranch, near Pontypool, organised tours for Howel Harris in Monmouthshire and other parts of south-east Wales, while other nonconformists assisted Harris in his missionary work in the north of the country.[33] It is unfortunate that this alliance was torn apart 'by theological differences and disciplines'.[34] The Independents and Methodists quarrelled due to Harris' intransigence, especially his refusal to allow his followers to form Independent churches.[35] Nevertheless some of these Methodists did so, and many others, who came under the Revival's influence, became ministers amongst the Independents. John Thomas, the hymn writer,[36] was influenced by Harris and Griffith Jones, Llanddowror, and became an Independent because of his dislike of denominationalism. In his autobiography, *Rhad Ras* (Free Grace), he observed that the churches he served or established were *anenwadol* (non-denominational).[37] In this respect the old vision was still alive. The Revival proved to be one of the turning points of Welsh religious history, and became a more potent force as it coincided with the beginnings of industrialisation in Wales and a massive expansion of the population. Moreover, the revival ensured that many working class migrants, who had moved from the rural areas into the industrial areas of south Wales, became nonconformists and literate as a result of the pioneering work of Griffith Jones, while their chapels became the centres of a new and confident culture. The style of worship also radically changed due to the effect of the Revival. Until the 1730s the Independents were known as 'Sentars Sychion' ('Dry Dissenters') and each Sunday a service would be held in the morning that could last for three hours. Their sermons were long and monotonous; some psalms were sung by the congregation whilst seated; and prayers were delivered by the minister while the congregation was standing.[38]

Further changes were also evident. The early Independents met in convenient buildings adapted for their gatherings, but from the 1690s chapels were built by the members. These were simple buildings with locally crafted furniture, such as benches or box-pews brought by the members, but many in the congregation remained standing on an earthen floor. In the centre of one of the walls was the pulpit with the communion table in its shadow and the 'Word' was elevated above the sacraments. Ministers supported themselves financially by following self-employed secular callings; some married wealthy women but they were mainly farmers, shop-keepers, craftsmen, even inn-keepers, while the most popular calling was that of a school-teacher. The minister was not a priest; he was an ordinary member of the church chosen by the members to give a lead in the worship and to study the scriptures. Daily services were held in the homes of members and led by the head of the family, and, therefore, great emphasis was laid on the '*allor deuluol*' (the family altar). It must be remembered that these were extended families with domestic servants and farmhands present. It was at these services, particularly when the minister or a visiting preacher was invited, that young men first showed signs of being called to the ministry. Consequently, they were actively encouraged by the congregation to receive a formal education to assist their calling.

The Evangelical Revival also occasioned a change in the style of preaching with the advent of the Welsh '*hwyl*'. David Davies (1763–1816), minister of Llangeler and later Swansea, was responsible for this development. He was the first dissenter to be ordained without receiving formal academic training, and became known as

the '*Utgorn Arian*' (Silver Trumpet) because of his powerful preaching. Hymn singing became increasingly popular as a result of the Revival with hymns being set at
first to popular tunes,[39] but it was not long before composers started to set them to
newly composed music. Since there were no hymn-books, the '*codwr canu*' (choir-
master/precentor) would recite the hymn one phrase at the time and the congregation
would sing it. In many churches the '*codwr canu*' would also set the tune, but in some
churches the fiddle or penny whistle would be used. The organ did not come to be
greatly used until after the mid-nineteenth century, even then there was great opposition to it. For example, in the 1860s when the recently appointed station-master first
introduced an organ into the chapel in Pencader, half the congregation walked out in
protest.

Towards the end of the eighteenth century, again as the result of the Revival, a
change occurred in the social composition of the leaders of the Independents. The
sons of people of humble origins became prominent, such as David Davies, who
was a publican's son. Indeed, one of the three generally recognised as the stal-
warts of the Welsh pulpit at the beginning of the century was William Williams
o'r Wern (1781–1840) who was born into a poverty-stricken family from the
highlands of Meirionnydd.[40] Williams' ministry represented the most energetic
and active period of the Independents in Wales as they took the lead in the formation of a nonconformity which developed into a radical socio-political as well as
a religious movement. As R. Tudur Jones observed the fundamental changes that
took place between 1790 and 1830 were 'so powerful that the Independents in
the middle of the twentieth century ... [were] still using the same agents believing that they have been in existence since apostolic times'.[41] An interest in the
welfare of overseas peoples became a concern which ensured the formation
and support of missionary movements such as the London Missionary Society
(LMS)[42] and the Bible Society.

The High Calvinist theology of the eighteenth century was effectively challenged by a brilliant theologian who became the principal of the Independent colleges at Abergavenny, Oswestry and Rotherham. Edward Williams of Glanclwyd
(1750–1813)[43] introduced the '*Sustem Newydd*' (New System) of Low Calvinism
which paved the way for the political and social radicalism that characterised the
nineteenth and twentieth centuries. Williams' first generation of disciples included
John Roberts of Llanbrynmair (1767–1834)[44] and Michael Jones of Llanuwchllyn
(1787–1853),[45] both of whom were forerunners of the radical leaders of the
Victorian era. By the early nineteenth century Independency in Wales developed into a more working class movement. It was also mainly a Welsh-language
movement which chimed with the cultural aspirations of the Welsh people. The
established church came to be regarded as a tool of the state and some Anglican
clergy were complicit in attempts to undermine the Welsh language. In turn, the
Independents, and other nonconformists, were regarded with great suspicion by the
English authorities. This was nothing new. They were seen as a 'fifth column' during the wars waged against Napoleonic France at the beginning of the nineteenth
century. This suspicion did have some basis in fact as many of the more radical
elements in Welsh dissent supported the principles of the French Revolution as

they had previously supported the American revolutionaries.[46] Moreover, during the first half of the nineteenth century Independent ministers, particularly David Rees of Llanelli (1801–1869), gave a prominent political lead. Davies' battle cry as the editor of a radical monthly *Y Diwygiwr* (The Revivalist) was *'Cynhyrfer! Cynhyrfer! Cynhyrfer!'* (Agitate! Agitate! Agitate!). He, and others, campaigned vigorously against injustices, such as the Corn Laws in the 1840s which kept the price of bread artificially high. With the increase in the levels of literacy, due to the work of the Sunday Schools, radical periodicals such as *Y Diwygiwr, Y Dysgedydd* (The Instructor) and *Y Cronicl* (The Chronicle) sold in their thousands and profoundly influenced the Welsh working class.[47]

This suspicion was intensified further by the radical activities of the Welsh working class and their nonconformist spokesmen during the first half of the nineteenth century. For example, *The Times* wrongly accused David Rees of Llanelli of being the leader of the Rebecca movement in the late-1830 and 1840s. The Government responded swiftly to suppress riotous activities and appointed a *Commission of Inquiry into the State of Education in Wales* which produced a three-volume report in 1847. This report was infamously dubbed 'Brad y Llyfrau Gleision' (The Treason of the Blue Books) because the Commissioners merely concluded that Wales was suffering from two major obstructions to progress: the Welsh language and nonconformity. R. Tudur Jones claimed that the reports were 'a great blessing for Wales' as they affirmed the radical attitudes of the Welsh people.[48] The response was immediate: it provoked a new sense of purpose among the Welsh, especially nonconformists who became the most committed defenders of cultural and religious freedom. Independent ministers took a leading role, including Evan Jones (Ieuan Gwynedd 1822–52),[49] William Rees (Gwilym Hiraethog 1802–83), regarded by some as the 'father of Welsh radicalism',[50] and Henry Richard (1812–88), known as the 'Apostle for Peace'.[51]

By the middle of the nineteenth century nonconformity had become more respectable and less controversial. The 1851 Religious Census demonstrated the extent to which the established church had lost ground to nonconformity, and the overwhelming transformation of Wales into a predominantly nonconformist nation. Well over half the population attended a place of worship on Sundays and of those over eighty per cent worshipped in a chapel rather than an Anglican church. While it has been demonstrated since that the Census was deeply flawed and its conclusions open to question, at the time nonconformist leaders were jubilant. Notwithstanding the dubious statistics, there is little doubt that the nonconformist confession was expanding rapidly. On average, chapels were being built at the rate of one every week, and communities were the focus of regular revivals, especially in the industrial valleys of south Wales. Between 1800 and 1851 the number of Independent ministers had grown from 74 to 319, and Independency was firmly established.[52]

Nonconformity was now closely identified with Welsh political, cultural and religious life, and as representing the socio-political aspirations of the working class. Prys Morgan emphasises that by the 1860s 'the Welsh way of life came to be identified with nonconformist and radical Wales'. Working people 'attended Sunday school, bought books, saved money to buy property, sent its sons to the ministry, and took political action against oppression'.[53] Henry Richard, who had been an Independent minister before becoming the first secretary of the Peace Society, successfully fought the election to become the Liberal Member of Parliament for Merthyr Tydfil in 1868, on the grounds there was a great need for members in the British Parliament to represent the beliefs and aspirations of the Welsh nation. Ieuan Gwynedd Jones identifies three main strands in Richard's beliefs: nationalism, nonconformity and the establishment of democracy.[54] Another radical Independent minister was Samuel Roberts (S. R.)[55] of Llanbrynmair (1800–1885). Richard and Roberts injected the strong element of pacifism into the nonconformist movement which has been one of the hallmarks of the Independents to the present day.[56] As Richard explained, 'we are pledged to the doctrine that all war is unchristian and unlawful, and cannot, whilst condemning it in the abstract, defend it in the concrete'.[57]

The Independent minister and college principal, Michael D. Jones (1822–1898), is widely regarded as the father of modern Welsh nationalism.[58] He was a visionary who believed that nonconformist culture could contribute to the creation of a new Wales, while his earlier ministry in America had taught him that emigration was not the answer to his country's problems. Yet he was pragmatic enough to acknowledge that the opportunities to make a new life would prove irresistible to those people whose living and working conditions were impoverished. He therefore supported and promoted the Patagonian venture. Jones' nationalism, decentralised socialism and his democratic principles were developments of his congregationalism, and his vision has formed the pattern of Welsh nationalism ever since.[59]

When the Union of Welsh Independents was first mooted, Jones was completely opposed to it and, as principal of Bala Theological College, he was involved in a bitter dispute about its constitution. Despite his opposition the Union was achieved in 1872,[60] and since that time there has been a tendency to regard Independency as a denomination. A similar dispute arose at the end of the twentieth century when an attempt was made to create a new denomination out of the four main denominations in Wales. Nevertheless the Union was formed to help churches, not to control them, and as R. Tudur Jones contemporary study emphasised the Union was 'a free and voluntary body'.[61] He recognised the underlying weakness of Welsh nonconformity between 1890 and 1914, the period of its greatest strength.[62] There was a tendency to stress the importance of outward respectability at the expense of tackling the more fundamental needs of Welsh people during the critical periods of war and depression, and the ensuing crisis of Welsh identity. This manifested itself in their negative response to the rise of socialism at the beginning of the twentieth century, and their support for the war effort had a detrimental effect on the churches. Gareth Evans observed that:

> most of the churches recognized the need for social reform, but they disagreed
> over the methods to achieve improvements. Nonconformists had spent the best
> part of two centuries trying to win liberties for the individual believer in the face
> of hostile state oppression. It was hardly surprising that they were deeply suspi-
> cious of the socialist creed with its apparent emphasis on nationalization and

state action. The traditional nonconformist message of individual responsibility and individual moral regeneration made the acceptance of a collectivist creed extremely difficult, if not impossible.[63]

Not all nonconformists were opposed to socialism. During the inter-war years many of the Independent radicals supported the rise of the Labour Party in Wales. T. E. Nicholas (1880–1971), a personal friend of Keir Hardie, was one the most prominent and colourful advocates. Others, however, such as Thomas Rees (1869–1924), John Morgan Jones (1873–1946) and D. Miall Edwards (1873–1941) tried to counter the challenge of socialist politics by emphasising the 'Social Gospel'. They believed that by putting into practice the principles of God's Kingdom a better society could be created. This emphasis on the 'Social Gospel' drew upon liberal politics that was gaining ground on the European continent. Welsh theologians such as David Adams (1845–1922) were strongly influenced by their German counterparts, and Adams became the main spokesman for this new theology. Since the Independents were not bound by any specific confession they were free to experiment with new ideas. As Robert Pope has explained:

the Older Dissent [i.e. Independents and Baptists] had a far more pronounced political tradition than that of the Methodists ... [they] also enjoyed at least theoretical freedom from confessions of faith, which enabled them to explore ideological areas officially declared off-limits for those of other traditions.[64]

As the Labour Party became more successful the Welsh working class increasingly abandoned the nonconformist chapels. Indeed, the 'ultimate failure' of nonconformity has been attributed to 'an inability, for a multitude of reasons, to retain the interest and allegiance of the working class'.[65] Robert Pope is nevertheless keen to exonerate Welsh nonconformity from neglecting their working-class members:

working-class withdrawal from the chapel could hardly have been due to a lack of social concern or a socially orientated theology on the part of Welsh nonconformists. This in itself is a point which needs to be made. Welsh nonconformity, certainly up to the Second World War, was distinctly social in its practical concern and in its theology.[66]

In time, the radical elements in Welsh nonconformity became disillusioned with a Labour Party that seemed to have abandoned both its Christian and Welsh roots, and became increasingly attached to Plaid Cymru, The Party of Wales.

One of the earliest leaders of Plaid Cymru was J. E. Daniel (1902–1962),[67] who was a professor at the Independent Theological College at Bangor. His essay, 'Gwaed y Teulu' (the Blood of the Family), was a landmark publication 'in the development of a specifically biblical philosophy of Christian nationalism in Wales'.[68] He also led the Barthian backlash to the dominant theological liberalism that predominated in Wales. Daniel was also a Christian pacifist, as were two of his successors as Presidents of Plaid Cymru, Gwynfor Evans (1912–2005) and Dafydd Elis Thomas.

Evans was elected President of the Union of Welsh Independents in 1953 and served as Treasurer during the 1960s, he was also a close personal friend of two of the most influential and radical Independents of the latter half of the twentieth century: Pennar Davies (1911–1996)[69] and R. Tudur Jones (1922–1998), principals of the Independent Theological Colleges at Swansea and Bangor. Although the two men were distinctive in their theology, they shared a commitment to Christian national- ism, radicalism and pacifism. They directly challenged the establishment by publicly supporting the activities of *Cymdeithas yr Iaith Gymraeg, CND Cymru* and other non-violent direct action groups. In this they, and many others, followed the best traditions of Welsh Independents from the conviction that anything else would be detrimental to the spiritual and cultural life of the Welsh nation. At the beginning of the twenty-first century when globalisation, cultural uniformity and nuclear annihi- lation threaten God's creation, there is a profound need for the radical Independent testimony that emphasises the value of diversity and the freedom to experiment in worship and ideas. Our greatest need is that the Independents themselves come to realise this and use their freedom to fulfil their great potential.

Notes

1. For a comprehensive study of Welsh Independents see R. Tudur Jones, *Hanes Annibynwyr Cymru* (Abertawe, 1966).
2. The 'Radical Reformers' are frequently, and incorrectly, referred to as 'Anabaptists'.
3. For general developments see G. R. Elton, *Reform and Reformation: England 1509–1558* (London, 1977); J. J. Scarisbrick, *The Reformation and the English People* (Oxford, 1982); M. J. Watts, *The Dissenters from the Reformation to the French Revolution* (Oxford, 1978); R. J. Acheson, *Radical Puritans in England, 1550–1660* (London, 1990).
4. For examples, see Thomas Rees, *History of Protestant Nonconformity in Wales* (2nd edn. London, 1883); G. Williams (ed.), *Welsh Reformation Essays* (Cardiff, 1967); G. Williams, *Recovery, Reorientation and Reformation: Wales 1415–1642* (Oxford and Cardiff, 1987); J. Gwynfor Jones, *Early Modern Wales, 1525–1640* (Basingstoke, 1994), ch. 4.
5. John Penri (or Penry) obtained his BA at Cambridge in 1584 and his MA at Oxford in 1586. For further details, see J. E. Lloyd and R. T. Jenkins (eds), *The Dictionary of Welsh Biography* (*DWB*) (London, 1959); Claire Cross, 'Penry, John (1562/3–1593)', in H. C. G. Matthew and Brian Harrison (eds), *Oxford Dictionary of National Biography* (Oxford, 2004); http://www.oxforddnb.com/view/article/21894 (accessed April 2010).
6. *DWB*; Stephen K. Roberts, 'Wroth, William (1575/6–1638x41)', in Matthew and Harrison (eds), *Oxford Dictionary of National Biography*; http://www.oxforddnb.com/view/article/30086 (accessed April 2010). See also R. G. Gruffydd, 'William Wroth a chychwyniadau Anghydffurfiaeth yng Nghymru', *Ysgrifau Diwinyddol* (Pen-y-bont ar Ogwr, 1988); Trevor Watts, 'William Wroth (1570–1641). Father of Welsh Nonconformity', *Congregational History Magazine*, 2, 5 (1989).
7. These events are summarised in Geraint H. Jenkins, *Protestant Dissenters in Wales, 1639–1689* (Cardiff, 1992), p. 14.
8. For details see C. Hill, 'Propagating the Gospel', in H. E. Bell and R. L. Ollard (eds), *Historical Essays, 1600–1750* (London, 1963), pp. 35–59; C. Hill, 'Puritans and the 'Dark Corners of the Land'', *Transactions of the Royal Historical Society*, 13 (1963), 77–102.
9. Stephen K. Roberts, 'Erbery, William (1604/5–1654)', in Matthew and Harrison (eds), *Oxford Dictionary of National Biography*; http://www.oxforddnb.com/view/article/8832 (accessed March 2010). See also B. Ll. James, 'The evolution of a radical: the life and career of William Erbery (1604–54)', *Journal of Welsh Ecclesiastical History*, 3 (1986), 31–48.

10. William Erbery, *Apocrypha* (1652), and quoted in Jenkins, *Protestant Dissenters in Wales*, p. 74.

11. See Geoffrey Nuttall, *The Welsh Saints 1640–1660* (Cardiff, 1957).

12. *DWB*; Stephen K. Roberts, 'Cradock, Walter (*c*.1606–1659)', in Matthew and Harrison (eds), *Oxford Dictionary of National Biography*; http://www.oxforddnb.com/view/article/6564 (accessed March 2010). See also Noel Gibbard, *Walter Cradock: A New Testament Saint* (Bridgend, 1977).

13. Walter Cradoc, *Mount Sion* (1649), and quoted in Nuttall, *Welsh Saints*, p. 28.

14. Walter Cradoc, from a sermon on 1 Corinthians 10:23, and printed in Iain Murray, The *Reformation of the Church. A Collection of Reformed and Puritan Documents on Church Issues* (Edinburgh, 1965), p. 322.

15. *DWB*. See also Stephen K. Roberts, 'Llwyd, Morgan (1619–1659)', in Matthew and Harrison (eds), *Oxford Dictionary of National Biography*; http://www.oxford dnb.com/view/article/16869 (accessed April 2010); Thomas M. Wynn, *Morgan Llwyd* (Cardiff, 1984); Thomas M. Wynn, 'Morgan Llwyd y Piwritan', in G. H. Jenkins (ed.), *Cof Cenedl*, III (Llandysul, 1988), pp. 61–88.

16. A useful study is provided in Robin Waterfield, *Jacob Boehme: Essential Readings* (Wellingborough, 1989).

17. Quoted in Nuttall, *Welsh Saints*, p. 42.

18. Gerald Morgan (ed.), *This World of Wales: An Anthology of Anglo-Welsh Poetry from the Seventeenth to the Twentieth Century* (Cardiff, 1968), p. 189. The poem entitled '1648' was written after Llwyd had been on a mission to north Wales in that year.

19. E. Bagshaw (ed.), *The Life and Death of Mr. Vavasor Powell, that Faithful Minister and Confessor of Jesus Christ* (London, 1671); *DWB*; R. T. Jones, *Vavasor Powell* (Abertawe, 1971); Stephen K. Roberts, 'Powell, Vavasor (1617–1670)', in Matthew and Harrison (eds), *Oxford Dictionary of National Biography*; http://www.oxforddnb.com/view/article/2266 (accessed April 2010).

20. Jenkins, *Protestant Dissenters*, pp. 25–6.

21. Pennar Davies, 'Episodes in the History of Brecknockshire Dissent', *Brycheiniog*, III, (1957), 23.

22. *DWB*; Brynley F. Roberts, 'Hughes, Stephen (1622?–1688)', in Matthew and Harrison (eds), *Oxford Dictionary of National Biography*; http://www.oxforddnb.com/view/article/68198 (accessed April 2010); G. H. Jenkins, 'Apostol sir Gaerfyrddin: Stephen Hughes, *c*.1622–1688', *Y Cofiadur*, 54 (1989), 3–23; Glanmor Williams, 'Stephen Hughes (1622–1688) : 'Apostol Sir Gâr' (The Apostle of Carmarthenshire)', *Carmarthenshire Antiquary*, 37 (2001), 21–30.

23. Zachary Mather, *Hugh Owen, Bronyclydwr: Apostol y Gogledd* (Wrecsam, 1899); *DWB*; J. E. Lloyd, 'Owen, Hugh (1639/40–1700)', rev. Stephen Wright, in Matthew and Harrison (eds), *Oxford Dictionary of National Biography*; http://www.oxforddnb.com/view/article/21006 (accessed April 2010).

24. There are many inaccessible 'sacred spots' such as Ogof Cwm Hwplyn, near Pencader, and Ogof Craig y Widdon, near Cefnarthen, both in Carmarthenshire, which have entered local folklore as places where the Independents worshipped during the time of persecution. See Jenkins, *Protestant Dissenters*, p. 51.

25. For detail see *DWB*; Edward Vallance, 'Maurice, Henry (1647?–1691)', in Matthew and Harrison (eds), *Oxford Dictionary of National Biography*; http://www.oxforddnb.com/view/article/18385 (accessed April 2010); R. Tudur Jones, *Congregationalism in Wales*, ed. Robert Pope (Cardiff, 2004), passim.

26. Quoted by Arthur Jones, 'Eglwys Llanigon a Henry Maurice', in Undeb yr Annibynwyr Cymraeg, *Eglwysi'r Annibynwyr* (Undeb yr Annibynwyr, 1939), p. 44.

27. *DWB*; Jones, *Congregationalism in Wales*, p. 97.

28. *DWB*; D. R. L. Jones, 'Jones, Samuel (1628–1697)', in Matthew and Harrison (eds), *Oxford Dictionary of National Biography*; http://www.oxforddnb.com/view/article/15080 (accessed April 2010); G. H. Jenkins, *The Foundations of Modern Wales, 1642–1780* (pbk edn. Oxford, 1993), p. 196.

29. For a study of this period see Jones, *Congregationalism in Wales*, ch. 7.

30. For details see ibid., p. 104.

31. *DWB*; R. M. J. Jones, 'Jones, Jenkin (1700?–1742)', rev. Dylan Foster Evans, in Matthew and Harrison (eds), *Oxford Dictionary of National Biography*; http://www.oxforddnb.com/view/article/15020 (accessed April 2010).

32. Williams' father was a deacon at Cefnarthen Independent church, while his mother had provided the land to build the chapel for the Calvinist Independents at Pentretygwyn after their secession from

Cefnarthen church which had become Arminian. Details are provided in *DWB*; Derec Llwyd Morgan, 'Williams, William (1717–1791)', in Matthew and Harrison (eds), *Oxford Dictionary of National Biography*; http://www.oxforddnb.com/view/article/29556 (accessed April 2010). As illustrated elsewhere in this volume, these 'Hen Ymneilltuwyr' (Old Nonconformists) made a valuable contribution to Welsh religious life, and laid the foundations for the enthusiastic awakening that was to follow. By publishing books in Welsh they ensured that the reading public had an expansive choice of religious works upon which to base their understanding and strengthen their personal devotions.

33. Jenkins, *Foundations of Modern Wales*, p. 362.
34. Ibid.
35. See Jones, *Congregationalism in Wales*, pp. 111–13.
36. *DWB*; R. Tudur Jones, 'Thomas, John (*bap.* 1730, *d.* in or before 1806)', in Matthew and Harrison (eds), *Oxford Dictionary of National Biography*; http://www.oxforddnb.com/view/article/62918 (accessed April 2010).
37. For Thomas' autobiography see John Thomas, *Rhad Ras* (Swansea, 1810; repr. ed. J. Dyfnallt Owen. Cardiff, 1949).
38. The change is discussed in Jones, *Congregationalism in Wales*, pp. 117–21.
39. Many of our modern hymn tunes are old Welsh folk-songs which underwent a process of change to suit Victorian tastes.
40. W. Rees, *Memoirs of the late the Rev. W. Williams, of Wern*, trans. James Rhys Jones (London, 1846); *DWB*; D. L. Thomas, 'Williams, William [Williams y Wern] (1781–1840)', rev. Mari A. Williams, in Matthew and Harrison (eds), *Oxford Dictionary of National Biography*; http://www.oxforddnb.com/view/article/29558 (accessed April 2010). The other two were the Baptist, Christmas Evans, and the Calvinistic Methodist, John Elias.
41. Jones, *Hanes Annibynwyr Cymru*, p. 169.
42. The LMS later amalgamated with other missionary societies in forming the Council for World Mission.
43. W. T. Owen, *Edward Williams, D.D. His Life, Thought and Influence* (Cardiff, 1963). See also *DWB*; J. E. Lloyd, 'Williams, Edward (1750–1813)', rev. S. J. Skedd, in Matthew and Harrison (eds), *Oxford Dictionary of National Biography*; http://www.oxforddnb.com/view/article/29497 (accessed April 2010).
44. *DWB*; D. L. Thomas, 'Roberts, John (1767–1834)', rev. Mari A. Williams, in Matthew and Harrison (eds), *Oxford Dictionary of National Biography*; http://www.oxforddnb.com/view/article/23761 (accessed April 2010); Samuel Roberts, *Cofiant y Parch. John Roberts, o Lanbrynmair* (Llanelli, 1837).
45. *DWB*.
46. Jones, *Congregationalism in Wales*, pp. 130–1.
47. The three named periodicals were edited by Independent ministers. See ibid., pp. 176–7.
48. Jones, *Hanes Annibynwyr Cymru*, p. 219; Jones, *Congregationalism in Wales*, pp. 170–1.
49. *DWB*; D. L. Thomas, 'Jones, Evan (1820–1852)', rev. D. Ben Rees, in Matthew and Harrison (eds), *Oxford Dictionary of National Biography*; http://www.oxforddnb.com/view/article/15001 (accessed April 2010).
50. *DWB*; R. A. Johnson, 'Rees, William [Gwilym Hiraethog] (1802–1883)', rev. Mari A. Williams, in Matthew and Harrison (eds), *Oxford Dictionary of National Biography*; http://www.oxforddnb.com/view/article/23290 (accessed April 2010); D. Ben Rees, *The Polymath: Reverend William Rees, ('Gwilym Hiraethog' 1802–1883) of Liverpool* (Liverpool, 2002).
51. *DWB*; Matthew Cragoe, 'Richard, Henry (1812–1888)', in Matthew and Harrison (eds), *Oxford Dictionary of National Biography*; http://www.oxforddnb.com/view/article/23527 (accessed April 2010); B. L. Davies, *Henry Richard: A Radical Dissenter and Education in Wales* (Aberystwyth, 1993).
52. Jones, *Hanes yr Annibynwyr*, p. 191.
53. Prys Morgan, *The Eighteenth Century Renaissance* (Cardiff, 1981), p. 157.
54. Ieuan Gwynedd Jones, 'Henry Richard ac Iaith y Gwleidydd yn y Bedwaredd Ganrif ar Bymtheg', in Jenkins (ed.), *Cof Cenedl*, III, p. 131.

55. He was the son of John Roberts, Llanbrynmair. See *DWB*; D. L. Thomas, 'Roberts, Samuel (1800–1885)', rev. D. Ben Rees, in Matthew and Harrison (eds), *Oxford Dictionary of National Biography*; http://www.oxforddnb.com/view/article/23773 (accessed April 2010).
56. A host of resolutions were adopted by the Union of Welsh Independents condemning the use of violence and the preparations for war during the twentieth century.
57. Jones, 'Henry Richard', p. 67.
58. He was the son of Michael Jones, Llanuwchllyn. See *DWB*; R. Tudur Jones, 'Jones, Michael Daniel (1822–1898)', in Matthew and Harrison (eds), *Oxford Dictionary of National Biography*; http://www.oxforddnb.com/view/article/49170 (accessed April 2010).
59. R. Tudur Jones, 'Michael D. Jones a thynged y Genedl', in Jenkins (ed.), *Cof Cenedl*, I (Llandysul, 1986), pp. 97–123.
60. For details see Jones, *Congregationalism in Wales*, pp. 198–204.
61. R. Tudur Jones, *Yr Undeb: Hanes Undeb yr Annibynwyr Cymraeg 1872–1972* (Abertawe, 1975), p. 414.
62. R. Tudur Jones, *Ffydd ac Argyfwng Cenedl: Cristionogaeth a Diwylliant yng Nghymru 1890–1914* (2 vols. Swansea, 1981–2).
63. D. Gareth Evans, *A History of Wales 1906–2000* (Cardiff, 2000), pp. 40–1.
64. Robert Pope, *Seeking God's Kingdom: The Nonconformist Social Gospel in Wales, 1906–1939* (Cardiff, 1999), pp. 37–8.
65. Robert Pope, *Building Jerusalem: Nonconformity, Labour and the Social Question in Wales, 1906–1939* (Cardiff, 1998), p. 249.
66. Pope, *Seeking God's Kingdom*, p. 31.
67. D. Densil Morgan, *Cedyrn Canrif: Crefydd a Chymdeithas yng Nghymru'r Ugeinfed Ganrif* (Caerdydd, 2001).
68. D. Densil Morgan, *The Span of the Cross: Christian Religion and Society in Wales 1914–2000* (Cardiff, 1999), p. 157.
69. For details of the life and work of Pennar Davies and R. Tudur Jones see Morgan, *Cedyrn Canrif.*

CHAPTER 3

BAPTISTS

D. Hugh Matthews

Although they have a shared inheritance, Welsh Baptists can boast a separate identity to their English counterparts. By the mid-eighteenth century, most of the Baptists
in Wales were Calvinist (or Particular) in their theology and closed communion in
their practice, resulting in the trust-deeds of the majority of Welsh Baptist churches
today describing them as 'Particular Closed Communion Baptists'.[1] Traditionally,
they have also been anti-clerical in their outlook but strongly in favour of the congregational and associational principle.

The first Baptists in Wales

There is no certainty concerning the arrival of Baptists in Wales. Individuals with
Baptist leanings may have formed part of the dissenting congregation at Llanfaches
in Monmouthshire in 1639, and in the following years Baptists were part of congregational churches when there was no Baptist fellowship nearby. In c.1646 Hugh
Evans, however, brought the teachings of the General (or Arminian) Baptists to mid-
Wales and formed the first all-Baptist fellowship in Brecon and Radnorshire, which
became known as 'Hugh Evans's People'. Hugh Evans of Llan-hir in Radnorshire
came into contact with a General Baptist church in Coventry while he was an appren-
tice to a clothier in the Midlands. There,

> being zealous in the Gospel, and his love much kindled towards God and man,
> and hearing that his country was destitute of that means of salvation, that is to
> say the preaching of the word and the ministration of the ordinance of Jesus
> [viz. believers' baptism], he was much moved with love to the truth and to his
> native country.[2]

Hugh Evans thereafter went to London to plead the cause of Wales before Jeremiah
Ives who ministered to the church in Old Jewry, and appears to have been commis-
sioned by that church to spread the gospel in Wales, gathering followers in the counties of Brecon and Radnorshire.[3]

The Particular Baptists

In 1649, John Miles (1620/1–83), a puritan preacher, became convinced of Baptist principles and subsequently was the chief organiser of the Calvinistic Baptists in Wales. A native of Newton Clifford in the Welsh-speaking part of Herefordshire, he was educated at Oxford and is assumed to have been a chaplain in the Parliamentary army and was based near Swansea.[4] In Spring 1649, accompanied by Thomas Proud, he arrived in London and was baptized at the Particular Baptist church, which met at the Glasshouse in Broad Street.[5] Encouraged to return to Wales to propagate the Baptist message, Miles returned to Glamorgan. On 1 October 1649, aware that there were many in Wales who questioned infant baptism in contrast to the acceptance of believers' baptism, he gathered a church at Ilston, on the Gower peninsula.[6] Indeed, it can be argued that Miles did more than anyone to establish the Baptists of Wales on a firmer foundation. He did this in two ways. First, he was an able organiser who established 'a quasi-Presbyterian' system of church government,[7] which kept the churches at Ilston (1649),[8] Olchon (1650), Hengoed (1650), Carmarthen (1651) and Abergavenny/Llanwenarth (1652) under strict control.[9] These churches were, in reality, 'regional' churches with more than one meeting-place for each of the five centres. Representatives of all the churches met together in a six-monthly General Meeting, which acted almost like a synod, with Miles as the main spokesman among the ministers.[10]

Next, Miles used the laws passed by Parliament during the Commonwealth to the advantage of Baptist witness in Wales. The Act for the Better Propagation and Preaching of the Gospel in Wales (22 February 1649/50) was an opportunity for chosen Commissioners and Approvers, including Miles, to promote a good quality puritan minister for each parish. This Act expired in 1653 and was not renewed, but in its place the Committee for the Approbation of Publique Preachers ('Triers') appointed 226 preachers to parishes in Wales. Many of the appointees under these measures were Baptists, and it was not unusual for the incumbent in the parish church at this time to be a Baptist without formal theological training, but a person 'sent forth' by one of the five Particular Baptist churches of south Wales. All of these ministers, including Miles, were paid by the state.[11] The acceptance of state payments was to become one of the early controversies which troubled the Baptists in Wales. Was it right to take the state's money to do the Lord's work? The Llanwenarth church, unwilling for ministers to receive state subsidies, decided in 1655 to distance itself from those who 'doe receive maintenance from the Magistrates'.[12] There is no evidence that this decision affected the other churches, and Miles's attitude to those who objected to state maintenance is summed up in his *An Antidote Against the Infection of the Times* (1656). Here he attacked the spiritually proud, Quakers in particular, whom he accused of being jealous of maintained ministers:

> often times they have nothing to justly charge them with, they cavil at their lawful maintenance, which God the wise disposer of all things hath ordained for them ... and by his providence gives unto them.[13]

Another controversy which had surfaced earlier concerned 'the singing of Psalms and hymns in Publicke worship'. At the General Meeting in Carmarthen in March 1651 the propriety of singing was raised, and churches were invited to consider the matter. Singing in public worship posed many problems for the dissenters: could words other than those from the Scriptures (the Psalms) be justified? Could the words of Scripture be versified in order to sing them? Would worshippers not perjure themselves before God if they sang words which did not convey exactly their own experiences and beliefs? At the General Meeting in Llantrisant in August 1654, the Abergavenny church raised the issue only for it to be deferred, while John Miles, David Davies and William Thomas were 'desired to state the point severally, according to Scripture'.[14] The response is not recorded, but it would appear that the singing of Psalms was, itself, acceptable. This can be assumed because Miles' defence of Baptist principles and doctrines in *An Antidote* contained advertisements for several books offering 'the singing of Psalms in Welsh'.[15] Nevertheless, although the singing of Psalms may have been acceptable and other singing 'in the Spirit' seems to have been practised, hymns for congregational singing were not fully accepted among the Baptist community until they became a feature of the Methodist revival of the eighteenth century.

In the 1650s a number of the Baptists at Llanwenarth and Olchon adopted the Arminian practice of imposition (or laying on) of hands on the newly baptized. They had possibly confused the names of two distinct Baptist meeting places in London, and thinking that they were dealing with the Particular Baptists of the Glass House, had contacted instead William Rider and the General Baptists of Glaziers' Hall. The question was raised in the General Meeting by the Carmarthen church in 1654 when its delegates inquired: 'Whether laying on of hands be an ordinance of Christ; and if it be so, then upon whom?'[16] The imposition of hands on those being set apart for the ministry of the Word and for offices within the churches became accepted practice, but insistence on laying hands on the newly baptized became a contentious issue, and this question was to dominate Baptist thinking in Wales for more than a century.

Open Communion Baptists

Along with Hugh Evans's People, Miles' Baptists favoured closed communion, but there was also a third group of Baptists in Wales. These were Particular in their theology, but favoured open communion and were often found in mixed congregations alongside Congregationalists. Open communion Baptists in south Wales had links with the Broadmead church in Bristol although they were never organised in the same way as Miles' churches. These three groupings were tolerant of one another and cooperated together, as well as with other dissenters, both during the Cromwellian period and in the dark days of oppression that followed the Restoration of the monarchy in 1660. Their co-operation during the 1650s is illustrated by the way in which the Commonwealth provisions for puritans of all descriptions were administered. If it was convenient to cooperate when state money was available to support the work of spreading the Gospel, it was prudent to be supportive of each other and cooperate after the Restoration. However, after the Act of Toleration in 1689, without ever losing their tolerance of each other and other dissenters or their willingness to cooperate, the three Baptist groupings recovered their own separate identities.[17]

Following the Restoration and John Miles' emigration to America in 1663,[18] the General Meeting of the Particular Baptists in Wales became redundant, but in 1689 the churches attended a meeting of Baptists called by the London churches and subsequently joined the Western Association of Baptist churches in 1692. Eight years later, in 1700, the Welsh churches formed themselves into an Association of Particular, Closed Communion churches and within a comparatively short time all the Baptist churches in Wales, with the exception of Wrexham, had joined.[19] The churches of this Association raised and supported their own ministers, stressed 'Believers Baptism, laying on of hands, the doctrine of personal election, and final perseverance'.[20] A fourth grouping of Baptists emerged briefly in 1750. They were led by Charles Winter who embraced Arminianism after he had taken issue with the Association over the question of Calvinism. The twenty-three members who were excommunicated by the church at Hengoed built a meeting-house at Craig-y-fargod, Bedlinog, and probably practised open communion.[21] The congregation eventually distanced itself from Arminianism and embraced Arianism, becoming Unitarian in its belief. It was never strong and eventually closed in 1830.

The Ministry of the Churches

Although a few of the first Baptist ministers in Wales were puritans who had received a university education for ministry in the Church of England, the majority appear to have received little formal education but were recognised by the churches as being gifted preachers. Such men were encouraged to develop their gifts and exercise them within closed meetings. These abilities were rigorously tested before approval was granted, with some candidates being permitted to exercise their gifts only in closed meetings, or while accompanied by other believers. Others were sent out as missionaries to preach in public meetings. Most of those recognised as gifted appear to have been farmers and artisans, although the occasional 'schoolmaster' was also found among their numbers. It was from the ranks of such 'gifted men' that churches replenished their stock of ministers, with each church providing its own pastors in the early years of Baptist witness in Wales.

Initially, the ministry adopted by the Baptists in Wales appears to have followed closely the six key point pattern described in a paper prepared by John Miles and other leading ministers, and presented to the General Meeting of the churches in Llantrisant in August 1654.[22] Thus, a pastor presided over each of the large, regional churches which had been established at Ilston, Hay, Hengoed, Carmarthen and Llanwenarth. The minister was assisted by teaching elders, who, like the pastor would have been 'set apart by the laying on of hands' (or ordained) for the work, and it was the teaching elder who presided over a branch of the regional church in the absence of the pastor. Ruling elders assisted in the discipline of these scattered branches, with deacons as the fourth tier. These, too, were set apart for their work by the laying on of hands. According to Joshua Thomas the lost records of the church in Blaenau Gwent showed that ordination of a deacon did not qualify him to serve as a ruling elder – further ordination was needed – nor did ordination as a ruling elder enable him to serve as a teaching elder. However, when a man had been ordained as a teaching elder, no further ordination was required should he be called to be a pastor.[23]

Widows and 'ordinary prophets' formed the two remaining tiers of the six-fold pattern of ministry described in the 1654 Declaration of Llantrisant. Widows were pressed into service to assist the deacons when propriety called for a woman's presence, and 'ordinary prophets', who appear to have been approved lay preachers, were called on to assist the church branches when necessary.[24] As each scattered regional church grew and subsequently divided into smaller, local churches, the need to follow the pattern laid down at Llantrisant became less pressing and fewer officers were needed by each church. Traces of the various tiers of ministry can nevertheless be found in some places as late as the nineteenth century, although the vast majority had adopted the two-fold pattern of ministry, the pastor and deacons, long before then.

Education

The English universities were closed to dissenters and nonconformists in the seventeenth and eighteenth centuries, but some of the ministers who had received a good education established non-denominational academies. For example, at Samuel Jones's academy at Brynllywarch, near Llangynwyd, in Glamorgan successive generations were given some instruction.[25] From 1720 promising Baptist preachers were sent to a Baptist academy in Bristol where they were given an education that was designed according to the candidate's ability and needs. Welsh churches made good use of this facility, although *every* candidate for the ministry did not receive formal training. The curriculum offered by Bernard Foskett at Bristol was wide-ranging and included English Grammar, the Classics, Hebrew, Chaldee, Philosophy, Logic, Ontology, Pneumatology, Antiquities and Geography.[26] Between 1732 and 1770 there was a Baptist Academy at Trosnant, Pontypool, which largely operated as a preparatory school for the Bristol Academy as almost all of the students who were educated in Trosnant later moved to Bristol to complete their studies.[27]

After the closure of Trosnant, primarily because of the lack of trained instructors after the initial years of success, Wales was without a Baptist academy until 1807 when one was established at Abergavenny. This removed to Pontypool in 1836 before relocating to Cardiff in 1893 to be near the newly-established University College of South Wales and Monmouthshire. A second academy was established at Llangollen in 1862, moving to Bangor in 1892 to be near the University College of

North Wales. A third academy was established at Haverfordwest in 1839, relocated at Aberystwyth in 1894, and closed its doors in 1899. The closure was the result of deliberations whereby the Welsh churches had determined that their needs would best be served by two colleges, one in the south and one in the north.[28]

Ministerial support and the Particular Baptist Fund

Ministers in the first Baptist churches received a stipend from a fund operated by the General Meeting, and from monies generated during the Protectorate when local commissioners utilised tithe returns to pay for ministers. Payments varied, but were generous in comparison to the levels of support provided during the seventeenth century. For example, William Morgan, a cobbler, was an itinerant preacher who received between £10 and £20 per annum from the state. John Miles's payment was considerably more, and in September 1657 he received 'an augmentation of £40 in lieu of the like sum formerly granted him as Minister in Llanelly'. A further augmentation was granted on 8 December and derived from the prebend of Whitchurch in Glamorgan.[29] This situation was not to last. The loss of state support and the oppression that followed the Restoration forced the churches and their ministers to provide their own financial assistance. Even William Pritchard, the first pastor of Llanwenarth, who survived the oppression and lived until 1713, appears to have supported himself as a schoolteacher for most of his ministry. Certainly, the Baptists of Llanwenarth who decided in 1654 that £30 per annum was reasonable maintenance for their pastor, were only paying his successor £1 per quarter (£4 per annum) a hundred years later.[30]

By the eighteenth century most ministers needed to be in a position to support themselves, with churches doing little more than reimbursing lost earnings and defraying the expenses ministers incurred while on church business. Many ministers kept smallholdings, and often the location would be determined by the churches which they served. Thus in 1762, Zachariah Thomas of Aberduar (Llanybydder) complied with the request of the Baptists in Cwmpedol (Caeo) and Bwlchyrhiw to rent a farm in the area in order to become their minister. Others opened schools, or like Evan Thomas of Molleston, who had a shop in Narberth, became tradesmen.[31] Moreover, by the mid-eighteenth century as most ministers were either farmers or schoolteachers a debate was held at the Association meeting in 1755 which explored fixing a suitable time, other than Whitsun, for holding the annual meeting of the Association. Clearly it was felt that

> Whitsun-week happened sometimes too early, before some had finished sowing barley, and before the horses were got strong to travel, and the grass grown sufficient for them. Others pleaded that the Whitsun-week was commonly a more leisure time, particularly for schoolmasters.[32]

This does not mean that ministers were affluent. Earlier in 1717, six wealthy London churches established the Particular Baptist Fund in order to help the impoverished Calvinistic Baptist ministers in England, while in June 1718, Thomas Hollis, a trustee of the fund, submitted a list of Welsh Baptist ministers 'to whom he was willing to give of his own Charity to be distributed by this Society'. A year later, Hollis and his brother, John, wrote to the fund:

> We have in our power £200 of our late honoured father's money which we are willing to add to your fund acquainting you with the particular regard he had to poor Baptist Ministers – whether pastors or teachers – in Wales. That they may be remembered to you now and hereafter in your Annual Distributions and that it may be entered in your register. When you have considered how it shall be disposed of for an annual improvement, the money is ready to be paid to the Treasurer or his order.[33]

The Hollis family came from Yorkshire and their connection with Welsh ministers is not known, but it was because of their generosity that Welsh Baptist ministers in the eighteenth century began receiving small annual gifts between £1 and £7 in order to supplement their income from the churches. For ministers to benefit, each church had to submit information about its numbers, income and annual disbursements. In addition, the minister's marital status, the number of children he had 'in their minority', his - or his wife's - personal wealth, and the number of hours he devoted to his ministry, had to be recorded. The generosity of the Hollis family brought the Welsh churches within the operations of the Particular Baptist Fund, while the trust deeds of the majority of eighteenth century Baptist meeting houses in Wales named the fund as the beneficiary if the church closed.[34]

The Laying on of Hands

As early as 1651 the Arminian practice of laying on of hands on the newly baptized had become part of the Welsh Baptist experience, most notably at Llanwenarth and Olchon, but clear references to this practice in confessions of faith and letters of transfer bear testimony to the influence of Rhydwilym – a church not founded until 1668. No entry was made in the Rhydwilym churchbook until after the 1689 Toleration Act had been passed. Then, as well as chronicling the history of its formation and noting the names of its founder-members, the churchbook records the church's confession of faith. This confession is identical to that written by the puritan preacher, Vavasor Powell, and recorded in *The Life and Death of Mr Vavasor Powell* (1671), except that the reference to open communion has been deleted. The Rhydwilym confession differs from the one adopted and signed by the Baptists of England and Wales, including representatives from Rhydwilym, who assembled in London in 1689 to celebrate their new-found freedom. The main difference in

Rhydwilym's confession was that the 'Laying on of hands is one of ye principles of ye doctrine of Christ and a gospel ordinance.'[35] The church at Rhydwilym took this principle so seriously that its representatives to an Assembly of Baptists in Bristol in 1693 questioned whether they should partake of communion with delegates who did not observe the practice. Such was Rhydwilym's insistence on the custom that, in the first half of the eighteenth century, no church wishing to join the Welsh Association (formed in 1700) was exempt from adherence to the practice of laying hands on the newly baptized.[36] This does not mean, however, that the custom went unchallenged.

Laying on of hands on the newly baptized is normally associated with General Baptists; Particular Baptists rejected its use because they considered that it introduced human agency into a process which they considered to be the prerogative of God alone. It is rarely seen in confessions prepared by English Particular Baptist churches, except where there is a Welsh influence, such as the *Confession of Faith of Limehouse Baptists* (1713), prepared by its minister, David Rees, a native of Hengoed. Such was Rhydwilym's strength and influence among Particular Baptists that soon the laying on of hands was an article of belief as important as believers' baptism and Calvin's theology. When writing about the Association meetings of 1737, Joshua Thomas noted that the Baptist churches in Wales had been 'very strict for laying on of hands on the baptized, ever since 1689, or soon after', and that it had not been a topic for discussion until 1736. It was, however, in 1737 that the church at Trosgoed (Maes-y-berllan) raised the matter for a second time. At this meeting a candidate for baptism had expressed doubt concerning the practice and the claim that it was sanctioned in Scripture. Furthermore, Philip Morgan, the minister of the church, and his assistant, William Herbert, had researched the subject and concluded that it was 'not properly a gospel ordinance'.[37]

Adherence to the custom had been questioned by the Association in 1736 when Trosgoed church had enquired 'whether persons of different sentiments might be admitted to, and continue in, communion'. The other churches of the Association had reaffirmed their belief in the practice during this time and restated their position in 1737, while at the same time permitting the Trosgoed church to follow its own conviction.[38] After this the practice was 'seldom used' by the Trosgoed church, suggesting that whenever anyone requested the laying on of hands, it was not denied them. While not expelling Trosgoed for its unorthodoxy, the Association insisted that only churches which practised the laying on of hands could be admitted as new members. The Particular Closed Communion Baptists of Glyn Ceiriog, near Llangollen,[39] sought membership of the Welsh Association in 1765, but as they were 'not under imposition of hands, the association would not then receive them into the connection'. Their application was, however, accepted in 1768, by which time the Association had become more tolerant and the practice had become optional.[40] The majority of Welsh churches nevertheless retained the practice. Protected by the barrier of the Welsh language, 'believers' baptism, laying on of hands, the doctrine of personal election and final perseverance' – and with the proviso from 1766 that 'others of the same sentiments' could receive fellowship without practising the laying on of hands – the Baptists in Wales had established the foundations on which they could build.[41]

The Mission to north Wales

The eighteenth century Methodist Revival in Wales challenged and invigorated the grave and more temperate centres of older religious dissent. In 1776, in response to Methodist activity, the Baptists sent missionaries to evangelise north Wales. Before this date the Baptists had been largely confined to south and mid-Wales.[42] The only Baptists in north Wales were those found in the north-east, particularly at Wrexham, where mixed Baptist/Independent churches dating back to puritan times had been established, or where Baptist communities had been gathered as a result of an English mission. The Welsh mission took the form of preaching tours to the north by ministers, most of whom were from mid-Wales. The first baptisms occurred in Anglesey in 1779, and a year later the Association admitted 'the Anglesea church' into fellowship.[43] From Anglesey, the Baptist witness quickly spread east and south, and several Baptist churches were founded in north Wales. By 1790, the Welsh Association had become unwieldy and divided itself into three Associations: the Northern (nine churches), including Anglesey, Caernarfonshire, Denbighshire and Merionethshire; the Eastern (nineteen churches) administering to mid- and south-east Wales, and the South Western (eighteen churches) based in west Wales.[44]

Schisms

Following closely on what appeared to be a new dawn for Baptists in Wales came events that were to undermine the Association. In north Wales, J. R. Jones, minister of Ramoth, Llanfrothen, the first church in Merionethshire, embraced and disseminated the teaching of Archibald Mclean, a Scottish Baptist. Jones accepted the main tenets of Calvinism and the Trinity, although he rejected the eternal regeneration of the Son;[45] he totally renounced the enthusiasm of the Methodist Revival, understanding faith as the intellect's response to the Gospel. Church communion was a weekly occurrence, with the kiss of peace, foot-washing and the *agape*.[46] also observed. He gained support among some of the churches and ministers of north Wales, and in 1798 withdrew from the 'Babylonian' Baptists of Wales.[47] At one time, nine of the thirty congregations and five of the ministers in the Northern Association had withdrawn in support of Jones.[48] The movement met with some success, but was itself divided from 1835 by the teaching of Alexander Campbell, with many churches becoming 'Disciples of Christ'. Four so-called 'Scotch Baptist churches' have persisted to this day: two at Harlech, one at Llanefydd and a further one at Ponciau.[49]

The schism within the South Western Association was prompted by an attempt to impose a Confession of Faith on the churches in response to the softening attitude of some members towards Calvinism. In 1799, the Association withdrew fellowship from churches and ministers that would not subscribe to the Confession of Faith. The Eastern Association followed suit and consequently the two Associations lost some ministers, either temporarily or permanently. Subsequently some churches that were decidedly Arminian in theology became Unitarian Baptists, joined with the Unitarians, or failed to recruit new members and declined.[50] The French Revolution also affected Welsh Baptists at the end of the eighteenth century. Two of its prominent ministers, William Richards of Lynn and Morgan John Rhys, the publisher of the pioneering *Cylchgrawn Cynmraeg* (The Welsh Magazine), believed in the political and social idealism of the Revolution. However, following its worst excesses and the outbreak of war between France and Britain in 1791, defenders of the Revolution were silenced and a cloud of suspicion surrounded dissenters. Welsh Baptists were deprived of an able leader when Morgan John Rhys emigrated to America in 1794, but suspicion still persisted.[51] Following the French landings in Fishguard in 1797, the homes of several prominent Baptist ministers in Pembrokeshire were searched, and at least one Baptist preacher, Thomas Jones, spent seven months in Haverfordwest prison as a result of his earlier support for the revolutionaries.[52]

The Nineteenth and Twentieth Centuries

After the turmoil of the last decade of the eighteenth century, the nineteenth century was a period of consolidation and growth. Controversies were rare, although there were heated exchanges over Andrew Fuller's challenge to a rigid Calvinism that allowed 'nothing spiritually good to be the duty of the unregenerate'.[53] Other developments included the spread of denominational publications, notably *Seren Gomer* (Star of Gomer from 1814), *Yr Athraw* (The Teacher, 1827), *Seren Cymru* (Star of Wales, 1851) and *Y Greal* (The Grail, 1852), and a change in the structure of the Baptist Association as the three regional Associations subdivided mainly along county lines. In 1866, the Baptist Union of Wales and Monmouthshire, which changed its name to the Baptist Union of Wales in 1959, was created when five of the nine existing Welsh-language Baptist Associations formed a Union. By 1881 the other four associations had also joined.[54]

As early as 1857, the formation of the Monmouthshire English Association, followed in 1860 by an Association of the English churches of Glamorgan and Carmarthen, pointed to a language problem and a division along language lines. These associations joined the Baptist Union of Great Britain, based in London. In 1914, the growing language problem led the Union to consider dividing itself into two wings, one Welsh and the other English, each having its own President, Assembly and Council, but with a central headquarters, secretariat and bureaucracy located in Swansea.[55] The English Assembly held its first meeting in September 1921.[56] In spite of these developments there are some English-language Baptist churches in Wales which continue their allegiance to the Baptist Union of Great Britain. Toward the end of the twentieth century there were unsuccessful attempts to unite all Baptist churches in Wales within one Welsh Union.[57] Unlike its sister Union in England, which had been formed in 1813, the Baptist Union of Wales is a Union of Associations. To belong to the Union, and take part in its activities, individuals and churches must first belong to one of the member Associations. Most of the churches that belong to the Union are still, nominally at least, Calvinist in their theology and, until the middle of the twentieth century, were almost exclusively closed-communion churches. Since the 1960s, many have become open-membership churches and most have embraced open-communion. A small number of churches still cling to the practice of laying hands on the newly baptised.[58]

In 1921, the Union established a corporation for property-holding purposes and the corporation is now the sole trustee or a co-trustee of many Baptist chapels in Wales. The Union also has a publishing arm, and services several committees designed to promote and strengthen Baptist witness and life in Wales.[59] Membership of 879 churches belonging to the Baptist Union of Wales reached 142,592 following the 1904/5 Revival. Since this period the Baptists have suffered the same malaise as other nonconformists. Recent statistical information (collected c.2008) indicates that there are now 431 churches in the eleven Associations which make up the Baptist Union of Wales with a total membership of 13,858.[60]

Notes

1. For details of the organisational qualities of the early Baptists, see B. R. White, 'The Organisation of the Particular Baptists, 1644–1660', *Journal of Ecclesiastical History*, 17, 1 (October, 1966), 209–26; Idem., 'John Miles and the structures of the Calvinistic Baptist Mission to South Wales, 1649–1660', in M. John (ed.), *Welsh Baptist Studies* (Llandysul, 1976), pp. 35–76. A thorough examination of the Baptist witness in Wales is provided in T. M. Bassett, *The Welsh Baptists* (Swansea, 1977).

2. John Price and William Bownd, *The Sun Outshining the Moon* (London, 1658), pp. 9–10.

3. Joshua Thomas, *Hanes y Bedyddwyr yn Mhlith y Cymry* ... (Pontypridd 1885), p. 257. The book was Thomas' manuscript 'Materials towards a History of the Baptists in Wales' translated and edited by Benjamin Davies, Pontypridd. Thomas also referred to the observations of John Walker in his *An Attempt Towards Recovering an Account of the Numbers and Sufferings of the Clergy of the Church of England* ... (London, 1714).

4. For details of John Miles, see Thomas Richards, 'John Miles (1621–83)', in John E. Lloyd, R. T. Jenkins and William Ll. Davies (eds), *Y Bywgraffiadur Cymreig hyd 1940* (London, 1953), pp. 595–6; Stephen K. Roberts, 'Miles, John (1620/1–1683)', in H. C. G. Matthew and Brian Harrison (eds), *Oxford Dictionary of National Biography* (Oxford, 2004); http://www.oxforddnb.com/view/article/19691 (accessed October 2009).

5. See B. G. Owens, *The Ilston Book: Earliest Register of Welsh Baptists* (Aberystwyth, 1996), pp. 165, 171ff.

6. Ibid., p. 9.

7. See White, 'John Miles', 65–71.

8. The original Ilston Churchbook is housed at Brown University, Rhode Island, MS 2–ZZN in the Sidney S. Rider Collection, while a facsimile edition is kept at the National Library of Wales (NLW), Aberystwyth. See NLW, Facs 863. See also the transcribed records in Owens (ed.), *Ilston Book*.

9. Details of 'closed' and 'open membership' Baptist communities and subsequent disputes are provided in Joshua Thomas, *A History of the Baptist Association in Wales 1650–1790* (London, 1795), p. 11; White, 'John Miles', 36–40.

10. The first General Meeting was held at Ilston between 6 and 7 November 1650. See Owens, *Ilston Book*, p. 25ff. For details of the five meetings and the supervision of the London church, see White, 'Organisation', 211–13; White, 'John Miles', 40–53.

11. See Thomas Richards, *A History of the Puritan Movement in Wales* (London, 1920), pp. 81–9; White, 'John Miles', 35.

12. Thomas, *Hanes y Bedyddwyr yn Mhlith y Cymru*, p. 215n.

13. John Miles, *An Antidote against the Infection of the Times* (London, 1656), and reprinted by the Welsh Baptist Historical Society, ed. T. Shankland (Cardiff, 1904), p. 25.

14. Thomas, *History of the Baptist Association*, p. 11.

15. Miles, *An Antidote*, p. 52.

16. Thomas Richards, 'William Rider', *Trafodion Cymdeithas Hanes Bedyddwyr Cymru* (1950), 5–10; D. Hugh Matthews, 'The Glass House or Glaziers' Hall: Two Seventeenth Century Baptist Meeting Houses – or One?', *Baptist Quarterly*, XXXIV (1973), 124–6.

17. This is clearly shown by reading the individual histories of each Welsh Baptist church in Joshua Thomas' *Hanes* which includes the histories of General and Open-communion Baptist churches. All of these churches, after some years of independence, eventually joined the Welsh Association.

18. Bassett, *Welsh Baptists*, p. 40.

19. For details of the re-establishment of the Association see ibid., pp. 48–52.

20. For example, see the Swansea church's letter of dismissal to emigrants in Pennsylvania given in Thomas, *Hanes y Bedyddwyr*, p. 111.

21. Bassett, *Welsh Baptists*, p. 40.

22. Details are provided in D. Hugh Matthews, 'Datganiad Llantrisant (1654): Ymgais i wthio Presbyteriaeth ar Fedyddwyr Cymru?', in J. Gwynfor Jones (ed.), *Agweddau ar Dwf Piwritaniaeth yng Nghymru yn yr Ail Ganrif ar Bymtheg* (Lampeter, 1991), pp. 147–65.

23. D. Hugh Matthews, 'Astudiaeth Hanesyddol o'r Weinidogaeth ymhlith y Bedyddwyr yng Nghymru', unpublished University of Wales, MA thesis, 1980, pp. 37–40.

24. For a discussion of the role of women in the Baptist Church from the early years of witness to the twentieth century see B. P. Jones, *Sowing Beside All Waters: The Baptist Heritage of Gwent* (Cwmbran, 1985), ch. 14.

25. G. H. Jenkins, *Protestant Dissenters in Wales 1639–1689* (Cardiff, 1992), p. 62.

26. D. Hugh Matthews, 'Myfyrwyr Bernard Foskett ym Mryste', *Trafodion Cymdeithas Hanes Bedyddwyr Cymru*, (1980), 8–9.

27. A brief outline of the Trosnant Academy is provided in Thomas, *History of the Baptist Association*, p. 51; John Rufus Williams (Rufus), *Hanes Athrofeydd y Bedyddwyr yn Sir Fynwy ...* (Aberdâr, 1863), pp. 5–21; Bassett, *Welsh Baptists*, pp. 67–9. Thomas suggests that the date was *c*.1736 when John Griffith rented a house at Trosnant for the double purpose of holding meetings and opening a school, while Rufus notes that it was 1732 when Griffith first rented the house in Trosnant for preaching and the education of ministers. However, 1736 is the date he gives for the admission of the first four students. Moreover, in the Breviats of the Association held in 1741 it was stated that 'there was an attempt of late to set up a Seminary at Pontypool for the benefit of the ministry'. For further information about Welsh nonconformist academies see H. P. Roberts, 'Nonconformist Academies in Wales (1662–1862)', *Transactions of the Honourable Society of Cymmrodorion* (1928–9), 63, 71.

28. See Bassett, *Welsh Baptists*, pp. 345–9. The South Wales Baptist College in Cardiff and the North Wales Baptist College in Bangor still prepare men and women for the Baptist ministry. They are both linked with the local University's Departments of Theology and Religion.

29. Thomas Richards, *Religious Developments in Wales, 1654–1662* (London, 1923), p. 108; Thomas Richards, 'Bedyddwyr Cymru yng Nghyfnod Lewis Thomas', *Trafodion Cymdeithas Hanes Bedyddwyr Cymru*, (1916–19), 10. For a detailed study of ministerial remuneration during the Commonwealth and post-Restoration, see Richards, *History of the Puritan Movement in Wales*, ch. 10; Bassett, *Welsh Baptists*, pp. 64–6.

30. NLW, MS. Dep. 410B. Llanwenarth Churchbook.

31. Thomas, *Hanes y Bedyddwyr yn Mhlith y Cymru*, p. 526; J. Ivor James, *Molleston Baptist Church Pembrokeshire. Reflections on the Founders' Tercentenary* (Carmarthen, 1968), p. 18.

32. Thomas, *History of the Baptist Association*, p. 57.

33. The letter is transcribed in the minutes of the Particular Baptist Fund (4 February 1719) and housed at Angus Library, Regent's Park College, Oxford. For a brief history of the Particular Baptist Fund, see Theo. T. Valentine, *Concern for the Ministry: The Story of the Particular Baptist Fund 1717–1967* (Teddington, n.d.). For a correct identification of Theo Valentine's wrongly transcribed Welsh place names (p. 10) see D. Hugh Matthews, 'Ôl Nodiad', *Trafodion Cymdeithas Hanes Bedyddwyr Cymru*, (1986), 52.

34. The Particular Baptist Fund is still in existence and in recent years has benefited greatly from Welsh chapel closures. It continues to aid impoverished college-trained Baptist ministers, and helps those who have suffered prolonged periods of illness or have retired without a pension.

35. The Rhydwilym Confession of Faith is reproduced in *Trafodion Cymdeithas Hanes Bedyddwyr Cymru*, (1979), 5–25.

36. Thomas, *History of the Baptist Association*, p. 62

37. Ibid., p. 48.

38. Ibid. See also Bassett, *Welsh Baptists*, p. 74.

39. A church established as the result of a mission from Warrington and Nantwich in England.

40. Thomas, *History of the Baptist Association*, p. 61; Bassett, *Welsh Baptists*, pp. 74–5.

41. Thomas, *History of the Baptist Association*, p. 61.

42. For a useful appraisal of the Baptist missions, see Bassett, *Welsh Baptists*, pp. 100–7; T. M. Bassett, *The Baptists of Wales and the Baptist Missionary Society* (Swansea, 1991).

43. Bassett, *Welsh Baptists*, p. 104.

44. Ibid., p. 107.

45. This is discussed in J. Idwal Jones, *J. R. Jones Ramoth a'i Amserau* (Llandysul, 1966), p. 45.

46. The 'love feast', said to be a re-enactment of the custom of churches in New Testament times, was *not* part of the communion service but involved partaking of 'a simple, rustic meal'. A hymn was sung at the beginning and end of the meal which was shared by members *between* the Sunday services. See J. D. Davies, 'Y Bedyddwyr Albanaidd a'r Bedyddwyr Campbellaidd yng Nghymru', *Trafodion Cymdeithas Bedyddwyr Cymru*, (1940), 77. This is the reason that in north Wales the Scotch Baptists became known as 'Batus bara caws' – 'bread and cheese Baptists'!

47. In a meeting in Ramoth towards the end of 1798, J. R. Jones referred to the 'Babylonian Captivity' of Baptists and it was then that he decided to break from the 'Babylonian' Baptists of Wales who did not share his views. See W. J. Rhys, *Penodau yn Hanes y Bedyddwyr Cymreig* (Swansea, 1949), pp. 147–50.

48. D. Hugh Matthews and John Rice Rowlands, 'Y dechreuadau hyd sefydlu'r Undeb, 1649–1866', in D. Densil Morgan (ed.), *Y Fywiol Ffrwd Bywyd a Thystiolaeth Bedyddwyr Cymru 1649–1999* (Swansea, 1999), p. 21. See also Bassett, *Welsh Baptists*, pp. 120–1.

49. The followers of J. R. Jones, Ramoth, became known as 'Scotch Baptists' since they adhered to the teaching of Archibald Mclean, who was a Scottish theologian. The movement was subsequently divided by the teachings of Alexander Campbell, the son of an Irish Presbyterian minister, who was, himself, a Presbyterian minister in Washington, Pennsylvania. The Campbellite movement became known as The Disciples of Christ and now forms part of the United Reformed Church. The ministry of Scotch Baptists was a bivocational ministry. After the Second World War, two of their ministers, T. W. Jones [later Lord Maelor] and James Idwal Jones became Labour MPs for Merioneth and Wrexham respectively. James Idwal Jones was later the author of *J. R. Jones Ramoth a'i Amserau*. A further high-profile Welsh figure, David Lloyd George, was also brought up a Scotch Baptist, though attending Castle Street Welsh Baptist Church while in London. The impact of both movements on the Baptists of Wales is traced in Davies, 'Y Bedyddwyr Albanaidd', 1–79; and W. Lliedi Williams, 'Y Bedyddwyr Campbellaidd' – a series of articles published in *Trafodion Cymdeithas Hanes Bedyddwyr Cymru* (1972, 1973, 1974 and 1975). J. D. Davies' essay was subsequently published as a monograph in 1941. See J. D. Davies, *Y Bedyddwyr Albanaidd a'r Bedyddwyr Campbellaidd yng Nghymru* (Blaenau Ffestiniog, 1941).

50. Rhys, *Penodau yn Hanes y Bedyddwyr Cymreig*, pp. 153–4.

51. Bassett, *Welsh Baptists*, pp. 109–13. For John Morgan Rhys see H. M. Davies, 'Transatlantic Brethren': A Study of English, Welsh and American Baptists with particular reference to Morgan

John Rhys (1760–1804) and his Friends', unpublished University of Wales, Ph.D. thesis, 1984. This has subsequently been published as *Transatlantic Brethren: Rev. Samuel Jones (1735–1814) and his Friends; Baptists in Wales, Pennsylvania and Beyond* (Bethlehem, Pa; 1995).

52. Bassett, *Welsh Baptists*, p. 111.
53. 'Andrew Fuller', in F. L. Cross (ed.), *The Oxford Dictionary of the Christian Church* (London, 1957).
54. Gareth O. Watts, 'Yr Adran Gymraeg, 1866–1999', in Morgan (ed.), *Y Fywiol Ffrwd*, pp. 34–5.
55. In December 2008, the Baptist Union of Wales removed its headquarters from Swansea and relocated on the site of Trinity College, Carmarthen.
56. Morgan (ed.), *Y Fywiol Ffrwd*, p. 37.
57. Papers relating to the discussions are housed in the Baptist Union of Wales headquarters.
58. The practice was never abandoned by the church at Rhydwilym or its daughter churches in Pembrokeshire; elsewhere, since 1766, it has been used intermittently, usually by ministers who have strong links with Rhydwilym or Pembrokeshire Baptists.
59. See the Baptist Union of Wales *Handbook*, published annually since 1868, and its Annual Reports for details of the various departments and Committees.
60. Peter M. Thomas (ed.), *Undeb Bedyddwyr Cymru ... Llawlyfr 2010 ...* (Caerfyrddin, 2009), p. 98.

CHAPTER 4

THE RELIGIOUS SOCIETY OF FRIENDS (QUAKERS)

Richard C. Allen

The 350th anniversary of George Fox's establishment of the Religious Society of Friends (Quakers)[1] was celebrated in 2002. In an article for the *Guardian* in May of that year Stephen Bates wrote that the 'Quakers aren't the sort to make a fuss of a 350th anniversary. Instead, they will get on with their work – quietly struggling to defeat the forces of violence and extremism'.[2] Indeed, from the mid-seventeenth century onwards the history of Quakerism has been well-documented,[3] and members have been renowned for their pacifism, philanthropic endeavours and the promotion of social reform. But what are the origins of the Friends in Wales and what do they believe in? How did they overcome the difficult years of persecution, and develop from a sect to a recognisable denomination? Finally, what contribution has the Society made to the religious life of Wales?

During the 1630s the Welsh puritan preachers William Wroth (1575/6–*c*.1641) and William Erbery (1604/5–1654) had already separated themselves from the established church and Archbishop William Laud's efforts to impose religious uniformity. Other dissenters soon followed them, and in November 1639 the first dissenting church was established at Llanfaches in Monmouthshire.[4] The Civil War years and Interregnum, *c*.1642–1660, also produced a number of radical political and religious movements, among them the Levellers, Diggers, Seekers, Ranters, and Fifth Monarchists. These movements, supported by the growth in printing and itinerant preaching, advocated novel social, economic and religious changes, and challenged the civil and ecclesiastical authorities.[5] Additional dissenting preachers, who had been forced to quit Wales before the civil wars, were, after the ejection of many Anglican clergymen, positioned in many Welsh parishes.[6] Here they were able to disseminate their radical religious principles in a variety of tracts and pamphlets, and more directly by holding impromptu religious services in markets, waste grounds and village churchyards. Friends, it has been argued, were, 'a by-product of the religious and social upheavals called the puritan revolution',[7] which led to the creation of new religious movements.

In this period of upheaval, George Fox (1624–1691) had a vision of a new community of believers. During Whitsun 1652 he gathered enthusiastic supporters, particularly in the north-west of England where Quakerism can be said to originate.[8] Shortly thereafter missionaries were dispatched throughout the British Isles, Europe and North America.[9] In 1653 John ap John (*c*.1625–1697), a member of Morgan

Llwyd's Independent congregation at Wrexham, visited George Fox at Swarthmoor Hall in Cumbria.[10] This was a significant meeting as ap John converted to Quakerism and, following his visit, Quaker missionaries from the north-west of England, notably Thomas Holme (1626/7–1666), a weaver from Kendal,[11] Richard Hubberthorne (1628–1662), a yeoman from Yealand Redmayne,[12] John Lawson, a shopkeeper from Lancaster, John Audland (1630–1664), a linen draper from Preston Patrick (1630–1664),[13] Thomas Ayrey (?–1665), a yeoman of Birkfield, Elizabeth Leavens-Holme (?–1665),[14] and Alice Birkett were dispatched to Wales.[15] In 1654, as a result of their efforts, meetings were held throughout the country and several of these have continued until the present day. Converts to Quakerism, who came from a variety of backgrounds, turned away from Anglicanism and from the dissenting congregations of the 1640s and early 1650s largely because they had failed to meet their spiritual needs. For example, Thomas Wynne (1627–1691), a physician of Caerwys in Flintshire, wrote

> I could find neither Bishop, Doctor, Prebend, Vicar nor Curat, to look after my soul, they were all fled and left me to the mercy of the Wolf that had worried them; and for many Years together there were none of them so much as visited me, nor sent me so much as an Epistle or Collect, nor any comfort or hopes … And it was at this time that the Lord raised many Witnesses … and made them exceedingly to Tremble.'[16]

Such conversions were naturally controversial as the feltmaker Richard Davies (c.1635–1708) of Cloddiau Cochion in Montgomeryshire recalled, 'it was the great talk of the country that I was become a Quaker'. A clergyman from Welshpool also informed them that Davies was 'distracted, and that they should see for some learned men to come and restore me to my senses'.[17]

Quaker preachers took advantage of the different interpretations of religious belief, particularly among the Baptist congregations which 'laid them all the more open to Quaker proselytising'.[18] Thus in mid- and south Wales Thomas and Elizabeth Holmes, and Alice Birkett, were able to quickly establish Quaker gatherings among former Baptists. In February 1655, Thomas Holme wrote to George Fox that in south Wales there were 'divers meetings wher[e] many ar[e] Convinced of the truth, of that peopell [people] called babtis [Baptists]; many of the Churches ar[e] broken in pecses [pieces]'.[19] Moreover, itinerant preachers as well as newly convinced Welsh Friends were prepared to engage in heated discussions concerning the nature of their beliefs as well as publish pamphlets defending them. For example, on 24 April 1657 John Moone, a Radnorshire Quaker, published his *The True Light hath made manifest darknesse*. This was a response to the stinging attacks against the Quakers and was particularly directed against Vavasor Powell and other leading Baptists in Wales.[20] It is not surprising, given their enthusiasm for preaching 'Truth', extravagant pronouncements and notorious behaviour, that Friends were singled out by hostile clergymen, as well as fellow dissenters such as Powell and John Miles, the Swansea Baptist minister, and were accused of being a 'deviant' people: papists or radical malcontents, possessed by the devil, witches or mentally unbalanced. The reality was the reverse, for these were serious-minded and devout individuals searching for salvation in an uncertain world. The radical approach of some early Friends to their evangelical work was, nonetheless, controversial and calculated to provoke a strong reaction. For Miles there needed to be an antidote to their proselytising.[21]

Doctrinal divisions between the Welsh dissenters, particularly those between Morgan Llwyd and Vavasor Powell, in the mid-1650s also may have led people to question the validity of early dissenting beliefs, and made them more amenable to the simple message of Quakerism.[22] Indeed, the conflict among the Welsh puritan 'Saints' may have caused alternative religious groups, such as the Quakers, to emerge. They filled a void for the discontented and those 'burdened perhaps by guilt, torment, resentment and disillusionment ... [who] ... passed from church to conventicle, and radical sect to radical sect, only to find each one wanting'.[23] This is evident in the journal of Margaret Ellis of Radnorshire, written many years after she became a Quaker, which revealed her inner torment. When she was fourteen, Margaret questioned her devotion to the established church, and sought the advice of the ministers and her family, friends and neighbours. Despite her soul-searching she became aware that celebrating the Eucharist did not resolve the problem. In response she turned to the Quakers who offered her a personal relationship with God that the more traditional churches could not provide.[24]

Converts to Quakerism did not accept a 'formulated creed demanding definite subscription ... liturgy, separated priesthood or outward sacrament'. Indeed, even the term 'the Society of Friends' does not appear to have been used until the late-eighteenth century, for in the seventeenth century they used epithets, such as 'Friends of Truth' and 'The Children of Light', or more commonly they referred to each other simply as 'friend'.[25] In this early period they rejected the prevailing Calvinist ideology, especially the doctrine of predestination, and in its place promoted the message of 'Inner Light' with the implication of salvation for all. Friends rejected many of the accessories of the established church by developing a movement founded upon simplicity and plainness, and upon their own spiritual experiences rather than complete reliance upon the Scriptures. They believed in a return to primitive Christianity and maintained that they had a personal and direct relationship with God; like the first Christians they thought that through the workings of the Holy Spirit they would be led to 'truth'.[26] Moreover, they regarded personal spiritual experience ('the inward light' or 'the light of truth') as greater than the ministrations of a state-sponsored Church, its 'hireling' ministers and rituals. They did not accept that there was a need to worship in a consecrated building, they refused to swear oaths, pay tithes or maintain the clergy, and declined to remove their hats to social superiors, while also addressing people 'thee' and 'thou'. Furthermore, members promoted silent worship as a simple communion with God, and demonstrated that, although the foundations of institutional worship were being torn apart, it was still possible for people, whatever their social status or gender, to find true Christian values in their meetings for worship.

In their opposition to more orthodox religious practices, the Friends condemned the beliefs of Independent ministers and succeeded in persuading some of their adversaries to join them, notably George White, an Independent preacher from Monmouthshire and Thomas Ellis, a former member of Vavasor Powell's congregation.[27] In these early years the responsibility for the welfare of new members fell upon the Quaker missionaries, particularly when they were subjected to verbal and physical attacks by clergymen and fellow dissenters. Personal problems and disputes could, however, impair the work of these early Friends. For example, the marriage of Thomas Holme and Elizabeth Leavens in 1654 and Elizabeth's pregnancy in 1656 caused the 'Mother of Quakerism', Margaret Fell, to reprove the couple as she believed that such actions undermined their missionary work and burdened recently 'convinced' Welsh Friends.[28] Elizabeth was determined to continue her missionary work and this can be measured by the fact that fifteen days after the birth of her child she was again preaching.[29] Clearly these itinerant Quaker ministers and their 'gathered' meetings attracted many adherents, while Friends were assisted by the religious liberty offered during the Commonwealth period. In a letter to Margaret Fell in April 1656, Thomas Holme observed that Friends in south Wales were able to hold at least ten meetings on a regular basis,[30] and as these meetings increased in size Holme was able to organise small communities of worshippers to meet in family homes or at other suitable venues throughout Wales.[31] These small meetings developed a sense of community which prevailed for several generations, and included men of wealth and influence, notably John Bevan and John Gawler of Glamorganshire, Walter Jenkins and Richard Hanbury of Monmouthshire, Edward Lord of Pembrokeshire, Rowland Ellis and Robert Owen of Merionethshire, and Thomas Lloyd of Montgomeryshire.

The success of the Quaker missionaries in gaining adherents did not pass unnoticed. By 1657 leading Friends, including George Fox himself, travelled to Wales to assist them,[32] and occasioned additional 'gatherings'. The dissemination of the Quaker message at these 'threshing' meetings was of seminal importance in the early years of Quakerism, but the meetings often proved to be provocative. As these evangelists continued to encourage Quakerism and enjoyed marked success, the civil and ecclesiastical authorities began to take more notice of this vociferous group. There was a widespread perception that the Quakers were socially and sexually deviant, and the unpredictability of some of their members provoked alarm and censure that far outweighed the numerical strength of the movement. Their hostile attitude towards magistracy and ministry, particularly the disruption of divine services, prophetic utterances, and their identification as 'children of the Light' also provoked criticism.[33]

Contemporaries recounting Friends' activities, particularly the James Nayler affair in October 1656, placed an emphasis on their blasphemous or radical and fanatical behaviour.[34] In this case Nayler's re-enactment of Christ's entry into Jerusalem proved to be a highly provocative act to the Bristol authorities and led to his arrest and conviction as a blasphemer.[35] A year earlier Joshua Miller, the puritan minister of St Andrew's Church in Cardiff, had openly disputed Quaker ideology with Francis Gawler and Tobias Hodges, ardent members of the Society.[36] Such was the ferocity of the Quaker's attack that Miller complained that the Friends were 'the saddest and most deplorable spectacles of revolted professors that ever I have heard or read of'. He observed that they often disrupted him during divine service or in public with a 'railing, reviling, brawling spirit', and compared them to the 'Oyster women of Billingsgate'.[37] Another critic of the Quakers was the Glamorgan Baptist preacher John Miles. In 1656, at the same time as Friends were persuading Baptists to join them in 'gathered' meetings, Miles condemned their activities suggesting that there needed to be an 'antidote against the infection of the times'.[38] Towards the end of the Protectorate and in the years following the restoration of the monarchy in 1660, the patience of the authorities had certainly worn thin against Quaker schismatics and their 'threshing meetings'. In the late-1650s instructions to magistrates focused on the arrest of those suspected of delinquency and vagrancy and, as a result, many Friends were roughly man-handled or incarcerated by constables, watchmen and churchwardens. Some Friends, such as Richard Davies, were accused of insanity or witchcraft. When he was brought before the magistrates at Welshpool in 1660, Davies was asked why he supported a 'strange religion'. He replied that it was 'the good old way', but this brought forth accusations that he was mad and suggestions that he ought to be whipped.[39] In spite of such accusations the Quakers continued to preach their persuasive message and to draw adherents into their movement.

Friends' willingness to continue 'open-air' meetings throughout Wales was a significant factor in the early development and success of the Quaker communities, while the personality of itinerant preachers, or a propertied convert who had first 'gathered' the meeting,[40] determined its future development. Thus, Quakers saw these meetings as serving a dual role. First, by preaching 'openly' they could persuade others to join their Society, but of greater significance was the belief that by preaching to those who 'are so much at ease in Sin, and so indifferent as to Religious Inquiry, that they resort to no Place of Worship',[41] Friends were providing a service that they felt the established church had failed to make available. At a meeting held at Shirenewton in Monmouthshire in 1659 there is more evidence on the nature of these 'open meetings', and the response of magistrates toward Friends. Walter Jenkins of Monmouthshire, Edward Edwards, a Denbighshire Friend, Elizabeth Holme and Francis Gawler were arrested, brought before the local puritan magistrates and informed that they had broken the law by unlawful assembly. This was not the first time as the magistrates commented: 'you have broken the Law in meeting together under the tree so near the Steeple-house, and we have several times warned you of it before'. In their reply the Friends acknowledged that they had not countermanded this law by arguing that 'the Law of the Nation giveth liberty to all for to meet together in the faith of Christ, in the which we meet together'.[42]

The period post-1660 was equally precarious, particularly when the Penal Code (1660–89) was rigidly enforced. The activities of Welsh Friends were perceived as highly provocative and this led to their persecution, but like the early Christians, whom they professed to emulate, members were prepared to undergo physical suffering.[43] It is estimated that from the early 1650s to the introduction of the Act of Toleration in 1689, 15,000 Friends were punished under a variety of laws, and that 450 consequently died in prison or from their ordeal.[44] Among them were several

Welsh Friends, including Walter Jenkins, a former magistrate in Monmouthshire, who died in 1661, and Humphrey Wilson of Montgomeryshire who died in 1665 from 'a Distemper contracted thro the coldness and unwholesomness' of his prison.[45] Moreover, years of continuous travelling and repeated imprisonment throughout Wales had a detrimental effect on the physical condition of Thomas and Elizabeth Holme. In March 1663 Holme informed George Fox that Elizabeth's health was extremely precarious:

> My wife hath been very sicke, more then ten days. And at present shee is very weke and sicke … She is trubled with the rising of the mother[46] in one side, and the splin in the other, beside the ston[e] doth much anoy hire besides sume other destempers, soe Hir body is all out of order.[47]

Two years later Elizabeth died at Kendal,[48] while in October 1666 Thomas Holme, aged 39, died and was buried at the Pont-y-Moel burial-ground in Monmouthshire.[49] Welsh Friends now had to rely on their own meetings and appointed ministers to take the Society into the next period of its development, while, at the same time, facing savage repression. They were, however, assisted by a second missionary visit throughout Wales, conducted by Fox, who helped the nascent Quaker communities establish a more permanent organisation, based on monthly and quarterly meetings.[50]

At the Bala Assizes on 6 August 1676, Justices Walcott and Eyton threatened to execute nine Merionethshire Quakers who had failed to attend church and swear the oaths of allegiance and supremacy. Although the Quakers had declared their faithfulness to the Crown, they would not go against the Biblical Commandment which forbade swearing. Walcott tried to prosecute them under fourteenth century heresy laws and other similar statutes, and warned that their refusal to comply would result in further court proceedings where they could be classified as traitors. If they were found guilty the men would be hanged and quartered, while the women 'were to be burned'. A second court appearance in September was met with the stern resolve of the Friends and they were imprisoned as traitors. They were denied any warmth from a fire, and one of the party, Edward Rees, who was over sixty, died that winter. The House of Commons reprieved the others, while Walcott was censured for his harshness. The respite was nevertheless brief and during the alleged Popish Plot of 1679 Friends again came under severe attack – this time as suspected papists. This was not just a religious imposition, but also the desire to make the Quakers conform to the letter of the law. If they would not comply they were to be reclassified as either outsiders, or far more seriously, as traitors.[51] Other punitive measures taken against the Friends were intended to ruin them financially, to restrict their movement, and ultimately to curtail their perceived subversive activities. A second example demonstrates this. In 1674, a magistrate and a number of soldiers broke up a Quaker meeting in Montgomeryshire. It was alleged that Thomas Lloyd of the Dolobran meeting had preached to them, and he was subsequently fined £20 for contravening the penal laws. Other Friends who attended the meeting were fined or had their property taken away.[52] This example was replicated throughout Wales in these troubled times until the passing of the Act of Toleration in 1689.

For many members in the 1680s the only alternative to persecution was emigration to the 'good and fruitful land' of Pennsylvania.[53] Welsh Friends who emigrated found that they could still conduct their lives according to the code of discipline established by George Fox in the post-Restoration period. This code acted as a moral guide for Friends, and aimed to provide members with a richer fellowship. By applying themselves to such a clear set of values, Welsh Friends were determined to make sure that no member of their community behaved in a manner that would bring the Society into disrepute. Thus, adherence to a prescriptive code helped the Society to regulate itself. Members who refused to acknowledge their failings faced the censure of the preparative, monthly or quarterly meeting. If they refused to condemn their actions and publicly submit a paper of recantation then they faced expulsion. Disownment from the Society was not a measure Friends took lightly, and it was only called upon if a member refused to submit to counselling from their local meeting. In many respects, however, by imposing these regulations Friends rejected many traditional and popular customs, such as theatrical performances, dancing, music, sporting events, and consequently set themselves apart from the wider community.[54] There are, of course, many examples where Welsh Friends did not comply with the exacting measures of the Society, or where their conduct clearly was at odds with the standard of behaviour expected. By the eighteenth century the rules on marriage, particularly to non-members, were rigorously enforced. This reflected a concern that mixed marriages would weaken the unity of the Society, but the large number of disownments for marrying non-members ('walking disorderly') would suggest that many Welsh Friends were unable to comply with the rules. This had a twin effect. It deprived the Society of a new generation of young and vibrant people, and thwarted any opportunity to increase their numbers.[55]

For Friends who were wealthy the struggle to resist the trappings of fashionable society was too strong, while for others the simple enjoyment of community activities either forced them to remain separate from their neighbours, or run the risk of censure and disownment from the Society. Welsh Friends deplored profligacy and the decadence of the seventeenth century. They sought to keep their clothes plain and reprimanded those who dressed immoderately. In 1689 the Welsh Yearly Meeting recorded that Friends ought to be 'plaine and desent in your habitts that you may be a good example to families and neighbours'.[56] Increasingly many Friends were unable to keep to these regulations. In 1777 the Yearly Meeting epistle complained of the lack of plainness in dress and modest behaviour. Members felt that this betrayed the legacy of earlier Friends, and they were worried that younger Friends would abandon Quakerism as well as the effect that their fashionable attitudes could have upon the whole Society.[57] Yet towards the end of the century, and especially in the nineteenth century, Welsh Friends were prepared to accept modifications in their customs and dress. For example, at a Quaker wedding at Neath between Mary Eliza Richardson and Henry Habberley Price Junior in 1864, 'the dresses of the ladies of the bridal party were chaste and elegant, but not gaudy. The bride was dressed in a white silk bonnet and lace fall, and bore in her hand a beautiful bouquet.' The children of Charles S. Price were also elegantly dressed in their 'knickerbocker dress of blue with white cashmere caps and feathers'.[58]

In most respects, however, the eighteenth century and the first half of the nine-teenth century was a depressed period for the Friends. In her study of Glamorgan Friends, Fay Williams commented upon the decline of the meetings in the eastern part of the county as a result of the death of leading Friends and a general apa-thy ('lukewarmness and indifference') which had set in amongst members there.[59] Elsewhere there were revivals, notably in west Glamorgan and in Pembrokeshire with the settlement of the Nantucket Island (Massachusetts) Quaker-whalers at Milford Haven in the 1790s.[60] But in general the Welsh Quaker meetings declined throughout the eighteenth and nineteenth centuries. For example, the last Welsh Yearly Meeting was held at Welshpool in 1797,[61] while in Radnorshire the 1851 religious census noted that there were only sixteen people attending worship at the Pales meeting. In 1860, Stanley Pumphrey observed that 'within the memory of many, there was here a flourishing congregation. Now the Meeting can hardly be said to exist. One infirm, lame old man, still crosses the hills at the hour of worship to sit there alone with God.'[62] Moreover, six years later there were only seventy-three in membership throughout Wales, while the Western Quarterly Meeting recorded in 1881 that many meeting-houses were no longer in use by Friends or had been rented out to other religious bodies.[63] The overall decline in Welsh Friends can be attributed to various factors, in particular the predominance of the English language in meetings in contrast to the largely monoglot Welsh population; the emigration of significant numbers of Friends to Pennsylvania; the challenge of Methodism; and the insular nature of the Quaker code of conduct, especially its clannishness and endogamous marriages.[64]

A recent study of Friends in Wales in the second half of the nineteenth century and the early years of the twentieth century by Gethin Evans nevertheless shows the tenacity of small numbers of Quakers in the country to keep meetings alive and the relationship of Welsh Friends with the London Yearly Meeting. In this study he explores the changing political, religious and social landscape of Wales as well as the attempts by Friends in Wales to provide a new home mission in this period of spiritual reawakening.[65] Despite these attempts to reverse the decline of meetings and embrace Welsh identity, the overarching London Yearly Meeting, in comparison with other nonconformist bodies, simply acted as an 'observer' in the religious-political issues of the day. They distanced themselves from the disestablishment of the Anglican Church in Wales and the thorny questions surrounding the 1902 Education Act. What is more noticeable is that the evangelical work was effec-tive in only the English-speaking urban areas of south Wales and not in the indus-trial valleys or in north Wales.[66] For example, at Swansea and Cardiff there was an increase in membership, and this was assisted by the efforts of the evangelical Home Missionary Committee (HMC). From being in a fragile condition in 1871 the Swansea Meeting[67] continued to wither between 1871 and 1896, but the work of B. J. Elsmere, formerly of Ledbury in Herefordshire, and the building of a new meeting-house in December 1897 proved to be a turning point and a second meeting-house, which had room for 250 seats, had been built by June 1899 for the large num-ber of attenders rather than for the modest number of members.[68] Yet disagreements between Friends in the meeting did much to undermine these achievements – a situation which continued to exist well into the twentieth century.[69] The Swansea meeting in the late-nineteenth and early twentieth centuries clearly shows the changing fortunes of a small meeting as membership fluctuated from 18 in 1861 to 3 in 1878, while a modest increase to 35 in 1901 did not last. Even the Welsh Revival of 1904–5 had no real impact with figures falling to 34 in 1906 and 17 in 1918.[70] This does not, however, take into consideration the number of regular attenders present at the Swansea meetings.

The Cardiff Meeting underwent a similar period of change. With no recorded members in *c*.1815 the Religious Census conducted in 1851 indicated that there had been a very modest recovery with five members attending the morning meeting of worship. Meetings were, until 1870, held in the home of Samuel Bevington, and through the efforts of Arthur Sessions, formerly of Gloucester, a mini-revival took place with twenty-seven members being recorded in 1875. Along with his brother, Frederick, they held a Preparative Meeting for Friends in Cardiff and Newport, while the organisational abilities of the Ulster Quaker William Hobson led to the building of a new meeting-house in Cardiff in February 1889.[71] Yet, as with the Swansea meeting, there were disagreements mainly about the evangelical direction the HMC was following. This led to the publication of a number of pamphlets by conservative Friends and their subsequent disownment from the Society.[72] The HMC appointed William Jesper Sayce in 1892 to replace Hobson and he noted a slight increase in membership. By 1895 there were seventy-eight members (and twenty-five regular attenders), but by 1916 membership had again declined to sixty-seven.[73]

The HMC may have been optimistic about its chances to secure a foothold in Welsh-speaking areas as the Western Quarterly Meeting observed in 1894 that

> we think there is an opening for Friends, among a population so disposed as they are to the reception of religious truth in its more simple forms, if any could be found, imbued with the principles of Friends willing to devote themselves to the work, and at the same time possessing a competent knowledge of the language.[74]

But, as Evans points out, the idea that the small number of Friends in Wales who spoke Welsh could provide a mission to Welsh-speaking communities was wholly unrealistic and rather patronising.[75]

Other towns, such as Newport and Neath, also witnessed a slight but unsustainable revival.[76] Likewise, in Radnorshire the American Quaker evangelist Yardley Warner inspired a revival in 1867 with his Tent Meetings on Pen-y-bont Common which led to new meetings at Pen-y-bont, Llanyre and Llandrindod Wells.[77] Such activity was supported by the organisation skills of Henry Stanley Newman who acted as clerk to the Hereford and Pales Monthly Meeting from 1869 to 1893. Indeed, the founding of meetings at Pen-y-bont and Llandrindod Wells were 'in large measure due to his aggressive efforts and to his eagerness to ensure that causes once founded should in due time be established'.[78] The continued existence of the Pales meeting was assisted with the creation of a day school in 1867 which, despite its often perilous finances, provided Friends with a clear attachment to the area. B. J. Elsmere and John Owen

Jenkins of Radnorshire similarly provided effective leadership and missionary oversight in Radnorshire and elsewhere in Wales in the late-nineteenth century and in the first quarter of the twentieth century.[79]

Despite the pessimistic mood of many of the annual reports that there was 'little fresh work or service to notice' at the turn of the twentieth century,[80] Quaker meetings continue to be held throughout Wales.[81] Modern-day attenders of Friends' meetings might, however, be attracted by the social and political activism as much as the religious ethos of the Society. In 1997 Welsh Friends produced a brief study of what it was to be a Friend in the twentieth century.[82] They noted that there were 900 Friends, although not birthright members, who were predominantly female and scattered throughout Wales. The majority described themselves as Welsh, a few spoke the Welsh language, and they were, like their forebearers, 'very active in community affairs, campaigning and [involved in] voluntary activities', notably in Greenpeace, CND, Oxfam, the British Heart Foundation, and the Aids Helpline.[83] A recent website gives more information about Welsh Friends suggesting that there are thirty-five meetings in Wales and provides details of Friends' beliefs, the location of meetings, events, advice to members and non-members, and a regular newsletter, *Calon*.[84] Currently, Friends are collectively structured into four Area Meetings encompassing Wales and the borders: North Wales Area Meeting;[85] Hereford and Mid-Wales Area Meeting;[86] South Wales Area Meeting;[87] and the Southern Marches Area Meeting.[88]

The Friends in Wales were originally, and for much of their history, an alternative community, existing largely 'outside the mainstream of life in the areas, in which they lived'.[89] They nevertheless played a significant role in the economic and social life of Wales as industrialists, pioneers of education, prison reformers, advocates of peace, and as humanitarians and philanthropists.[90] This was particularly noticeable in the late-1920s and throughout the 1930s when they offered considerable support during the period of mass employment in the south Wales valleys, particularly in the Rhondda and at Brynmawr.[91] Under the guidance of William Noble, Margaret Pitt, and Emma and Peter Scott, they provided an education centre at Maes-yr-Haf, Trealaw, as well as financial assistance and practical help by providing craft workshops for the large number of unemployed.[92] As a final comment this is how a recent member of the public described the Friends: 'I've been to a Quakers' meeting. I quite enjoyed the silence and the stillness, but I rather objected when people spoke! I know they're expected to, but it sort of destroyed my own train of thought. I enjoyed the informality, having been brought up high church, but I liked most the fact that it wasn't – what's the expression – happy-clappy type!'[93] Friends are, therefore, recognized and respected even if some of the descriptions, like this one, do not necessarily pay sufficient attention to them as a Christian community.

Notes

1. The more common term 'Quaker' was in fact a term of abuse employed in 1650 by a magistrate, Gervase Bennet of Derby, to expose the alleged uncontrolled behaviour of some members of the Society. See John L. Nickalls (ed.), *The Journal of George Fox* (Cambridge, 1952), p. 58.

2. Stephen Bates, 'Peace of the Action', *Guardian*, 22 May 2002, pp. 2–3.
3. The most accessible overviews of early Quakerism are William Braithwaite's two-volume study. See W. C. Braithwaite, *The Beginnings of Quakerism* (2nd edn. York, 1981), and *The Second Period of Quakerism* (2nd edn. Cambridge, 1961); P. Dandelion, *An Introduction to Quakerism* (Cambridge, 2007). Texts specified elsewhere in this chapter provide information on the development and decline of the Society.
4. T. Richards, *A History of the Puritan Movement in Wales* (London, 1920), ch. 1–2.
5. For details, see C. Hill, *The World Turned Upside Down* (Harmondsworth, 1975); M. Watts, *The Dissenters from the Reformation to the French Revolution* (Oxford, 1978), ch. 2; G. H. Jenkins, *The Foundations of Modern Wales* (Oxford, 1987), ch. 1–2.
6. Richards, *History of the Puritan Movement*, ch. 3–9.
7. J. W. Frost, 'The Dry Bones of Quaker Theology', *Church History*, 89 (1970), 504.
8. Recent studies of Fox include H. L. Ingle, *First Among Friends: George Fox and the Creation of Quakerism* (New York and Oxford, 1994).
9. E. E. Taylor, *The Valiant Sixty* (London, 1947).
10. Library of the Society of Friends, London (hereafter LSF), MS. Vol. 366. Mediations upon a summer's evening, dated 21.5.1673. Details of the life of John ap John are provided in W. G. Norris and N. Penney (eds), 'John ap John, and early records of Friends in Wales', *Journal of the Friends' Historical Society* (hereafter *JFHS*) Supplement 6 (1907); T. Shankland, 'Pwy oedd John ap John a Chatrin ei Wraig', *Cymru*, 56 (1919), 177–83; W. A. Bebb, 'John ap John, Apostol y Crynwyr yng Nghymru', *Cymru*, 62 (1922), 187–8; T. M. Rees, *A History of the Quakers in Wales and their Emigration to North America* (Carmarthen, 1925), pp. 16–22; Richard C. Allen, 'John ap John (*c.*1625–1697)', in H. C. G. Matthew and Brian Harrison (eds), *Oxford Dictionary of National Biography* (Oxford, 2004); http://www.oxforddnb.com/view/article/61973 (accessed January 2010).
11. Richard C. Allen, 'Holme, Thomas (1626/7–1666)', in Matthew and Harrison (eds), *Oxford Dictionary of National Biography*; http://www.oxforddnb.com/view/article/61971 (accessed January 2010).
12. Catie Gill, 'Hubberthorne, Richard (*bap.* 1628, *d.* 1662)', in Matthew and Harrison (eds), *Oxford Dictionary of National Biography*; http://www.oxforddnb.com/view/article/14018 (accessed January 2010).
13. Caroline L. Leachman, 'Audland, John (*c.*1630–1664)', in Matthew and Harrison (eds), *Oxford Dictionary of National Biography*; http://www.oxforddnb.com/view/article/69073 (accessed January 2010).
14. Details are provided in Allen, 'Holme, Thomas'.
15. See Taylor, *Valiant Sixty*; Nickalls (ed.), *Journal of George Fox*, p. 174; LSF, Swarthmore Collection, MS. IV. 66. John Lawson to Margaret Fell, Chester *c.*1653; MS. VII. 4. John Audland to George Fox, Bristol, 8.3.1654; MS. VII. 18. Journal of John Audland 27.4–30.7.1654; MS. I. 194. Thomas Home to Margaret Fell, 10.10.1654; MS. I. 197. Thomas Holme to Margaret Fell, Chester, 28 August 1655; MS. IV. 247. Thomas Holme to George Fox, Cardiff, 27 February 1655.
16. Thomas Wynne, *An Antichristian Conspiracy Detected ...* (London, 1679), pp. 8, 9.
17. Richard Davies, *An Account of the Convincement, Exercises and Services and Travels of ... Richard Davies* (London, 1877), pp. 26–7. See also J. Gwynn Williams, 'Davies, Richard (*bap.* 1635, *d.* 1708)', in Matthew and Harrison (eds), *Oxford Dictionary of National Biography*; http://www.oxforddnb.com/view/article/7256 (accessed January 2010).
18. M. F. Williams, 'Glamorgan Quakers 1654–1900', *Morgannwg*, 5 (1961), 54.
19. LSF, Swarthmore Collection, MS. IV. 247. See also Craig Horle, 'Quakers and Baptists 1647–1660', *Baptist Quarterly*, 26 (1976), 354.
20. John Moone, *The True Light hath made Manifest Darknesse ...* (London, 1657). See also Richard Hubberthorne and John Lawson, *Truth Cleared ... An Answer to a Printed Paper wherein are Certaine Untruths and False Aspersions, Cast Upon a People, Called Quakers, by Some Members of the Church of Wrexham in Wales* (London, 1654).
21. John Miles, *An Antidote against the Infection of the Times ...* (London, 1656).
22. R. C. Allen, *Quaker Communities in Early Modern Wales: From Resistance to Respectability* (Cardiff, 2007), ch. 1.

23. G. H. Jenkins, *Protestant Dissenters in Wales* (Cardiff, 1992), p. 34.

24. Haverford College, Pennsylvania. Quaker Special Collections, MS. 975B, the diary of Margaret Ellis, written *c*.1739–1752, p. 1.

25. E. H. Milligan, *Britannica on Quakerism* (London, 1965), p. 3.

26. Helpful studies on the origins and doctrines of the Society are provided in G. F. Nuttall, 'Puritan and Quaker Mysticism', *Theology*, LXXVIII (October, 1975), 518–31; Frost, 'Dry Bones', 503–23; B. Reay, 'Quakerism and Society', in J. F. McGregor and B. Reay (eds), *Radical Religion in the English Revolution* (Oxford, 1984), ch. 6.

27. On 6 October 1648 White was approved as minister of the parish, but he adopted the principles of Friends and became a leading spokesman. See *Journal of the House of Lords*, X, 531; Lambeth Palace, MS. 639 (Codices Tenisoniasni) fo. 186 - Episcopal Returns, 1669. For other conversions, including Ellis, see N. Penney (ed.), *The First Publishers of Truth* (London, 1907), pp. 323–5.

28. LSF, Swarthmore Collection, MS. I. 195. Thomas Holme to Margaret Fell, Frandley Great Budworth, *c*.October 1654; MS. I. 203. Thomas Holme to Margaret Fell, Newport, 30 April 1656; C. Trevett, *Women and Quakerism in the 17th Century* (York, 1991), pp. 98–9.

29. LSF, Swarthmore Collection, MS. I. 205. Thomas Holme to Margaret Fell, Cardiff, 4 June 1656.

30. Ibid., MS. I. 203.

31. Allen, *Quaker Communities in Early Modern Wales*, pp. 27–32.

32. Nickalls (ed.), *Journal*, pp. 289–94, 297–307; Allen, *Quaker Communities in Early Modern Wales*, p. 29.

33. For accounts of the provocative actions of Friends and the response of magistrates and clergy-men see Francis Gawler, *A Record of Some Persecutions in South Wales* (London, 1659), passim; Rees, *History of the Quakers in Wales*, ch. 4; Allen, *Quaker Communities in Early Modern Wales*, ch. 4.

34. For examples of 'deviant' behaviour, see Donald F. Durnbaugh, 'Baptists and Quakers – Left wing Puritans?', *Quaker History*, 62, 2 (Autumn 1973), 67–82; K. L. Carroll, 'Early Quakers and 'Going Naked as a Sign', *Quaker History*, 67, 2 (Autumn 1978), 69–87; C. L. Cherry, 'Enthusiasm and Madness: Anti-Quakerism in the Seventeenth Century', *Quaker History*, 73, 2 (Autumn 1984), 1–24.

35. See L. Damrosch, *The Sorrows of the Quaker Jesus: James Nayler and the Puritan Crackdown on the Free Spirit* (Cambridge, Mass. 1996).

36. For contrasting accounts, see Joshua Miller, *Antichrist in Man, the Quakers Idol* (London, 1655), pp. 6–14; Gawler, *A Record of Some Persecutions*, pp. 13–14.

37. Miller, *Antichrist*, pp. 6–7.

38. John Miles, *An Antidote Against the Infection of the Times* (London, 1656), and reprinted in *Transactions of the Welsh Baptist Historical Association* (1904), 1–52. For the Quaker reply, see George Fox, *The Great Mistery of the Great Whore Unfolded* (London, 1659). This was reprinted in the 1904 transactions, 214–16. Insights into early Quaker and anti-Quaker rhetoric are provided in G. H. Jenkins, 'Quakerism and anti-Quaker Literature in Wales from the Restoration to Methodism', *Welsh History Review*, 7 (1975), 403–26.

39. Davies, *Account*, pp. 42–3.

40. Leading Friends such as Richard Hanbury, the ironwork's owner of Pont-y-Moel, welcomed, if not relished, the opportunity to dispute theological arguments with church ministers in public. One meeting poster that is certainly forthright in its message can be seen in the Bodleian Library, Oxford. Tanner MS. 37. fo. 119R. (5mo 17d. 1680).

41. Theodore Eccleston, *A Reply to Tho. Andrews Letter to a Parishioner of Pontypool* (London, 1708), p. v.

42. Gawler, *A Record of Some Persecutions*, p. 9–13.

43. See LSF, Great Book of Sufferings, II. For assessments of Quaker persecution in Wales, see Williams, 'Glamorgan Quakers', 51–9; G. H. Jenkins, 'The Friends of Montgomeryshire in the Heroic Age', *Montgomeryshire Collections* (1988), 17–24; Allen, *Quaker Communities in Early Modern Wales*, ch. 4.

44. Milligan, *Britannica on Quakerism*, p. 6.

45. Jenkins, 'Friends of Montgomeryshire', 18

46. Panic or hysteria.

47. LSF, Swarthmore Collection, MS. IV. 251. Thomas Holme to George Fox, Kendal, 1 month 1663. Presumably Elizabeth Holme had a kidney stone or some other debilitating medical condition.
48. Penney (ed.), *First Publishers of Truth*, p. 260.
49. National Archives, Society of Friends Registers. No. 677, p. 42.
50. See Allen, *Quaker Communities in Early Modern Wales*, p. 32, ch. 3 (organisation of the Welsh meetings); Nickalls (ed.), *Journal of George Fox*, pp. 514–22.
51. For details of the laws by which Quakers could be punished and their response, see C. Horle, *The Quakers and the English Legal System, 1660–1688* (Philadelphia, 1988).
52. Rees, *Quakers in Wales*, p. 134.
53. G. H. Jenkins, *Literature, Religion and Society in Wales 1660–1730* (Cardiff, 1978), pp. 178–9; R. C. Allen, 'In Search of a New Jerusalem. A Preliminary Investigation into Welsh Quaker Emigration to North America c.1660–1750', *Quaker Studies*, 9, 1 (September, 2004), 31–53.
54. Welsh Friends occasionally published attacks on popular activities, see Evan Bevan, 'Of the evils of Cockfighting', *Glocester Journal*, 13 April 1731, p. 2; R. C. Allen, 'An Alarm Sounded to the Sinners in Sion': John Kelsall, Quakers and Popular Culture in Eighteenth-century Wales', in J. Allen and R. C. Allen (eds), *Faith of Our Fathers: Popular Culture and Belief in post-Reformation England, Ireland and Wales* (Newcastle, 2009), pp. 52–74.
55. Williams, 'Glamorgan Quakers', 67.
56. Glamorgan Archive Service (hereafter GAS), D/DSF/2 (Yearly Meeting minutes), p. 492. Studies on Quakers and plainness include J. Kendall, 'The Development of a Distinctive Form of Quaker Dress', *Costume*, 19 (1985), 58–74; D. J. Hall, 'Plainness of Speech, Behaviour and Apparel in Eighteenth-Century English Quakerism', *Studies in Church History*, 22 (1985), 307–18; R. C. Allen, 'A Pilgrim's Progress. A Welsh Quaker's Spiritual Journey. Four papers written by Thomas Lewis of Shirenewton, Gwent. c.1741–2', *JFHS*, 58, 2 (1998), 136–62.
57. GAS, D/DSF/2, p. 922.
58. *Neath Gazette*, 12 March 1864. For a fuller account, see M. F. Williams, 'The Society of Friends in Glamorgan, 1654–1900', unpublished University of Wales, MA thesis, 1950, pp. 141–2.
59. Williams, 'Glamorgan Quakers', 63–6.
60. Ibid., 66, 67–70; R. C. Allen, 'Nantucket Quakers and the Milford Haven Whaling Industry, c.1791–1821', *Quaker Studies*, 15, 1 (September, 2010), 6–31.
61. The last Welsh Yearly Meeting was held in Welshpool and Friends thereafter met at a Half-Yearly Meeting. For the last Yearly Meeting see GAS, D/DSF/2, pp. 1049–54.
62. H. S. Newman, *Memories of Stanley Pumphrey* (London, 1883), p. 23, and cited in T. Macpherson, 'A Measure of Grace. Quakers in Radnorshire', *Transactions of the Radnorshire Society*, 69 (1999), 8–33.
63. Owain Gethin Evans, '"Benign Neglect": The Activities and Relationship of London Yearly Meeting of the Religious Society of Friends (Quakers) to Wales, c.1860–1918', unpublished University of Birmingham, Ph.D. thesis, 2009, p. 17 and Table 2. Tabular Returns for the Quarterly Meetings with meetings in Wales, c.1862–1897; Worcester Record Office (WRO), Western Quarterly Meeting WQM), Report 19.4.1881.
64. Jenkins, 'Friends of Montgomeryshire', 24–30; Allen, *Quaker Communities in Early Modern Wales*, ch. 7.
65. Evans, 'Benign Neglect'.
66. For details of the objectives and activities of the Home Mission Committee see ibid., pp. 140–9.
67. Ibid., pp. 163–73.
68. There were twenty-eight members in the morning meeting and sixty-five in the evening. Ibid., p. 166.
69. Ibid., pp. 165–72.
70. Ibid., p. 173.
71. Ibid., pp. 173–7.
72. Ibid., pp. 177–85. See also R. C. Allen, 'An Example of Quaker Discipline: The Case of Dr Charles Allen Fox and the Cardiff Quakers', *Journal of Welsh Religious History*, New Series, 1 (Winter 2001), 46–73.
73. Evans, 'Benign Neglect', pp. 189, 190.
74. WRO, WQM, Report 18.4.1894, and cited in ibid., p. 148.

75. Evans, 'Benign Neglect', pp. 148–9.
76. Ibid., pp. 190–7.
77. Macpherson, 'A Measure of Grace', p. 31; Evans, 'Benign Neglect', pp. 159–63.
78. LSF, Minutes and Proceedings of the Yearly Meeting of Friends, pp. 254–9 (testimony to Newman c.1913), and cited in Evans, 'Benign Neglect', p. 147. For details of his life see H. M. Newman, *Henry Stanley Newman* (London, 1917).
79. Evans, 'Benign Neglect', pp. 149–63.
80. *Minutes and Proceedings of the Yearly Meeting of Friends*, c.1912; and cited in ibid., p. 221.
81. In 1960 it was recorded that there were approximately 202,000 Friends in the world, with 123,000 in North America and less than 25,000 in Britain. See Milligan, *Britannica on Quakerism*, p. 3.
82. D. Rowland and P. Stoner, *Mae'r gân yn y galon. Quakers in Wales Today* (Llandybie, 1997). A comprehensive study of the Friends in Wales in the period after the First World War, however, has not been undertaken.
83. Rowland and Stoner, *Mae'r gân yn y galon*, pp. 11–12, 15.
84. http://www.quakersinwales.org.uk/default.aspx (accessed August 2010).
85. This includes meetings at: Bangor, Colwyn Bay, Holyhead, Llangollen, Mold, Oswestry, Porthmadog, Pwllheli, Ruthin, and Wrexham. See http://www.northwalesquakers.org/home.html (accessed August 2010).
86. There are meetings at: Aberystwyth, Dolgellau, Dolobran, Llanidloes, Machynlleth, and Newtown. See http://www.hmwquakers.org.uk/index.html (accessed August 2010).
87. Meetings are currently provided at: Brecon, Bridgend, Caerleon, Cardiff, Cardigan, Lampeter and Llanybydder, Milford Haven, Narberth, Neath, Penarth, St Davids , Swansea, and Trealaw (Rhondda). For details of Bridgend, Neath and Swansea meetings see http://www. bridgendquakers. org.uk/; http://www.neath quakers.org/; http://www.Swansea quakers.org/ (accessed August 2010).
88. This was formerly part of the Hereford and Mid Wales Area Meeting. Meetings are held at: Abergavenny, Almeley Wootton, Clun Valley, Hay-on-Wye, Hereford, Ledbury, Llandrindod, the Pales, Ludlow, and Ross-on-Wye.
89. Williams, 'Glamorgan Quakers', 73.
90. Ibid., 74–5; Rees, *Quakers in Wales*, ch. 8; H. Lloyd, *The Quaker Lloyds in the Industrial Revolution* (London, 1975).
91. B. Naylor, *Quakers in the Rhondda, 1926–1986* (Chepstow, 1986); Pamela Manasseh, *Quaker Relief Work and the Brynmawr Experiment* (Birmingham, 2000) and her later doctoral study, 'The Brynmawr Experiment 1928–1940: Quaker Values and Arts and Crafts Principles', unpublished University College, Falmouth, Ph.D. thesis, 2009.
92. For a brief summary see Manasseh, 'Brynmawr Experiment', pp. 86–9, 91–110.
93. Rowland and Stoner, *Mae'r gân yn y galon*, p. 17.

CHAPTER 5

ROMAN CATHOLICISM

Trystan O. Hughes

With the 1536 and 1543 Acts of Union, the Reformation was imposed onto Wales and was initially welcomed by only a few. During the following 150 years, instructional literature was produced to keep *yr Hen Ffydd* (the Old Faith) alive[1] and Welsh Catholics were persecuted and martyred.[2] The seventeenth century especially was a depressing period for Catholics in Wales. The allegiance of many leading Catholic families to Charles I during the civil wars of the 1640s and early 1650s perpetuated fears that parts of Wales were spawning grounds for papist agitators.[3] The restoration of the monarchy in 1660 did not provide much respite, as Elizabethan recusancy laws were again employed to enforce conformity of worship.[4] Rumours of foreign invasion and secret intrigues between 1678 and 1679, occasioned by an alleged Papist Plot, caused a wave of mass hysteria whipped up by Titus Oates. This led to the summary executions of several important Catholic priests, the most notable of whom was David Lewis, the superior of the Jesuit College at Llanrothal on the Monmouthshire-Herefordshire border.[5] These events had major ramifications for the Welsh Catholic population, priests and laity alike.

By the end of the seventeenth century, however, the influence of Protestant dissenters, recusant persecution, and a shortage of priests ensured that Roman Catholicism had all but died in Wales. It was kept alive only in pockets in the south-east and north-east corners of the country, and largely by gentry families. Garfield Lynch observed that protection was afforded to priests in 'safe-houses' at Llanarth and Abergavenny,[6] while a gradual decline in gentry patronage was a significant factor in the weakening of Catholicism throughout Wales. Eighteenth-century Catholic registers would nevertheless suggest that there was a body of support on the borders, but, with Wales' zealous embracing of the evangelical revival in the eighteenth century, the possibility of a Catholic revival seemed remote. Yet, by the beginning of the twentieth-first century Roman Catholicism was not only one of the two largest single denominations in Wales (alongside the Anglican Church in Wales), but also stood as an accepted, intrinsic, and revered element in the religious makeup of Wales.

The modern history of the Roman Catholic Church in Wales essentially begins with the vast influx of Irish workers to the industrial centres of south-east Wales in the 1840s. Irish immigration had certainly begun earlier.[7] Catholics in Cardiff, for example, grew from 'a few Catholic families' in the 1820s to 1,200 in 1840.[8] Yet it was the growth in the next two decades that was particularly striking. By 1851 the number had increased to 4,000 and by 1861 it had more than doubled to 9,800.

Likewise, there was only one Catholic in Merthyr Tydfil in 1801. The Catholic population increased to 300 by 1828, and to 4,049 by 1855. Similar expansion was seen in other industrial south Wales towns, especially Newport and Swansea. The Greenhill area of Swansea was even given the epithet 'Little Ireland', while there were smaller Catholic communities in a number of north Wales towns, such as Holywell, Wrexham, and Bangor. With the restoration of the Catholic diocesan hierarchy in 1850, the Diocese of Newport and Menevia was established in the southeast, while the rest of Wales became part of the Diocese of Shrewsbury. Thomas Joseph Brown was appointed as the first bishop of Newport and Menevia. Heavy Catholic immigration had led to the desperate need for priests to minister to the new communities. Brown ensured a sufficient presence of priests by appealing for the help of religious orders. Among the numerous orders that moved into Wales to assist during the nineteenth century were the Franciscans, the Benedictines, the Fathers of Charity, and the Jesuits.[9] Likewise, many Irish secular priests crossed the Irish Sea to minister to their compatriots, who were more than often living in abject poverty. Still, money was raised for the building of many churches and schools. The number of Catholic churches in Wales grew from 14 in 1840 to 123 in 1910. In the same year, the number of Catholic schools in Wales stood at 71.[10]

During the nineteenth century, Rome considered Wales as little more than a district of England. In 1895, however, Cardinal Vaughan of Westminster announced that 'Wales ought to be treated as an independent state rather than as an appendage of England.'[11] The Vicariate of Wales was established in that year and Francis Mostyn, of the recusant family of Talacre, near Holywell, was appointed Vicar Apostolic. The Vicariate comprised all the Welsh counties except Glamorganshire and Monmouthshire. With the comparatively low number of Catholics outside of the south-east, the Vicariate reminded Catholics of the need to see Wales as a missionary field. Three years later the Vicariate was elevated to a Diocese and the ancient title 'Menevia' was revived. Mostyn became the first bishop of Menevia in modern times. With the formation of the Province of Wales in 1916, the diocese of Menevia becoming a suffragan See to the new metropolitan archdiocese of Cardiff, which included the counties of Glamorganshire, Monmouthshire and Herefordshire. A Catholic historian later described this 'natural and almost inevitable development'[12] as the completion of 'the evolution of Wales'.[13] The structure of the Welsh Catholic Church, however, was not to be fully completed until 1987, when it was changed to its present three-diocesan structure – with the archdiocese of Cardiff in the south-east, the diocese of Menevia in the south-west, and the diocese of Wrexham in the north.

Such diocesan changes were themselves necessary because of the increase in the numbers of Catholics in Wales. This phenomenal growth continued during the twentieth century.[14] In 1911 there were only 54,055 Catholics in the whole of Wales, by 1921 this number had increased to 69,521, by 1931 to 100,977, and by 1941 to 105,580. In 30 years, the number of Welsh Catholics had almost doubled, and this was at a time when the population of Wales was falling. After the Second World War, expansion continued. By 1951 the number of Catholics had increased to 113,600, by 1961 to 128,500, and by 1973 to 143,276. The increase in churches and Catholic schools at this time was likewise impressive. The number of churches increased from 95 in 1901 to 269 in 1973, and the number of schools from 71 in 1911 to 125 in 1973.[15]

Numerous public events were testimony to the growing number of Welsh Catholics and the confidence and triumphalism that this engendered. Not least were the annual Corpus Christi celebrations with their attendant colourful processions. In the south Wales towns these were particularly impressive, especially during the inter-war years. In Cardiff, the mile-long procession to the Castle grounds saw around 6,000 children take part annually, with about 30,000 visiting the ground and up to 120,000 spectators in the streets.[16] At Newport around 20,000 took part,[17] while around 10,000 took part at Swansea.[18] Even in the diocese of Menevia, large Catholic rallies were frequent – at Trefriw in 1931, Colwyn Bay in 1935, Llandrindod Wells in 1938, and at the Calvinistic Methodist stronghold of Bala in 1954.[19] The latter attracted around 20,000 Catholics, making the number of Catholics to have visited the small Catholic church at Bala to 140,000 in six years.[20] The numbers at all these celebrations were astonishing, and it is little wonder that many locals were apprehensive at the sight of such great rallies, especially those in the staunchly nonconformist areas of Wales.

Numerous reasons can be posited for this Catholic expansion. Certainly Catholic immigration from Ireland remained intense, and subsequently moulded the practices of the Church itself. The nineteenth century had seen the growth of a strong Irish community in the industrial south-east. During the first sixty years of the next century, the influx from Ireland again became heavy, but now it was not only the south-east that was affected. Higher wages and better working conditions attracted Irish workers to every part of Wales. In north Wales, the percentage of Irish-born inhabitants increased in every single county. Both Anglesey and Caernarfonshire recorded their highest-ever figures of Irish born in 1951, with two and half per cent of Anglesey's population having been born across the Irish Sea.[21] It was estimated that between 1945 and 1960 as many as 4,000 southern Irishmen a year had found employment in Wales. This meant that between 45,000 and 60,000 Irishmen had entered Wales in this period, a figure not including wives and children.[22] Many of the larger immigrant communities clung to their Irish identity, an identity strengthened by incoming Irishmen. Up to the 1930s in the south-east, for example, Gaelic was encouraged, Irish societies thrived, and Republican banners were paraded. Yet, the rapid loss of this fervent Irish cultural identity did not result in a Welsh Catholic Church. The Church instead became Anglo-Irish. English in its language and attitudes, yet with a continuing sentimental affection for all things Irish. The popularity of St Patrick and St Patrick's day, with its Shamrock and Gaelic service, far surpassed that for the Patron Saint of Wales, and even among second, third, and fourth generation immigrants there remained an often superficial affiliation with 'auld Oireland'.[23]

As well as from Ireland, immigration from other countries also strengthened the Church. Migration from England was certainly a factor. During the Second World War, wholescale evacuation into Wales was witnessed and, although many returned to their homes after the war, others stayed behind, either through choice or because of the difficulties in obtaining housing in the devastated cities. Likewise, English workers were attracted to post-war Wales by the tourist industry, in north Wales especially, and by the other revitalised industries. Many also moved to Wales to retire. By 1966 one in five people living in Wales was of non-Welsh origin. Most of these had come from cities where Catholicism was strong, such as Liverpool and Manchester, and so served to strengthen the formerly small Welsh Catholic communities. For example, in the Catholic parish of Aberystwyth by 1955 the number of faithful born in England (31%) far outnumbered those born in Wales (22%) or Ireland (15%).[24] That parish also reveals how continental Catholics had numerically strengthened the Welsh Catholic Church during the twentieth century. Thus twenty per cent of Aberystwyth Catholics had been born in Italy (5% more than had been born in Ireland) and eight per cent were Polish immigrants.[25] In other Welsh Catholic communities, immigrants from Germany, Spain, Yugoslavia, and Hungary were to be found, alongside those from Italy[26] and Poland. Many of these continental Catholics had been refugees, others had been kept at Welsh prisoner-of-war camps, while others had simply moved to Wales to find work.

It was claimed during this time that the remarkable increase in the numbers of Catholics in Wales was due to evangelistic success. Rome, it was maintained, was winning over many native converts. In 1959 Catherine Daniel wrote that 'in spite of the [Catholic Church in Wales's] often foreign appearance it draws a steady stream of converts'.[27] Between 1916 and 1961 there were over 300 converts annually in Wales. The high-points in this development were in the late-1920s and again in the late-1950s, with numbers reaching as high as 700 converts annually. At an estimate there were over 20,000 converts to Roman Catholicism in Wales between 1920 and 1960. In 1955 almost a quarter of the Catholic population of Aberystwyth were converts.[28] There were also a good number of high-profile and well-publicised Welsh conversions. Among these were Saunders Lewis (the playwright and Plaid Genedlaethol Cymru's first president), Catherine Daniel (the wife of Plaid's second president), R. O. F. Wynne (the Squire of Garthewin), David Jones (the poet, artist and sculptor), and a number of non-Catholic clergymen and ministers.[29] Yet it is questionable whether Catholic fervent missionary endeavours had anything close to their original intentions. In truth, the vast majority of converts were either lapsed Catholics who had returned to the fold, or non-Catholics who had converted at their marriage to a Catholic. They were therefore 'Catholics' in name and nothing more. Superficial successes, therefore, masked the reality that immigration was the real key to the increase.

Whatever the reasons for the growth, the twentieth-century expansion of Catholicism was in striking contrast to the fortunes of the Welsh chapels at this time. No other Welsh Christian body could boast an increase in numbers anywhere close to that of the Roman Church, and many of the others were decreasing at almost the same rate as Catholicism was increasing. This gave a flourishing and triumphalistic Church further confidence. From the 1920s onwards, the misplaced Catholic claim that Wales was on the verge of converting *en masse* to Rome became popular. At a crowded meeting in Cardiff in 1936, speaker after speaker announced that the conversion of Wales was imminent. Michael McGrath, bishop of Menevia and future archbishop of Cardiff, declared that 'North Wales is moving fast with all Wales back to the faith of the fathers.' Fr Owen Dudley continued by proclaiming that he was certain of one thing, that 'there has never been since the Reformation an opportunity such as is ours to-day. Protestantism is on its death-bed.'[30] Similar enthusiasm continued up to the early 1960s, when one *Western Mail* correspondent claimed that 'by 2050 AD Wales will be a second Ireland in religious outlook'.[31]

The natural result of Catholic confidence was Protestant trepidation and fear. This was channelled into anti-Catholic hostility and prejudice. Aside from Northern Ireland and the streets of Liverpool and Glasgow, nowhere in Britain was this more fervent than in Wales. Rather than being at a local level, however, this opposition was largely found in chapel conferences and publications, and was largely expressed by ministers, deacons, and clergymen. These either virulently dismissed suggestions of the conversion of Wales to Rome as sectarian propaganda, or else sternly warned of the dangers of Papism. The absurdity of such animosity is best shown in the oft-made claim, even by chapel ministers, that it would be better if Wales turned to atheism than Papism.[32] Anti-Catholic sentiment was, indeed, frequent and virulent. In 1926, E. Griffith-Jones, Principal of the United College, Bradford, warned that were the Papacy to win over Wales and Britain, it would be in a position to take over the world: 'Nothing would be more calamitous than for this country to become Roman Catholic.'[33] Four years later, the nonconformist newspaper *Y Faner* proclaimed its opinion that 'nothing but evil can come from the success of Roman Catholicism in Wales, and everywhere else'.[34] As late as 1951, an article by the Rev. E. Lewis Evans of Pontarddulais showed the extent and frenzy of Protestant fear. 'Nothing can hide from the Papists', he warned, 'they walk from conquest to conquest . . . they attempt to win over the whole world'.[35]

A number of factors made this hostility all the more trenchant. First, the Anglo-Irish nature of the Catholic Church in Wales was regarded as a threat to the Welsh language and way of life. However much Welsh Catholics emphasised that their Church was not alien to the nation, but rather the pre-Reformation faith of Wales, there could be no denying that modern Catholics in Wales were a motley collection of immigrants and their descendants. At a Methodist Synod at Llangefni in 1931, the Rev. Lewis Edwards summarised the belief held by many nonconformists at this time. 'There is no disguising the fact', he wrote, 'that Roman Catholics are opposed to everything the Welsh people hold dear in their national life'.[36] Such accusations lost much of their potency as the result of, firstly, a succession of bishops who were sympathetic to the Welsh cause, and, secondly, the formation of the Welsh Catholic Society (*Y Cylch Catholig*) in the early 1940s. The *Cylch*, led by a string of able and patriotic Catholics, did much to persuade Welsh nonconformists that there were both native and immigrant Catholics who were dedicated to Welsh culture and even nationalism.[37]

The second factor leading to hostility towards Catholicism, was that, up to the 1950s, Catholicism was seen as a political and not merely a religious threat to Wales. In the inter-war years especially, there was an atmosphere in chapel circles that could almost be described as hysterical or frenzied. It was truly believed that Rome was a real political threat to Wales. In 1930, *Y Faner* announced that 'the Papist danger is not a false dream, not vague imaginings. Roman Catholicism today is as daring as ever . . . let Wales be watchful. Watch every move. Catholics are crafty, you never know what direction their plots will come to light.'[38] As late as 1940, W. J. Gruffydd, editor of *Y Llenor*, insisted that 'a strong section of the Catholic Church has been working out of sight, in every direction in life, not only to restore the Church's control over individual men's morals but to restore its power and sovereignty over the state'.[39]

Furthermore, this political Papal menace was perceived as a Fascist threat. It was the Church's hatred of communism, its authoritarian structure, and its Italian, Spanish, and German sympathies, which led to accusations that Rome's devious political plans were centred around Fascism. In 1937, the Rev. M. Watcyn-Williams gave a stern warning against the subtle combination of Fascism and Catholicism 'which, under the guise of religion, threatens to stamp out the liberty of Christians'.[40] When the President of the Welsh Nationalist Party, Saunders Lewis, converted to Catholicism, the situation became all the more anxious. With a number of other prominent Plaid Cymru members following Lewis to Rome, concern was expressed that they were merely a front for Papal Fascism. In a bitter attack on the Welsh Nationalist Party in 1942, the Rev. Gwilym Davies warned his fellow countrymen that the party's aims were all too clear: 'in the independent, totalitarian, fascist, and papist Wales, there will only be one party, one church and one language'.[41] The most shocking fact is that many Plaid Cymru members defended their party, not by asserting that there was nothing wrong with Catholic leadership, but by claiming that Plaid was not actually a Catholic party, but essentially a nonconformist party. 'Ninety Nine percent of the members of Plaid Cymru', wrote D. J. Thomas of Dyserth in *Y Faner* in 1950, 'are all ordinary people of Wales and zealous Nonconformists'.[42]

The third factor that exacerbated hostility towards Catholicism was the absence of Catholics in ecumenical discussions. Up until the 1960s, the Catholic Church clung rigidly to its position of *extra ecclesiam nulla salus* (outside the Church no salvation). It alone was the true Church, with all other denominations being heretical. Although ecumenical unity was increasingly seen as the ideal amongst non-Catholics, the Roman Catholic Church remained as aloof and remote as ever from the other denominations in Wales, with Catholics strictly forbidden to attend non-Catholic services. In the words of Archbishop Francis Mostyn of Cardiff in 1932, Christian unity could happen 'in no other way than by the submission of those outside the Catholic Church to the teaching and authority of that Church. Without this the unity of Christendom is a mere pious wish, which can never be attained.'[43] In the atmosphere of ecumenism, this spirit was regarded more than ever as intolerant, narrow, exclusive, and conceited. In 1928 the Rev. J. Gower Jones, an Anglican clergymen, claimed that Mostyn's use of the label 'heretics and schismatics' to describe his fellow Welshmen was 'an exhibition of pride and arrogance and totally incongruous with the humility of Christ'.[44] Likewise, in 1937 in the *Western Mail* the Rev. M. Watcyn-Williams ridiculed Rome's 'ridiculous' and 'arrogant' claims,[45] while another correspondent expressed horror at 'the mentality of Roman Catholics today'.[46] Even on the eve of the Second Vatican Council, which would transform Catholic attitudes to ecumenism in Wales as elsewhere, Welsh Catholics continued their staunch disdain for other denominations and were still resolute in their insistence on the unique position of their Church.[47]

While these factors made anti-Catholic animosity all the more trenchant, there could be no denying that hostility was generally a reaction to the growth in strength and numbers of the Church. Aside from specific reactions to the Church's expansion, however, anti-Catholicism took various forms. Non-Catholic Welshmen were, for example, hostile to, and intolerant of, Catholic doctrinal issues. Largely expressed through conferences and the Welsh press, the attacks on Catholic beliefs were impassioned. Few beliefs and practices were left unscathed. Catholics were regarded as being superstitious, unscriptural, ostentatious, and in bondage to the past. Papal infallibility, Marian dogmas, transubstantiation, and devotion to martyrs were the butt of Welsh hostility, as was the authoritarian temper of the Papacy. In the opinion of the Rev. Vyrnwy Morgan, those who tested Roman doctrines by reason, history, and Scripture repudiated them as being the 'essence of superstition, idolatry and error'.[48] Many nonconformists condemned Catholicism as blasphemous. For Anne Lodwick Lewis, Catholic beliefs were 'a substitute for Christianity. The Pope claims to be a substitute for Christ. The sacrifice of the Mass is a substitute for our Lord's sacrifice on Calvary. Mary and the Saints take the place of Christ in the hearts of Roman Catholics.' She concluded that, in Wales, 'our dire need is for another Martin Luther'.[49] In 1950 Y Goleuad, in reacting to the 'modern' dogmas of Papal Infallibility and the Bodily Assumption of the Virgin Mary, exemplified such attitudes to Roman doctrine by announcing that 'at the root of all these calamitous superstitions is a lack of a complete faith in God and Christ'.[50] In face of such enmity, Welsh Catholics used their newly-found optimism and confidence to counter-attack the beliefs of nonconformists and Anglicans. 'The Welsh nation has to be won back from a cold, individualistic and sterile religion', wrote J. T. F. Williams, 'into the warm, corporate, and active profession of Catholic Christianity'.[51]

Anti-Catholic hostility also came to the fore in opposition to Catholic schools. In Wales, more than in any other part of Britain, Catholic insistence on their own schools caused a fervent reaction. The burden on the Catholic community of financing a separate system of education was great, but the impassioned hostility of the Local Education Authorities (LEA) served to make the situation far worse. Up to the 1950s, Catholics in Wales struggled tirelessly against LEAs that defied the government by not allowing Catholics their own schools. In 1949 H. W. J. Edwards wrote that the educational difficulties which Catholics were experiencing in Wales 'may amount to that degree of hostility known as persecution'.[52] Although the LEAs claimed that financial reasons were behind their defiance, the sectarian and anti-Catholic motives behind resistance was all too clear. At Colwyn Bay in the 1930s and at Flint in the late-1940s, there were particularly fervent controversies where LEAs refused to allow Catholic schools to be built. At Flint, one councillor had even warned Catholics that he intended to make the Reformation itself pale into insignificance compared to this religious war.[53] 'We are a reformed Church', announced the Principal of Aberystwyth Theological College in his support of the Flintshire's Council's stand, 'and cannot sit back and allow our country to be taken over to the Roman Catholic faith without some protest'.[54]

Up to the 1960s, then, Wales' attitude to the Catholic Church was characterised by perpetual bigotry. Surprisingly, however, alongside this hostility was evidence of a gradual change in attitudes. An abating of prejudice and hostility occurred for a number of reasons. First, hostility subsided with the integration of immigrant Catholics into Welsh society. Once Catholics were settled into specific areas and became part of everyday life, they became accepted quite quickly. Anti-Catholic prejudice was often the fear of the unknown rather than blind hatred and malice. Second, respect for individual Catholics helped decrease hostility, as saintly and hard-working individual Catholics were recognised and valued. Third, Catholic social efforts and moral stands had a positive consequence. In the 1930s, relief work among the poverty-stricken folk of south Wales ensured increasing admiration for the Church. 'In South Wales today,' the *Tablet* noted, 'there is every kind of com-plication – racial, moral, national, economic and social – but it may be a sign of new times that even the poorest, and once the most bigoted, are now making the enigmatical remark so often heard in England: "If I were anything I would be a Catholic"'.[55] Likewise, many of the Catholic moral stands, particularly on issues such as divorce, sex, violence in films, war, and euthanasia, were respected. At the Calvinistic Methodist General Conference in 1933 the Rev. D. Jones even admitted that 'the Church of Rome says some things that the Protestants should have said clearly a long time ago'.[56]

A fourth factor that contributed to the lessening of prejudice was due to the efforts of a significant Catholic minority to foster a Welsh consciousness among their fellow Catholics. This was true of some, though not all, members of the hierarchy. Archbishop Mostyn of Cardiff and Bishop Vaughan of Menevia had some command of the Welsh language, while Mostyn's successor at Cardiff, Archbishop McGrath, an Irishman, learnt Welsh so fluently that he became a Welsh scholar and befriended a number of prominent Welsh poets, including T. Gwynn Jones. Later bishops, such as Bishop Mullins of Menevia and Bishop Regan of Wrexham, continued the episcopal Catholic support of Welsh language and heritage. As early as the 1930s, one Welsh non-Catholic was writing that 'the gibe that Roman Catholicism in our midst is merely an Irish and an Italian mission is rapidly becoming untrue'.[57] *Y Cylch Catholig*, which is still in existence today, further helped change Welsh attitudes to the Church. By the 1970s, J. Heywood Thomas, a Welsh nonconformist lecturing at the University of Durham, could even claim that 'it is one of the glories of contemporary Welsh Catholicism that it has supported the determined efforts of Welshmen to preserve their language and the Christian tradition it enshrines'.[58]

Ironically, the fifth and final factor that led to a lessening of anti-Catholicism in Wales was the growth of secularism. As the twentieth century progressed, Wales experienced increasing religious indifference and an onslaught of religious apathy. Anti-Catholic hostility therefore decreased according to a scale set by this waning of religious sentiment. Bishop Petit of Menevia recognised this when he wondered in 1952 whether the hostility of the Welsh towards Catholicism could be 'softened before it is removed by the tolerance that springs from indifferentism'.[59]

Despite this secularism, the Roman Catholic Church today continues to play an important part in Welsh Church life. Boosted by an influx of Polish immigrants to many parts of the country since the expansion of the European Union in 2004, church numbers in Wales continue to be relatively healthy. Furthermore, the new attitude towards ecumenism in the Church since the Second Vatican Council (1962–5) has transformed denominational relations. Today, the Church is a prominent member of CYTUN (Churches Together in Wales), both at a national and a local level,[60] and, in November 2002, it launched a Welsh-language edition of its ecumenical document, *The Search for Christian Unity*.[61] The past century, then, had seen a great change in attitudes towards, and also within, the Catholic Church in Wales. Up to the 1960s, a virulent prejudice and hostility towards the Church had been witnessed in many areas of Welsh life. Yet, accompanying this, there was also a gradual change of attitude towards the Church that had been evident since the First World War. It was this tolerance that eventually won the day and led to the Catholic Church becoming accepted as an important and respected member of the family of Welsh Churches.

Notes

1. For example, *Y Drych Cristnogawl* (The Christian Mirror) (1600).
2. For example, Richard Gwyn in 1584.
3. K. J. Lindley, 'The part played by the Catholics in the Civil Wars in Lancashire and Monmouthshire', unpublished University of Wales, MA thesis, 1965.
4. Most notably the Marquis of Worcester at Raglan Castle and other leading gentlemen in Flintshire and Monmouthshire. See R. P. Matthews, 'Roman Catholic Recusancy in Monmouthshire 1608–89. A demographic and morphological analysis', unpublished University of Wales, Ph.D. thesis, 1996.
5. M. M. Cusack O'Keefe, 'The Popish Plot in South Wales and the Marches of Gloucester and Hereford', unpublished University of Galway, MA thesis, 1970.
6. Garfield Lynch, 'The Revival of Roman Catholicism in South Wales in the late eighteenth and nineteenth centuries', unpublished University of Wales, MA thesis, 1941. See also Philip Jenkins, '"A Welsh Lancashire?": Monmouthshire Catholics in the Eighteenth Century', *Recusant History*, 15, 3 (May, 1980), 176–88.
7. For details, see Paul O'Leary, *Immigration and Integration: The Irish in Wales, 1798–1922* (Cardiff, 2000).
8. Daniel J. Mullins, 'The Catholic Church in Wales', in Alan McClelland and Michael Hodgetts (eds), *From Without the Flaminian Gate: 150 Years of Roman Catholicism in England and Wales 1850–2000* (London, 1999), p. 273.
9. Mullins, 'Catholic Church', pp. 272–94.
10. John Williams, *Digest of Welsh Historical Statistics* vol. I (Cardiff, 1985).
11. Donald Attwater, *The Catholic Church in Modern Wales: A Record of the Past Century* (London, 1935), p. 125.
12. *Tablet*, 12 February 1916, p. 200.
13. Martin V. Sweeney, 'Diocesan Organisation and Administration', in G. A. Beck (ed.), *The English Catholics 1850–1950* (London, 1950), p. 148.
14. See Trystan Owain Hughes, *Winds of Change: The Roman Catholic Church in Wales 1916–62* (Cardiff, 1999), pp. 6–43.
15. Williams, *Digest of Welsh Historical Statistics*.
16. *St Peter's Parish Magazine*, 5, 5 (1925), 207. See also Paul O'Leary, 'Processions, Power and Public Space: Corpus Christi at Cardiff, 1872–1914', *Welsh History Review*, 24, 1 (June, 2008), 77–101.
17. *Newport Catholic Magazine*, 1, 7 (1928), 208.
18. Gerard Spencer, *Catholic Life in Swansea 1847–1947* (Swansea, 1947), p. 71; *Tablet*, 3 June 1933, p. 704.
19. Cf. Hughes, *Winds of Change*, pp. 9–12, 14–15.
20. Cf. *Western Mail*, 5 July 1954, p. 5.
21. John Archer Jackson, *The Irish in Britain* (London, 1963), pp. 16, 20.
22. *Western Mail*, 15 March 1960, p. 4.

23. For 'Irish' processions see Paul O'Leary and Neil Evans, *Claiming the Streets: Processions and Urban Culture in South Wales, c.1830–1880* (Cardiff: forthcoming).
24. Menevia Diocesan Archives, Swansea. Aberystwyth File. An Unpublished manuscript written by Michael P. Fogarty entitled 'A Social Survey of the Parish of Aberystwyth' (1955), p. 2.
25. Ibid.
26. See Colin Hughes, *Lime, Lemon and Sarsaparilla: The Italian Community in South Wales 1841–1945* (Bridgend, 1991).
27. *Menevia Record*, 7, 2 (1959), 17.
28. Fogarty, 'Social Survey of the Parish of Aberystwyth', p. 3.
29. Cf. *Western Mail*, 19 December 1947, p. 3; 13 March 1952, p. 1.
30. *Western Mail*, 10 February 1936, p. 5.
31. *Western Mail*, 24 February 1960, p. 4.
32. *Y Cymro*, 10 June 1933, p. 15; 24 June 1933, p. 7; 15 June 1933, p. 5.
33. *South.Wales News*, 26 March 1926, p. 9.
34. *Baner ac Amserau Cymru*, 24 June 1930, p. 4.
35. *Y Dysgedydd*, 9 (1951), 218–21.
36. *Tablet*, 23 May 1931, p. 672.
37. Cf. Hughes, *Winds of Change*, pp. 179–203.
38. *Baner ac Amserau Cymru*, 1 July 1930, p. 4.
39. *Y Llenor*, XIX, 3 (1940), 121–6.
40. *Western Mail*, 8 April 1937, p. 10.
41. *Y Traethodydd*, July 1942, p. 107.
42. *Baner ac Amserau Cymru*, 12 April 1950, p. 2.
43. Francis Mostyn, Cardiff Lenten Pastoral 1928.
44. *Western Mail*, 23 February 1928, p. 7.
45. Ibid., 17 August 1937, p. 9.
46. Ibid., 28 August 1937, p. 11.
47. Cf. Ibid., 25 February 1960, p. 4; 8 March 1960, p. 4; these are reactions to M. J. Williams of Welshpool's claim that 'for a group of finite, fallible beings to call itself the Body of Christ, to me, is utter blasphemy'.
48. J. Vyrnwy Morgan, *The Welsh Mind in Evolution* (London, 1925), p. 190.
49. *Western Mail*, 15 March 1960, p. 4.
50. *Y Goleuad*, 6 December 1950, p. 5.
51. J. T. F. Williams, 'The Conversion of Wales', *Month*, 167, 861 (1936), 256–7.
52. *Tablet*, 22 January 1949, p. 55.
53. *Menevia Diocesan Yearbook* (1952), p. 106.
54. *Western* Mail, 18 June 1954, p. 7.
55. *Tablet*, 28 November 1936, p. 734.
56. *Y Cymro*, 10 June 1933, p. 13.
57. E. E. Thomas, 'Wales and Catholicism', *Welsh Outlook*, XIX, 2 (1932), 47.
58. *Tablet*, 11 November 1972, p. 1081.
59. *Menevia Diocesan Yearbook 1952*, p. 14.
60. Cf. Daniel J. Mullins, *The Catholic Church in Modern Wales* (Cardiff, 2001), pp. 42–3.
61. The launch of *Chwilio am Undod Cristnogol* (London, 2002) took place at the Welsh National Centre for Ecumenical Studies, based at the University of Wales, Trinity Saint David, Carmarthen.

CHAPTER 6

CALVINISTIC METHODISM

Eryn M. White

Calvinistic Methodism was the first version of the Protestant faith which could be said to be indigenous to Wales. Rather than being imported from outside the country, it was the outcome of the Evangelical Revival which emerged in mid-eighteenth century Wales. Its initial development was, therefore, entirely independent of English Methodism and, if anything, preceded it. From somewhat humble beginnings, Calvinistic Methodism succeeded in transforming the religious complexion of Wales by the nineteenth century, as it gave an impetus to the general growth of nonconformity. Starting out as a marginal movement of the middling sorts in rural Wales, it became a dominant force in Welsh religion and society. Although the nickname 'Methodist' was soon adopted officially, the movement was also commonly and affectionately known as the *Cyfundeb* (Connexion) or the *Hen Gorff* (Old Body or Connexion) of Daniel Rowland, Howel Harris, William Williams and George Whitefield.[1]

The year 1735 tends to be accepted as the start of the Revival in Wales since that was when the main leaders, Daniel Rowland and Howel Harris, were converted. The two first met and began to co-ordinate their activities in 1737, by which time both had begun to make an impact through fervent and itinerant preaching. Although the message was by no means original, consisting of a reiteration of the principles of the Protestant faith, the intensity was fresh and attracted converts, most notably Howel Davies and William Williams. Both Rowland and Harris soon realised that they had to make some sort of provision for those who had been affected in order to sustain them in their conversion. It was this necessity which led to the development of the Methodist society.[2]

The societies were the lifeblood of the early Methodist movement. Their aim was to offer fellowship and support to those who had been through the life-changing experience of conversion. The disparate societies were brought together under the care of the Association, which determined the rules and order of the movement. The Association was the assembly of clergy and exhorters, as the Methodist lay preachers were called, which became the governing body of Methodism in Wales. The General Association met for the first time on 7 January 1742 and the first joint Association of Welsh and English Calvinistic Methodism was held on 5 January 1743, presided over by George Whitefield as Moderator. The driving force of the Association was Howel Harris, who emerged as the major organiser and administrator, and was appointed general superintendent of the societies. A system was

set in place to ensure supervision of the entire membership through the appointment of stewards and private exhorters in each society under the supervision of local
superintendents. Each superintendent reported to the General Association and also
to a monthly society which met in each county. In this way the decisions of the
Association were passed on to the various localities and the condition of the societies
in each area was reported back.[3]

During the early years of the Association and the alliance with Whitefield,
the Welsh Methodists had made plain their adherence to Calvinist theology. The
split which occurred in English Methodism in 1741 between the Calvinists under
Whitefield and the Arminian disciples of the Wesley brothers was avoided in
Wales, where the Calvinistic branch of Methodism would always overshadow the
Wesleyans.[4] Calvinistic Methodism attracted support in the rural areas of mid and
south Wales, especially from among the middling sorts, the same sections of the
community who had been drawn to old dissent. The movement initially met with a
hostile response in the towns, particularly in the north of the country, but was able
to continue its gradual, steady growth until the late-1740s when internal tensions
eventually led to the division between the main leaders, Harris and Rowland, and
their respective followers in 1750.[5]

The seeds of the division had probably been sown years before, at the foundation of the Association, when there had been some uncertainty over who should be
regarded as the movement's main leader. George Whitefield had been invited to act
as Moderator, possibly in order to avoid giving either Rowland or Harris supremacy
over the other. Even so, there was increasing tension apparent in the Association
meetings, particularly from around 1746, as questions arose regarding the orthodoxy
of Harris's preaching. Harris was suspected of Moravian tendencies, although he
was by no means the only Methodist to be deeply influenced by Moravian ideas.
There were more serious implications to the accusations of Patripassianism levelled
against him. Patripassianism promoted the idea that it was God who had died on the
cross and not simply the mortal body of Christ. This was clearly contrary to accepted
Christian doctrine and there is little doubt that Harris had indeed preached this message.[6] The storm clouds were already gathering, therefore, by the late-1740s when
Harris's relationship with Madam Sidney Griffith gave rise to further controversy.
Harris met Sidney Griffith when on a visit to north Wales in 1748 and subsequently
they became spiritual companions. He believed her to be a prophetess who had
revealed God's will, which, for him at least, necessitated her presence in Association
meetings, an honour not granted to any other woman during this period. Rumours
and insinuations implied that theirs was an adulterous relationship, although it does
not appear that Harris's closest colleagues believed him guilty of more than a lack
of wisdom and discretion in this respect. Harris's diaries reveal his deep regard and
love for Griffith, along with his fervent conviction that God had designed them for
each other. This implied that God would determine the death of their respective
spouses so that they could be a couple. Madam Griffith was indeed soon widowed,
but died well before Anne Harris, in 1752, a loss which Harris mourned to the end
of his days.[7]

By 1750, the liaison with Sidney Griffith had proved to be the final straw for Daniel Rowland and most of the other leading Methodists. Rowland and his supporters met in Llantrisant on 23 June 1750 in Harris's absence and agreed that he should be expelled from the movement.[8] Rowland, William Williams and Howel Davies, as ordained clergy, seemed to represent authority and orthodoxy for many in the movement and were backed by George Whitefield, who had already banned Harris from his London Tabernacle. It became apparent that they commanded the greatest following and the largest geographical area, including Rowland's own stronghold of south-west Wales. Harris was left with a reduced party of exhorters and societies to organise and maintain. By 1752 his support had dwindled to the point that they could not viably continue in competition with the exhorters and societies who were loyal to Rowland and the Methodist clergy. Harris ordered his remaining exhorters to go where they felt called to serve and retreated to his home at Trefeca, where he set up a co-operative religious community known as the 'Family'. The intention was for Harris to act as father and Sidney Griffith as mother of the Family, but Griffith's untimely death shattered Harris's dreams in that respect. He was, however, ably assisted first by Sarah Bowen and later by her sister Hannah, who acted as a sort of matron at Trefeca, as the growing community attracted over a hundred members who supported themselves through their labours.[9]

During the years of division, the Methodist movement undoubtedly suffered as a result of the quarrel and the loss of Harris's commitment and organisational skills. It was a diminished movement which limped its way through the 1750s, whose very survival seemed in jeopardy. It was widely acknowledged that Rowland lacked Harris's penchant for directing the Association and ordering the exhorters. Yet, it was Rowland's ministry at Llangeitho, in association with the development of William Williams as a truly inspired hymn writer, which breathed new life into the movement in 1762.[10] The Llangeitho Revival, as it became known, gave Welsh Methodism fresh impetus and dynamism. New members were attracted in substantial numbers after many years of decline and contraction. In addition, by 1763, Harris was reconciled with his old friends and recommenced his itinerant preaching, although never on the same scale as his tireless efforts in the 1740s. Welsh Calvinistic Methodism was poised to make the breakthrough from a minority movement to a major religious influence in the country.

From the 1770s onwards, Methodism amassed a more widespread following beyond its original heartland in rural mid and south Wales. The movement was beginning to take on the more permanent form of a denomination as an increasing number of societies contributed funds in order to build chapels in which to meet.[11] Despite this, it was largely its flexibility as a movement which could meet in ordinary dwelling houses which enabled Methodism to gain ground in the new industrial communities of south Wales during the last quarter of the eighteenth century. The Church, in comparison, was hamstrung by its institutional reliance on consecrated buildings and ordained clergy, and was slow to adapt to the needs of the burgeoning population of industrial areas.[12] Methodism also managed to overcome much of the initial opposition encountered in north Wales, so that between 1774 and 1784 some twenty-five chapels were built in the north.[13] This development was aided by the fact that a new generation of leaders emerged who were based in the north, including Thomas Charles. Born in Carmarthenshire, Charles is firmly associated with Bala, the town in which he ministered for years, and with the creation of the Sunday School Movement. He was one of the many for whom the experience of hearing Daniel Rowland preach at Llangeitho led to conversion. Charles subsequently attended Jesus College, Oxford, before being ordained in the Anglican Church in 1778.[14] As the first generation of leaders passed away, their mantle fell to a large extent on Charles. Harris died in 1773, Rowland in 1790 and Williams in 1791. During their lifetime, they had striven to ensure that the Methodists remained in the communion of the Anglican Church; after their passing, that position became increasingly untenable.

That Welsh Calvinistic Methodism would ultimately emerge as a separate non-conformist denomination with hindsight appears almost inevitable from its very beginnings. Once the movement had instituted a governing body in the form of the Association and had formulated its rules and regulations, the foundation for a separate denomination had been laid. The determination of the founding fathers to remain within the Church in the end merely postponed secession rather than pre-vented it. Even so, it was not without considerable heart-searching and reluctance that Thomas Charles agreed to lead the Methodists away from the mother Church. He and David Jones, Llangan, one of the most eminent of the Methodist clergy, for some time resisted the arguments in favour of secession. These focussed chiefly on the pressing need for the sacraments of baptism and communion to be administered within the societies. Yet there were insufficient ordained clergy within the Methodist ranks to fulfil these obligations for the members. For example, by 1811 there were approximately ten ordained Methodist clergymen in the south and only three in the north.[15] A substantial proportion of the members were unwilling to receive commu-nion from the hands of the Anglican clergy or to suffer them to baptise their children. The result was that several were driven to seek these sacraments from dissenting ministers, as the lesser of two evils. This was a particular problem in Pembrokeshire, where Nathaniel Rowland held sway following the death of his father-in-law, Howel Davies, in 1770. The younger Rowland has frequently been held responsible for the relative weakness of Methodism in Pembrokeshire because of his refusal to adminis-ter the sacrament anywhere but in the three chapels used for that purpose by Howel Davies: Monkton, Woodstock and Capel Newydd.[16] Methodists in the area turned to other denominations for succour, especially to the Baptists who gained considerable ground in the county.

Leading Methodists, notably Thomas Jones of Denbigh, had witnessed the dis-tress such circumstances caused those under their care, and felt that forcing their members to seek the sacraments outside the movement was contrary to God's word and to the universal custom of God's Church.[17] In 1810 Thomas Jones summarised his arguments in 'The Complaint of the Calvinistic Methodists in Wales On Account of their being destitute of the Ordinances of Christ in his Churches. Viz Baptism and the Supper of the Lord', translated into English by Ebenezer Richard.[18] This document also outlined the methods and principles that they might follow as a free church ordaining their own ministers. Jones felt compelled to follow his own guidelines when on 8 March 1810 he baptised a child in its parents' home. On 18 March 1810 he performed a baptism in the chapel in Denbigh for the first time, a significant step towards separation.[19] As others followed suit, Thomas Charles realised that he could not continue in his opposition and found himself in the position of having to implement change. He drew up a revised set of rules authorising the administration of sacraments in the societies which were approved by the Association and enshrined in the 1823 *Confession of Faith*. This was not achieved without some difficulty, as Charles admitted:

> I never had so delicate a subject under my consideration as I had prejudices of an opposite nature to combat with. However, thro' the Lord's blessing upon my endeavours, I hope I have succeeded. To pass incensured by different parties I do not expect; but I am happy that the body of Welsh Calvinistic Methodists seem to have been, by the means adopted, by all appearances more firmly compacted than ever; and by that means likely [to] be more extensively useful in promoting knowledge and reformation thro' the whole country.[20]

A number of Anglican Methodists, including David Griffiths, Nevern, could not follow his lead and refused to countenance the separation. However, the monthly meetings in each county were urged to select suitable candidates to act as assistants to the Methodist clergy and perform the sacraments of baptism and communion. The first ordination of Methodist ministers took place between 19 and 20 June 1811 in a simple, unceremonious meeting of the Association in Bala, followed by a similar ordination between 10 and 11 July for south Wales at Llandeilo, Carmarthenshire. The candidates were questioned by Thomas Charles regarding the principles of their faith and their candidature approved by a unanimous show of hands. Those present at these two assemblies were obviously touched with a sense of awe at the significance of the occasion. After three quarters of a century as a church within a church, the Calvinistic Methodist Church of Wales was finally established by the events of 1811.[21] Its doctrines were confirmed in the 1823 *Cyffes Ffydd* (Confession of Faith), and its status as a separate Christian body registered by the Court of Chancery in 1826. In 1864, the General Assembly was formed to bring together the work of the southern and northern Associations and has met annually since.[22]

One of the first to be ordained in 1811 was John Elias. Born in 1774, he was approved as a preacher by the Caernarfonshire monthly meeting at the age of twenty and was based in Anglesey from 1799 onwards. He became one of the foremost preachers of his day and one of the most prominent Methodists, to the extent that he was referred to as the 'Methodist Pope'. John Elias has been regarded in a somewhat unsympathetic light by historians, particularly for what has been perceived as his dictatorial control over the Connexion and his tendency towards High Calvinism, expressed in the *Confession of Faith*. More recently, historians, including R. Tudur Jones, have shown that the stricter interpretation of Calvinism apparent in the *Confession* was one from which John Elias later retreated, nor was he the only Methodist to hold this view since the wording of the *Confession* was approved at the time.[23] However, it was most likely that it was John Elias who was responsible for the sentence in Article XVIII of the *Confession* which stated that Christ died only for the elect chosen by God and not for all.[24]

John Elias's influence has also been blamed for the political conservatism of the Methodists in the early nineteenth century, given his distrust of the emerging political radicalism of the period. It would probably be fairer to view this in the context of the long-standing Methodist tradition of loyalty to authority and of demonstrating allegiance to the government of the time in order to avoid the accusations of sedition and treason which had plagued the movement for much of its history. The founding fathers had been compelled to express loyalty to the Crown at the time of the 1745 rebellion, when the societies were suspected of being secret Jacobite cells. Subsequent leaders felt a similar compulsion during the Napoleonic Wars, which led to the publication of Thomas Jones's *Gair yn ei Amser* (A Word in Season, 1797) and Thomas Charles's *Welsh Methodism Vindicated* (1801).[25] The Methodists tended to take the view that the government of the day was to be obeyed as a matter of principle.[26] This was confirmed at the Bala Association of 1837, which noted that it was not the role of believers to interfere in politics in any way.[27] Methodist coalminers were even forbidden to join trade unions during the 1830s.[28] It was from the 1840s onwards that Methodists began to move away from this position of political neutrality towards a closer affinity with Liberalism. It has been suggested that the reasons for this change included the death of John Elias in 1841 and the emergence of a younger generation of ministers, particularly Roger Edwards and Lewis Edwards.[29] The influence of the Oxford Movement on the Anglican Church may also have played a part in distancing the Methodists from a mother church which now seemed to have more in common with Catholicism than with its erstwhile children in the Connexion. Although the Methodists had ceased to be Anglicans in 1811, it took considerably longer for them to cut the emotional and traditional ties that still bound them to the Church. It was probably the furore surrounding the Education Commission of 1847, or the treachery of the Blue Books, which forced them to come to terms with the reality that they were indeed nonconformists, who might do better to seek common ground with old dissent rather than the established church.[30]

Having made the momentous decision to ordain its own ministers, the denomination had to organise some dedicated training, especially as nonconformists were still excluded from university education when the separation occurred in 1811. In 1836 Lewis Edwards, one of the great preachers and theologians of the nineteenth century, married Jane Charles, the granddaughter of Thomas Charles, and settled in Bala. There, along with his brother-in-law, David Charles, he established a school to prepare candidates for the Calvinistic Methodist ministry in 1837. The school became a denominational college in 1839 and did much to raise educational standards among ministers. However, there was very little emphasis on instruction through the medium of Welsh, despite the fact that it was the language of the majority of congregations. The question of how to cater for an increasingly bilingual population was one which caused considerable debate in the nineteenth century. Lewis Edwards became a prominent advocate of the 'English cause', as it came to be known. He believed that the spread of English was part of God's plan, as he explained to the General Assembly in Dolgellau in 1880:

As the kingdom is going English, we must follow suit, and there is a danger for us in battling against the English language that we lose sight of people's souls, and battle instead against the progress and survival of the Connexion.[31]

This was a controversial viewpoint and one which provoked a heated debate with Emrys ap Iwan among others.[32] Despite this, the Conference of English Churches was formed in 1881, with separate meetings for north and south which were united in 1889. By 1899, 239 English churches with 17,000 members had been established,[33] while in 1947 the Association in the East was inaugurated so that the English-medium congregations would have the right to discuss and determine their own affairs.[34]

From their earliest beginnings, the Methodists had been alive to the value of literature for disseminating religious knowledge and to the importance of the printing press in achieving this end. The need to produce, translate and print material for the members had been a topic for discussion from some of the earliest meetings of the Association onwards. A strong literary tradition had been established through the verse and prose of Williams Pantycelyn, Peter Williams's edition of the Bible and Thomas Charles's *Geiriadur Ysgrythyrawl* (Scriptural Dictionary). The denomination built on this foundation throughout the nineteenth century, supplying the growing demand for Sunday School literature and for catechisms such as *Rhodd Mam* (A Mother's Gift).[35] The nineteenth century also witnessed an unprecedented growth in the publication of denominational periodicals.[36] The Connexion produced, among other titles, *Y Drysorfa* (The Treasury) from 1831 and *Trysorfa y Plant* (The Children's Treasury) for children from 1862, along with *The Treasury* for English members from 1864. Yet, perhaps its most notable contribution was *Y Traethodydd* (The Essayist), which appeared for the first time in 1846 under the joint editorship of Lewis Edwards and Roger Edwards, who sought to use the journal to introduce contemporary ideas and scholarship to the readership. The circulation figures for these periodicals were remarkable. *Trysorfa y Plant*, whose readership extended to children from other denominations as well, soon achieved a circulation of 44,000 copies a month, making sufficient income to pay the production costs of both *Y Drysorfa* and *Y Traethodydd*.[37] *Y Drysorfa* played an important part in bringing Daniel Owen, the novelist, to the attention of the reading public by serialising his first major works *Y Dreflan* (The Village, 1881) and *Rhys Lewis* (1885).[38] Daniel Owen's works were grounded in his experience with the Methodists, as a member, a lay preacher and as a student at Bala College. He demonstrated in his novels the hypocrisy of some members of the congregation during the second half of the century, for whom middle-class respectability seemed more important than true faith.[39]

Although questions might be raised about the commitment of some of the members, there was no doubting the numerical strength of the Connexion during the nineteenth century. The Religious Census of 1851, despite its flaws, was the first serious attempt to count those who attended a place of worship and it demonstrated quite clearly that the majority of worshippers in Wales (87%) chose the nonconformist denominations rather than the Anglican Church. Nonconformity in general was in the ascendancy in Welsh-speaking areas and Calvinistic Methodism was particularly strong in north Wales.[40] The Calvinistic Methodists in 1851 had 807 chapels and those who attended those chapels on the three services on Census Sunday, 30 March 1851, numbered 76,274, 57,747 and 120,734. By 1905 the denomination consisted of 1,411 chapels with 170,617 members.[41] On the eve of the First World War, it was the largest of the nonconformist denominations in Wales with 185,000 members.[42]

Throughout this period it retained something of its evangelical force, reinvigorated by periodical revivals, some of which were local in their influence, whilst others, particularly the 1859 revival, were of national significance.[43] Such revivals frequently served to coax the adherents or hearers, who were not full members, into the fold and thus increase the membership. There seemed to be a recurring cycle of revival, whereby each outbreak of activity was followed by a period of quiet and stability. These years of tranquillity would almost inevitably be followed by concerns regarding the state of religion and the active campaigning for revival. This gave rise to the only slightly tongue-in-cheek suggestion by Emrys ap Iwan that a revival was expected every ten years by the late-nineteenth century. The last of the series of revivals to inject new life into the Connexion was the 1904–5 Revival, which is most frequently associated with Evan Roberts's ministry.[44] This revival was also the product of concern regarding prevailing apathy amongst worshippers, which led certain Methodist ministers in south Cardiganshire to hold meetings to pray for renewal. Joseph Jenkins of New Quay and his nephew, John Thickens of Aberaeron, did much to foment revival by organising conferences in New Quay and the surrounding area as well as inviting successful evangelists, such as Seth Joshua, to speak to their congregations. They also drew upon some of the methods employed by the Forward Movement which had been formed in 1891. Revival was already stirring amongst the young people of New Quay before Evan Roberts's famous spiritual experience at Blaenannerch Chapel in September 1904. Roberts and other preachers attracted substantial congregations over the following months and large numbers were recruited to the nonconformist denominations. Yet the increase proved to be temporary and many of those who joined in the fervour of revival were later to abandon their membership.[45]

During the twentieth century the Connexion appeared to be distancing itself from the previous emphasis on Calvinism. The Methodists emerged from the First World War conscious of the need for reform. The Reconstruction Commission was reluctant to replace the *Confession of Faith* in such a climate of uncertainty, yet had to acknowledge that it could scarcely be said to represent the views of the denomination as it stood. The solution was to issue a *Declaratory Statement of Common Faith and Practice* which was endorsed by 1923. It was inclusive in nature, avoided controversy and steered clear of any discussion of the Calvinist doctrine of election. Further debate produced the *Declaratory Articles* of 1924 which contained a more detailed statement of faith. These Articles would form the basis of the Parliamentary Act of July 1933 which detached the Connexion from the *Confession of Faith* and christened it with its new name as the Presbyterian Church of Wales.[46] The Articles allowed for a more liberal interpretation of doctrine, whilst reassuring the more conservative that traditional orthodoxy had not been abandoned. Indeed, on the eve of the name change, John Roberts argued that Methodism had long since leant towards Presbyterianism.[47] A crucial development in this respect was that Thomas Charles had persuaded the Association in 1800 that each society should choose its own elders, and that the elders should be members of the Association and thus have the right to select and ordain ministers.[48] Prior to this decision, the leaders of each society had been appointed by the Association and not elected by the members. There were, therefore, obvious Presbyterian elements to Methodist organisation, which might be seen to justify the change of name to the Presbyterian Church of Wales.

In the meantime, as these discussions continued, the Connexion had been rocked by doctrinal controversy in the case of the Rev. Thomas Nefyn Williams, or Tom Nefyn, as he was more commonly known. Tom Nefyn became minister of Ebenezer Church in Tumble, Carmarthenshire, in 1926. He first attracted attention for some of his more unconventional practices, notably allowing smoking in the services. It was his theology, however, which caused him to be suspended from the Methodist pulpit in 1929 for his idiosyncratic views on the Trinity, the Virgin Birth and the resurrection in his pamphlet, *Y Ffordd yr Edrychaf ar Bethau* (The Way I Look at Things) which he produced in 1928.[49] The 220 members of Ebenezer were excommunicated for supporting their pastor, but they established the Tumble Christian Fellowship in a new meeting house at Llain y Delyn. The instigator of the whole affair, Nefyn, returned to his native north Wales and in a remarkable change of direction in 1931 agreed to accept the principles of the *Confession of Faith* and was reinstated in the ministry of the Calvinistic Methodist Church.[50] Theological debate and uncertainty would continue, however, as rapid social change gave rise to radical theology and old certainties were questioned. By the 1960s the work of J. R. Jones, a member of the Presbyterian Church and professor of Philosophy at Swansea University, on the 'Crisis of Meaninglessness' provoked a strong response as it questioned the need for traditional Christianity in a modern, technological age.[51]

The twentieth century was an increasingly testing time for the Connexion, with its membership continuing to decline as society became more secular in its outlook. Even though Welsh nonconformity, as a whole, reached its numerical peak in 1926 with a total of 530,000 adult communicants, the numbers of adherents who were not full members, or those who were children, continued to decline – a fact which boded ill for future recruitment.[52] During the second half of the twentieth century, all denominations, except for the Roman Catholics, suffered a decline in numbers, although the Anglican Church seemed to fare somewhat better than the nonconformists. The gradual decline witnessed from around 1926 onwards speeded up considerably after the end of the Second World War. Between 1945 and 1950, the Presbyterian Church lost 13,327 members, from 172,954 to 159,627. The number of communicants declined further to 136,716 by 1960, 108,064 by 1970, 85,400 by 1978 and 55,690 by 1993.[53] The number of churches also declined from the peak of 1,504 in 1927 to 1,014 in 1970 and to 977 in 1993.[54]

Methodism had always benefited from the social opportunities it offered its members, with the chapel as a focus for a number of meetings and activities during the week as well as on Sunday. However, it faced growing competition from a range of modern, secular entertainments including the cinema, radio and television. At the same time, the Welsh language which had been so strongly associated with nonconformity was also experiencing a steady decline. Traditional sabbatarianism was on the wane with the Licensing Act of 1960 introducing seven-year polls regarding Sunday opening. Moreover, only four counties, Anglesey, Caernarfonshire, Merionethshire and Cardiganshire, remained 'dry' by 1968. This is an outcome which Kenneth O. Morgan has described as 'a somewhat pathetic commentary on the waning authority of organized religion'.[55] The chapels were no longer able to exercise control over their members as they had done in the past. There was an associated decline in the numbers attracted to the ministry, which in turn had implications for the viability of some of the denomination's institutions. The Colleges at Bala and Trefeca closed in 1964. The closure of the remaining centre, the United Theological College at Aberystwyth, in 2003 brought to an end a long and honourable history of education within the Connexion. With ministers in increasingly short supply, some congregations did continue to thrive, but, in many rural areas in particular, the closure of Presbyterian chapels became a commonplace event.

There have nevertheless been some constructive developments. In the light of such decline it was not surprising that ecumenical initiatives and closer co-operation between the Christian groups within Wales were accepted as an important way forward.[56] The Council of Churches for Wales was replaced in 1990 by Cytûn, which included the Catholic Church. In some areas, ministers are shared with some of the other nonconformist denominations to form ecumenical pastorates. As full-time ministers become increasingly scarce, there is greater use of part-time ministers to help fill the breach. The strategy formulated by the Connexion in recent years has encouraged congregations to unite to form more vibrant churches and even in some cases to build new places of worship. The old College at Bala became a youth centre in 1969 and Trefeca is now a centre for lay training, conferences and retreats. In 1978 a woman was ordained minister for the first time by the Presbyterian Church of Wales. The response to the publication of the revised version of the Bible in 1988 and the interdenominational hymn book, *Caneuon Ffydd*, in 2001 demonstrated that there was still a market for some religious literature. Yet there is no doubt that the Connexion, like all the other traditional Protestant nonconformist groups in Wales, faces a serious challenge to its survival as a new century dawns and as it approaches its tercentenary in 2035.

Notes

1. Gomer M. Roberts, *Hanes Methodistiaeth Galfinaidd Cymru* (2 vols. Caernarfon, 1973–8), I: *Y Deffroad Mawr*; II: *Cynnydd y Corff*; Derec Llwyd Morgan, *The Great Awakening in Wales* (London, 1988); Eryn M. White, *Praidd Bach y Bugail Mawr: Seiadau Methodistaidd de-orllewin Cymru* (Llandysul, 1995). For a wider context, see Michael Watts, *The Dissenters I: From the Reformation to the French Revolution* (Oxford, 1978); David Hempton, *Methodism and Politics in British Society 1750–1850* (London, 1984); David W. Bebbington, *Evangelicalism in Modern Britain: A History from the 1730s to the 1990s* (London, 1989); W. R. Ward, *The Protestant Evangelical Awakening* (Cambridge, 1992); Mark Noll, David W. Bebbington and George A. Rawlyk (eds), *Evangelicalism: Comparative Studies of Popular Protestantism in North America, the British Isles and Beyond 1700–1990* (New York, 1994); G. M. Ditchfield, *The Evangelical Revival* (London, 1998); David Ceri Jones, *A Glorious Work in the World: Welsh Methodism and the International Evangelical Revival, 1735–1750* (Cardiff, 2004).

2. For Harris see Geoffrey Nuttall, *Howell Harris, 1714–1773: The Last Enthusiast* (Cardiff, 1965); Gomer M. Roberts, *Portread o Ddiwygiwr* (Caernarfon, 1969); Eifion Evans, *Howell Harris, Evangelist, 1714–1773* (Cardiff, 1974); Geraint Tudur, *Howell Harris: From Conversion to Separation, 1735–50* (Cardiff, 2000). For Rowland see Eifion Evans, *Daniel Rowland and the Great Evangelical Awakening in Wales* (Edinburgh, 1985); and for Williams, see Gomer M. Roberts, *Y Pêr Ganiedydd* (2 vols. Aberystwyth, 1949–58); Glyn Tegai Hughes, *Williams Pantycelyn* (Cardiff, 1983); Derec Llwyd Morgan, *Williams Pantycelyn* (Caernarfon, 1983); Derec Llwyd Morgan (ed.), *Meddwl a Dychymyg Williams Pantycelyn* (Llandysul, 1991).

3. White, *Praidd Bach y Bugail Mawr*, pp. 51–64; Tudur, *Howell Harris*, pp. 63–91.

4. See A. H. Williams, *Welsh Wesleyan Methodism, 1800–1858* (Bangor, 1935); Rupert Davies and Gordon Rupp (eds), *A History of the Methodist Church in Great Britain* (London, 1965); Lionel Madden (ed.), *Methodism in Wales: A Short History of the Wesley Tradition* (Llandudno, 2003); John Munsey Turner, *John Wesley: The Evangelical Revival and the Rise of Methodism in England* (London, 2002).

5. Evans, *Howel Harris*, pp. 45–57; Tudur, *Howell Harris*, pp. 151–94; Eryn M. White, '"A Breach in God's House": The Division in Welsh Calvinistic Methodism, 1750–63', in Nigel Yates (ed.), *Bishop Burgess and His World: Culture, Religion and Society in Britain, Europe and North America in the Eighteenth and Nineteenth Centuries* (Cardiff, 2007), pp. 85–102.

6. For instance, 'He was God everywhere on the Cross and in the Grave'. See NLW, Calvinistic Methodist Archive (CMA), Diary of Howel Harris, 130, 30 April 1748.

7. For this relationship see Roberts, *Portread o Ddiwygiwr*, pp. 112–28; Tudur, *Howell Harris*, pp. 195–228.

8. NLW, CMA, Diary of Howel Harris 145, 24 June 1750.

9. For the history of the Family, see Alun Wynne Owen, 'A Study of Howell Harris and the Trevecka 'Family' (1752–60) based upon the Trevecka letters and Diaries and other Methodist archives at the NLW', unpublished University of Wales, MA thesis, 1927; Alun Wyn Owen, 'Yr Ymraniad', in Roberts (ed.), *Hanes Methodistiaeth Galfinaidd Cymru*, I, pp. 314–55; White, 'A Breach in God's House'.

10. R. Geraint Gruffydd, 'Diwygiad 1762 a William Williams o Bantycelyn', *Journal Historical Society of the Presbyterian Church of Wales* (*JHSPCW*), 54 (1969), 68–75; 55 (1970), 4–13; Derec Llwyd Morgan, *The Great Awakening*, trans. Dyfnallt Morgan (London, 1988), p. 101; Evans, *Daniel Rowland*, p. 309.

11. See Roberts (ed.), *Hanes Methodistiaeth Galfinaidd Cymru*, II.

12. See E. T. Davies, *Religion in the Industrial Revolution in South Wales* (repr. Cardiff, 1987), and his 'The Church in the Industrial Revolution', in D. Walker (ed.), *A History of the Church in Wales* (Penarth, 1976); *Religion and Society in the Nineteenth Century* (Llandybïe, 1981), pp. 47–60.

13. Gomer M. Roberts, 'Ennill Tir 1774–1784', in Roberts (ed.), *Hanes Methodistiaeth Galfinaidd Cymru*, II, pp. 114–17.

14. R. Tudur Jones, *Thomas Charles o'r Bala: Gwas y Gair a Chyfaill Cenedl* (Cardiff, 1979), pp. 11–16.

15. Gomer M. Roberts, 'Ymwahanu oddi wrth Eglwys Loegr', in Roberts (ed.), *Hanes Methodistiaeth Galfinaidd Cymru*, II, p. 300.

16. Euros W. Jones, 'Nathaniel Rowland (1749–1831)', *JHSPCW*, 7 (1983), 40.

17. Idwal Jones, 'Notes on the Ordination Controversy, 1809–10', *JHSPCW*, 29 (1944), 116–19.

18. NLW, MS. 11335A; see also B. G. Owens, 'A Petition for the Ordinances by Ebenezer Richards', *JHSPCW*, 23 (1938), 62–78.

19. Idwal Jones (ed.), *Hunangofiant Thomas Jones o Ddinbych* (Aberystwyth, 1937), pp. 51–4, and his 'Notes on the Ordination Controversy', 109–19; Frank Price Jones, *Thomas Jones o Ddinbych 1754–1820* (Denbigh, 1956), pp. 41–62.

20. D. E. Jenkins, *Life of Thomas Charles* (3 vols. Denbigh, 1908), III, p. 264.

21. Ibid., III, pp. 263–90.

22. Eifion Evans, 'The Confession of Faith of the Welsh Calvinistic Methodists', *JHSPCW*, 59 (1974), 2–11; R. Buick Knox, 'Methodistiaeth ac Eglwysyddiaeth', in Elfed ap Nefydd Roberts (ed.), *Corff ac Ysbryd: Ysgrifau ar Fethodistiaeth* (Caernarfon, 1988), pp. 69–78.

23. See R. Tudur Jones, *John Elias, Prince Amongst Preachers* (Bridgend, 1974).

24. J. Ellis Wynne Davies, 'Sylwadau ar John Elias', *JHSPCW*, 1 (1977), 37–50.
25. See R. Watcyn James, 'Ymateb y Methodistiaid Calfinaidd Cymraeg i'r Chwyldro Ffrengig', *JHSPCW*, 12, 3 (1988–9), 35–60.
26. Ieuan Gwynedd Jones, *Explorations and Explanations: Essays in the Social History of Victorian Wales* (Llandysul, 1981), pp. 109–10.
27. *Y Drysorfa*, 7 (1837), 245.
28. J. E. Caerwyn Williams, 'Roger Edwards Yr Wyddgrug', *JHSPCW*, 4 (1980), 14.
29. Harri Williams, '*Y Traethodydd* a Gwleidyddiaeth', *JHSPCW*, 5 (1981), 25–44.
30. Prys Morgan, 'From Long Knives to Blue Books', in R. R. Davies et al (eds), *Welsh Society and Nationhood: Historical Essays Presented to Glanmor Williams* (Cardiff, 1984), p. 210; Ieuan Gwynedd Jones, *Mid-Victorian Wales: The Observers and the Observed* (Cardiff, 1992), pp. 156–65.
31. R. Tudur Jones, 'Nonconformity and the Welsh Language in the Nineteenth Century', in G. H. Jenkins (ed.), *The Welsh Language and its Social Domains 1801–1911* (Cardiff, 2000), p. 260. For further discussion of the 'English Cause' see Frank Price Jones, 'Yr Achosion Saesneg', *JHSPCW*, 58 (1973), 2–11; Ieuan Gwynedd Jones, 'The Religious Frontier in Nineteenth-Century Wales', *JHSPCW*, 5 (1981), 3–24.
32. Robert Ambrose Jones (Emrys ap Iwan, 1848–1906). See D. Myrddin Lloyd, *Emrys ap Iwan* (Cardiff, 1979).
33. Jones, 'Yr Achosion Saesneg', 7.
34. J. E. Wynne Davies, 'The Association in the East', *JHSPCW*, 21 (1997), 5–63.
35. See Brynley F. Roberts, 'The Connexion in Print', *JHSPCW*, 16–17 (1992–3), 9–31.
36. Huw Walters, 'The Periodical Press to 1914', in Philip Henry Jones and Eiluned Rees (eds), *A Nation and its Books: A History of the Book in Wales* (Aberystwyth, 1998), pp. 197–208.
37. Aled G. Jones, *Press, Politics and Society: A History of Journalism in Wales* (Cardiff, 1993), p. 102.
38. This was subsequently published by Owen, see Daniel Owen, *Hunangofiant Rhys Lewis, gweinidog Bethel* (Wyddgrug, 1885).
39. See Glanmor Williams, *The Welsh and their Religion* (Cardiff, 1991), pp. 64–8; Derec Llwyd Morgan, *Pobl Pantycelyn* (Llandysul, 1986), pp. 111–30; Robert Rhys, *Daniel Owen* (Cardiff, 2000).
40. Davies, *Religion and Society in the Nineteenth Century*, pp. 27–30; Jones, *Explorations and Explanations*, pp. 217–35.
41. R. Tudur Jones, *Ffydd ac Argyfwng Cenedl: Hanes Crefydd yng Nghymru 1890–1914* (2 vols. Swansea, 1981–2), I, p. 49, and his *Faith and the Crisis of a Nation: Wales 1890–1914*, trans. Sylvia Rhys Jones and ed. Robert Pope (Cardiff, 2004), p. 32.
42. D. Densil Morgan, *The Span of the Cross: Christian Religion and Society in Wales* (Cardiff, 1999), pp. 17, 23.
43. Eifion Evans, *Fire in the Thatch* (Bridgend, 1996), pp. 186–225.
44. See Eifion Evans, *The Welsh Revival of 1904* (Bridgend, 1969); Jones, *Ffydd ac Argyfwng Cenedl*, II, pp. 122–7, and his *Faith and the Crisis of a Nation*, pp. 283–69; Noel Gibbard (ed.), *Nefol Dân: Agweddau ar Ddiwygiad 1904–5* (Bridgend, 2004); D. Densil Morgan, 'Diwygiad Crefyddol 1904–5', in Geraint H. Jenkins (ed.), *Cof Cenedl, XX* (Llandysul, 2005), pp. 167–200.
45. Jones, *Faith and the Crisis of a Nation*, pp. 362–4.
46. Morgan, *Span of the Cross*, pp. 107–30.
47. John Roberts, *Methodistiaeth Galfinaidd Cymru* (London, 1931), pp. 123–42.
48. Ibid., p. 125.
49. Tom Nefyn Williams, *Y Ffordd yr Edrychaf ar Bethau* (Dolgellau, 1928).
50. Robert Pope, *Building Jerusalem: Nonconformity, Labour and the Social Question in Wales, 1906–39* (Cardiff, 1998), pp. 208–11. See also William Morris (ed.), *Tom Nefyn* (Caernarfon, 1962); Harri Parri, *Tom Nefyn* (Caernarfon, 1999).
51. Dewi Z. Phillips, *J. R. Jones* (Cardiff, 1995); Morgan, *Span of the Cross*, pp. 224–30.
52. D. Densil Morgan, 'The Welsh Language and Religion', in Geraint H. Jenkins and Mari A. Williams (eds), *'Let's Do Our Best for the Ancient Tongue': The Welsh Language in the Twentieth Century,* (Cardiff, 2000), p. 379.

53. John Williams, *Historical Digest of Welsh Statistics* (Cardiff, 1985), p. 295; Morgan, *Span of the Cross*, p. 265; Presbyterian Church of Wales, *Agenda of the General Assembly* (Caernarfon, 1994), p. 48.
54. Williams, *Historical Digest*, pp. 294–5; *Agenda of the General Assembly*, p. 48.
55. Kenneth O. Morgan, *Rebirth of a Nation: Wales 1880–1980* (Cardiff, 1981), p. 355.
56. See Noel A. Davies, 'The Ecumenical Dimension: Past Trends, Future Prospects', chapter 21 in this volume.

CHAPTER 7

WESLEYAN METHODISM

David Ceri Jones

The history of the branch of Welsh Methodism most closely associated with John Wesley[1] has unfortunately been over-shadowed by the longevity and dominance of Calvinistic Methodism (after 1933 the Presbyterian Church of Wales).[2] In eighteenth century Wales, the Calvinistic Methodists quickly established a connexional structure to rival that which John Wesley (1703–91) established in England in the mid-1740s; but Wesley himself made no attempt to extend his influence into Wales in a co-ordinated way. This is not to say that Wesley ignored Wales altogether. From 1739 until his death in 1791, Wesley visited or travelled through Wales on at least forty-six separate occasions, but the origins of a distinctly Wesleyan Methodist presence in Wales owed more to a number of small pockets of Wesley sympathisers scattered around the country. They took the lead in creating embryonic societies in the country, often without Wesley's explicit support and, as a consequence, these societies were not fully incorporated into the national Wesleyan Methodist movement until some considerable time after Wesley's death.

Wesley's first itinerary in Wales, during October 1739, set the pattern for the majority of his subsequent visits. Probably at the invitation of Howel Harris (1714–73), Wesley first preached in Wales on the outskirts of Chepstow, before proceeding along a pre-arranged itinerary that saw him inspect some of the infant Methodist communities which had been established by Harris in south-east Wales, including the strategically important society at Cardiff.[3] Echoing the words of Whitefield a few months earlier,[4] Wesley thought 'no part of England so pleasant . . . as those parts of Wales I have been in. And most of the inhabitants are indeed ripe for the gospel.'[5] But by the time of his second visit in April 1740, again at Harris's invitation, the controversy that Wesley had ignited among the English Methodists by his decision to preach against the moderate predestinarian theology of most of the Methodists in Bristol,[6] conspired to severely limit his audience in Wales. Subsequently, Wesley's opportunities to establish societies in Wales were radically curtailed as the Calvinistic Methodists, including Harris at times, became increasingly reluctant to welcome the controversial Wesley to Wales. Coupled with this development, the overwhelming bulk of Wales was still monoglot Welsh speaking and Wesley, without Harris's enthusiastic support after 1741, and with few sympathetic Welsh-speaking supporters to translate for him, found this 'confusion of tongues'[7] an insurmountable obstacle. His itineraries therefore tended to be concentrated on those areas of the country that had a significant bilingual or majority English-speaking population.[8]

He was helped when the Methodist society at Cardiff sided with him after the schism between the followers of George Whitefield (1714–70) and Wesley into Calvinist and Arminian camps in 1741, a foothold that was consolidated when the Cardiff Wesleyans raised sufficient funds to build a permanent meeting-place in 1742.[9] Wesley's visits to Wales after this date were therefore informed by his need to bolster the position of this society and some of the splinter societies that had been established in other parts of south-east Wales by Methodists who had come into contact with the Cardiff society. At Wesley's first Conference, the lack of Wesleyan converts in Wales dictated the establishment of only one circuit to cover the whole of the country and, despite the success of the Cardiff society, the Conference decided that it would be better if these groups were known as preaching stations, rather than be given the more formal designation of society.[10] By 1748 there were still only four Wesleyan clusters in Wales, though in 1749 they were joined by three more embryonic societies at Bedwas in Monmouthshire, and at Llanwynno and Llantrisant in Glamorgan. The Wesleyan Methodist presence in south-east Wales was given an enormous boost by the support that it received from two wealthy and well-placed local landowners. Robert Jones (1706–42), of Fonmon Castle in the Vale of Glamorgan, converted to Methodism and became a strong supporter of Wesley in 1741. He was subsequently able to use his patronage and influence as a local magistrate to ensure the safety of both Calvinist and Arminian Methodist preachers in Wales.[11] Marmaduke Gwynne (1692–1769) of Garth in Breconshire,[12] despite close links with Howel Harris, associated himself ever more closely with the Wesley brothers throughout the 1740s, particularly after his daughter Sarah's marriage to Charles Wesley (1707–88) in 1749.[13]

Without either the ability or resources to make significant in-roads into Welsh-speaking communities, Wesley practically resigned himself to only minimal influence in Wales. When controversy erupted over some of his followers' attempts to establish an Arminian society at Neath in 1746, in direct competition to the Calvinist society in the town, Wesley agreed, at an amicable meeting of Calvinists and Wesleyans from England and Wales at Bristol in January 1747, not to attempt to establish a society in any place where there was already a thriving Calvinistic society. However, Wesley still reserved the right to establish English-speaking societies wherever possible, especially in places where they would not immediately threaten any Calvinistic societies already in existence.[14] A. H. Williams has, with some justification, suggested that Wesley, in effect, handed Wales over to his Calvinistic co-religionists, reassured that their obvious success made his attentions largely superfluous.[15] In the aftermath of the division between the followers of Howel Harris and Daniel Rowland (1711–90) in 1750, Wesley made only two visits to Wales during the whole of the following decade, admirably staying away rather than creating potential for further problems in Wales by an aggressive proselytising strategy.

The rekindling of Wesley's interest in Wales was largely brought about by the activity of Thomas Taylor (1738–1816).[16] Taylor was sent to work in south Wales in 1761 and his success in parts of Gower and in those areas of Pembrokeshire that had remained untouched by the ministry of Howell Davies (1716–70), opened up some of the more anglicised areas of south and west Wales to Wesleyan influence for the first time. His ground-breaking work resulted in the creation of three separate Methodist circuits in south Wales, centred on Pembrokeshire, Glamorgan and Breconshire.[17] Consequently, for the next fifty years or so Wesley's visits to Wales were of two kinds. Some were little more than brief visits as he travelled through the country, preaching at various strategic points *en route* to Ireland.[18] Other more extended itineraries were constructed in a manner that enabled him to oversee those communities that were beginning to look to him for leadership. In August 1753, for example, Wesley travelled west from Bristol to Cardiff and Fonmon before returning to England[19] and, on a slightly longer itinerary in August 1768, he travelled south from Shrewsbury to Haverfordwest through south Wales via Gower, Neath and Cardiff before once more heading back to Bristol.[20] Both visits indicate that the Wesleyans had made significant inroads into a few of the more anglicised parts of south Wales by the early 1760s. A similar story may be told of Wesleyan incursions in north Wales from the mid-1750s onwards. Thomas Olivers (1725–99),[21] who had been converted under the preaching of George Whitefield, became one of Wesley's itinerants in 1753. In 1758 he was stationed at Chester and from there extended his influence by preaching throughout north-east Wales. His activities in Flintshire eventually led to the establishment of a Wesleyan society at Mold in 1762, followed shortly after by the foundation of another similar society at nearby Wrexham. After a visit by Wesley in August 1769 to Welshpool and Newtown in Montgomeryshire, a small group of Methodists began meeting at the home of a local farmer, John Evans.[22] Supported by Wesleyans from neighbouring Breconshire, a small society was established in 1778 and a permanent chapel built twenty years later,[23] a pattern typical of the way in which Wesleyan itinerants could over time extend their influence into hostile territory.

John Wesley's relations with the leaders of Welsh Calvinistic Methodism fluctuated throughout his lifetime. Whilst his closest friend, Howel Harris, was active in the leadership of the movement, Wesley was able to move among the Calvinists with slightly less suspicion.[24] But once Harris has been ousted from the movement in 1750, Wesley no longer had a natural ally and found it difficult to gain a hearing in Wales without being accused of either causing unnecessary dissension or proselytising. Rehabilitated, Harris was welcomed back into the Welsh revival in the early 1760s and his presence enabled Wesley to return to Wales, free of at least some suspicion. During his subsequent visits, he visited Harris regularly and, on a few occasions, was invited to meetings that included some of the other Welsh revivalists. In August 1769, for example, he preached at the first anniversary of the Countess of Huntingdon's college at Trefeca, sharing the platform with Harris, Daniel Rowland and William Williams (1717–93),[25] and three years later Harris invited him to preach again at Trefeca.[26] But Harris's death in 1773 restricted Wesley's activities in Wales once more. Both Daniel Rowland and William Williams were far less prepared to allow Wesley free rein among their societies, and were much more cautious in their dealings with him. Subsequently, therefore, Wesley's visits to Wales tended to concentrate almost exclusively on those areas where his own preachers had already made inroads. Despite the admirable pioneer endeavours of a handful of far-sighted and resourceful individuals, by the time of Wesley's death in 1791 the number of Wesleyan Methodists in Wales was still extremely small. With barely 600 members, only seven preachers and just three circuits concentrated almost exclusively in English-speaking areas, mostly along the English border and in Pembrokeshire, Wesleyan Methodism appeared chronically ill-equipped to compete with the larger and much more aggressive Calvinistic movement.

Before 1800 Welsh Wesleyan Methodism did not exist as a separate entity within the national Wesleyan Methodist movement. Missionary efforts had occurred as the result of incursions by Wesley himself and the far-sighted labours of a few ambitious preachers stationed at various points along the Welsh border. But responsibility for the transformation of the small clusters of Wesleyan societies in Wales into a more coherent and unified body belongs to Thomas Coke (1747–1814), Wesley's immediate successor as the leader of Methodism and instigator of Methodist missions.[27] Coke, a native of Brecon, had become familiar with the failings of the largely English-speaking Welsh Wesleyan preachers during his frequent journeys through parts of north Wales on his way to Ireland. Persuaded of the need for a more concerted missionary enterprise in the Welsh language, particularly in north Wales, Coke won over the Methodist Conference in 1800 to his idea of a Welsh mission and managed to get it to agree to the appointment of Owen Davies (1752–1830)[28] and John Hughes (1776–1843)[29] as Welsh-speaking preachers in north Wales. A year later they were joined by the recently admitted Welsh-speaking itinerant, John Bryan (1776–1856).[30]

Davies and Hughes concentrated on north-east Wales, building on the pioneering work of Edward Jones, Bathafarn (1778–1837), who had opened a preaching-house at Ruthin in 1800 and established a society in the town shortly after.[31] Their efforts were extremely successful. Their natural abilities, coupled with their determination to preach in Welsh had the desired effect, and precipitated a growth in the numbers of Wesleyan Methodists in Wales as well as the establishment of a number of new districts, including one at Ruthin and another in Caernarfonshire. In south and mid Wales there was also significant growth after 1805 and further new districts were added to the 'Welsh mission', particularly at Llanidloes and Aberystwyth. Owen Davies had also persuaded Conference to send missionaries to south Wales, while Edward Jones, Bathafarn, and William Davies had been breaking new ground in south-west Wales.[32] By 1810 the Wesleyan presence in Wales had undergone dramatic growth. There were 5,549 Wesleyan Methodists in the North Wales District, served by forty-nine ministers, accommodated in sixty chapels[33] and held together by their own highly successful 'denominational' periodical, *Yr Eurgrawn Wesleyaidd* (1809–1983; after 1933 *Yr Eurgrawn*) under the editorial direction of John Bryan.[34] Although not originally intended as an entirely Welsh language periodical, *Yr Eurgrawn Wesleyaidd* rapidly became the main voice of Welsh-speaking Wesleyans. In its early years it depended heavily on translations of English material, especially from the *Wesleyan Methodist Magazine*, but it quickly reached the point where most of its contents were original contributions by native Welsh speakers.

This period of growth was, however, relatively short-lived. The unexpected death of Thomas Coke in 1814 robbed Wales of its strongest advocate at the annual Methodist Conference. In the years immediately following, Conference withdrew many of the most committed and successful Welsh-speaking preachers, including Owen Davies, John Bryan and Edward Jones, relocating them to various parts of England, while financial resources for new preachers were also re-allocated to other areas. Membership consequently declined sharply, so that by 1817 there were little more than 4,000 Wesleyans in south Wales.[35] In the wake of this crisis, Wesleyan Methodism in Wales became introspective as its members sought to protect what had already been achieved, developing the apparatus of denominational life and revitalising their grass-roots members through the widespread proliferation of Sunday schools whose membership, crucially, included adults as well as children. By 1822 the Welsh Wesleyan movement could boast over 140 schools, 11,638 scholars and 1,460 teachers.[36] Despite not engaging in very much fresh evangelism during these years, the Wesleyans proved to be resilient enough to withstand the depredations of other stronger Methodist groups, particularly the Calvinists and some of the other more radical groups that had broken away from the original Wesleyan body.

The first half of the nineteenth century saw the fairly rapid splintering of English Wesleyan Methodism into an array of separate Connexions, but not all of these groups made their presence felt in Wales. It was only the Bible Christians, established by William O'Bryan (1778–1868) in 1815, and Hugh Bourne's Primitive Methodists who made any concerted attempt to recruit members in Wales. Both groups concentrated their attentions in south Wales and in predominantly English-speaking areas, but enjoyed only limited success.[37] However, the split that occurred in the Welsh-language Wesleyan society in Liverpool in 1818 when Thomas Jones (1785–1865) and some disgruntled followers aligned themselves with the Independent Methodists,[38] after they had objected to the Liverpool society's decision to begin paying its ministers, was much more damaging. Jones moved to Wales shortly after the split and caused further dissension among the Welsh-speaking societies in north Wales by trying to persuade others, who he knew had also expressed unease about the payment of ministers, to join him.[39]

Thomas Jones's activities seem to have paid dividends when some local preachers, mainly from Anglesey and Caernarfonshire, began to voice concerns about the authority of their ministers and the intrusiveness of Conference. Wanting a greater variety of preaching, particularly from laymen, by a more frequent interchange of personnel between one district and another, and the proper remuneration of local preachers when they preached in circuits other than their own, some of the agitators planned a meeting at which they proposed to station preachers in north Wales. It was suggested that each circuit send a preacher and a leader to the meeting, but the Connexion's ordained ministers were strongly discouraged from attending. This challenge to the authority of the ministers and, by extension, the British Conference, led to the expulsion of seven leading 'reformers' in Anglesey in October 1831. More widespread secessions followed in the succeeding months as Methodists from Caernarfonshire and Anglesey grouped together, quickly becoming known as 'Y Wesle bach' (The Minor Wesleyans).[40] The new Methodist group was strongest in north Wales and quickly threw in their lot with Thomas Jones and his Independent Methodists. At the North Wales District Meeting of the Wesleyan Methodists in 1832, Jabez Bunting (1779–1858), the architect of the Wesleyan Methodist Church,[41] estimated that eight chapels, twenty-three preachers and almost 600 members had been lost as a result of the agitation.[42] Although only a small group, the Minor Wesleyans were part of a much wider national challenge to the authority and auto-cratic government of Bunting and the Methodist Conference. Groups, such as the Minor Wesleyans as well as the Wesleyan Methodist Association and, perhaps to a lesser extent, the Primitive Methodists in England,[43] all protested about the same fundamental problem. Despite having a variety of individual grievances, they all objected to the power of the Methodist Conference and its ministers, and they all wished to give their lay membership a greater role in the day-to-day life of their churches.[44] But despite grand ambitions to launch a new denomination to rival the old Wesleyan establishment, the Minor Wesleyans found life outside the Wesleyan fold difficult. Financial difficulties and the slow seepage of members back to the old group took their toll. In 1838 they were forced to throw in their lot with the Wesleyan Methodist Association,[45] who initially seemed prepared to plough more money into sending missionaries into north Wales.

By 1850 Wesleyan Methodism's quarter century of dissension was largely at an end. Many of the rival groups that coalesced into English Wesleyanism, and precipi-tated the loss of considerable numbers of adherents among the original Wesleyan body, had only a marginal impact on Wales. The Primitive Methodists had a presence in Wales but this was small and, on the whole, fairly insignificant. The Wesleyan Reformers, which came into being after the expulsion of three ministers in 1849 resulted in the secession of over 100,000 members in the years that immediately followed. Despite the efforts of Samuel Dunn (1797–1882) and William Griffith (1806–83), two of the three ministers who had been ejected in 1849,[46] the Reformers had little success in Wales. By 1853 there were only four Wesleyan Reform societies in Wales, one at Tredegar, another at Merthyr and two at Aberdare. In north Wales, in spite of their efforts to capitalise on the efforts of the Minor Wesleyans, whose grievances were on the surface remarkably similar, reform missionaries received a sharp rebuff.[47]

Despite so many disputes and secessions, Wesleyan Methodism in Wales had wit-nessed steady, if unspectacular, growth during the first half of the nineteenth century. In 1828 north Wales could boast well over 4,000 Wesleyans, while in the south there were just over 3,000 members.[48] In the statistics gathered for the Religious Census in 1851, out of the 898,442 sittings in Welsh places of worship recorded on Census day, twelve per cent of the worshipping population attended Wesleyan Methodist cha-pels.[49] Whilst the Wesleyans in Wales were nowhere near as strong as their English counterparts who enjoyed well over 1.5 million members by this time,[50] they never-theless represented a significant minority within the larger nonconformist commu-nity. Yet the Welsh Wesleyans still suffered from something of an image problem. To many they seemed to be little more than an extension of English Methodism, without a separate identity and with insufficient resources to mount a concerted evangelistic effort aimed at expanding their numbers and carving out a distinct identity. This situation was rectified to some extent by the ground-breaking decision to establish a Welsh Home Mission Fund in 1856.[51] The fund, the brainchild of the newly appointed Chairman of the North Wales District, Thomas Aubrey (1808–67),[52] was sustained by a one shilling levy upon each member of the denomination. It was created in order to consolidate the position of the existing circuits and chapels, release funds to establish new circuits and pioneer mission stations, and to provide adequate houses for ministers. The fund enabled Welsh Wesleyan Methodists, especially in north Wales, to gradually free themselves from their financial dependence on England, thereby giving them a measure of autonomy for the first time.

As with every other Welsh nonconformist denomination in the early and middle years of the nineteenth century, the spirituality of Wesleyan Methodism was moulded by the ebb and flow of religious revivalism. There had been numerous small-scale local religious awakenings in Wales, which affected the Wesleyans to a greater or lesser extent, throughout the first half of the century, but it was not until the 1857–9 awakening that the Wesleyans moved into the mainstream of Welsh evangelical nonconformity. The revival had its immediate origins in the mid-day prayer meetings that Jeremiah Lanphier (1809–90), an undistinguished city missionary employed by a Dutch Church in New York, tentatively began in September 1857.[53] After a slow beginning the prayer meetings were enormously successful as thousands began to attend. They returned to their own places of worship energised by their involvement, and thereby spread the revival far and wide. It was carried to Wales by Humphrey Jones (1832–95) who had left Tre'rddol in Cardiganshire in 1854 to join his family in Wisconsin and, after a short period as a candidate for the ministry of the Methodist Episcopal Church, had become a peripatetic preacher among some of his fellow expatriates. During this period he learned about Charles G. Finney's (1792–1875) 'New Measures' revivalism,[54] and on his return to Wales in 1858, having experienced the excitement of the New York revival for himself, he was determined to experiment with some of Finney's techniques. Initially, he was highly successful as an awakening quickly got underway in his native north Cardiganshire. He was soon joined by the Calvinistic Methodist minister at nearby Ysbyty Ystwyth, Dafydd Morgan (1814–83), and they both superintended the revival until Jones had to withdraw on account of complete mental and physical exhaustion.[55]

The revival was an unqualified success and spread from Cardiganshire to many other parts of Wales with an estimated 100,000 new converts being added to the various nonconformist denominations in its immediate aftermath. Among the Wesleyans, numbers, in both the North and South Wales Districts combined, grew remarkably from 11,839 members in 1858 to 16,388 just two years later, an increase in excess of forty per cent.[56] Significantly, the awakening coincided with a move among nonconformists in Wales towards greater cooperation in protection of their own distinctive rights. Prior to the 1850s Wesleyans in Wales had been largely conservative in their political opinions and had tended to keep their distance from most of the other nonconformist denominations. However, the infamous report of the Royal Commission on the state of education in Wales, published in 1847 and better known as the 'Blue books', revolutionised their attitudes to Wales and its nonconformist establishment. The Wesleyans did not escape from many of the criticisms made by the Commissioners. They too were included in the scurrilous attacks mounted on the language, culture, religious preferences and morals of the Welsh who, according to the Commissioners, were the most 'ignorant, depraved, idle, superstitious, drunken, debauched, lewd, and lying population on the face of the earth'.[57]

The stinging attack of the Commissioners, together with the harshness of the injustices suffered by many of those who had sided with the Liberal Party in the General Elections of 1859 and 1868, radicalised many of the nonconformist denominations. Among the Wesleyans a growing number of its ministers had adopted Liberal political opinions, at least by the early 1860s, and *Yr Eurgrawn*, the official mouthpiece of the denomination, had begun to publish articles in support of issues such as education reform, land reform and, of course, the disestablishment of the Church of England in Wales. By the 1880s and 1890s many of these ministers, and their successors, had become enthusiastic champions of the policies of the Liberal party's radical Welsh nationalistic group, *Cymru Fydd,* and strong supporters of Thomas Edward Ellis (1859–99) and David Lloyd George (1863–1945).[58] Over disestablishment for example, the Wesleyans switched from their traditionally conservative stance. This had been inherited largely from the days of John Wesley's reluctance to leave the Church of England, but attitudes changed once the full impact of the Oxford Movement became apparent during the middle years of the nineteenth century.[59] By the 1880s and 1890s the Wesleyans had become some of the most vehement supporters of disestablishment, sending countless petitions to the Prime Minister, Gladstone, in support of his efforts to get the legislation through a reluctant Parliament.[60]

Although he spent much of his adult life outside Wales, nobody exemplified this new emphasis on the twin commitments of radical political action and enthusiastic evangelical preaching more than the Carmarthen born Methodist statesman, Hugh Price Hughes (1847–1902). Hughes became Superintendent of the first West London Mission in 1884 which had been established in an attempt to reconnect the chapels with the sprawling masses of the urban poor in some of the main population centres of England and Wales. This effort quickly became known as the 'Forward Movement' and it began to sponsor the building of Central Halls, the first of which opened in Manchester in March 1886. Largely secular in architecture, they attempted to bridge the gap between the chapels and the poor by providing a viable alternative to either the pub or the music hall and, in their heyday until the outbreak of the Second World War, they provided valuable social assistance before the advent of the Welfare State.[61] For Hughes though they were part of a more ambitious reorientation of Christian endeavour that sought to address the material as well as the spiritual needs of men and women. The development of Central Halls and Hughes's prolific journalism as editor of the *Methodist Times* after 1885 ensured that social issues were constantly raised as part of the 'Nonconformist Conscience', particularly in regard to temperance, gambling and wider issues relating to social morality.[62]

His efforts were greeted with enthusiasm in Wales and he inspired many others to follow his example. In 1893 John Evans, Eglwysbach (1840–97), superintended a mission with its headquarters at Pontypridd, in the heart of the poverty-stricken south Wales coalfield. But, according to Glyn Tegai Hughes, the mission 'produced only moderate results'.[63] Despite the popularity of Evans's charismatic preaching and the success of the ministry of mercy that he established, his untimely death in 1897 brought the work to an abrupt halt.[64] The later half of the nineteenth century were the years of Welsh nonconformist dominance, religiously, politically and culturally. By aligning itself with the broader currents of Welsh nonconformity, Wesleyan Methodism benefited from the massive growth in numbers experienced by the whole nonconformist enterprise. By the outbreak of the First World War in 1914 there were 41,422 Wesleyans in Wales,[65] a figure significantly lower than the Calvinistic Methodists or the Congregationalists, but nonetheless a substantial achievement, particularly in the light of the marginal place that the denomination had occupied in Welsh religious life for much of the eighteenth and nineteenth centuries.

By the eve of the twentieth century, therefore, there seemed little indication that the apogee of nonconformist power had already been passed. Numbers were still healthy and a series of administrative changes designed to cope with ever greater expansion were intended to position the Wesleyans to meet the fresh challenges of the twentieth century head on. By 1903 the North Wales District had grown to such an extent that the decision was taken to divide the District between eastern and western regions. Perhaps more significantly in 1899 a new Welsh Assembly (*Y Gymanfa*) was established to oversee Welsh language Methodism. The Assembly wielded considerable power and took over the responsibility of ordaining Welsh language ministers from the British Conference. It survived until 1974 when it was wound up and replaced by a different body, also called *Y Gymanfa*. This was designed to represent the whole of Methodism in Wales in both languages for certain specific purposes, particularly mission and ecumenical relations.

Whilst the Great War undoubtedly undermined the faith of many people, for others the churches became the chief sources of comfort and reassurance, especially for those who had suffered the inhumanity of the trenches at first hand.[66] There was therefore no mass turning-away from religion after 1918, but rather a period of quiet consolidation and regrouping. The Wesleyans initiated negotiations with the other main Methodist churches which resulted in the formation of the unified Methodist Church of Great Britain in 1932. This was an amalgamation of the United Methodist Church, which had been created in 1907 after the merger of the Methodist New Connexion, the Bible Christians and United Methodist Free Churches, with the Primitive Methodists and the original Wesleyan Connexion.[67] This re-organisation, whilst reinvigorating the denomination for a while, did little to arrest the beginnings of a serious decline in membership, a decline mirrored in all of the mainline denominations in Britain. Callum Brown has recently demonstrated that religious adherence in Britain remained at a fairly high level throughout the first half of the twentieth century, and that decline and rapid secularisation only really undermined the dominant position of Christianity during the 1960s.[68] Although there is plenty of evidence to suggest that the haemorrhaging of members from Wesleyan Methodism was well underway before the 1960s there is little doubt that the denomination, like so many other churches, found it difficult to respond to the new challenges that the permissive society presented. But by this time the signs of terminal decline were already apparent. When a new all Cymru District was established among Welsh-speaking Wesleyans in 1974, the number of members only amounted to about 11,000.[69] Subsequently decline has been even more catastrophic. In 2003 the Cymru District could muster little more than 2,700 members,[70] and there has been a chronic lack of candidates for the ministry. Despite the efforts of a large number of lay volunteers, who have dedicated themselves to learning Welsh and serving in predominantly Welsh-speaking areas, the long-term future of the Cymru District seems to be less assured than ever before. On the other hand, English-speaking Wesleyan Methodism has not declined to quite the same extent. The total membership of the English-speaking districts in 2001 was just over 12,500, making it roughly four times the size of the Cymru District.[71]

It is easy to paint an unremittingly gloomy picture of the inexorable decline of Welsh Wesleyanism and Christianity in twentieth century Wales. There have been plenty of signs of vibrant spirituality and among some a determination to make their faith relevant to the modern world. Wesleyanism had its share of radical political thinkers in the early part of the century. The pacifist preacher David Gwynfryn Jones (1867–1954),[72] David Thomas (1880–1967), Robert Richards (1884–1954), the economist and historian who became Labour MP for Wrexham in 1922, and George Thomas, Viscount Tonypandy (1909–97), who served as Secretary of State for Wales and later became the distinguished Speaker of the House of Commons,[73] each in radically different ways attempted to relate their faith to socialist politics. Later, writers like E. Tegla Davies (1880–1967)[74] and D. Tecwyn Evans (1876–1957), historians such as Griffith T. Roberts (1912–91) and A. H. Williams (1907–96), the founder of the Wesleyan historical journal *Bathafarn* in 1946, and gifted communicators and biblical scholars, notably John Roger Jones (1879–1974), contributed to the vibrancy of twentieth century Wesleyan spirituality. Wesleyans in Wales also responded creatively to the challenges presented by the Ecumenical Movement after the foundation of the World Council of Churches in 1948. They have been involved in discussions over cooperation between denominations on a local level for many years and have taken an active role in the success of Cytûn (Churches Together in Wales), founded in 1990 with the aim of uniting 'in pilgrimage those churches which, acknowledging God's revelation in Christ, confess the Lord Jesus Christ as God and Saviour according to the Scriptures'.[75] Other currents that have refashioned many other denominations in the late-twentieth century have been largely absent within Welsh-speaking Wesleyan Methodism. Charismatic renewal of the kind experienced, to a greater or lesser extent, by most denominations seems to have largely passed it by, and it is only in some of the more progressive English-speaking congregations that there have been some attempts to make the Church relevant to the post-1960s generation.

Like all the traditional denominations in Wales, Wesleyan Methodism, both English and Welsh-speaking alike, faces many seemingly insurmountable challenges if it is to maintain its distinctive identity and survive as a viable expression of Christian witness in Wales in the coming years. In the new millennium numbers are perilously low and, despite plenty of committed lay members, there is a potentially crippling lack of ministers and too few ministerial candidates coming through to plug the gaps. There is a very real sense in which the denomination is now closer to something approaching the size it had been when Wesley himself visited Wales so frequently in the latter half of the eighteenth century but, crucially, there seems to be no later-day John Wesley on the horizon to revitalise its fortunes.

Notes

1. For the growth and emergence of Wesleyan Methodism see Rupert Davies, A. Raymond George and Gordon Rupp (eds), *A History of the Methodist Church in Great Britain* (4 vols. London, 1965–88), I (1965); Henry D. Rack, *Reasonable Enthusiast: John Wesley and the Rise of Methodism* (London, 1989); David Hempton, *Methodism: Empire of the Spirit* (New Haven, 2005).

2. For the development of Welsh Calvinistic Methodism see the chapter in this volume by Eryn M. White; Derec Llwyd Morgan, *The Great Awakening in Wales* (London, 1988); Geraint Tudur, *Howell Harris: From Conversion to Separation, 1735–1750* (Cardiff, 2000); David Ceri Jones, *'A Glorious Work in the World': Welsh Methodism and the International Evangelical Revival, 1735–50* (Cardiff, 2004).

3. A. H. Williams, 'The First Methodist Society in Wales', *Bathafarn: Cylchgrawn Hanes yr Eglwys Fethodistaidd yng Nghymru* (hereafter *Bathafarn*), 15 (1960), 21–37.

4. Iain H. Murray (ed.), *George Whitefield's Journals* (London, 1960), p. 230.

5. Nehemiah Curnock (ed.), *The Journal of the Rev. John Wesley A. M.* (London, 1932), II, p. 296.

6. Herbert McGonigle, *Sufficient Saving Grace: John Wesley's Evangelical Arminianism* (Carlisle, 2003), pp. 107–29.

7. A. H. Williams, *John Wesley in Wales, 1739–1750: Extracts from his Journal and Diary relating to Wales* (Cardiff, 1971), p. 36.

8. See Eryn M. White, 'The Established Church, Dissent and the Welsh Language *c*.1660–1811', in Geraint H. Jenkins (ed.), *The Welsh Language Before the Industrial Revolution* (Cardiff, 1997), pp. 264–9.

9. Williams, 'The First Methodist Society in Wales', 35–7.

10. Donald K. Knighton, 'English-Speaking Methodism', in Lionel Madden (ed.), *Methodism in Wales: A Short History of the Wesley Tradition* (Llandudno, 2003), pp. 3–4.

11. John Edward Lloyd and R. T. Jenkins (eds), *Dictionary of Welsh Biography down to 1940* (hereafter *DWB*) (London, 1959), p. 307; John A. Vickers (ed.), *A Dictionary of Methodism in Britain and Ireland* (hereafter *DMBI*) (Peterborough, 2000), p. 185; E. Athan Morgan, 'The Wesleys and Fonmon Castle, Glamorgan', *Bathafarn*, 9 (1954), 38–41.

12. *DWB*, pp. 331–2; *DMBI*, p. 145; A. H. Williams, 'The Gwynne's of Garth *c*.1712–1809', *Brycheiniog*, XIV (1970), 79–96.

13. Frederick C. Gill, *Charles Wesley: The First Methodist* (London, 1964), pp. 125–42.

14. National Library of Wales, Aberystwyth (NLW), Calvinist Methodist Archive (CMA) (Trevecka Group) MS. 2946, pp. 21–7, entry dated 'Bristol, Jany 22d 1747'; NLW, CMA, Diary of Howel Harris, 125, 22–4 January 1747.

15. A. H. Williams, *Welsh Wesleyan Methodism, 1800–1858: Its Origins,Growth and Secessions* (Bangor, 1935), p. 31.

16. *DMBI*, 346. Donald M. Lewis (ed.), *The Blackwell Dictionary of Evangelical Biography 1730–1860* (hereafter *BDEB*) (Oxford, 1995), pp. 1087–8.

17. Griffith T. Roberts, 'Methodism in Wales', in Davies, George and Rupp (eds), *History of the Methodist Church in Great Britain*, III (1983), p. 256.

18. For example, see Williams (ed.), *John Wesley in Wales*, pp. 26–8, 97–9.

19. Ibid., p. 49.

20. Ibid., pp. 76–8.

21. *DMBI*, pp. 259–60; Glyn Tegai Hughes, 'Thomas Olivers of Tregynon, 1725–1799', *Montgomeryshire Collections*, 91 (2003), 71–87.

22. Williams (ed.), *John Wesley in Wales*, p. 79.

23. See Knighton, 'English-Speaking Methodism', p. 6.

24. Harris's diplomacy is examined in more detail in David Ceri Jones, '"The Lord did give me a particular honour to make [me] a peacemaker": Howel Harris, John Wesley and Methodist Infighting, 1739–50', *Bulletin of the John Rylands University of Manchester Library*, 85 (2003), 73–98.
25. Williams (ed.), *John Wesley in Wales*, pp. 81–2.
26. Ibid., p. 86.
27. *DMBI*, pp. 72–3; John Vickers, *Thomas Coke: Apostle of Methodism* (London, 1969).
28. *DWB*, p. 145; *DMBI*, p. 88.
29. *DWB*, p. 381; *DMBI*, p. 168.
30. *DWB*, p. 55; *DMBI*, p. 46.
31. *DMBI*, pp. 183–4; Williams, *Welsh Wesleyan Methodism*, pp. 63–8.
32. A. H. Williams, 'The Origins of Welsh Wesleyan Methodism in South Wales, 1805–09', *Bathafarn*, 5 (1950), 44–51.
33. Glyn Tegai Hughes, 'Welsh-Speaking Methodism', in Madden (ed.), *Methodism in Wales*, p. 28.
34. Lionel Madden, 'Literature, Hymns and the Book Room', in Madden (ed.), *Methodism in Wales*, pp. 64–6.
35. Hughes, 'Welsh-Speaking Methodism', p. 30.
36. Ibid., p. 31.
37. Thomas Shaw, *The Bible Christians, 1815–1907* (London, 1965); Michael J. L. Wickes, *The West Country Preachers: A History of the Bible Christians, 1815–1907* (Bideford, 1987); Julia S, Werner, *The Primitive Methodist Connexion: Its Background and Early History* (Madison, Wisconsin, 1984).
38. The Independent Methodists were established in some of the industrial towns of Lancashire and Yorkshire in 1806, and they were among the most radical and politically active of the early Methodist communities. See Deborah M. Valenze, *Prophetic Sons and Daughters: Popular Religion and Social Change in England, 1790–1850* (Princeton, 1985).
39. *DMBI*, p. 185; Williams, *Welsh Wesleyan Methodism*, pp. 195–219.
40. This secession is covered in considerable detail in Williams, *Welsh Wesleyan Methodism*, pp. 221–52. See also Roberts, 'Methodism in Wales', pp. 260–1.
41. See W. R. Ward (ed.), *Early Victorian Methodism: The Correspondence of Jabez Bunting 1830–1858* (Oxford, 1976), pp. ix–xxiii.
42. Hughes, 'Welsh-Speaking Methodism', 31–2.
43. The Primitive Methodists had been founded by Hugh Bourne (1772–1852) and William Clowes (1780–1851) in 1810. See R. W. Ambler, *Ranters, Revivalists and Reformers: Primitive Methodism and Rural Society, South Lincolnshire, 1817–1875* (Hull, 1989); Geoffrey E. Milburn, *Primitive Methodism* (Peterborough, 2002); John Munsey Turner, *John Wesley: The Evangelical Revival and the Rise of Methodism in England* (Peterborough, 2002), pp. 151–76.
44. For a more detailed discussion of Wesleyan Methodism's most fractious decade see W. R. Ward, *Religion and Society in England 1790–1850* (London, 1972), pp. 135–76.
45. *DMBI*, p. 385.
46. The impact of this secession is discussed in considerable detail in Oliver A. Beckerlegge, *The Three Expelled* (Peterborough, 1996).
47. For the 'Reformers' efforts to win over Methodists in north Wales see Williams, *Welsh Wesleyan Methodism*, pp. 253–65.
48. Roberts, 'Methodism in Wales', p. 261.
49. John Davies, *A History of Wales* (London, 1990), p. 423. See also Ieuan Gwynedd Jones and David Williams (eds), *The Religious Census of 1851: A Calendar of the Returns relating to Wales* (2 vols. Cardiff, 1976–81), I, pp. xi–xxv.
50. Henry D. Rack, 'Wesleyan Methodism, 1849–1902', in Davies, George and Rupp (eds), *History of the Methodist Church in Great Britain*, III, p. 123.
51. Williams, *Welsh Wesleyan Methodism*, p. 187.
52. *DMBI*, p. 14; *BDEB*, p. 37.
53. For the wider context of the 1858–9 awakening see Kathryn Teresa Long, *The Revival of 1857–58: Interpreting an American Religious Awakening* (New York, 1998); Janice Holmes,

Religious Revivals in Britain and Ireland, 1859–1905 (Dublin, 2000); Kenneth S. Jeffrey, *When the Lord Walked the Land: The 1858–62 Revival in the North and East of Scotland* (Carlisle, 2002).

54. William G. McLoughlin Jr., *Modern Revivalism: Charles Grandison Finney to Billy Graham* (New York, 1959); Richard P. Carwardine, *Trans-Atlantic Revivalism: Popular Evangelicalism in Britain and America, 1790–1865* (Westport, Conn., 1978), pp. 3–56; Charles E. Hambrick-Stowe, *Charles G. Finney and the Spirit and American Evangelicalism* (Grand Rapids, Michigan, 1996).

55. Richard Carwardine, 'The Welsh Evangelical Community and Finney's Revival', *Journal of Ecclesiastical History*, 29, 4 (1974), 266–93; Eifion Evans, *Revival Comes to Wales: The Story of the 1859 Revival in Wales* (Bridgend, 1979); Eifion Evans, *Two Welsh Revivalists: Humphrey Jones, Dafydd Morgan and the 1859 Revival in Wales* (Bridgend, 1985).

56. Hughes, 'Welsh-Speaking Methodism', p. 36.

57. Quoted in Ieuan Gwynedd Jones, '1848 and 1868: 'Brad y Llyfrau Gleision' and Welsh Politics', in Ieuan Gwynedd Jones, *Mid-Victorian Wales: The Observers and the Observed* (Cardiff, 1992), p. 158. See also Gwyneth Tyson Roberts, *The Language of the Blue Books: A Perfect Instrument of Empire* (Cardiff, 1998).

58. For an introduction to the achievements of the Welsh Liberals see Kenneth O. Morgan, *Wales in British Politics, 1868–1922* (Cardiff, 1968).

59. Peter Freeman, 'The Response of Welsh Nonconformists to the Oxford Movement', *Welsh History Review*, 20 (2001), 435–65.

60. On the disestablishment debate in Wales, see K. O. Morgan, 'The Campaign for Welsh Disestablishment', in K. O. Morgan, *Modern Wales: Politics, Places and People* (Cardiff, 1995), pp. 142–76.

61. Christopher Oldstone-Moore, *Hugh Price Hughes: Founder of a New Methodism, Conscience of a New Nonconformity* (Cardiff, 1999). For the influence of the social gospel in Wales at the end of the nineteenth century and beyond see Robert Pope, *Building Jerusalem: Nonconformity, Labour and the Social Question in Wales, 1906–1939* (Cardiff, 1998); Robert Pope, *Seeking God's Kingdom: The Nonconformist Social Gospel in Wales, 1906–1939* (Cardiff, 1999).

62. For the background to the development of the 'Nonconformist Conscience' see D. W. Bebbington, *The Nonconformist Conscience: Chapel and Politics, 1870–1914* (London, 1982); R. J. Helmstadter, 'The Nonconformist Conscience', in Gerald Parsons (ed.), *Religion in Victorian Britain, IV: Interpretations* (Manchester, 1988), pp. 61–95; Ian Bradley, *The Call to Seriousness: The Evangelical Impact on the Victorians* (London, 1976).

63. Glyn Tegai Hughes, 'Pulpit and Pew', in Madden (ed.), *Methodism in Wales*, p. 95.

64. Owen E. Evans, E. H. Griffiths and Hugh Rowlands, 'The Church in Society', in Madden (ed.), *Methodism in Wales*, pp. 114–15.

65. D. Densil Morgan, *The Span of the Cross: Christianity and Society in Wales, 1900–2000* (Cardiff, 2000), pp. 22–3.

66. See D. Densil Morgan, '"Christ and the War": Some Aspects of the Welsh Experience', *Journal of Welsh Religious History*, 5 (1997), 73–91.

67. John Musney Turner, *Conflict and Reconciliation: Studies of Methodism and Ecumenism in England, 1740–1982* (London, 1982), 173–93; Adrian Hastings, *A History of English Christianity, 1920–2000* (London, 2001), pp. 262–4; Doreen Rosman, *The Evolution of the English Churches, 1500–2000* (Cambridge, 2003), pp. 320–2.

68. Callum Brown, *The Death of Christian Britain: Understanding Secularisation, 1800–2000* (London, 2001). See also Hugh McLeod and Werner Ustorf (eds), *The Decline of Christendom in Western Europe, 1750–2000* (Cambridge, 2003).

69. Hughes, 'Welsh-speaking Methodism', p. 37.

70. *Yr Eglwys Fethodistaidd, Llawlyfr a Chyfeiriadur: Talaith Cymru (30), 2003–2004* (Dinbych, 2004), p. 19.

71. *Minutes of Conference and Directory* (London, 2002), p. 69.

72. *DMBI*, p. 183.

73. Greg Rosen (ed.), *Dictionary of Labour Biography* (London, 2001), pp. 566–9; George Thomas, *George Thomas, Mr Speaker: The Memoirs of Viscount Tonypandy* (London, 1986).

74. Pennar Davies, *E. Tegla Davies* (Cardiff, 1983).

75. For more on Cytûn and its activities see http://www.cytun.org.uk (accessed March 2010).

CHAPTER 8

THE MORAVIAN CHURCH[1]

John Morgan-Guy

The closure in 1957 of the Moravian Chapel on St Thomas' Green, Haverfordwest effectively brought to an end more than two centuries of missionary endeavour and ministry by the *Unitas Fratrum*[2] in Wales. Haverfordwest, the first Moravian Society established in the country, was, by the date of the closure of its chapel, also the sole survivor.[3] In 1920 M. H. Jones called the Moravians 'one of the most missionary sects in the world',[4] and more recently J. C. S. Mason has recorded in impressive detail their signal contribution to what 'is now seen as the beginning of the modern British missionary movement'[5] both at home and abroad in the eighteenth century. Wales was to be one, modest, sphere of that Moravian missionary activity, yet, truth to tell, it never fulfilled its initial promise. Nonetheless, the story of the Moravians in Wales deserves to be better known – the last book on the subject was published in 1938.[6] In a sense, the full story still awaits the telling, as Jenkins, in that same book, drew attention to the then surviving, but largely unexploited, primary source material for a fuller and more detailed study to be made than he had been able to undertake.[7] In the compass of this short paper it is only possible to touch briefly on that story,[8] and to advance some suggestions as to why the Moravians' Welsh initiative ultimately foundered.

Although its roots lie in the religious history of the fifteenth century, and in particular with the disciples of Jan Hus in Bohemia,[9] it would not be inaccurate to say that the modern story begins in Saxony between 1722 and 1727 on the estate of Count Nicholas von Zinzendorf.[10] Energetic, committed, zealous and autocratic, Zinzendorf had from 1722 given refuge on his Berthelsdorf estate to refugee remnants of the *Unitas Fratrum*, those, mainly German, survivors of the persecutions and disruption the Brethren had endured in the Catholic Reformation and during the religious wars of the seventeenth century. As R. T. Jenkins pointed out, it was from the 1720s that 'Moravianism' was

> Extensively transformed. Zinzendorf was a Lutheran, and had also been a disciple of the Pietists (Spener, Francke, etc – the spiritual forbears of Griffith Jones and Howell Harris) though he reacted against them in some respects; nor should it ever be forgotten that he was an aristocrat. The characteristics, and the anomalies, of the eighteenth century Brethren's Church are the resultant of the mutual impact of Zinzendorf and Moravianism.[11]

The early years of the community at Berthelsdorf, whose settlement came to be known as Herrnhut, 'The Watch of the Lord', were bedevilled by discord and controversy, but on 13 August 1727, at a service of Holy Communion, 'all present felt an overwhelming sense of unity in the Lamb of God, the Lord Jesus Christ. All discord ceased, and they were united in their desire to share this experience of the love of God by His Holy Spirit with everyone.'[12] This 1727 experience provided the Moravians with their missionary dynamic, and, at least in the early years, the organizing ability and dominant personality of Zinzendorf gave form to the purpose. Within a year of the 1727 experience, Moravian Brethren had found their way to England, established a centre for meeting and worship in London, and were making contact with like-minded Christians both in the international commercial and mercantile world of the city and beyond.

It should not therefore surprise us that there were London Welshmen among the earliest of those attracted by the Moravians. William Holland (1711–1761),[13] a native of Haverfordwest but a successful house-painter in London by the time he was twenty, was certainly associated with the Moravians in the 1730s, and when the official congregation was established in Fetter Lane in 1742, his name stood first in the list of its members. Another early adherent was William Griffith (1704–1747)[14] who had been born at Penmorfa, Caernarfonshire. Both Holland and Griffith were to be involved in Moravian missionary activity in their native Wales. In 1743 Holland was appointed 'correspondent for Wales' and subsequently undertook missionary tours there, and in the same year Griffith did the same in Pembrokeshire. Nor should it surprise us that, at least in these early days, Moravians and Methodists were intimately connected. As Rupert Davies noted, in the German Pietism which so strongly influenced Zinzendorf

> We have, unmistakably, the ingredients of Methodism – the distinctive type of Churchmanship which sets about reforming the inner life of the Church, the orthodoxy which is never questioned, but tends to remain in the background, the intensely personal devotion to God in Christ, the striving towards holy love, the groups which practise fellowship in the Spirit rather than in formal acts of worship, without neglecting the 'means of grace', the desire to make known the love of Christ to those who have passed it by, and, most plainly, the hymns.[15]

No small wonder that men of the calibre of John and Charles Wesley, George Whitefield and Howel Harris were initially attracted by and associated with the Moravianism of the 1730s. More locally, over and over again, especially in the leadership of the Moravian societies in Wales in the eighteenth century, there is discernable evidence of the close association between the *Unitas Fratrum* and Methodism. After all, there was at this date a distinct identity of purpose between the Moravians and the Methodists. As R. T. Jenkins wrote of the former,

The Brethren's main task, as they conceived it, was to stimulate spiritual life, undenominationally as it were, within the bosom of the existing religious bodies – and in effect principally within the established church.[16]

Almost precisely the same could have been said of the infant Methodist societies, both in England and Wales. It was after 1740 that strains, tensions and misunderstandings resulted in estrangement between the Brethren and, for example, the Wesleys, Whitefield and Harris. The decade after 1740 also saw a gradual move to a settled 'denominationalism' by the Moravians. In 1742 they leased the Fetter Lane Chapel, which became thereafter 'an expressly Moravian Church',[17] the home of a distinct and distinctive congregation. In 1749 an Act of Parliament recognized the Moravians as an 'ancient Protestant Episcopal Church',[18] though full communion with the established church of England was to take nearly another two and a half centuries to achieve. It was, however, this increasingly settled 'denominationalism' of the Moravians which caused some members, such as William Holland, to disassociate themselves from the Brethren. Holland had, throughout his years with the Moravians, remained loyal to the established church, and in 1747 was forced to make a choice. After his Welsh mission, his obvious unease led to him being deprived by the Moravians of his 'labourer's' commission, and he soon after left the society.[19]

On the other hand, and perhaps more so in Wales, the Moravians increasingly attracted those whom Jenkins called 'unsettled Methodists'.[20] Those, that is, who

Found themselves in increasing revolt against the hardening Calvinism of the predominant Methodist wing in Wales, yet precluded, by their traditional repugnance to official Dissent, from attaching themselves (even where that was geographically feasible) to the Arminian Independents or the Arminian Baptists.[21]

Further, the controversies and divisions within Welsh Methodism, which centred upon the clash between Howel Harris and Daniel Rowland in the 1740s,[22] and which caused confusion bordering on chaos, with its inevitable concomitants of disillusionment and disaffection, also provided an impetus and an opportunity for Moravian activity in Wales. Here the refugees from Methodism found the same fervent, warm, committed spirit that had characterized the early years of the 'Great Awakening', but without the doctrinal wrangling that was now embittering the relationship of that Awakening's leaders. The Moravian societies in north and south-west Wales, in Caernarfonshire and Haverfordwest, date from this period, and in both cases the leaders were disaffected Methodists.

John Sparks (1726–1769),[23] a Haverfordwest tradesman, had been associated with Howel Harris, and had been recognized in 1745 as a Methodist 'exhorter', but in 1751, in the fall-out of the dispute between Harris and Rowland, he joined the Moravians, and, in company with another of Harris' former supporters, George Gambold, a schoolmaster in the town, began holding services in a warehouse on the quay.[24] In 1757 in north Wales, although there had been earlier sporadic contacts with the Moravians, the first serious and organized mission was undertaken, by the society based in Bristol, where one-third of the membership was Welsh-born.[25] The early years of the mission were beset with problems[26] and, as in Pembrokeshire, the first leaders, William Jones and Edward Oliver, were both former Methodists.[27] Jones was an attorney from the Vale of Clwyd, and Oliver (1720–1777), a carpenter, had for a short while been a member of Howell Harris' 'family' at Trefeca.

The Moravian presence in Wales, then, effectively dates from the time of the disruption in Methodism in the 1740s, which culminated in the separation between Harris and Rowland in 1750.[28] Moreover, its leadership, and arguably much of its membership in this early period, was composed of disaffected Methodists. Sadly, the Moravian initiative was hampered from the outset by the quality of its leadership. Sparks, the effective founder of the Moravian society at Haverfordwest, proved to be a difficult and autocratic man, who eventually had to be disciplined and 'silenced'.[29] Such personality problems as this dogged the other initiatives in Wales. In north Wales, William Jones proved a broken reed, and poor Edward Oliver, faithful and humble-minded though he evidently was, was also, in both church and personal life muddled and disorganized.[30] David Mathias (1738–1812) who to all intents and purposes took over the mission from him, at first sight might seem an ideal choice.[31] Welsh-speaking and well-connected (his father John was a landowner in Pembrokeshire, and himself a Moravian), he was energetic and experienced. He had been resident at the major Moravian settlement at Fulneck, Leeds, and was a recognized preacher. Yet, like Sparks, he proved to be of a 'haughty temper and lacking in tact'.[32] He abruptly left Wales in 1776, deserting his scattered flock, and no successor was found. By the time he returned to the north Wales mission in 1788, all initiative had been lost to a reinvigorated Methodism, and the work, centred upon Caernarfon, did not flourish. Mathias, appearing 'a little unhinged and confused',[33] again abandoned his post in 1793. His departure this time dealt a fatal blow to organized Moravianism in north Wales.[34]

The woeful story is not at an end. At Laugharne a society had been founded in 1768,[35] and put in the care of Francis Pugh (1720–1811), who was in deacon's orders.[36] Again, Pugh seemed a good choice. Welsh-speaking, he was a former neighbour of Howel Harris and previously a Methodist.[37] He even had experience as pastor of the church at Leominster. Yet again he proved to be a man of intractable temper – he and his wife Elizabeth Logg were described as 'irritable and stiff-necked'[38] – and his long ministry at Laugharne, with Carmarthen from 1772–3, was turbulent and troubled.[39] At Carmarthen, potentially an important centre, he quickly alienated the well-meaning Lazarus Thomas, the initiator of the society there. By 1788 the membership numbered only nine, Pugh, claiming ill-health, was refusing to minister there, and about 1790 the initiative foundered.[40]

The Moravian work in Wales was seriously, almost fatally, hampered by its leadership at the very time that, because of the confusion in Methodism, it could have been most fruitful. It is difficult to escape the conclusion that men like Sparks, Mathias and Pugh in particular were temperamentally incapable of accepting direction, leadership and authority. Moreover, they were arrogant and abrasive in the exercise of it. The organization of the church also left a great deal to be desired. The chapels and preaching centres that were established were controlled from two centres, Haverfordwest and Leominster. Indeed Haverfordwest (after 1763) was the only recognized 'congregation' in Wales.[41] The subsidiary chapels and preaching stations, many in private houses (Haverfordwest had twenty in 1763, for example) were dependent therefore on distant leadership and oversight, a weakness which conspired against the effective control of men like Sparks, Mathias and Pugh. There was also no Moravian 'settlement' or colony such as Fulneck (Yorkshire) in Wales. Mathias, to be fair to him, realized that such a settlement, perhaps on Anglesey, could have been a powerhouse and stabilizing influence for the whole of the north Wales' mission, but the idea came to nothing.[42] Between 1768 and 1771 a more serious attempt was made to acquire land at Cilycwm, Carmarthenshire, for the founding of a settlement, which would have been a valuable link between the Leominster and Haverfordwest 'congregations', but distant Fetter Lane in London, which held the purse-strings, prevaricated and delayed, and the opportunity was lost.[43]

The subsequent history of Welsh Moravianism was that of the quiet, congregational life of a small, settled denomination, a life such as that so well recorded by Dennis Monger in his history of the Brockweir chapel in the Wye Valley.[44] One by one, the chapels and preaching stations, such as Fishguard, Narberth, Tenby, Pendine, Rhosgoch (near Hay-on-Wye) and Builth closed down, until only Haverfordwest remained.[45] The closure in 1957 of the chapel there, and the withdrawal of the last pastor, brought to an end a fascinating, if often sad and troubled, era in Welsh religious history.

Notes

1. R. T. Jenkins called this the 'undenominational denomination'. See R. T. Jenkins, *The Moravian Brethren in North Wales. An Episode in the Religious History of Wales* (London, 1938), pp. 4–5.
2. Unity of Brethren (trans).
3. M. H. Jones, 'Moravian Chapels in Wales', *Journal of the Calvinistic Methodist Historical Society*, 5, 1 (1920), 30.
4. Ibid., 31.
5. J. C. S. Mason, *The Moravian Church and the Missionary Awakening in England 1760–1800* (Woodbridge, 2001), p. 1.
6. Jenkins, *Moravian Brethren in North Wales*.
7. Ibid., particularly in the preface, pp. xv–xxii. The records of the Haverfordwest chapel and of Moravian activity in Pembrokeshire are a case in point. They are divided between the National Library of Wales and the Public Record Office.
8. For wider studies useful as background see Colin Podmore, *The Moravian Church in England 1728–1760* (Oxford, 1998); J. Taylor Hamilton and Kenneth G. Hamilton, *History of the Moravian Church. The Renewed Unitas Fratrum 1722–1957* (2nd edn. Bethlehem, Pa., 1983). The latter is a comprehensive one-volume introduction to the worldwide activity of the Moravian Church.
9. Jenkins, *Moravian Brethren in North Wales*, pp. 1–2 gives a very short introduction to the early history of the Moravians.
10. Not surprisingly, there is an extensive literature on Zinzendorf. For example, see A. J. Lewis, *Zinzendorf the Ecumenical Pioneer: A Study in the Moravian Contribution to Mission and Unity* (London, 1962); Arthur J. Freeman, *An Ecumenical Theology of the Heart: The Theology of Count Nicholas Ludwig von Zinzendorf* (Bethlehem, Pa., 1998).

11. Jenkins, *Moravian Brethren in North Wales*, pp. 2–3.

12. J. D. Monger, *'Like a Tree Planted':The Story of Brockweir Moravian Church 1833–1983* (Magor, n.d. *c*.1983), p. 2.

13. *The Dictionary of Welsh Biography down to 1940* [hereafter *DWB*] (London, 1959), p. 363; Jenkins, *Moravian Brethren in North Wales*, pp. 18, 21, 27, 92, 129.

14. *DWB*, p. 301; Jenkins, *Moravian Brethren in North* Wales, pp. 21–5, 28, 79, 92, 129.

15. Rupert E. Davies, *Methodism* (London, 1963), p. 23.

16. Jenkins, *Moravian Brethren in North Wales*, p. 11.

17. Ibid., p. 10.

18. For the background and discussion of this recognition see Hamilton and Hamilton, *History of the Moravian Church*, pp. 119–31. The Moravian Church had, and has, retained the historic threefold order of ministry, bishop, priest (presbyter) and deacon.

19. *DWB*, p. 363. The fact that Holland thereafter became associated with Wesleyan Methodism is indicative of his desire for an evangelical Christianity within the established church and not, as he was evidently beginning to perceive it, within a separate and distinct society as Moravianism in England was becoming. The ultimate impossibility of 'undenominational denominationalism' was beginning to manifest itself.

20. Jenkins, *Moravian Brethren in North* Wales, p. 15.

21. Ibid., pp. 15–16. Moravian patterns of worship would also prove attractive to such 'unsettled Methodists', and its predominant theological 'strand' was Lutheran not Calvinist.

22. See Geraint Tudur, *Howell Harris. From Conversion to Separation 1735–1750* (Cardiff, 2000), pp. 151–94 for the most recent discussion of this.

23. *DWB*, p. 920.

24. Ibid., p. 273. George Gambold's elder brother John was a distinguished Moravian, who was consecrated a bishop in the church in 1753, the first non-German to be elevated to the episcopate after the renewal of 1722–7. A fine scholar, he was responsible in 1770 for the publication of a Moravian hymn-book in Welsh, *Ychydig Hymnau allan o Lyfr Hymnau Cynulleidfaoedd y Brodyr* (A Few Hymns out of the Hymn-book of the Fellowship/Congregation of the Brethren). Twelve of his own hymns, mainly translations from Latin and German into English, can still be found in the *Moravian Hymn Book* (London, 1975). At the end of his life Bishop Gambold returned to his native Haverfordwest as pastor of the Moravian church there. He died in 1771. See Daniel Benham, *Life of Bishop Gambold* (London, 1865).

25. Jenkins, *Moravian Brethren in North Wales*, p. 45.

26. Ibid., especially pp. 45–93.

27. For Jones, see Ibid., pp. 45–87, passim. Oliver was a native of Montgomeryshire, interestingly also the birthplace, at Tregynon, of his contemporary Thomas Oliver(s), 1725–1799, the hymn-writer, Methodist preacher, and friend of John Wesley. It is not known if they were related. Ibid; *DWB*, p. 688.

28. For additional work on Methodism in Wales see chapters by Eryn White and David Ceri Jones in this collection.

29. *DWB*, p. 920. Sparks went bankrupt in 1766, and died three years later.

30. Jenkins, *Moravian Brethren in North Wales*, p. 76. He ended his days as a shopkeeper and Moravian preacher at Fishguard.

31. For Mathias, see Ibid., pp. 95–159; *DWB*, pp. 619–20.

32. Jenkins, *Moravian Brethren in North Wales* provides a vivid picture of his strengths and failings.

33. Ibid., p. 142. Like Oliver before him, Mathias ended his days as a shopkeeper in Fishguard, where he died in 1812.

34. By 1785, after Mathias' first desertion of his north Wales mission, the little society was in the care of the Dublin church, founded in 1749. See J. H. Foy, *Moravians in Ireland* (Repr. Belfast, 1989), p. 2; Jones, 'Moravian Chapels in Wales', 31. After his second desertion in 1793, in the vivid words of Michael Roberts of Pwllheli, 'the Moravians vanished from the land even as the morning dew disappears in the heat of May'. Quoted in Jenkins, *Moravian Brethren in North Wales*, p. 155.

35. Jenkins, *Moravian Brethren in North Wales*, p. 30.

36. For Pugh, see *DWB*, p. 812 and notes Jenkins, *Moravian Brethren in North Wales*, pp. 12, 20, 45, 48, 49, 52, 55, 101, 112, 132–3, 142; R. T. Jenkins, 'The Moravian Brethren in Carmarthenshire', *Journal of the Calvinistic Methodist Historical Society*, XXI, 2–3 (1936), 61–8.

37. He had been expelled in 1746 and then joined the Moravians.

38. Quoted in *DWB*, p. 812.

39. Ibid. After his wife's death in 1793 those sent to Laugharne to assist him 'found him quite impossible to work with'. The congregation relocated during Pugh's ministry to a new chapel within the borders of Pendine parish. By 1850 the allegiance had passed to Methodism.

40. Jenkins, 'Moravian Brethren in Carmarthenshire', especially 61–4.

41. Jenkins, *Moravian Brethren in North Wales*; Jones, 'Moravian Chapels in Wales', outline the rather cumbersome local structures of the Moravian church in England and Wales at this date.

42. Jenkins, *Moravian Brethren in North Wales*, p. 8; Jenkins, 'Moravian Brethren in Carmarthenshire', 64. He quite rightly makes the point that Howel Harris' Trefeca 'family' was a parallel example of such a settlement, but that it had not been founded in imitation of them. Harris in his diary for 1736, three years *before* his first contact with the Moravians, had expressed a wish to found such a community. It was the common inspiration of the German Pietists, Jenkins insists, which led to a parallel development. After Harris' death in 1773 the Trefeca 'family' became more overtly sympathetic to Moravianism. Jenkins, *Moravian Brethren in North Wales*, p. 14. See also Geraint Tudur, *Howell Harris*, p. 152 and further references there.

43. For an account of the abortive negotiations, see Jenkins, 'Moravian Brethren in Carmarthenshire', 64–8.

44. Monger, *'Like a Tree Planted'*. Founded on the Gloucestershire side of the river, but on the initiative of a resident of Tintern, Monmouthshire. There was no convenient bridge between the Welsh and English banks, so the Brockweir Moravians, in the early years, would cross to Tintern by boat for celebrations of the Holy Communion in the parish church there.

45. Jones, 'Moravian Chapels in Wales' gives a very brief outline of the decline of the Moravian mission in Wales.

CHAPTER 9

UNITARIANISM

Euros Lloyd

In 1726 the first Welsh anti-trinitarian cause was established in Cardiganshire, in an area commonly referred to as 'Y Smotyn Du' (The Black Spot). The Black Spot is a parochial circle of about twenty miles that expands out from Ciliau Aeron to Llandysul and Lampeter, and remains to this day the Unitarian stronghold in Wales. Unitarian causes in Wales and England were usually urban, a tendency that was often seen throughout the history of nonconformity.[1] It is possible that being an Unitarian was easier in an urban environment, where more radical ideas would be able to prosper, and because towns and cities tended to have a mixture of various people with different theological ideas. Urbanization attracted people from various backgrounds, and it was more common for urban communities to be diverse in nature.

The exception to this pattern with regards to the development of nonconformity was the Unitarian cause in the Black Spot. The Unitarian churches of the Black Spot are located in various local parishes which include Llandysul, Llanwenog, Llandysiliogogo, Llanwnnen, Llanfihangel Ystrad, Llangybi, Cellan and Ciliau Aeron. The area was nicknamed the 'Black Spot' by the Methodists because of their failure to establish their own causes in the vicinity. It is no surprise that the presence of Unitarians in this area was to the Methodists annoyance and frustration. Every Unitarian church was within twenty miles of Llangeitho, namely one of the Methodist strongholds under the guidance of Daniel Rowland. By the early nineteenth century, Unorthodox Arians and Unitarians had created in south Cardiganshire:

> A triangular fortress of churches whose members tenaciously rebuffed all attempts by Calvinist evangelists to win them over to their cause. As a result, the heretics' sphere of influence was demonized as 'Y Smotyn Du' (The Black Spot) by revivalists at nearby Llangeitho, and hostility between the rival camps remained mutual and long-lasting.[2]

All anti-trinitarian thought throughout the centuries received scathing criticism by Trinitarians, as was the case in west Wales. Laws were also put in place in the mid- to late-seventeenth century in an attempt to restrict the development of anti-trinitarianism by making it illegal. After the civil wars, Charles II passed numerous religious acts that would shape the pattern of religion in Wales and England for years to come.

These measures included the Corporation Act 1661, the Uniformity Act 1662, the Five Mile Act 1665, the Test Act 1673, the Toleration Act 1689 and the Blasphemy Act 1698.[3] The Toleration Act of 1689 gave nonconformists the freedom to worship as they wished, but this particular measure only granted Trinitarian nonconformists the freedom to worship. Unitarians were not included in the Toleration Act in a deliberate attempt to hinder their development. Therefore oppression continued for anti-trinitarian Christians and Unitarianism was not finally legalised until the Doctrine of the Trinity Act in 1813.[4] Michael Watts has noted that Unitarians were 'both excluded from the benefits of the Toleration Act and, under the Blasphemy Act of 1698, liable to three years imprisonment for propagating their beliefs. Such measures, though, failed to halt the growth of heresy.'[5]

Despite criticism from other denominations, and the popularity of the Calvinistic Methodists, the Black Spot in south Cardiganshire and north Carmarthenshire was Unitarianism's main success story and created a unique religious pattern in Wales. The remainder of the Unitarian churches were peppered across south Wales. By the nineteenth century there were thirteen Unitarian churches in the Black Spot, though five of these were established in the second half of the seventeenth century, far before Unitarianism developed in the area. These five churches represent the early remains of the Presbyterians in the region, but by the eighteenth century they all followed an Arminian theology that rejected the predestinarian theology of Calvinism.

The churches in the Black Spot enhanced their theological beliefs by embracing the ideas of Arianism that held that Christ was God the Father, a teaching that was roundly condemned by the majority of Christian denominations. The five anti-trinitairian churches in question were Alltyblaca, Caeronnen, Ciliau, Cribyn and Llwynrhydowen. The establishment of Llwynrhydowen in 1726 by Jenkin Jones[6] was an important milestone for the anti-trintarian movement, as it was the first recognisably Arminian church in Wales.[7] By the time Jones died in 1742, the anti-trinitarian movement had developed further with the establishment of Alltyblaca between 1740 and 1741. These two churches maintained close links for over a hundred years with the same ministers serving their causes.

A key time in the history of Llwynrhydowen and Alltyblaca came with the appointment of David Evans to collaborate as minister of the pastorate with D. Lewis Jones in 1830. David Evans was the minister who cut the close ties between Alltyblaca and Llwynrhydowen, with the former being tied to Caeronnen. During the 1830s, David Evans introduced Unitarian theological ideas to his Alltyblaca congregation. Even though Alltyblaca and Caeronnen were developing and modernising their theologies, Llwynrhydowen maintained its Arian beliefs until William Thomas ('Gwilym Marles')[8] became minister. It was he who introduced the Unitarian ideas of Theodore Parker as Llwynrhydowen developed into a modern Unitarian congregation.

Another of the churches established in the seventeenth century was the aforementioned Caeronnen. During the first half of the eighteenth century, the church had developed from being an Arminian church to being one which adopted the Arian theology. But in 1846, when a new building was opened for the Caeronnen cause, Unitarian ideas were well and truly established amongst the members.[9] Caeronnen's sister church, Ciliau, hails from the same period and also adopted Arminian theology.

These two churches had the same six ministers starting with Rees Powell (1653–65) and ending with Evan Davies (1726–37), but Ciliau began to follow a more comprehensive Arian outlook from *c*.1760 under the leadership of Daniel Gronw. The separation of beliefs was more evident after a faction of Calvinist members seceded from the church in Graigwen. Certainly by the time of Gronw's successors, Dafydd Dafis[10] and Dafydd Llwyd, Ciliau was an Arian church. During the 1760s Ciliau began to cut ties with Caeronnen to work more closely with Llwynrhydowen, and when Daniel Gronw left the church for Bala in 1769, Ciliau had totally relinquished ties with its sister church while Llwynrhydowen's ministers were responsible for the congregation. But Ciliau failed to prosper like the other anti-trinitarian churches of the Black Spot. This was because of its geographical location on the extremity of the Cardiganshire stronghold which meant that it was surrounded by various Christian denominations who disagreed with anti-trinitarian beliefs.

The final of the five original churches established in the Black Spot before the introduction of Unitarian theology, was Cribyn. Cribyn was established in 1790 with the assistance of Dafydd Dafis of Castell Hywel, and Evan Davies of Cwmbedw. It is fair to say that Dafydd Dafis played an instrumental part in developing anti-trinitarian causes in the Black Spot. But Dafis' ministry occurred during a time of significant change with regards to the development of anti-trinitarian theology, with more publications appearing that inspired some to develop their theology more fully in the direction of Unitarianism. By the beginning of the nineteenth century there was a dispute within Dafis' churches as they embraced Arianism rather than Arminianism. Despite this development, there were members of the Llwynrhydowen, Alltyblaca and Ciliau congregations who believed that the theology of these churches was too backward, a barrier against a more fully defined Unitarian theology being established.[11] The result of this incompatibility was the establishment of the first Unitarian causes in Cardiganshire in 1802 with the help of Charles Lloyd. These causes were Pantydefaid, y Groes[12] and Rhyd-y-gwin (Llanfihangel Ystrad). The same ministers served y Groes and Pantydefaid churches until 1818, with well-known names in Unitarian history, such as David Jenkin Rees, Dr Charles Lloyd, John James and John Thomas, occupying the pastorate. These two churches went from strength to strength with the assistance of the missionary James Lyons, who visited the area in 1811, describing y Groes as 'the largest of Unitarians I saw in Wales'.[13]

The early years of the nineteenth century were a time of change for the anti-trinitarians. On 8 October 1802 the Welsh Unitarian Society was established at Gellionnen with Iolo Morganwg, Dafydd Dafis, Josiah Rees, Thomas Morgans, Thomas Davies and John Rowlands as leaders. The purpose of this society was to protect, defend and unite the supporters of Unitarian thought from across Wales.[14] Consequently the South Wales Unitarian Society, also established in 1802, covered the Unitarian causes of the Black Spot and any other Welsh speaking causes throughout Wales. But this order was changed when it was realised that the societies would work more effectively by protecting and servicing causes by regional location.[15] When the Unitarian missionary, Richard Wright visited Wales between 1816 and 1819 he was pleased with the progress of Unitarianism in the south of the country, observing that 'the seeds of Unitarianism have been widely scattered in south

Wales'.[16] He nevertheless believed that there was much more that could be done to strengthen and develop the Unitarian causes, notably with the publication of periodicals in the Welsh language and further missionary work.[17] Moreover, it was not until 1890 that an English language Unitarian society was established in Wales. This was the work of the Rev. W. A. Clarke of Swansea who sought provision for the English speaking causes throughout the country.

The Unitarians continued to establish and develop still more causes during the first half of the nineteenth century with two additional churches. In 1811 Bwlchyfadfa was established followed by y Graig in 1846, the two being daughter churches of the Llwynrhydowen congregation. The cause at Bwlchyfadfa was founded as a result of a dispute between Dafydd Dafis and his co-pastor, John Jones – a situation that mirrored the conflict between Dafis and Charles Lloyd and had led to the founding of Pantydefaid. Geographical reasons also played a part in the setting up of new causes, notably at Bwlchyfadfa which ensured that there was a purer Unitarian church in the area. Yet in the early period of Blwchyfadfa's history there was a division within the congregation. Members supporting the Calvinistic cause left Bwlchyfadfa to establish Pisga Independent Chapel. Meanwhile John Jones also left Bwlchyfadfa and founded Carmel chapel at Prengwyn, but with the assistance of Dafydd Dafis and Llwynrhydowen, the cause at Bwlchyfadfa was able to survive. Another daughter church of Llwynrhydowen was the Graig church in Llandysul.[18] It is thought that anti-trinitarian ideas took root here around 1811, as this is the first reference to the cause. By 1828 a cause had been established in Cwrtnewydd that would lead to the formation of the Bryn church, and in 1833 the Bryn Bach church was built with Unitarian ministers of the district serving the cause. Uncertainty dogged this cause for nearly fifty years before the congregation felt sufficiently able to build the Bryn church in 1882.[19]

With the publication of the 1851 census it became clear that the percentage of the population which belonged to the Unitarian cause in Cardiganshire was 3.5 per cent. This was a small number compared to the 38 per cent of Methodists, 22 per cent of Independents and 22.5 per cent of Anglicans.[20] The 1851 census noted the existence of eleven Unitarian churches in Cardiganshire. Llwynrhydowen church in Llandysul's parish had the strongest congregation with 500 regularly attending services on a Sunday. The Groes church had 300 members while the remainder of Unitarian churches had less than 300 regularly attending their services.[21] David Williams has argued that the Unitarians were flourishing at the turn of the nineteenth century with the establishment of new churches and the rebuilding of others, including the influential Llwynrhydowen church in 1791.[22]

During the final quarter of the nineteenth century, the final two Unitarian churches were established in the Black Spot. The first of these was Caeronnen's daughter church, Brondeifi which was established in 1874.[23] The youngest church amongst the Unitarian congregation of the Black Spot was the Cwm church in Cwmsychbant. The cause was set up in 1886, but it was twenty years later that the church was finally built, to ensure that the local Unitarians had a place of worship in close proximity. The Unitarians of the Black Spot were able to maintain their causes through to the twentieth century. With so many churches in close proximity, they were able to create a Unitarian fortress that protected the causes from the influence of other denominations, especially the Calvinistic Methodists.

By the start of the twentieth century fifteen of the thirty-four Unitarian churches in Wales were located along the rivers of the Teifi and Aeron.[24] The majority of the rest were to be found in Glamorganshire, with one, Cefncoedcymer, located in Breconshire.[25] In a letter in 1908, a local minister, the Rev. Arthur Thomas, wrote that the Cardiganshire churches are 'somewhat stationary'.[26] He stated that depopulation had greatly affected the causes, but added furthermore that the churches were actually 'holding their own'.[27] In neighbouring Carmarthenshire, the Unitarian cause was not as strong in comparison with Cardiganshire. Despite the first Unitarian cause being established in Carmarthenshire by Tomos Glyn Cothi in 1792,[28] Unitarianism was never as popular in the county in comparison with Cardiganshire.[29] Tomos Glyn Cothi is regarded as a leading figure in the Welsh Unitarian cause. He made a large contribution to the cause by translating the work of the English pioneers of Unitarian thought, Theophilus Lindsey and Joseph Priestley, into the Welsh language. This gave the Welsh the chance to read for themselves the theology of the key English Unitarian authors.

The establishment of Cwm Cothi Church was obviously an important development to the cause, with other churches being established in Cardiganshire and Carmarthenshire in the early years of the nineteenth century. An Unitarian cause followed in Onnenfawr at the turn of the nineteenth century under the ministry of John Griffiths. The congregation was evicted from the church in 1838, and despite building a new church for the cause, the church closed in 1886. Cwmwrdu church in Brechfa was built on the land of the Rev. William Rees on his own expense in 1832. By this time the cause at Cwm Cothi had deteriorated because of depopulation and emigration. The Unitarian cause of Cwmwrdu also failed in the second half of the nineteenth century, with many blaming its remote location. On the edge of Carmarthenshire in the village of Drefach, Penrhiw church was established in 1777 and in its early years relied on the Arminian ministers of Llwynrhydowen.[30] This reliance continued with Unitarian ministers of the various churches of the Black Spot contributing to maintaining the cause at Penrhiw. But the cause closed before the end of the nineteenth century. Penrhiw was moved and the chapel building reconstructed at the National Folk Museum of Wales in Cardiff.

The Graig church in St Clears was established in 1827, but closed at the turn of the twentieth century. This was another example of an Unitarian church failing to maintain its cause. Rhydypark church, near St Clears, was originally established as an Arminian cause in 1788, but moved towards Unitarian theology early in the nineteenth century. Once again, as with many other Unitarian churches, Rhydypark failed to outlast the nineteenth century. There was also an anti-trinitarian cause in the town of Carmarthen itself. Park-y-Velvet church was under the leadership of the tutors of the Carmarthen Presbyterian College. The theology of the church depended upon the tutor in charge and it fluctuated between Trinitarian and anti-trinitarian thought. There was also a mixed cause of Trinitarians and anti-trinitarians in Priory Street Chapel in the early nineteenth century following the visit of the missionary James Lyons to the town in 1811.[31]

One of the key establishments that helped Unitarianism progress was Carmarthen Presbyterian College, which was situated conveniently close to the Black Spot. A. G. Prys-Jones agrees that the college was an important factor in ensuring that students from west Wales were able to receive higher education in the area until the introduction of secondary schools and universities at the end of the nineteenth century.[32] Dewi Eirug Davies notes that the Carmarthen College was well known for its liberalism, particularly under the leadership of Thomas Perrot.[33] This, in turn, attracted a variety of students from different denominations because of the freedom given each individual to work out their theological position for themselves.[34] The majority of students attending the college from the second half of the eighteenth century to the twentieth century belonged to either the Congregationalists or Unitarians.[35] The college contributed to the success of Unitarianism in Wales, particularly in Cardiganshire.

It is difficult to judge if the Unitarian cause would have been as powerful in the Black Spot without the close proximity of the college in Carmarthen. It has been described as 'one of those pioneering institutions of advanced education which provided some opportunity for those of humbler means in Wales'.[36] H. P. Roberts believed it made a key contribution to providing education for generation after generation.[37] The location of the college was convenient for the Black Spot to be able to retain local students as well as attract students from different areas of Wales to stay on and support the cause after graduation. Carmarthen Presbyterian College was influential and a number of students who attended from Congregationalist backgrounds turned to Unitarian theology whilst studying there.[38]

Outside the Black Spot, the fortunes of the Unitarian cause were very different. Causes and churches were established, but many of them proved difficult to maintain in the long term, some even failing to outlast the nineteenth century. The Unitarian churches beyond west Wales were established in the towns and cities of south Wales. Most of these churches were the result of urbanization with supporters of the Unitarian cause often residing in some of the industrial areas of south Wales, including Merthyr Tydfil and Aberdare, while the Unitarian causes in Cardiganshire and Carmarthenshire were affected after the migration of members to these industrial centres. But this helped to establish Unitarian causes in south Wales, as Unitarians from all over the country came together and established new places of worship. Causes were established in Pontypridd, Aberdare, Cardiff, Swansea, Merthyr Tydfil and Bridgend. But many of the Unitarian causes were short-lived and disappeared in the late-nineteenth and early twentieth centuries. Unitarian causes in Aberdare remain to this day with Highland Place and Cefn Coed Cymer still open, but Cwmbach chapel, on the outskirts of the town, closed in 1935. The Aberdare causes were linked with the Unitarian church in Cardiff, especially when in 1971 J. Eric Jones took over responsibility for their pastoral care. There is a Unitarian cause on High Street in Swansea and a small rural congregation in the village of Nottage, near Porthcawl.

Unitarianism failed to gain much support in north Wales despite attempts by missionaries sent to stimulate anti-trinitarian ideas in the region. In 1893 an official Unitarian missionary, Dr William Griffiths, was sent to north Wales with the purpose of igniting support for their cause, but on his travels there was very little support for either him or his message. In Caernarfon he spoke to an audience who did not agree with his theology. He then travelled to Pwllheli and Ffestiniog where he was refused any opportunity to propagate his Unitarian beliefs. Griffiths was allowed to speak at a meeting in Llanberis and was also heard by 350 people at Talysarn, but the mission to north Wales proved largely unfruitful.

The nineteenth century was evidently a golden age of publishing in Wales, and denominational periodicals were among the most commonly printed items.[39] The Unitarians followed the other Welsh nonconformist denominations by publishing hymn books which contributed to giving the movement a measure of identity. In 1812 Iolo Morganwg publishing his first volume of hymns, *Salmau'r Egwlys yn yr Anialwch* (The Churches' Psalms in the Wilderness), another volume was published posthumously by his son, Taliesin, in 1834, and both volumes were published in a combined edition of 423 hymns in 1857.[40] By 1896, the Unitarians had published the first volume of the *Perlau Moliant* (Pearls of Praise), which to this day is their official hymn book. The first volume was very popular and it was re-published in 1918. The *Perlau Moliant* was amended in 1924 and again in 1929. The latest edition, still in active use today, appeared in 1997. During this time the Unitarians also established their own periodical called *Yr Ymofynydd* (The Inquirer), the first issue of which appeared in 1847. The Unitarians thought that they had to establish and finance their own periodical because of their different and radical views.[41] This proved to be a highly effective way of spreading their theology and ideas throughout Wales, as well as giving the movement better organisation. The *Ymofynydd* is still being published today, making it one of the oldest religious periodicals in Wales.

By the start of the twentieth century the Unitarians embarked on a new way of spreading their ideas by means of what they called the Van Missions. From 1906 the movement would send one or two missionaries around the country for months at a time to hold meeting in various towns and villages to discuss Unitarian thought. There would be a meeting in the morning for children with adults attending another one later in the day. It was an attempt to introduce the ideas of the Unitarians to a wider community, while also attempting to avoid the worst extremes of conversionist rhetoric.[42] John Roberts wrote

> The Unitarian Van Mission is one of the best things we have attempted. Too long have we waited for people to come to us. They couldn't do it. Afraid of doing anything ecclesiastically '*infradig*' we have hidden our light under a corn measure. We have at last discovered, however, that 'boldness has genius, power, and magic in it', that men who have been in the habit of speaking to a mere handful of unresponsive but dignified hearers are able to draw congregations numbering several hundreds.[43]

But the Van Mission was restricted to south Wales travelling only to Newport, Aberdare, Rhondda and the Merthyr valleys. Even with this new form of missionary work, Unitarianism could not establish any new causes as a consequence of the initiatives of the Van Missions.

It could be said that the Unitarians were actually more interested in maintaining the established causes already in existence, rather than trying to set up new ones by this time. Anti-trinitarians endured substantial criticism from other denominations which must have had an effect on the morale of the movement. The Unitarians were always having to defend their beliefs and were worried that they could lose support. This resulted in an emphasis on defending and reinforcing their existing causes. That could be deemed one of the reasons for the local success of Unitarianism in the Black Spot. When you consider the Welsh Unitarian movement in its entirety, it is a different situation entirely. Unitarianism in Wales cannot be considered to be a very powerful or influential movement, especially in comparison with the other Christian denominations in Wales. Unitarianism proved unable to compete with the strength of the Calvinistic and Wesleyan Methodists, as well as the Congregationalists and Baptists. Yet Unitarianism made a vital contribution in the counties of Cardiganshire and Carmarthenshire. While it is not possible to compare the religious pattern of the Black Spot with any other area in Wales, no other denomination was able to have such influence on a particular locality as the Unitarians enjoyed in this corner of west Wales. The Unitarians have managed to survive to the present day, and they continue to meet the spiritual needs of the communities which they serve. Despite the criticism and opposition they have faced over the years because of their very different theological views, this did not prevent the movement from developing, and even dominating in a unique area of Wales.

Notes

1. Alan Everitt, *The Pattern of Rural Dissent: The Nineteenth Century* (Leicester, 1972), p. 16.
2. *Yr Ymofynydd* (1913–15), p. 474.
3. A condition of the Blasphemy Act made it illegal to deny the Holy Trinity.
4. The Doctrine of the Trinity Act amended the Blasphemy Act which allowed Unitarians to worship freely.
5. Michael Watts, *The Dissenters: From the Reformation to the French Revolution* (Oxford, 1978), p. 327.
6. Jenkins was described by T. Oswald Williams as 'the father of Arminianism in Wales' in his *Undodiaeth a Rhyddid Meddwl* (Llandysul, 1962), p. 116.
7. For more information, see Aubrey J. Martin, *Hanes Llwynrhydowen* (Llandysul, 1977).
8. Unitarian minister (1834–1879). For more information see Nansi Martin, *Gwilym Marles* (Llandysul, 1979).
9. See T. Oswald Williams, *Hanes Cynulleidfaoedd Undodaidd Sir Aberteifi* (Llandysul, 1930), p. 12.
10. Minister and schoolmaster of Castell Hywel (1766–1829). For more information, see D. Elwyn Davies, *Cewri'r Ffydd* (Llandysul, 1999).
11. E. G. Bowen, 'The Teifi Valley as a Religious Frontier', *Ceredigion*, VII (1972), 10.
12. Goronwy Evans (gol.), *Fflam Ddwy Ganrif: Daucanmlwyddiant Capel y Groes* (Llandysul, 2002).
13. D. Elwyn Davies, *They Thought For Themselves* (Llandysul, 1982), p. 48.
14. Edward Williams, *Rheolau a Threfniadau Cymdeithas Dwyfundodiaid yn Neheubarth Cymru* (London, 1803), pp. 6–9.
15. Davies, *They Thought For Themsleves*, pp. 147–7.
16. Quoted in D. Elwyn Davies, *Y Smotiau Duon* (Llandysul, 1980), p. 134.
17. Ibid.
18. For more information, see D. Elwyn Davies, *Y Graig Llandysul* (Llandysul, 1984).

19. For more information, see D. Elwyn Davies, *Capel y Bryn 1882–1982* (Aberaeron, 1982).

20. David Williams, 'The Census of Religious Worship of 1851 in Cardiganshire', *Cylchgrawn Cymdeithas Hynafiaethwyr Sir Aberteifi*, IV (1960–3), 123. See also, John Williams, *Digest of Welsh Historical Statistics* (2 vols. Cardiff, 1985), II, pp. 352–3.

21. Ibid.

22. Ibid, p. 123.

23. For more information, see, D. J. Goronwy Evans, *Hanes Eglwys Undodaidd Brondeifi, Llanbedr Pont Steffan, 1874–1974* (Llandysul, 1974).

24. D. Densil Morgan, *The Span of the Cross: Christian Religion and Society in Wales, 1914–2000* (Cardiff, 1999), p. 11.

25. Ibid.

26. National Library of Wales, MS. FR9/1. The Rev. Arthur Thomas to R. J. Jones, 1 March 1908.

27. Ibid.

28. For more information, see Geraint Dyfnallt Owen, *Tomos Glyn Cothi* (Swansea, 1967).

29. Davies, *They Thought For Themselves*, p. 105.

30. For more information, see D. J. Goronwy Evans, *Penrhiw* (Llandysul, 1977).

31. Davies, *They Thought For Themselves*, p. 116.

32. A. G. Prys-Jones, *The Story of Carmarthenshire* (2 vols. Llandybie, 1959–1972), II (1972), p. 285.

33. Thomas Perrot became head of the Carmarthen Presbyterian College in 1719.

34. Dewi Eirug Davies, *Hoff Ddysgedig Nyth* (Swansea, 1976), p. 41.

35. Davies, *They Thought For Themselves*, p. 155.

36. G. E. Jones and G. W. Roderick, *A History of Education in Wales* (Cardiff, 2003), p. 42.

37. H. P. Roberts, 'The History of the Presbyterian Academy Brynllywarch-Carmarthen. Part 2', *Transactions of the Unitarian Historical Society*, 5, 1 (1931), 34.

38. Ibid.

39. For details see Huw Walters, *Y Wasg Gyfnodol Gymreig 1735–1900* (Aberystwyth, 1987), p. 4.

40. Dafydd Evans, *Y Perlau Moliant* (Llandysul, 1929), p. 5.

41. D. Elwyn Davies, 'Education and Radical Dissent in Wales in the Eighteenth and Nineteenth Centuries', *Transactions of the Unitarian Historical Society*, 19, 2 (1988), 192.

42. Davies, *Y Smotiau Duon*, p. 138.

43. John Roberts, 'The Van Mission', *Transactions of the Unitarian Historical Society*, 16, 4 (1978), 191.

CHAPTER 10

SALVATION ARMY

Jenty Fairbank

An eighteen-month Cornish revival campaign, during which an estimated 7,000 professed conversion, drew to a close in February 1863 when one-time Methodist New Connexion minister William Booth and his wife Catherine were invited to Cardiff by a group of nonconformists.[1] Foremost among these were well-known ship and colliery owners, John and Richard Cory, a Methodist and a Baptist respectively.[2] 'The Wesleyans, who are very revivalistic [sic] here, will not come and help us in a Baptist chapel!', wrote Catherine Booth from Cardiff, 'but we have reason to believe they will come to the circus'.[3] A wooden circus building, then, not only provided a neutral meeting place for denominational differences, but also proved to be an attraction for the non-church-going masses.[4] More than two years before the advent of the Christian Mission, forerunner of the Salvation Army, William and Catherine Booth had laid an important foundation for their future work in Wales. At the conclusion of the circus mission the Booths conducted services at Newport, Monmouthshire, before resting at Weston-super-Mare in the company of wealthy Cardiff contractor Jonathan Billups and his wife. Twenty years later this friendship would still stand, as the Booths' eldest son, Bramwell, used the Billups' home at Barry for meetings with his fiancée, Florence Soper.[5]

Eleven years after the Cardiff circus meetings, the *Christian Mission Magazine* disclosed 'very cheerful facts' regarding Booth's expanding national mission.[6] Having spread beyond its east London beginnings, its 265 preachers and exhorters were at work in nineteen mission stations in England. A year later the number of stations had risen to twenty-eight, one of which was in Cardiff. This had been a locally-run independent mission, which, at the end of 1874, had been taken over by the Christian Mission, with the aim of reaching working class people:

> The Gospel Hall ... is a good, substantial building, capable of containing ... four hundred people ... It is right to the front of one of the most crowded streets – indeed, in the best spot for our work in the whole town. It has recently been purchased ... by John Cory, Esq.[7]

John Allen was chosen to establish this new branch. When he first met the Christian Mission at an open-air service in Poplar, London, in 1868 he was described as a swearing, drinking, fighting navvy. Yet,

God laid hold of him and he was deeply convinced of sin ... After some two years of faithful labour in his leisure time for God, he was appointed an evangelist ... He went to Cardiff in November 1874, and was not merely enabled to form a large Mission Society, but was blessed to the salvation of sailors in great numbers.[8]

Intriguingly, it was as a result of accounts given by a group of sailors converted during the Booths' 1863 Cornish revival that the Cory brothers had invited the Booths to Cardiff.[9] It was not, however, a straightforward process for Allen to establish the Christian Mission in 1874. Passive resistance from those already associated with the Gospel Hall was immediately apparent. George Scott Railton noted that 'the Christians sat and looked on ... as if I had done them some wrong', and 'some of the Ministers are wondering what a navvy knows about Gospel truths'.[10]

Battling against ill-health brought on by overworking in Spartan conditions, Allen's soul-saving work nevertheless began slowly to prosper.[11] A local paper referred to these developments:

His powerful voice is often heard in the most crowded parts of Cardiff, at street corners, and in some of the most degraded and neglected bye-ways of the town; and though often interrupted, mocked, jeered at, and occasionally insulted, nothing daunts the spirit or quenches the zeal of this soldier of the Cross. Mr Allen is doing a good work in Cardiff, and Christians of every denomination may do well to take a leaf out of his book.[12]

Not only were indoor congregations so great that it was necessary for Allen to seek out larger premises, but his open-air meetings were attracting crowds of up to 1,500.[13] On Sunday evenings, the Cory brothers placed at his disposal the Stuart Hall, a music hall accommodating 2,000 people that would in 1881 become the permanent home of the Salvation Army's Cardiff One Corps. The Hall quickly earned the nickname 'Cory's Coffin' because of its shape.[14] Allen also borrowed a smaller hall in Canton for a few years.[15] By October 1875 the crowds gathered at his open-air meetings were so large that Allen was summoned, convicted, and fined for obstructing the thoroughfare. Such was the publicity surrounding the case, greater crowds than ever turned out and a second summons was issued. Indignation among the townsfolk was at fever pitch. A public meeting was called and the Watch Committee and Superintendent of Police were vilified.[16] Allen died at Portsmouth in 1878, aged only 35 years old, leaving a wife, four children and sizeable congregations in many parts of the United Kingdom,[17] not least in Cardiff.

At Whitechapel, London, in August 1878 the Christian Mission had 'met in Congress to make War'.[18] The increasingly popular description of the Mission as a 'salvation army' in the battle against sin took hold on the collective imagination, and within weeks its members were donning uniforms and calling themselves soldiers. Mission stations became known as corps, evangelists were termed officers, and William Booth, the Mission's General Superintendent, became the Army's General. Within a month the number of field officers had risen from 88 to 102 and the number of corps from fifty to sixty,[19] seven of them in Wales. By August 1879, of the one hundred corps in Britain, thirteen were in Wales.[20] Even the Anglican Rector of Merthyr expressed his admiration for the mission work in the valleys conducted by Kate Watts and her successors. 'Look at those Mission Women, "Evangelists" as they call themselves, who have been working in this parish now for fifteen months or more,' he wrote in February 1879, 'they are doing a great work, for I call it a great work if one soul is saved, and my honest belief is they have saved many'. His praise, however, was not unadulterated, as he added that he believed that they were 'not orthodox' and they were 'peculiar in their ways'. Still, he could not deny that they had 'made drunkards sober ... infidels believers ... communicants at the holy table of men who neither believed in God nor anything else but beer'.[21] Kate Watts reported in the *Christian Mission* in August 1878 that she had the names of some 500 or 600 converts in the valleys, the majority of whom were native Welsh people.[22] The leadership in London soon realised that the specific 'Welsh' dimension was a problem that had to be faced. Their answer came in the shape of Mother Shepherd, described in a confidential document as a 'regular virago'.[23] Mother Shepherd had been cook and hall-keeper at the Whitechapel headquarters. Although she had been brought up in east London, she had been born in Wales and the Welsh language was her native tongue. She and her four daughters, then, set off to launch the fledgling Salvation Army on an unsuspecting Aberdare at the end of September 1878.[24] It was to have repercussions beyond their expectations.[25]

No sooner was soul-saving work underway in Aberdare than Kate, at seventeen the oldest Shepherd daughter, was sent to the Rhondda Valley. Within weeks the *Western Mail* reported that the upper part of the Rhondda was 'in a ferment in consequence of a remarkable religious revival', which was affecting people from a plethora of backgrounds. Attributing this revival specifically to the Spirit-filled enthusiasm and charisma of 'a young English lady, Miss Kate Shepherd', the paper described her influence as 'most extraordinary' and even went as far as to compare the situation to 'the great revivals'.[26] While Kate was spearheading revival in the Rhondda, back at Aberdare her mother's work grew apace. Among her many converts was a young Jonah Evans. In December 1879 the front page of the first edition of the *War Cry* carried a command from General Booth to 'SEIZE NORTH WALES!', authorising George Scott Railton 'to raise a special force for the salvation of Wales, to be called "The Mountaineers" ... to commence by seizing the counties of Flint and Denbigh as soon as possible'.[27] A month later, in January 1880, the *War Cry* noted Railton's response. He claimed he could already boast twenty volunteers, and was hoping for a further '200 names from which to select sufficient to sweep the Principality'. The newspaper appealed for 'translations of our songs into Welsh, or Welsh songs of some sort with literal English version, so that officers may know exactly what each verse says'. It also reported, however, that the date of 'invasion' would be deferred until further arrangements were made for relieving Railton of other duties.[28] Within days it materialised that Railton's other duties were to consist in leading the Salvation Army's imminent invasion of the United States.

On 23 October 1881, Captain Munns and her lieutenant set about fulfilling General Booth's command to 'Seize North Wales' by 'opening fire' on Wrexham.

Within two months, 300 were regularly attending meetings in what the terminology of the day called the 'barracks', which, in turn, quickly became known as the 'Glory Shop'.[29] Five years later on 5 September 1886, Caernarfon solicitor John B. Allanson, who had been converted at the Army's Regent Hall in London's Oxford Street, was instrumental in establishing the Welsh-speaking Salvation Army in his hometown. Pioneer officers Major and Mrs Jonah Evans appealed for more Welsh-speaking officers,[30] and within months the work had spread to Ffestiniog, Llanberis, Llanwrst, Nantlle, Deiniolen, Porthmadog and beyond. By March 1887, *Y Gad Lef* (The War Cry) was circulating 10,500 copies and a Welsh Salvation Army Song Book had been published. Three months later, General Booth was welcomed by 300 soldiers of *Byddin Yr Iachawdwriaeth* (The Salvation Army) with banners flying, but no brass band. Allanson reported in the *War Cry* on 9 July 1887 that 'the people thoroughly understand vocal music and sing far too well and too heartily for anyone to care to spoil the melody of good singing by indifferent instrumental music'.[31] Less than a year later he was spearheading the Army's 'invasion' of Holyhead.[32] By November 1905 the Army's (unpublished) Corps Index of the British Isles showed that of the 5,023 soldiers and recruits belonging to eighty-one corps (evangelical centres) in Wales, 312 of them belonged to eleven Welsh-language corps. Penrhyndeudraeth, the last of these centres to be established, survived into the late-1950s,[33] having been led for forty of those years by the redoubtable Envoy Mrs Bessie Davies.[34]

The missionary work of the Salvationists, therefore, proved to be very successful, but was borne out of hard graft. Indeed, as far back as 1869 William Booth realised 'no one gets a blessing if they have cold feet, and nobody ever got saved while they had the toothache'.[35] Even in its Christian Mission beginnings, the Salvation Army ministered to the bodies as well as the souls of those it sought to save. In Wales it was no different. In 1875, a 'fallen girl' attended an open-air meeting in Cardiff and was helped to find refuge.[36] Eleven years later in November 1886, the *War Cry* appealed for funds to enlarge the Cardiff Rescue Home, and on 23 April 1887 it revealed Mother Shepherd as its Matron.[37] By the 1890s a 'salvation lodging house', police court work and a servants' registry office were all active in the city.[38] Since then there have been hostels for men and women, homes for children and for unmarried mothers, and over many years hundreds of boys sent from the courts to the Army's 'House o' the Trees', near Penycraig, Glamorgan, have emerged at the end of their training as responsible and law-abiding citizens.

The philanthropic attitude is certainly one of the major characteristics of the Salvation Army. Indeed, the slogan, 'Where there's need, there's the Salvation Army' has been well illustrated in Wales. On Tuesday, 14 October 1913, 900 men went to work at the Universal Colliery, Senghenydd. An ominous roar made the village tremble, dense smoke rose from the pit shaft, and more than 400 men were dead, entombed in the galleries of the blazing mine in what was described at the time as the greatest coal mining disaster Britain had ever known. The ranks of the Salvation Army itself were thinned by the tragedy as ten of its local bandsmen having lost their lives. Day-after-day Salvation Army officers undertook mortuary duty, conducted funerals, prayed with, cleaned and cooked meals for families of mothers too stunned by sorrow to cope.[39] Throughout Britain, Salvationists rallied to show their sympathy in a practical way, contributing £1,659. 7s. 8d. – the largest donation made to the Lord Mayor of Cardiff's relief fund.[40]

During the worse years of the inter-war depression, however, the Salvation Army's work throughout Wales suffered as many Salvationists relocated to other parts of Britain in search of work. Nevertheless, Army worship halls throughout the poverty-stricken valleys were turned into centres for the relief of unemployed men and their families. 'Farthing breakfasts' of bread, jam and cocoa were served, and nourishing soup for the mid-day meal could be had for a penny a jug. If the people were poor, so were the Salvationists, but they identified themselves with local need without stopping to count the cost.[41] In October 1966, the Salvation Army was again on-hand to offer support to the victims of another Welsh coal-mining community disaster. In the *Scotsman* later that month, John Rafferty wrote: 'I have made my last joke about the Salvation Army.' He acknowledged how they had been ridiculed in the past, but was aware that at Aberfan,

> They showed their worth, they, with the Red Cross, were the organisations with the apparatus, the techniques, the expertise, and the long-prepared systems of working, who knew exactly how to harness the willingness of the rescue workers, and how to supply them and the rescued with food, clothing and accommodation … Nobody knows for sure who were the first welfare organisation into Aberfan but, if there is any betting, newspaper men who cover disasters will have a few bob on the Salvation Army. When there is a disaster they are always there, whether it be at a pithead, a train smash or a fire, and nobody who works is ever short of a cup of tea or a sandwich. [42]

By the time of the disaster, just over a hundred years after William and Catherine Booths' Cardiff circus mission, the Salvation Army was operating seventy-seven evangelical centres in Wales (six of them in the north), three community centres and five social service centres – not to mention a significant number of Welsh-language Salvationists who were active in Patagonia. Those sailor converts, bearing news to the Cory brothers of the 1862–3 Cornish revival, could scarcely have foreseen the far-reaching outcome of their witness.

Notes

1. F. de L. Booth-Tucker, *The Life of Catherine Booth: The Mother of the Salvation Army* (2 vols. London, 1893), II, p. 70.
2. Cf. Bramwell Booth, *Echoes and Memories* (London, 1925), p. 37; Booth-Tucker, *Life of Catherine Booth*, II, p. 79.
3. Undated letter of Catherine Booth to her parents, quoted in Catherine Bramwell-Booth, *Catherine Booth: The Story of Her Loves* (London, 1970), p. 218. Specific directions with regards hiring buildings were provided in *Orders and Regulations for The Salvation Army* (undated, but issued c.1880). For example, 'Your main object will naturally be the largest buildings – Theatres, Music Halls, Circuses, Town Halls, Mechanics' Institutes, Temperance and Lecture Halls, used and fitted for meetings. But any large warehouse, storeroom, Rink or other building standing empty, or which could be fitted up and used for meetings, should be examined as well.'

4. W. T. Stead, *General Booth. A Biographical Sketch* (London, 1891), p. 57.
5. Soper was the daughter of a doctor in Blaina; cf. Bramwell-Booth, *Life of Catherine* Booth, p. 221.
6. *Christian Mission Magazine* (hereafter *CMM*), 31 March 1874.
7. Ibid., December 1874.
8. Ibid., December 1878, 309.
9. Bramwell-Booth, *Life of Catherine Booth*, p. 217.
10. George Scott Railton, *The Salvation Navvy* (London, 1881), pp. 90–1.
11. Allen had stated that, 'The doctor tells me I am very weak; my heart is in a very bad state and I am likely to fall down dead while speaking.' Ibid., p. 93.
12. Cited in ibid., p. 99.
13. Ibid., p. 105.
14. Keith Griffin, *Forth in Thy Name. A History of the Cardiff Canton Corps of the Salvation Army 1879–1979* (Cardiff, 1979), p. 2.
15. Railton, *Salvation Navvy*, p. 100.
16. Ibid., p. 109.
17. *CMM*, December 1878, 309.
18. Ibid., September 1878.
19. Ibid., October 1878, 253.
20. Ibid., August 1879, 199.
21. Ibid., February 1879, 34.
22. Cf. ibid., August 1878.
23. Salvation Army's International Heritage Centre, London. Unpublished MS. 'Disposition of Forces, 1883/4'.
24. Robert Sandall, *The History of the Salvation Army* (8 vols. London, 1947–2000), II (1950), p. 12.
25. *CMM*, October 1878, 256.
26. *Western Mail*, 4 March 1879.
27. *War Cry*, 27 December 1879.
28. Ibid., 24 January 1880.
29. *Wrexham Corps Centenary Brochure* (1981).
30. *War Cry*, 18 September 1886, 5.
31. Ibid., 9 July 1887.
32. This information is extracted from the *Caernarfon and Denbigh Herald*'s coverage for the 90th anniversary. See *Caernarfon and Denbigh Herald*, 8 January 1982.
33. Ibid., 11 April 1986.
34. *War Cry*, 26 September 1942.
35. Sandall, *History of the Salvation Army*, I (1947), p. 139.
36. Railton, *Salvation Navvy*, p. 96.
37. *War Cry*, 6 November 1886, 23 April 1887.
38. Jenty Fairbank, *Booth's Boots: The Beginnings of Salvation Army Social Work* (London, 1983), pp. 81, 90, 102.
39. *War Cry*, 25 October 1913.
40. Ibid., 22 November 1913.
41. *The Salvation Army Year Book*, 1974.
42. *Scotsman*, 29 October 1966.

CHAPTER 11

PENTECOSTALISM

David Ceri Jones

No account of the religious life of Wales from 1700 to the present day can afford to overlook the existence of perhaps the most recent religious group to feature in this entire work, Pentecostalism. The statistics relating to the rise and advance of Pentecostalism since the revival at Azusa Street, Los Angeles, in 1906 are remarkable. According to David Barratt, in 1997 Pentecostal and charismatic Christians numbered over 497 million worldwide, constituting an estimated twenty-seven per cent of the worldwide Christian population.[1] Events in Wales in the early years of the twentieth century were an important catalyst to the foundation of the Pentecostal movement, and Welshmen made important contributions to the beginnings of at least two of the Pentecostal denominations that were established in the British Isles in the immediate aftermath of the 1904–5 Welsh revival.

Like most labels, the term 'Pentecostal' can be misleading since it is usually used to apply to a wide array of, what appear on the surface to be, apparently very different religious groups. The incredible growth of Pentecostal churches in large swathes of South America, Africa and South-East Asia, not to mention the patchwork of Pentecostal denominations in North America also, all reflect, to a greater or lesser extent, the indigenous cultures in which they are situated. In these diverse areas, Pentecostalism has proved to be hugely dynamic and able to accommodate itself to widely different cultural contexts. It could therefore be argued, with some justification, that the movement has been informed more by local and individual responses to highly emotional religious experience than by a coherent and universally agreed set of core theological ideas. However, this functional interpretation does not do justice to the distinctiveness of the movement.

Walter J. Hollenweger, the foremost historian of Pentecostalism, has written that the movement should be viewed as an expression of oral and narrative spirituality,[2] while Harvey Cox regards it as a resurgence of 'primal spirituality, the fulfilment of the human longing for a direct experience of God, rather than being rooted in abstract religious ideas'.[3] Both interpretations capture at least something of the essence of the movement. However, like most evangelical groups around the world, Pentecostals take a very conservative stance on almost all doctrinal matters, but according to David Martin, 'the heart of its distinctive appeal lies in empowerment through spiritual gifts offered to all' rather than in its traditional biblicist theology.[4] Today, as Allan Anderson has recently demonstrated, this vibrant, kaleidoscopic body of charismatic and Pentecostal Christians is the fourth largest variety of worldwide Christianity after Orthodoxy, Catholicism, and Protestantism.[5]

The emergence of Pentecostalism was the result of the confluence of a number of tributaries. These included the many Wesleyan Holiness groups which proliferated in parts of America in the wake of the 1859 revival; the highly influential Keswick Convention, first held in the Lake District town in 1875; and elements of highly emotive premillenial dispensationalism. This was popular among Fundamentalists in the United States and given particular prominence in Britain during the latter half of the nineteenth century by the Plymouth Brethren and the activities of visionary individuals in the United States who possessed an indomitable assurance following their experience of what they called the 'baptism of the Spirit'. These influences all converged in the early years of the twentieth century to create the favourable conditions for the 'fire from heaven' to fall.[6] Most accounts of the beginnings of Pentecostalism pay considerable attention to one or other of these elements, but few accord the Welsh Revival of 1904–5 the prominence it undoubtedly deserves. As significant as each of these elements were, Frank Bartleman, one of the first Pentecostal historians, was quick to admit that the Azusa Street revival of 1906 had been 'rocked in the cradle of little Wales'.[7]

Following the saturation coverage given to the career of Evan Roberts (1878–1951) in the *Western Mail*, and the critique of the revival that appeared from the pen of the Dowlais Congregational minister Peter Price, interpretations of the 1904–5 awakening have tended to regard it as little more than the 'Evan Roberts Revival'. Such an interpretation masks both the complexity and scope of the revival and the extent to which it was carried on in some localities without the direct input of Roberts. It is, therefore, better to regard the revival as the culmination of a remarkable period of evangelistic activity, which began at the end of the nineteenth century in some of the rapidly growing urban centres of south Wales. John Pugh's (1846–1907) 'Forward Movement', which he established within the Calvinist Methodist Church in 1872, proved remarkably adept at reaching the unchurched in parts of industrial south Wales during the late-1880s and the 1890s.[8] Pugh's pioneering work was later taken-up by two remarkable brothers, Seth (1858–1925) and Frank Joshua (1861–1920), and it was at meetings at Blaenannerch, Cardiganshire, led by Seth Joshua at the end of September 1904, that Roberts had his experience of personal surrender. This 'bending to the Spirit', as he preferred to call it, was accompanied by a vision in which Roberts was assured that 100,000 Welsh souls were soon to be won for Christ.[9]

The revival did not, however, just grow out of Roberts' Blaenannerch experiences. The spirituality of the Keswick convention, with its emphasis on entire sanctification obtainable through the experience of the baptism of the Spirit, had been remarkably popular in Wales, and the establishment of Wales's own Keswick Convention at Llandrindod Wells in 1903 led many to hope that a more widespread religious awakening might be imminent.[10] Among those who benefited from the Convention was R. B. Jones (1869–1933), the Baptist minister at Porth, Rhondda, who went on to play a prominent supplementary role in the revival, and whose fundamentalism set him apart from many of the excesses of those closely associated with the Evan Roberts circle.[11] There was also evidence of a small awakening at the Calvinistic Methodist chapel at Newquay, Cardiganshire, and it was not until the influential Methodist patriarch, Evan Phillips (1829–1912), at nearby Newcastle Emlyn, confirmed Roberts's commission that he decided to return home to Loughor and began holding his own revival meetings at Moriah chapel.

It was not long after Roberts's first meeting at Moriah before news spread of the sensational phenomena that seemed to accompany him wherever he went. The 1904 revival was unlike many of the earlier religious revivals that had shaped Welsh nonconformity so decisively.[12] Roberts consistently downplayed the importance of preaching and appeared to have little respect for the traditional structures of the churches in which he worked. He rarely preached in the formal sense of the term, but travelled from place to place with his brother, Dan, and close friends Sidney Evans and Sam Jenkins. More controversially, he was usually accompanied by a small band of female helpers who were largely responsible for leading the singing at revival meetings, but they were also known to occasionally address meetings themselves. The message Roberts took with him on his travels was rudimentary and theologically crude, consisting of little more than four simple exhortations. He passionately urged his listeners to separate themselves from all sin, renounce all morally dubious behaviour, obey the immediate promptings of the Holy Spirit and publicly confess their faith in Christ.[13] However, it was the wildly enthusiastic displays of emotion that took place in Roberts's meetings that were most controversial. Public participation was normal and shouting out, crying, repetitious singing, the charismatic gifts of tongues and prophecy, as well as more disturbing psychic manifestations were commonplace.[14] The revival's relative lack of theology as well as the egalitarian and spontaneous nature of many of the experiences that lay at its core attracted many from among the working classes. The young and women were drawn to the revival in particularly large numbers at a time of profound social dislocation. The continued rapid industrialization of south Wales, the drift from the land and the decline of traditional industries all contributed to what Russell Davies, in reference to Carmarthenshire, has called a sense of 'rootlessness' among the rural population of west Wales.[15] It was amongst many of these socially, economically and politically disenfranchised individuals that the exciting pieties of the revival seemed to be most attractive.

By mid-November invitations from all over Wales flooded into Loughor and Roberts embarked on his first itinerary, which saw him conduct revival meetings throughout eastern Glamorgan for much of the following month.[16] From there he moved further west conducting meetings in Swansea, Neath, and Merthyr Tydfil. But it was during February 1905 that the revival seemed to reach its peak as Roberts traversed the Ogwr, Neath, and Afan valleys. His famous six days of silence during this trip indicates the extent to which Roberts was suffering from almost complete physical and mental exhaustion by this time.[17] Nonetheless he re-emerged from his silence and travelled to Liverpool where he conducted meetings among the expatriate Welsh community for two weeks from the end of March until the beginning of

April. The meetings witnessed some of the most bizarre manifestations of the whole revival, and were the occasion for considerable conflict with some of the ministers from the local community.[18] Roberts's subsequent tour of parts of north Wales was much more sedate by comparison. By this time, much of the initial enthusiasm of the revival had abated and Roberts's later itineraries in both north and south Wales lacked the same emotional intensity of those just a few months earlier. By the end of 1905 the revival appeared to be largely over. Roberts tried to keep going into 1906, but his final itinerary in Caernarfonshire during January clearly proved that the revival was a spent force. In its aftermath, a dejected Evan Roberts retreated from public life, emotionally, physically, and spiritually exhausted, and spent much of the following twenty years at the home of Jessie Penn Lewis (1861–1927) and her husband in Leicester.[19] Here, with Penn-Lewis's guidance, he wrote *War on the Saints* (1912) in which he offered his considered reflections on the revival and included his famous repudiation of many of its excesses.[20]

News of the Welsh revival raised the spiritual temperature of many radical Protestant groups around the world who had been praying and looking for something similar. However, it would be a mistake to assume that the Welsh revival automatically gave rise to Pentecostalism. In Wales, as in Britain more generally, it was among those individuals who had been caught-up in the revival that Pentecostalism emerged, possibly in response to the frustration that many of them felt as they returned to the more mundane routines of everyday church life. Perhaps one of the most important visitors to Wales in 1905, particularly in the light of later developments, had been Alexander Boddy (1854–1930), the Anglican vicar of Sunderland. Boddy had an almost insatiable appetite for out-of-the-ordinary religious phenomena, and his visits to Wales, and to Norway to meet T. B. Barratt (1862–1930), a pastor in the Methodist Episcopal Church who had led a revival in Oslo,[21] led him to organise a convention for those interested in furthering spiritual renewal along the lines of what had occurred in Wales. The Sunderland Convention ran from 1908 until 1914 and its supporters were kept regularly informed of Pentecostal developments around the world by the publication of a magazine that Boddy characteristically entitled *Confidence*.[22] For a short time, the magazine gave a measure of coherence to British Pentecostalism and many of its early supporters were to be instrumental in the establishment of Pentecostal churches and denominations. However, with its foundation the focus of Pentecostal activity had largely shifted to the United States, as a revival had begun at the instigation of the African American preacher and son of freed slaves, William J. Seymour (1870–1922) at Azusa Street, Los Angeles, during April 1906. Seymour had been a student at Charles Fox Parham's (1873–1929) Bethel Bible College at Topeka, Kansas, where he had witnessed Agnes Ozman (1870–1937) speak in tongues after Parham had laid hands on her during January 1901. In the wake of this development, Parham and his students had established Apostolic Faith churches in various parts of the United States, and it was to one of these congregations that Seymour was invited to hold the meetings that led to the outbreak of the revival at Azusa Street. Seymour led a fully inter-racial leadership team, and for three years Azusa Street became the powerhouse of Pentecostalism. A number of affiliated Pentecostal churches were established in California, and thousands of visitors made the trip to Azusa Street, received the baptism of Spirit and returned to their homes determined to establish Pentecostal churches.[23] This revival, together with the highly publicised 'Korean Pentecost'[24] and the awakening at Pandita Ramabai's (1858–1922) Mukti mission at Poona in the Maharashtra region of West India,[25] which had been the focus of attention during the interval between the Welsh revival and events in California, proved to be the catalysts for the formation of new Pentecostal associations in many parts of the world.

The first British Pentecostal congregation was established in Bournemouth by William O. Hutchinson (1864–1928) in 1908 and, within three years, Hutchinson had also established the Apostolic Faith Church, Britain's first Pentecostal denomination.[26] The new group became a focus for many of those in Wales who had been affected by the 1904–5 revival, and had found it impossible to re-adjust to the regular life of their old denominations. Many of the 'children of the revival' began to abandon the churches in which they had spent most of their lives in favour of independent mission halls, many of which were committed to the sort of Pentecostal spirituality that characterised Hutchison's Apostolic Faith churches.[27] Hutchison tried to take advantage of this situation by planting his own churches in south Wales and it was to one of these congregations in Swansea, led by James Brooke,[28] that Daniel P. Williams (1882–1947) was drawn soon after his experience of baptism with the Spirit at Aberaeron in Cardiganshire during 1909.

Following his experience of the fullness of the Spirit, 'Pastor Dan', as he was affectionately known, began attending a mission hall at Pen-y-groes near Ammanford in Carmarthenshire. Predictably, it did not take long for controversy to disrupt the congregation and Williams soon left to establish a more radical congregation nearby. It was at this time that he also began attending Brooke's meetings in Swansea and he was persuaded to affiliate the Pen-y-groes mission to Hutchison's Apostolic Faith Church. In 1910, Hutchison formally ordained Williams and made him overseer of the Pen-y-groes assembly and, at the 1914 Apostolic Faith Convention, Williams was set-apart as an Apostle. Once again this arrangement did not last long. Tensions quickly escalated between the two bodies over issues relating to the oversight of the new 'denomination'. Consequently, in 1916 Daniel P. Williams severed his ties with Hutchison and formed his own independent Apostolic Church with its headquarters at Pen-y-groes. After a brief period of internal reorganisation, Williams settled the Apostolic Church's doctrinal position by drawing up eleven articles of faith and linked his group with three other similar groups in other parts of the British Isles. Andrew Turnbull's congregation in Glasgow became a member of the Apostolic Church in 1919, while Edgar Frank Hodges affiliated his congregation in Hereford with the Welsh and Scottish groups in 1920. In 1922, Williams linked his congregations with those that had been established by Herbert Victor Chanter in and around the Bradford area, and shortly afterwards the united Apostolic Church was finally formed.[29] During the same year, an important additional step was taken when the Apostolic Church Missionary Movement was set up. The headquarters was located at Bradford and D. P. Williams became its first President, commissioning its first missionary, who was sent to Argentina in 1922. The Apostolic Church has subsequently been involved in missionary activity in over fifty countries around the world.

The Apostolic Church grew steadily, and between 1922 and 1930 three new districts were added in the north of England, London, and Ireland. In 1933 these seven districts were reorganised and unified under a centralised administration at Pen-y-groes, although the headquarters of the missionary wing of the denomination remained at Bradford and financial oversight was devolved to Glasgow. Despite their somewhat anti-intellectual reputation, Pentecostals in Britain have been keen to establish their own educational facilities for the training of ministers and church leaders. Foremost among these institutions has been the grandly named Apostolic Church International Bible School, which was opened at Pen-y-groes in 1933. Its first principal was W. H. Lewis, a schoolteacher from Birchgrove near Swansea, and for the next forty years teaching posts in the school were filled by prominent Apostolic ministers, who, more often than not, had received no formal academic training. The school eventually closed in 1982 because numbers had rapidly declined, but it was reopened in 1990 with a new name, 'The Apostolic Church School of Ministry'. In 2000 there was a further re-organisation when the denomination's National Council decided to establish a school of ministry. This new school took over the site of the old Pen-y-groes college and offers long and short-term courses, some of which were, until recently, validated by Bangor University, to students who wished to study on a full and part-time basis. The majority of students at the school have tended to come from West Africa, particularly Nigeria which boasts the largest number of Apostolics in the world, and over sixty students graduated from the college at the end of the 2003–4 academic year.[30]

Following re-organisation in 1933, the Apostolic Church lost its radical edge and many felt that the new highly centralised structure actually drained the denomination of much of its vitality and energy. By 1939, the Apostolic Church could boast just forty-three paid ministerial staff in the British Isles and there seemed grave uncertainty about the long-term sustainability of the denomination.[31] Henry Llewelyn has outlined in considerable detail how the Church also lost impetus following the controversy over the teaching of the 'Latter-Rain Movement' which first emerged in Canada during the late-1940s.[32] A number of congregations seceded from the national Apostolic Church, particularly in and around Bradford, led by the influential Cecil Cousen (1908–64), and some of these were to play a prominent role in the emergence of the Charismatic Movement during the 1960s. Controversies of this nature and the secessions that invariably followed had a highly damaging impact on the morale of what was already a small and beleaguered denomination. The emergence of the Charismatic renewal led to further confusion and forced a reassessment of the Apostolic Church's position to a new interdenominational renewal movement that clearly resembled it in so many respects. In response, the Apostolic Church has been required to reorganise on a number of occasions. Though the Church has consistently reaffirmed its distinctive beliefs, its constitution has been simplified on a number of occasions, including as recently as 1985 and 1987, and the administrative offices of the denomination have now been centralised in Swansea.

For many Pentecostals today, the Apostolic Church is best known for its Convention held every August. The Pen-y-groes Annual Convention was first convened in 1917 and attracted over 1,000 delegates. By 1921, ever increasing numbers, including many from England, Scotland and Ireland, forced the Convention to hire more substantial premises and it was not long before the Convention developed a strong international focus, as Apostolic missionaries returned once a year to report on their progress. In 1933 a permanent Apostolic Temple was opened in Pen-y-groes and the Convention has continued to play a central role in the life of the denomination. More recently, a substantial growth in the number of people wishing to attend necessitated the Convention's move to the campus of Swansea University, for the first time in 2003. The move has proved to be a great success. Over 1,500 adults attended the 2003 Convention, and the programme diversified to provide activities for children and young people.[33] In the early years of the twenty-first century, the Apostolic Church nationwide remains relatively small, boasting just 5,312 members worshipping regularly in 110 congregations.[34] In Wales there are only thirty-nine Apostolic congregations listed on the denomination's website, the majority of which are small and aging, and concentrated almost exclusively in the south Wales valleys and parts of eastern Carmarthenshire.[35]

The second major British Pentecostal denomination, whose roots also lay in the 1904–5 revival, is the Elim Foursquare Gospel Alliance. George Jeffreys (1889–1962) and his brother, Stephen (1876–1943), were born at Nantyffyllon, near Maesteg. After their conversions during the Welsh Revival, George, always the more ambitious of the two, received his baptism with the Spirit and began speaking in tongues in 1911.[36] His desire to enter the ministry was accepted at an independent Apostolic Church at Maesteg in 1912 and he quickly enrolled at Thomas Myerscough's Bible School at Preston in Lancashire. The short duration of the course offered at the college was to George's liking and enabled him to devote a considerable proportion of his time to evangelistic work, linking up with his brother to hold evangelistic campaigns all over south Wales. It was one of these missions, at Cwm-twrch in the Swansea valley in 1913, which launched the Jeffreys brothers onto the national stage. On completion of his studies in 1915, George founded the Elim Evangelistic Band in County Monaghan, Ulster, and in 1916 the first Elim church was established in Belfast.[37] He subsequently embarked on an ambitious and rigorous itinerant preaching ministry throughout England, Wales and Ireland, holding mass evangelistic campaigns in some of the biggest auditoriums, including the Royal Albert Hall every Easter in the 1930s, during which he linked up with the controversial American Pentecostal preacher Aimee Semple McPherson (1890–1944).[38] In 1921, the first Elim church in England was established at Leigh-on-Sea, Essex, and by 1926 George Jeffreys's group seemed to have achieved a measure of credibility. Consequently, he decided to rename it the Elim Foursquare Gospel Alliance of the British Isles with its permanent headquarters located in London.

Following his establishment of Elim in 1916, George Jeffreys does not seem to have had too much further direct contact with Wales, although he did establish churches in Swansea and Cardiff in 1929. Despite building up the denomination in such a short space of time, relations within the new body were marred by disagreements and personality clashes. Stephen Jeffreys left to work with the Assemblies of God, while George severed his links with the denomination he had established in 1939 as a result of a schism over the best form of government to administer the growing number of Elim congregations. Jeffreys, true to his Welsh congregational roots, wanted to ensure that each congregation remained as autonomous as possible. However, in 1933 the first national conference of ministers met and in the following year a deed poll transferred control of the churches to an executive council consisting of nine ministers, three nominated by Jeffreys and four by the conference, thereby leaving Jeffreys without overall control of the denomination for the first time. Jeffreys subsequently resigned to found his own Bible Pattern Church Fellowship at Nottingham in 1940. Unfortunately, Elim's decision to revise its constitution and introduce a quasi-Presbyterian structure in 1942 was too little, too late for Jeffreys.[39]

During the middle years of the twentieth century the most influential figure among the Welsh Elim churches was Pastor P. S. Brewster. Brewster conducted a remarkably long and successful ministry at Cardiff's City Temple between 1939 and 1974, and from that base he was able to establish more than ten Elim congregations. Most of these congregations were in the south Wales valleys, but he was also responsible for founding a church at Aberystwyth in 1941 and another at Brecon in 1951. Despite remarkable initial success, Jeffreys' departure from Elim in the late-1930s marked the beginning of the most difficult period in the life of the denomination since its foundation. The Charismatic Movement forced Pentecostals to reassess their purpose and mission, and gave further impetus to those within Elim pressing for still more congregational autonomy. In the 1990s, there was further modernisation and considerable investment in the provision of graduate and post-graduate courses at the denomination's Regent Theological College at Nantwich in Cheshire. By 2000, Elim had undergone a period of further growth and could boast 76,200 members attending 635 congregations across the country, all of whom were under the oversight of the denominational headquarters at Cheltenham.[40] The picture in Wales is rather different. Elim has never made Wales a priority and has consequently never developed specifically Welsh structures to meet the different needs of the country. Today, there are just thirty-three Elim congregations in Wales, although some of them, including Cardiff's City Temple, are large, thriving, multi-cultural churches, meeting the needs of a population way beyond those who regularly attend their services.

Elim and the Apostolic Church are the only two Pentecostal groups whose origins have direct links with Wales. Latterly, the main Pentecostal denominations have been augmented by a vast array of Pentecostal and charismatic churches, some of which are parts of smaller denominational groups, others part of Pentecostal parachurch organisations. Of these groups, the largest and most influential is the Assemblies of God. Begun in the United States in 1914,[41] the group's origins in Britain were far more fluid. It seems that it had its origins in W. F. P. Burton's (1886–1971) attempt in the early 1920s to draw together many of the scattered independent Pentecostal assemblies which had proliferated in previous years. At a convention in Sheffield in 1923, Burton, Nelson Parr (1886–1976) and John Carter (1893–1981), recommended the formation of a Provisional Council to assist congregations scattered throughout the country. Parr, worried at rumours that the south Wales assemblies were considering affiliating to the American Assemblies of God, wanted to expand the remit of this body and organised a further meeting in Birmingham in February

1924. This was followed with another meeting in May 1925 to establish an administrative structure that would safeguard the autonomy of individual congregations, whilst at the same time providing a structure that would commit the assemblies to closer co-operation.[42] The British Assemblies of God was established, therefore, in 1924, and thirty-eight Welsh assemblies affiliated to the new body, making them the largest segment of the young movement.[43] The new body grew steadily. By 1929 there were 200 affiliated congregations throughout the British Isles, ten years later there were 350, and by the end of the 1950s there were well over 500.[44] In Wales, growth was slower as newly established churches gradually affiliated to the group once they were strong enough, such as the assembly in Newtown, Montgomeryshire. Founded as a result of the endeavours of some particularly far-sighted Assemblies of God evangelists in 1948, the congregation in Newtown joined the Assemblies in 1951 and has grown to become one of the more successful and vibrant assemblies in the whole of Wales, having renamed itself Hope Community Church in 2006.[45]

Unfortunately, this has not been true of the majority of Welsh Assemblies. Where the British Assemblies of God have experienced a number of periods of growth, particularly on the back of the Charismatic Movement in the late-1960s and 1970s, the Welsh assemblies have tended to stagnate. Their reputation in the larger movement has also been mixed. Although there was a tradition of thronged Easter meetings and conventions in some places, there has also tended to be a spirit of legalism and small-mindedness, characteristic of much of mid- and late-twentieth century evangelical nonconformity, that has marred their growth and effectiveness. The Assemblies of God website lists forty-seven assemblies in Wales, ten in the north and thirty-seven in the south,[46] making them just a fraction of the 646 assemblies and 54,000 members nationwide.[47]

Other Pentecostal groups are much more amorphous and therefore difficult to account for. There are many independent Pentecostal congregations which do not readily appear in church statistics. These tend not to be affiliated to any larger body, and were often formed as the result of splits from other Pentecostal churches. The large numbers of immigrants into Britain from the West Indies during the 1950s and 1960s also had an effect on the Pentecostal churches. Initially many churches were reluctant to incorporate immigrants into their congregations because of the perceived disruptiveness of their exuberant spirituality, and consequently this led to the growth of distinctive African Caribbean Pentecostal churches. The largest of these groups is now the New Testament Church of God, which has almost 100 congregations in England and is affiliated to the International Church of God, Cleveland, Tennessee, but it has no major presence in Wales.[48] The extent to which these churches have become part of mainstream British religious life is borne out by the fact that a minister from the New Testament Church of God, Joel Edwards, was the general director of the Evangelical Alliance until December 2008.[49]

The distinctiveness of many Pentecostal denominations has been compromised since the 1960s by the emergence of the Charismatic Movement. Allan Anderson has recently drawn attention to the ambiguity that exists between the terms 'Pentecostal' and 'charismatic'. 'Pentecostal' still appears to refer to many of the groups discussed in this chapter, but the term 'charismatic' is now taken to refer to all those churches, both within and outside of the traditional denominations, where the exercise of the gifts of the Spirit and the experience of the baptism of the Spirit are seen to be central. Although Pentecostals still maintain that the baptism of the Spirit is always accompanied by the gift of tongues, a position that most charismatics would not accept, in many other respects, what was once unique to Pentecostalism is now no longer exceptional. The overall result is that it has become almost impossible to distinguish between the two groups.[50]

The beginning of the Charismatic renewal has been traced to the Spirit baptism received by Dennis Bennett (1917–91), the Episcopalian rector of Van Nuys in Los Angeles during 1959. The storm of controversy that this created became the catalyst for the rapid spread of charismatic influences throughout the North American churches.[51] However, in Britain the renewal initially owed more to the influence of a number of leading Pentecostals, including the South African David du Plessis (1903–87)[52] and Donald Gee (1891–1966), the principal of the Assemblies of God college and editor of *Pentecost*, the highly visible magazine of the World Pentecostal Fellowship.[53] It found its most enthusiastic early supporters in the Church of England, particularly at All Souls Church in central London, where, despite the unenthusiastic approach of its rector, John Stott, Michael Harper who was his curate, worked to further renewal among sympathetic Anglican parishes. In 1963, the Anglican parish of St Mark's in Gillingham, Kent, became a model of what the renewal could achieve on a local level, but it was possibly Michael Harper's decision to found the Fountain Trust in the same year that had the most far-reaching consequences. Soon there was a network of influential charismatic clergymen and ministers throughout the country, some of whom like David Watson (1933–84), the rector of St Michael the Belfry in York, had remarkable international ministries. In Wales, the Charismatic Movement at first found it much more difficult to gain a foothold. The Anglican Renewal Ministries has had some success in drawing together members of the Church in Wales united by their charismatic experiences,[54] but others, most notably those within the evangelical and reformed constituency, gradually transferred their hostility away from the liberalism of the traditional denominations towards the much more threatening charismatics.

During the 1970s, the energies of the Charismatic renewal were channelled into the 'House Church Movement'.[55] Arising from the disillusionment that many charismatics felt with the structures of the traditional denominations, house churches, which were at first literally churches meeting in houses, were informal groupings of Christians intent on recapturing the spirit of the New Testament Church. Many of them adopted a 'Restorationist' concept of church government, wishing to restore the pattern of ministry outlined in Ephesians 4:11. It is difficult to account for the number of House Church congregations with any degree of accuracy. Some have been linked to larger quasi-denominational structures like Terry Virgo's New Frontiers churches or Roger Forster's Icthus churches,[56] but others are simply local associations drawing together groups of like-minded members. Many of them have attracted controversy because of their often authoritarian structures and the rigorous control which their leaders have tended to exert over many of their members. House churches, therefore, have a tendency to split and divide regularly, and this has prevented many of them from exerting a more profound influence in their communities.[57]

In the very recent past, the Charismatic Movement itself has undergone further significant evolution. The so-called third wave of renewal, which has followed on from classical Pentecostalism, which has been designated as the first wave; and the original Charismatic Movement, which was called the second, has altered the landscape still further. The name most commonly associated with this development has been John Wimber (1934–97). His theology of 'power evangelism', particularly that the proclamation of the Gospel had to be authenticated by 'signs and wonders', has proved remarkably popular. His network of Vineyard churches now have an international presence, although in Wales there are only two congregations, one in Cardiff and the other in Wrexham.[58] The Vineyard churches received a significant boost during the mid-1990s as a result of the 'Toronto Blessing'. The first stirrings were heard at the Toronto Airport Vineyard Church in 1994, and the blessing quickly spread to other parts of the world after the enthusiastic support given to it by Wimber. According to Rob Warner, Wimber's endorsement of the blessing enhanced his already high reputation among English charismatics and made the blessing, which included the controversial gift of 'holy laughter', more acceptable than it might otherwise have been.[59] However, as the excitement associated with the 'Toronto Blessing' began to fade another 'revival' began during 1996, this time at an Assemblies of God congregation at Brownsville, near Pensacola in Florida. Television flashed pictures of the revival around the world, leading many Pentecostals to believe that it was just the beginning of a much more extensive awakening. Despite subsiding as quickly as they first burst on the scene, both events have proven to be crucially important to Pentecostals as they have provided them with models of revival from which to draw inspiration other than the Welsh or Azusa Street revivals.

Specific figures about the number of charismatic churches in Wales are almost impossible to verify. Within the Church in Wales there are a number of prominent churches, such as St Michael's in Aberystwyth,[60] which act as the focus for most of the charismatic activity within the Church. There are also charismatic churches within the traditional nonconformist denominations and plenty of independent house churches. But in many respects, the research necessary for historians to assess accurately both the strength and contribution of overtly charismatic churches in Wales has not yet been carried out.[61] However, it would be safe to say that the Charismatic Movement has had a significant impact on the atmosphere of Welsh Evangelical Christianity as a whole. Many churches, while not wishing to call themselves charismatic, and uneasy with some of the charismatic emphases on the continuation of the gifts of the Holy Spirit, have nevertheless adopted charismatic forms of worship. Exuberant styles of worship, and the singing of contemporary worship songs have become commonplace in evangelical churches throughout the British Isles.[62] Often influential agencies in furthering Charismatic renewal have been the large numbers of individuals, mostly young, who have regularly attended one or more of the annual charismatic conventions, such as Soul Survivor, New Wine and the Stoneleigh International Bible Week, which itself attracted 26,000 delegates in 2001.[63] Other conventions, like Spring Harvest and Green Belt, while not overtly charismatic in their theology, have popularised charismatic-style worship. Delegates have often returned to their home churches determined to introduce a more contemporary charismatic-like style of worship. However, a lack of sensitivity has often led to bitter conflict within many evangelical churches in Wales and the unfortunate division of many struggling congregations. While in some ways the Charismatic renewal has improved the morale of many Christians in Wales since the 1960s, it has also had a more unsavoury side with increased instances of the abuse of power within churches, and this has often proved to be a disruptive force within many more traditional evangelical churches.

What is deeply ironic about the story of Pentecostalism in Wales is that, despite the Welsh origins of so many of its leaders and organisations, the country has largely missed out on the tremendous growth in Pentecostal, and more recently charismatic, activity which has occurred in many parts of the world.[64] Philip Jenkins has recently traced the dramatic globalisation of Christianity, and has argued that at the core of this growth has been the unprecedented success of Pentecostal and charismatic churches in many parts of the developing world. So significant has this growth been that he has concluded that Pentecostals may now be the 'largest segment of global Christianity, and just conceivably a majority'.[65] This astonishing achievement has its origins in the series of events that took place in different parts of the world during the early part of the twentieth century. None of these revivals turned out to be as far-reaching in their importance or influence as the revival that brought Wales to the forefront of the worldwide Christian community for a short time at the end of 1904 and during much of 1905. The growth of Pentecostalism has consequently become the chief legacy of the Welsh revival, and perhaps a sign that despite the unremittingly gloomy tale of religious decline in Wales during much of the twentieth century, there have at least been a few signs of vibrant spiritual life.

Notes

1. D. R. Barrett, 'Annual Statistical Table of Global Mission 1997', *International Bulletin of Missionary Research*, 21, 1 (1997), 24–5.
2. Walter J. Hollenweger, *The Pentecostals* (London, 1972).
3. Harvey Cox, *Fire from Heaven: The Rise of Pentecostal Spirituality and the Reshaping of Religion in the Twenty-First Century* (London, 1996), p. 5.
4. David Martin, *Pentecostalism: The World Their Parish* (Oxford, 2002), p. 1.
5. Allan Anderson, 'The Future of Protestantism: The Rise of Pentecostalism', in Alister McGrath and Darren C. Marks (eds), *The Blackwell Companion to Protestantism* (Oxford, 2004), p. 439.
6. For more on these tributaries see Vinsan Synan, *The Holiness-Pentecostal Tradition: Charismatic Movements in the Twentieth Century* (Grand Rapids, Michigan, 1997); Grant Wacker, *Heaven Below: early Pentecostals and American culture* (Cambridge, Mass., 2001); Charles Price and Ian Randall, *Transforming Keswick: The Keswick Convention, Past, Present and Future* (Carlisle, 2000); George M. Marsden, *Fundamentalism and American Culture: The Shaping of Twentieth-Century Evangelicalism, 1870–1925* (New York, 1980).
7. Quoted in Edward J. Gitre, 'The 1904–05 Welsh Revival: Modernisation, Technologies, and Techniques of the self', *Church History: Studies in Christianity and Culture*, 73, 4 (December, 2004), 792.
8. Geraint Fielder, *Grace, Grit and Gumption: The Exploits of Evangelists John Pugh, Frank and Seth Joshua* (Fearn, Ross-shire and Bridgend, 2000).
9. Brynmor P. Jones, *Voices from the Welsh Revival, 1904–1905* (Bridgend, 1995), pp. 19–20.

10. Brynmor Pierce Jones, *The Spiritual History of Keswick in Wales, 1903–1983* (Cwmbrân, 1989).

11. For more on R. B. Jones see Eifion Evans, *The Welsh Revival of 1904* (Bridgend, 1969), pp. 31–3; Brynmor Pierce Jones, *The King's Champions: Revival and Reaction, 1905–1935* (Cwmbrân, 1986).

12. For the development of different interpretations of religious revivals, see Janice Holmes, *Religious Revivals in Britain and Ireland, 1859–1905* (Dublin, 2000); Kenneth S. Jeffrey, *'When the Lord Walked the Land': The 1858–62 Revival in the North-East of Scotland* (Carlisle, 2002), pp. 1–48.

13. See Evans, *Welsh Revival of 1904*, pp. 163–6; William Kay, 'Revival: Empirical Aspects', in Andrew Walker and Kristin Aune (eds), *On Revival: A Critical Examination* (Carlisle, 2003), pp. 187–91.

14. For further discussion see John Harvey, 'Spiritual Emblems: visions of the 1904–5 Welsh Revival', *Llafur: Journal of Welsh Labour History*, 6, 2 (1993), 75–93; Nigel Wright, 'Does Revival Quicken or Deaden the Church? A Comparison of the 1904 Welsh Revival and John Wimber in the 1980s and 1990s', in Walker and Aune (eds), *On Revival*, pp. 130–2.

15. Russell Davies, *Secret Sins: Sex, Violence and Society in Carmarthenshire, 1870–1920* (Cardiff, 1996), pp. 203–9. See also Robert Pope, *Seeking God's Kingdom: The Nonconformist Social Gospel in Wales, 1906–1939* (Cardiff, 1999), pp. 1–4.

16. This itinerary is outlined in minute detail in D. M. Phillips, *Evan Roberts: The Great Welsh Revivalist and His Work* (London, 1923), 249–378. See also Geraint Tudur, 'Evan Roberts and the 1904–5 Revival', *Journal of Welsh Religious History*, 4 (2004), 87–94.

17. Evans, *The Welsh Revival of 1904*, pp. 134–6.

18. Jones, *An Instrument of Revival*, pp. 123–30; R. Tudur Jones, *Faith and the Crisis of a Nation: Wales 1890–1914* (Cardiff, 2004), pp. 321–6.

19. See Peter Prosser, 'Jessie Penn Lewis', in Dyfed Wyn Roberts (ed.), *Revival, Renewal and the Holy Spirit* (Milton Keynes, 2009), pp. 116–28.

20. Brynmor Pierce Jones, *The Trials and Triumphs of Mrs. Jessie Penn-Lewis* (Plainfield, N.J., 1997), pp. 228–30.

21. For more on Barratt see 'Thomas Ball Barratt: from Methodist to Pentecostal', *Journal of the European Pentecostal Theological Association*, XIII (1994), 19–40.

22. See Edith Blumhofer, 'Alexander Boddy and the Rise of Pentecostalism in Britain', *Penuma: Journal of the Society for Pentecostal Studies*, 8, 1 (1986), 31–40; William K. Kay, *Inside Story: A History of the British Assemblies of God* (Mattersey, 1990), 17–42.

23. Synan, *Holiness-Pentecostal Tradition*, pp. 84–106; Joe Creech, 'Visions of Glory: The Place of the Azusa Street Revival in Pentecostal history', *Church History*, 65 (1996), 405–24; Alan Anderson, *An Introduction to Pentecostalism: Global Charismatic Christianity* (Cambridge, 2004), pp. 39–45.

24. William Blair and Bruce Hunt, *The Korean Pentecost and the Sufferings which followed* (Edinburgh, 1977).

25. E. L. Blumhofer, 'Pandita Ramabai', in Timothy Larsen (ed.), *Biographical Dictionary of Evangelicals* (Leicester, 2003), pp. 536–8; Samsundar M. Adhav, *Pandita Ramabai* (Madras, 1979).

26. Malcolm R. Hathaway, 'The Role of William Oliver Hutchison and the Apostolic Faith Church in the Formation of British Pentecostal Churches', *Journal of the European Pentecostal Theological Association*, XVI (1996), 40–57.

27. For more on some of these congregations, see Brynmor Pierce Jones, *How Lovely are Thy Dwellings* (Newport, 1999).

28. Henry Byron Llewellyn, 'A Study of the History and Thought of the Apostolic Church in Wales in the Context of Pentecostalism', unpublished University of Wales, MPhil. thesis, 1997, pp. 29–33.

29. James E. Worsfold, *The Origins of the Apostolic Church in Great Britain with a Breviate of its Early Missionary Endeavours* (Wellington, New Zealand, 1991), passim.

30. I am indebted to Bryn Thomas, Dean of Studies at the Apostolic Church School of Ministry, for this information.

31. Ian M. Randall, *Evangelical Experiences: A Study in the Spirituality of English Evangelicalism, 1918–1939* (Carlisle, 1999), p. 213.

32. Synan, *The Holiness-Pentecostal Tradition*, 212–13; Richard Riss, 'The Latter Rain Movement of 1948', *Pneuma: Journal of the Society for Pentecostal Studies*, 4, 1 (1982), 32–45; Llwyelyn, 'A Study of the History and Thought of the Apostolic Church in the Conquest of Pentecostalism', pp. 54–73.

33. Worsfold, *Origins of the Apostolic Church in Great Britain*, pp. 184–5.
34. Peter Brierley (ed.), *UK Christian Handbook, Religious Trends, 3, 2002/3* (Beckenham, Kent, 2001), 9.9.
35. For details see http://www.apostolic-church.org/ (accessed February 2005).
36. For the Jeffreys brothers' early lives in Wales see Desmond Cartwright, *The Great Evangelists: The Remarkable Lives of George and Stephen Jeffreys* (Basingstoke, 1986), pp. 13–35.
37. James Robinson, *Pentecostal Origins: early Pentecostalism in Ireland in the context of the British Isles* (Milton Keynes, 2005), especially ch. 6 and 7.
38. Malcolm R. Hathaway, 'The Elim Pentecostal Church: Origins, Development and Distinctives', in Keith Warrington (ed.), *Pentecostal Perspectives* (Carlisle, 1998), pp. 17–18; Edith L. Blumhofer, *Aimee Semple McPherson: Everybody's Sister* (Grand Rapids, 1993).
39. Hathaway, 'Elim Pentecostal Church', pp. 21–4; Bryan R. Wilson, *Sects and Society: The Sociology of Three Religious Groups in Britain* (London, 1961), pp. 39–56.
40. Brierley (ed.), *UK Christian Handbook*, 9.9.
41. Edith L. Blumhofer, *Restoring the Faith: The Assemblies of God, Pentecostalism and American Culture* (Urbana, 1988).
42. This is dealt with in considerable detail in Kay, *Inside Story*, pp. 69–83.
43. William K. Kay, *Pentecostals in Britain* (Carlisle, 2000), p. 28.
44. Ibid.
45. For more on its establishment and subsequent development see http://www. hope-community-church. org.uk/ (accessed May 2010).
46. http://www.aog.org.uk/locations (accessed April 2010).
47. Kay, *Pentecostals in Britain*, p. 31.
48. http://www.ntcg.org.uk (accessed April 2010). Significantly, no reference is made to the existence of any African American Pentecostal churches in Wales. See Paul Chambers, 'Religious Diversity in Wales', in Charlotte Williams, Neil Evans and Paul O'Leary (eds), *A Tolerant Nation? Exploring Ethnic Diversity in Wales* (Cardiff, 2003), pp. 125–38.
49. See http://www.eauk.org (accessed April 2010). His replacement as director general is Steve Clifford.
50. Anderson, *Introduction to Pentecostalism*, p. 144.
51. Hollenwenger, *Pentecostals*, pp. 4–6.
52. Rick Howard, 'David du Plessis: Pentecost's Ambassador-at-large', in Wonsuk Ma and Robert P. Menzies (eds), *The Spirit and Spirituality: Essays in Honour of Russell P. Spittler* (London, 2004), pp. 271–97.
53. Donald Gee's life is analysed in Richard Massey, *Another Springtime: The Life of Donald Gee, Pentecostal Leader and Healer* (Guildford, 1992).
54. See http://www.anglicanrenewalministries-wales.org.uk (accessed April 2010).
55. For more on the movement see Andrew Walker, *Restoring the Kingdom: The Radical Christianity of the House Church Movement* (London, 1988); Nigel Scotland, *Charismatics and the New Millennium: The Impact of Charismatic Christianity from 1960 into the New Millennium* (2nd edn. London, 2000), pp. 20–5; William K. Kay, *Apostolic Networks in Britain: New Ways of Being Church* (Milton Keynes, 2007).
56. Virgo's New Frontiers International is the only one of these groups to have a presence in Wales, with one congregation in Cardiff. See http://www. newfrontiers.xtn.org (accessed April 2010).
57. Some of the tensions within the House Churches have been examined in a Welsh context in Paul Chambers, '"On or Off the Bus": Identity, Belonging and Schism. A Case Study of a neo-Pentecostal House Church', in Stephen Hunt, Malcolm Hamilton and Tony Walter (eds), *Charismatic Christianity: Sociological Perspectives* (Basingstoke, 1997), pp. 140–59.
58. See www.vineyardchurches.org.uk (accessed April 2010).
59. Rob Warner, 'Ecstatic Spirituality and Entrepreneurial Revivalism: Reflection on the Toronto Blessing', in Walker and Aune (eds), *On Revival*, pp. 221–38. For a defence of the blessing, see Guy Chevreau, *Catch the Fire: The Toronto Blessing: An Experience of Renewal and Revival* (London, 1994), and for a more balanced critique see David Hilborn (ed.), *'Toronto' in Perspective: Papers on the new Charismatic Wave of the mid-1990s* (Carlisle, 2001).
60. See http://www.stmikes.org.uk/ (accessed April 2010).

61. The most reliable indicator to date is Kay, *Apostolic Networks in Britain*, passim.
62. Some of these changes have been usefully charted in an Anglican context in James H. S. Steven, *Worship in the Spirit: Charismatic Worship in the Church of England* (Carlisle, 2002).
63. See http://www.newfrontierstogether.org/Groups/98997/Newfrontiers/AboutUs/Hist%20ory/Bible_Weeks/Bible_Weeks.aspx (accessed April 2010).
64. For the globalisation of Pentecostalism see Simon Coleman, *The Globalisation of Charismatic Christianity: Spreading the Gospel of Prosperity* (Cambridge, 2000); Martin, *Pentecostalism*.
65. Phillip Jenkins, *The Next Christendom: The Coming of Global Christianity* (New York, 2002), p. 8.

CHAPTER 12

UNITED REFORMED CHURCH

Robert Pope[1]

At least in one sense, the United Reformed Church was 'born' at 1.26 on the morning of 21 June 1972, when the United Reformed Church Bill was voted upon and passed in the House of Commons.[2] The uniting assembly took place on 5 October at the Central Hall, Westminster,[3] followed by an ecumenical celebration in Westminster Abbey. Much consideration was given to the name of the new church and it has been greatly misunderstood since. However, the name 'United Reformed Church' reflects the Church's basic theological presuppositions, and any understanding of it must take that name as its starting point. First, and perhaps foremost, the Church is 'United' because it was formed from the union of two Churches, the Congregational Church of England and Wales and the Presbyterian Church of England. Their union came as the result of a wave of ecumenical fervour following the Second World War and very careful negotiation between representatives of the two Churches stretching back over many decades. This was the first occasion since the Protestant Reformation when Churches in Britain united across denominational lines.[4] The only subsequent cross-denominational unions have also involved the United Reformed Church and they are outlined below.

There is no specifically 'Reformed' tradition in Britain as there is, for example, in mainland Europe.[5] Nevertheless, it was considered important to include the term in the name because the two Churches trace their ancestry back to the Protestant Reformation, finding their particular theological roots in varying forms of Calvinism. Congregationalists and Presbyterians differed in their understanding of the nature and order of the Church. For Congregationalists, the Church was (and still is) a gathered community of believers, covenanted together for the worship of God and mutual support. Each Church was to be an independent body, separate from the rest of society and from the state. Only when a local congregation could not come to an agreement over an issue was the wider body to be called together in Synod.[6] Initially, the Congregationalists came together in the Congregational Union of England and Wales (1832) which, strictly speaking, was not a denomination but a gathering of independent churches which sought mutual edification and assistance. It had no authority over the running of any of them. In 1966, the Congregational Union voted to become a Church (or a denomination) in recognition of the relationships and thinking which had developed among the Churches of the Union.[7] Not all congregations joined the new 'Church' and only those which did participated in the talks for union.

Presbyterians, on the other hand, originally maintained a parish system but sought to impose on it a system of discipline focussed on an eldership elected to work in partnership with the minister. At one time it appeared that the national Church may well have been established under a Presbyterian system, as it is in Scotland, but with the restoration of the monarchy in 1660 the Presbyterians too found themselves excluded from an episcopal establishment. Presbyterian churches were under the oversight of presbyteries consisting of ministers and elders in council. During the eighteenth century, many, though by no means all, of the original Presbyterian churches became Unitarian under the influence of Enlightenment thought and the inability of the presbyteries to exercise any theological control. It was not these churches that came to union in 1972 but those of the Presbyterian Church of England, which was established on 13 June 1876 as the union of the Presbyterian Church in England and the United Presbyterian Synod of England, both being the products of Scottish migration.[8] These churches, too, exercised oversight through the gathering of ministers and elders in council, though, unlike north of the border, neither had adopted a parish system. Finally, the United Reformed Church is a 'Church' because it consists of a gathering of believers who agree to meet together in the name of Jesus Christ, for worship, for mutual edification and for service and witness in the local community.

It is worth noting that the Bill debated in the House of Commons in June 1972 had as its goal the establishment of a new Church and not the uniting of two others. While possibly shocking at the time, this concept is an important one for any hope of achieving organic union, yet it is one that seems to have been forgotten since. Two Churches whose ancestries stretched back over three hundred years had to cease to exist in order for another to be created. One of the significant figures who planned and instigated the union, the Rev. Dr John Huxtable,[9] General Secretary of the Congregational Church and later joint General Secretary of the United Reformed Church (with the Rev. Arthur MacArthur,[10] General Secretary of the Presbyterian Church of England), observed:

> The fact that in law you cannot simply stick two churchly bodies together with appropriate amounts of ecclesiastical glue was a timely reminder that to achieve Christian unity there has to be a death and resurrection sequence without which the goal cannot be achieved.[11]

From its inception, the United Reformed Church has been committed not only to ecumenism but to the organic union of the Church of Christ on earth. The Church's witness has been hampered by division and disunity, and the United Reformed Church was formed under the conviction that only organic union could ensure effective witness and demonstrate obedience to Christ's prayer in John 17:11 that his followers 'be one' in reflection of the unity between the divine Father and Son. Consequently, the United Reformed Church united in 1981 with the Churches of Christ. The first congregation of the Churches of Christ, whose polity was characterized by weekly communion and believer's baptism, had been founded in Nottingham on 25 December 1836. Its background was among Scotch

Baptists who had come under the influence of the former Presbyterian Alexander Campbell. In 2000, union occurred with the Congregational Church of Scotland and the Church became the United Reformed Church in Great Britain, serving three nations.[12]

Faith and Order

Faith and order in the United Reformed Church is governed by the Basis of Union. This document provides information concerning the ethos, theology and ecclesiastical practice of the Church. In theology, the Basis of Union affirms that the United Reformed Church is orthodox Trinitarian and regards the Word of God as discerned in the Old and New Testaments as authoritative for the Church's life (following the Reformation principle of *sola Scriptura*). It is through preaching from and studying the Scriptures that God's saving will is made known. True to the tradition of British dissent, the creeds are affirmed and accepted, though not made a condition of membership. Instead, they are confirmed as historical and contextual expressions of Christian faith. Two sacraments are observed: baptism is the entry into the Church, and the Lord's Supper is the remembrance of Christ's sacrificial redemption in which he is present, both risen and ascended.[13]

The Reformed tradition is characterized by the three slogans of the Reformation: *sola gratia*, *sola fide* and *sola Scriptura* – salvation by grace through faith and according to the Scriptures alone. This remains a fundamental aspect of the United Reformed Church's theology, though there is also the sense that God's will is worked out from the Scriptures under the guidance of the Holy Spirit whenever the Church meets together in council. This suggests that, for the United Reformed Church, God's Word is an active, dynamic entity which is to be discerned by God's people in every age. The Scriptures offer the supreme authority for the life and faith of the Church, but they must be interpreted under the power and guidance of the Holy Spirit. In effect, this reflects the primary characteristic of the dissenting and nonconformist traditions in Britain, which united the Reformed insistence on the authority of Scripture with what could be termed the charismatic emphasis on the guidance of the Spirit.

The United Reformed Church is a conciliar church governed by lay and ordained people meeting in council and recognizing that ministry is exercised by the whole people of God. Oversight is exercised through officers of the local church and through the councils of the wider church. Each local congregation has a certain degree of autonomy in conducting its business through the Church Meeting in which all members of that congregation are eligible to vote and which the elders' meeting advises. The local Church Meeting is responsible for the witness and nurture and service of the Church in any given locality. The elders' meeting consists of representatives from the congregation elected by the Church Meeting and duly ordained.[14] Elders share in pastoral oversight and leadership in the local Church, collectively exercising care of the congregation's spiritual life.

From the inception of the United Reformed Church, local Churches were gathered together into Districts and the District Council comprised representatives of the churches in a given area 'grouped together for the purpose of fellowship, support, intimate mutual oversight and united action'.[15] Each District Council was presided over by a president who could be lay or ordained and was elected from among the membership of the District Council, usually for a period of two years. District Councils were grouped together into Synods. However, shortage of resources and the perceived need to reduce bureaucracy led the United Reformed Church to disband the District Councils (called Area Councils in Scotland) in 2006. As a result, local Churches now relate directly to the Synod and, currently, there are thirteen in the United Reformed Church, two of which, those of Wales and Scotland, are national rather than provincial synods. Each Synod is presided over by a moderator who is elected from among the ordained ministers initially for a seven year period. He or she can then be re-elected for periods of five years.

Until 2006, representatives of the whole Church would meet annually in council at a General Assembly which is presided over by an Assembly moderator who was elected to the office for one year and could be a lay person or an ordained minister. According to the Basis of Union, the General Assembly

> Shall embody the unity of the United Reformed Church and act as the central organ of its life and the final authority, under the Word of God and the promised guidance of the Holy Spirit, in all matters of doctrine and order, and in all other concerns of its common life.[16]

However, from 2008 General Assembly has met biannually with two moderators, one an ordained minister and one an elder, who serve for two years prior to the Assembly over which they will preside and for the two years following their election.

The General Assembly elects a Mission Council made up of Synod representatives which is empowered to act in its name 'in matters of urgency' between meetings of the General Assembly. The administrative offices for the Church are located at 86 Tavistock Place, London, where staff look after various aspects of the Church's life. Day-to-day affairs are ultimately the responsibility of the General Secretary and since 2008 this has been the Rev. Roberta Rominger. She trained for ministry in the United States of America and was ordained there in the Churches of Christ, serving in California. She came to Britain in 1985 and served churches in Surrey and in the north-east of England before being appointed Moderator of the Thames North Synod (the London area) in 1998.

The structure of the Church, then, is one which values the Congregational emphasis on the ability of the Church Meeting to discern the will of God and also the Presbyterian emphasis on the need for church leaders to meet in council. Each council of the Church, the Elders' Meeting, the Synod and the General Assembly, is, in effect, a 'Church Meeting' in the same way as the local Church gathers in council. Such a structure is undergirded by the conviction that all God's people, lay and ordained, are entrusted with the task of ministry and all can discern the will of God.

The United Reformed Church in Wales

Prior to the formation of the United Reformed Church, some consideration was given to locating the north Wales churches with those of Merseyside, while those of the south would form a separate province. This was not pursued and the Welsh churches formed a distinct Synod, following the way in which the Congregational Unions of North Wales, South Wales and Monmouthshire had been presided over by a single moderator. It is noteworthy that, thirty years later, such an idea could not even be contemplated due in part to the increasing recognition of Wales as a distinct national unit which possesses an ecumenical outlook distinct from that of England and is increasingly developing its own political identity, particularly following the establishment of the National Assembly for Wales in 1998.

At the formation of the Church, there were 172 congregations in Wales which voted to join together with three Presbyterian churches (St Andrews, Swansea; St Andrews and Windsor Place, both in Cardiff).[17] It should be said that, partly because this Presbyterian presence was so small, a latent Congregationalism has lingered in the Wales Synod, and this has remained over the thirty years of its existence - an ironic situation for a proto-Presbyterian Church to find itself in and one that is difficult to explain when so many among its membership in recent years have no background in Congregationalism. The first moderator of the Wales Synod was the Rev. William Samuel, affectionately referred to as 'Bill Sam'. He was trained at the Memorial College, Brecon, and had pastorates at Garn, Abercarn (1940–1947), Park, Llanelli (1947–1952) and Gnoll Road, Neath (1952–1961). In 1962, he became moderator for the Congregational Unions of North Wales, South Wales and Monmouthshire, a position which he held until 1977. Working from offices in Cardiff, 'Bill Sam' rarely ventured out of south Wales, which resulted in a Synod where there was a polarization between the churches of the north and those of the south. The forging of a distinct identity as the Synod of Wales would be left to his successors. He died on 11 July 1990. In 1977, the time came to appoint a new moderator and the mantle fell upon the Rev. Dr John I. Morgans. Dr Morgans had trained at the Memorial College (which had, by that time, moved to Swansea), Mansfield College, Oxford[18] and Hertford Theological Seminary, USA.[19] Pastorates followed at Llanidloes (1967–1974) and Manselton, Swansea (1974–1977), prior to taking up the position of moderator. A passionate preacher, Dr Morgans offered the new Church fervent and informed leadership for twelve years.

Although there is no rule to say that a moderator cannot be elected to a third term of office, there is an expectation that he or she will remain in post for no more than two terms. Towards the end of his second term, Dr Morgans indicated that he did not wish to be re-appointed. By that time he had moved to the Penrhys Estate, perched on a mountain top between the two Rhondda Valleys. By the 1980s, Penrhys held a reputation for crime and deprivation, suffering all the social consequences that come in the wake of ninety per cent unemployment. Eight denominations were committed to ecumenical witness on the estate and this culminated in the establishment

of the Penrhys Uniting Church in 1989 and the opening of Llanfair, a set of buildings including a worship area and space for community projects, in 1992. Following
his period as moderator, Dr Morgans accepted the call to become minister of the
Church. Subsequently, pioneering work has been undertaken in establishing links
between the voluntary, business and statutory sectors resulting in a Church involved
in many aspects of community life ranging from a café, boutique and launderette
to providing homework, music and art classes. Certainly, 'Llanfair is one model of
church life in this century, and through its inclusiveness, its participatory pattern of
doing theology and offering worship to God, and service to community, it is helping
to point towards the future.'[20]

The Synod was left looking for a new moderator and the call was issued to the Rev.
John Ll. Humphreys. He was born in north Wales, raised in Surrey and educated at
the University of Wales, Aberystwyth, Northern College, Manchester, and Princeton
Theological Seminary, New Jersey, USA. A seven year pastorate at Bridgend and
Pontycymmer ended in 1985 when he went to work with the Reformed Church in
Hungary. Over the following years the Wales Synod developed close links with the
Reformed Church in Hungary which resulted in exchange visits by parties of young
people from the two countries. As moderator, John Humphreys spent much time tra-
versing the awkward highways and byways of Wales in a largely successful attempt
to forge a greater unity between the churches of the north and those of the south. A
thoughtful man, with a considered and catholic approach, he instigated a wholesale
re-evaluation of Church life in the Synod under the conviction that the Church must
move into the twenty-first century if it wants to survive and remain relevant. The
process – named 'Re-imagining the Future' after a phrase from the American Old
Testament scholar and minister of the United Church of Christ Walter Brueggemann –
continued after John Humphreys' time as moderator came to an end in 2000. He
took his vast experience into a temporary post in the Mersey Synod prior to becoming Training and Development Officer for the infant Synod of Scotland in 2001.
In a move that is almost unprecedented, John Humphreys was called by the Synod
of Scotland to become its moderator, a post which he took up in April 2005, thus
becoming the first minister to hold the moderatorial office in the United Reformed
Church in two different synods.

With John Humphreys' departure, the Synod of Wales was once again charged
with looking for a new moderator, and the name which came from the selection
process was the Rev. Peter C. Noble, a native of Gwent who was trained at the
Northern College, Manchester. He had been minister at the Plough Church, Brecon,
and Libanus (1983–1989), Caerphilly and Ystrad Mynach (1989–1995), prior to
becoming Training Officer for the Synod and chaplain to Cardiff University. He was
inducted to the position in 2000, bringing to it wide pastoral experience and an interest in modern theology and its interface with contemporary culture. Such concerns
are vital as the churches face an apparently transitional period in which the past
has to be left behind while no-one is quite sure what the shape of the future should
be. The years ahead will not be easy, but Peter Noble offers a leadership in which
he is willing to think the unthinkable and this is sure to challenge the Church into

're-imagining' a more effective witness and service in the twenty-first century. He was reappointed to serve for a second term in 2007.

It has to be admitted that, for the United Reformed Church, like other mainstream, traditional denominations in Wales, the years between 1972 and 2002 have constituted a period of decline, as a perusal of the statistics reveal.

Figures for the United Reformed Church in Wales, 1972–2008[21]

Year	Places of Worship	Membership	Children	Adherents[22]
1973	175	12,675	5,138	
1974	172	12,179	5,098	
1975	171	11,617	4,873	
1976	170	11,182	4,564	
1977	172	10.280	3,933	
1978	169	10,147	4,108	
1979	169	10,018	4,080	
1980	164	8,871	3,493	
1981	163	8,656	3,348	
1982	163	8,235	3,054	
1983	163	8,092	2,910	
1984	161	6,378	2,353	
1985	159	7,514	2,152	
1986	157	7,306	1,958	
1987	154	7,044	2,790	
1988	154	6,813	3,005	
1989	153	6,578	3,078	976
1990	153	6,383	3,133	777
1991	167	6,053	3,071	1,106
1992	155	5,982	3,411	1,293
1993	154	5,700	3,307	1,713
1994	152	5,525	4,248	1,951
1995	146	5,108	3,000	1,740
1996	145	4,960	3,563	1,695
1997	143	4,812	3,335	1,896
1998	143	4,693	3,257	1,258
1999	141	4,483	3,339	1,159
2000	139	4,275	3,113	1,025
2001	138	4,168	2,953	949
2002	131	3,950	2,816	
2003	128	3,814	2,639	937
2004	128	3,677	2,224	907
2005	122	3,501	2,162	813
2006	119	3,304	2,054	827
2007	118	3,159	2,258	764
2008	115	2,997	2,015	524

Between 1974 and 2008, over sixty churches seem to have closed their doors, while membership in 2008 was under one third of the membership figure during the first years of the United Reformed Church's existence. As is the case in other Christian bodies in Wales, the figures show a steady flow away from religion rather than a dramatic exodus, and they fail to reveal to what extent this is due to older congregations losing members naturally through death and those members not being replaced. Furthermore, decline in church membership is higher in the Welsh Synod than for the Church as a whole. For the United Reformed Church, there was a fifty-one per cent drop in membership between 1972 and 1997, while in Wales the figure was nearer sixty-three per cent. By 1997 the United Reformed Church accounted for three per cent of the worshipping congregations in Wales.[23]

It is a little disturbing to have to record that the decline between 1982 and 1995 was one of thirty-six per cent, while the Anglican Church in Wales lost only nine per cent of communicants during the same period. The current shape of the United Reformed Church in Wales would appear, then, to be one of congregations that are growing older and smaller and are, by and large, failing to attract new members. Of course, that is not the whole picture as it fails to take real account of the number of children and adherents involved in local Churches. Furthermore, it makes no assessment of the way in which Christians are being sustained in their churches to face the vicissitudes of twenty-first century life or of the way in which a smaller membership is becoming increasingly active and committed to witness in the world.

The Future

Wales in the twenty-first century appears to be secular and pluralistic, and increasingly forgetful of and ambivalent towards its Christian past and heritage. Indeed, this heritage is at times considered to have been limiting and oppressive, and for many the loosening of the moral and cultural dominance of the 'chapel' is to be welcomed. The United Reformed Church's task, like that of other denominations, is to discover how it can still be 'the Church' among people who, to all appearances, can live life well enough without it. Current experience for Christians in Wales has been characterized in one study by using the Old Testament motif of Exile, where the people of Israel experienced the shocking transformation from being 'God's people' to being 'Not God's people.'[24] Israel knew what it was to exist in a foreign land where 'singing the Lord's song' proved difficult if not impossible (Ps. 137). They were sustained by discovering new meaning in their past traditions and by the promise of restoration. As the contemporary Church increasingly finds itself in a context which is ambivalent, even alien and hostile, it too must re-discover meaning and respond to the challenge of a secular, post-modern and post-Christian context in which it must compete to be heard, valued and believed. There may not be such a clear promise of 'restoration', even if such a thing would be desirable. But the challenge is just as clear as it was for the Israelites as they had to learn to cope with and remain faithful in their Babylonian captivity.

In response to both the statistical decline and the mentality of decline that haunts the Churches in Wales, the United Reformed Church has begun a process which recognizes that the Church had reached crisis point and required wholesale transformation in order to survive and develop. The fact that the message and consequence of the Gospel has eternal significance requires the retention of something from the past in recognition of the Church's apostolicity – the fact that it is sent into the world with a mission inaugurated by Christ. As a result, change has to do with form rather than content and the Synod began 're-imagining the future' by encouraging study of aspects of church life in order to discover what it is that must be carried into the future.[25] This study was then taken further by a consultation which met in Aberystwyth in September 2002 with a view to encouraging vision and expectation and taking the process forward.

In October 2002, the process of 're-imagining the future' was overtaken by events in the denomination as a whole when the Mission Council established a steering group charged 'urgently and radically to re-think the Church's priorities, programmes and processes'. This group has spearheaded a new consultative and challenging process under the title 'Catch the Vision'. The aim is to rethink the structures of the Church in such a way that is appropriate for the new millennium while also challenging local churches to explore the idea of 'emerging church' – namely novel ways of being church which begin 'with the desire to express church in the culture of the group involved'. As such, emerging church 'is church shaped by the context, not by "This is how we have always done it".'[26] The 'Catch the Vision' steering group has produced a vision statement based on the Five Marks of Mission – (1) to proclaim the good news of the Kingdom; (2) to nurture and teach new believers; (3) to respond to human need in loving service; (4) to seek to transform unjust structures of society; (5) to safeguard creation and sustain and renew the earth – and has received responses to it from the churches.

Catch the Vision seemed initially to concentrate on streamlining bureaucracy and enabling decisions to be made more quickly. This resulted in recommendations being made to dissolve Districts and to meet as General Assembly every two years. These administrative changes gave way to a more theological reappraisal of church life and the re-focussing of priorities to ensure that the United Reformed Church's finite resources were devoted to mission. From this has developed the 'Vision 4 Life' initiative which asked local Churches to sign up to a year of Bible study (from Advent 2008), a year focussing on prayer (from Advent 2009) and a year dedicated to evangelism (from Advent 2010). The process is intended to bring 'transformation to the URC and its partner churches'.[27] Further initiatives are planned as the United Reformed Church seeks to respond positively to the challenge of being 'the Church' in the twenty-first century.

There can be little doubt that Church life will be different in the future from what it has been, or that it must be one which is contemporary and relevant. The specific task entrusted to the United Reformed Church is to find how it can be both catholic, in the sense that it is in continuity with the Church in all times and places, and Reformed, in the sense that it conveys the insights of the Protestant Reformation regarding salvation by faith, the authority of the Scriptures and the ministry of the whole people of God. The years ahead, then, could be exciting and dynamic as the Church seeks to take its mission seriously and to do so in light of the needs, aspirations and culture of twenty-first century Wales. The United Reformed Church has begun to realize this. Only time will tell what fruits it will produce.

Notes

1. I am grateful to the Rev. C. Keith Forecast for reading through and commenting on an earlier draft of this chapter.
2. Stephen Koss notes that the chamber was crowded for the debate and that all the members who contributed spoke in favour of this step towards unity. See S. Koss, *Nonconformity in Modern British Politics* (London, 1975), pp. 7–8.
3. The story of the Church's institution and its antecedents is told in David G. Cornick, *Under God's Good Hand: A History of the Traditions which have come together in the United Reformed Church in the United Kingdom* (London, 1998).
4. D. M. Thompson, *Where Do We Come From? The Origins of the United Reformed Church* (London, n.d.), p. 1.
5. There are historical reasons for this. Though created during the Reformation, the Anglican Church was more a compromise with Catholicism than a specifically 'Reformed' church. Many of those who wished to see the Reformation pursued further, known initially as 'puritans', ultimately became dissenters and nonconformists due to their belief that the government of the Church ought to be separate from the government of the state. It is this 'dissenting' or 'nonconformist' tradition that has been Britain's inheritance from the Reformation and to which the antecedents of the United Reformed Church belong. The United Reformed Church's Basis of Union maintains the belief that the Church and state are distinct entities.
6. See John Owen, *The True Nature of a Gospel Church and its Government* (1689), and edited by W. J. F. Huxtable (London, 1947), p. 126ff. It ought to be mentioned that terms such as 'presbyterian' and 'congregationalist' were, for much of the seventeenth century, interchangeable rather than representative of clearly defined and separate entities.
7. Legally, the Congregational Church was still regarded as a Union which meant that when the vote to become the United Reformed Church was taken, each local congregation had to vote separately on the issue. Though not intimated at the time, with hindsight it can be seen that this earlier vote facilitated the later ballot for union with the Presbyterian Church of England.
8. Cornick, *Under God's Good Hand*, pp. 123–31.
9. For John Huxtable (1912–1990), see his autobiography *As it Seemed to Me* (London, 1990). His commitment to ecumenism was recognized by the Archbishop of Canterbury, Michael Ramsey, who conferred on Huxtable the Lambeth DD in 1973.
10. For Arthur MacArthur (1913–2008), see his recollections in *Setting up Signs: Memories of an Ecumenical Pilgrim* (London, 1997).
11. W. John F. Huxtable, *A New Hope for Christian Unity* (London, 1977), pp. 38–9.
12. Prior to this union there were seven United Reformed Churches in Scotland which had originally been Churches of Christ and belonged to English Synods. The union with the Congregational Church of Scotland allowed the formation of the Synod of Scotland, strengthening the United Reformed Church presence in that country.
13. The wording of the Basis of Union is ambiguous reflecting concerns in the Reformed and dissenting traditions about the nature of 'presence' in the sacrament. The wording could be interpreted as referring to Christ's presence in the church where two or three gather in Christ's name (Mt.18.20). However, it is more likely to be affirming Calvin's conciliatory position that Christ is present by mystery, the elements remaining as bread and wine.

14. Ordination here, as with that of ministers of Word and Sacraments, is seen to be the setting apart by the Church of individuals for a specific ministry. However, only the ministry of Word and Sacraments and eldership are subject to ordination. See Basis of Union.
15. Ibid.
16. Ibid.
17. Voting on union took place differently in the two churches. In the Congregational Church, each local congregation had to vote and attain a sufficient majority in order to enter the union. In the Presbyterian Church, this vote was taken by the General Assembly. See Cornick, *Under God's Good Hand*, p. 175.
18. Here he undertook research for the degree of BLitt into the work of the early Welsh Puritan dissenter William Erbery.
19. At Hertford, he was awarded a Ph.D. for his work on puritan literature. Dr Morgans published extracts from his diary offering a revealing insight into his own thoughts as well as into the social and religious history of Wales as *Journey of a Lifetime: From the Diaries of John Morgans* (Private Publication, 2008).
20. *Ten for Joy* (Cardiff, 2001), pp. 18–25.
21. *United Reformed Church Yearbooks 1972–2002*.
22. Traditionally in nonconformist churches a distinction has been made between those who have taken full membership and those who simply attend services. The latter are referred to as 'adherents'.
23. *Yr her i newid: canlyniadau arolwg eglwysi Cymru/Challenge to change: results of the 1995 Welsh churches survey* (Swindon, 1997). See also, Robert Pope, *The Flight from the Chapels: The Challenge to Faith in a new Millennium* (Cardiff, 2000).
24. Peter Cruchley-Jones, *Singing the Lord's Song in a Strange Land: A Missiological Interpretation of the Ely Pastorate Churches, Cardiff* (Berlin, 2001).
25. The Synod published study material in a number of booklets: *Reformed? Yes Reformed*; *Ten for Joy*; *Body Language*; *Change? All Change! How?*
26. Michael Moynagh, *Emergingchurch.intro* (Oxford, 2004), p. 11.
27. See www.vision4life.org.uk

CHAPTER 13

SEVENTH-DAY ADVENTISM

Brian Phillips

The Seventh-day Adventist movement grew out of the religious ferment in the New England States of North America in the early part of the nineteenth century. According to James White, one of the founders, a nucleus was gathered from a plethora of denominations, including 'Methodists, Regular Baptists, Freewill Baptists, Seventh-day Baptists, Presbyterians, Congregationalists, Episcopalians, Disciples (of Christ), Dutch Reformed, Christian (Connection), Lutherans, Catholics, United Brethren, Universalists, worldlings and infidels'.[1] The movement's origins can be dated back to the winter of 1843 when a Seventh-day Baptist, Rachael Oakes, visited the Christian Connection Church in Washington, New Hampshire. Most of the congregation were Millerite Adventists but Rachael Oakes convinced them that they should keep the Seventh-day Sabbath.[2] Thus today the town proclaims itself as being the first to call itself Washington and to be the birthplace of Seventh-day Adventism.

Adventist theology was influenced by a number of the denominations it grew from, but one strand of theology came from George Storrs who had written tracts and advocated Conditional Immortality in his preaching.[3] By 1845 many were convinced that Storrs was right, but some avoided speaking on the subject so as not to split the group.[4] Quite quickly leaders began to emerge, like Joseph Bates, James and Ellen White and others who began propagating such teachings, and promoted a series of Bible Conferences which took place at various venues in New England between 1848 and 1851. Here they drew together the disparate strands of doctrine that had developed since 1844,[5] and by the end of 1848 it was decided to publish a magazine that would inform the world of their distinctive message.[6] For the first eighteen months it was called *Present Truth*, then it took the name the *Advent Review and Sabbath Herald*. It still continues as the International Church Magazine of Seventh-day Adventists, but has undergone several changes in name and is called today, the *Review*.[7]

Like the experience of many new religious movements there was a reluctance on the part of the founders to establish an organised denominational framework. However, the events of the American Civil War made them realize that a form of organization would be necessary to ensure that the status and credibility of their ministers would be recognized by the government. The Seventh-day Adventist Church was formally organized in 1863 and its headquarters were established at Battle Creek, Michigan. The words 'Seventh-day' were decided upon to express the organisation's conviction that the fourth commandment should be kept as a memorial to creation, while 'Adventist' was included to indicate the church's belief in the imminent return of Jesus.[8]

Rapid development took place in the activities of the denomination. Following the lead taken on health in the writings of Ellen White, a Sanatorium and Health Food Company was established at Battle Creek. Dr John Harvey Kellogg became the director of the Sanatorium and began inventing the breakfast cereals his brother W. K. Kellogg would afterwards market![9] Although the breakfast food industry began among Adventists in Battle Creek others were to exploit the world market. Adventists, however, continued to promote a physically healthy life style, which they believed would encourage people to maintain a healthy spiritual existence.

In 1872 a pamphlet was produced that included a statement of 'Beliefs held among us'. The preamble, however, noted that the 'The Bible is our only creed',[10] and as such early Adventists were of the opinion that a creed would potentially lead to their doctrines becoming set in concrete, while any newly perceived biblical teaching would be designated a heresy. From this period there have been few doctrinal changes, and the current beliefs can be found in *Seventh-day Adventists Believe – A Biblical Exposition of 27 Fundamental Doctrines.*[11] Seventh-day Adventism is, therefore, a Bible-based denomination, whose basic belief system is similar to several other evangelical denominations. It holds to the Trinity of Father, Son and Holy Spirit, and maintains that salvation is a gift from God that is imparted to the believer through faith. Adventists hold to the regeneration of believers, who are then justified before God as though they have never sinned. Being justified by faith, they are then to live a life of faith guided by the Holy Spirit that will enable them to grow in grace through a continual process of sanctification. It is readily accepted that God wants Christians to grow spiritually, but they will not become perfect until they receive their glorified bodies at the Second Advent of Christ. As the name suggests Adventists have a particularly focussed group of teachings surrounding the events at the end time, the Judgment, the Millennium, and the signs of Christ's return. Entrance into the Church is normally through baptism, by immersion, for those who are of an age of understanding.

Millerite Adventists had long sent books and magazines to relatives in Europe detailing the specifics of their faith, and Seventh-day Adventists continued this tradition. As early as 1864, M. B. Czechowski, a former Roman Catholic Priest, acted as a missionary to Europe and began Seventh-day Adventist work in Italy, Switzerland and Romania. Ten years later, J. N. Andrews continued pioneering work in Switzerland and began the publication of a French-language journal in 1876.[12] On his way to Europe, Andrews passed through Britain and wrote to the leaders in America that a missionary Headquarters should be established in England. The British headquarters was established in Southampton in 1879 and moved to Grimsby in 1884. A. A. Johns, an American of Welsh descent, was a missionary in Grimsby from 1882 to 1885 and it was from there that he moved to Wales in 1885.[13]

Johns moved to Aberystwyth and reported that he was finding difficulty in communicating with the Welsh. He noted that the population of Wales was 1,200,000, with one third reading and writing in Welsh, one-third understanding both Welsh and English and the remaining speaking English alone. However, he did produce several tracts in Welsh and did try and learn the language himself.[14] After a series of tent meetings at Llanbadarn, he claimed three converts to Seventh-day Adventism. At the same time several groups of missionary workers had come to Britain from America and a method was developed to gain converts. First, a missionary magazine called *Present Truth*[15] was sold door-to-door, next, meetings would be held in a tent or hired hall, and lastly, Bible studies would be given prior to baptism. This method was used in Bath over a period of several years and culminated in the baptism of eighty converts in 1894.[16]

A group of American missionaries and converts from Bath soon began work in Newport, Cardiff and elsewhere in south Wales between 1894 and 1900. Two early converts, Griffith Francis Jones, from Llanerfyl, near Welshpool, and William Henry Meredith, from Tredegar, Monmouthshire, were to have a widespread influence on the future of the Seventh-day Adventist Church. Jones was born in 1864 and as a young boy sang in the Anglican church choir at Llanerfyl. At the age of fifteen he became a seafarer and in 1890 passed the Master Mariner's examination in Liverpool.[17] When travelling from Newport, Monmouthshire, to the West Indies in 1893 he found a copy of the magazine *Present Truth* on the deck and after reading the magazine he decided that he would give his life to the proclamation of the Gospel. On becoming a Seventh-day Adventist he began selling the *Present Truth* in many parts of Britain and Ireland, but feeling a need for further training, he crossed the Atlantic and enrolled at the Keene Academy, Texas. After a year's training, he and his wife pioneered Seventh-day Adventist work in the French speaking Society Islands in the Pacific. Jones was ordained in 1903 and sent to the Cook Islands before undertaking pioneering work in Singapore, the Solomon Islands, New Guinea, the Loyalty Islands and many other islands in the West and South Pacific. On some of the islands he faced hostility, on others he found cannibals. From his base in Australia he sailed the Adventist missionary ship, the 'Melanesia', to many parts of the Pacific and was the first white man to be seen on some of these islands. Wherever possible he built a church and a school, and within six weeks he attempted to preach in the local language or dialect. When he died in Australia in 1940 his obituary told some of the story:

> Griffith Francis Jones ... was a man of deep piety and high culture. He was kind hearted, humble, and very courageous. He possessed a wonderful faculty of dependence upon divine help and guidance and could inspire others with his interesting experiences of providential openings into the darkened heathen lands. In the Islands, where the name of 'Jones' is well known and revered ... scores of men and women ... will hear of his passing with profound sorrow. In all, he and his wife held services in thirty-eight different countries and islands, using thirty-four languages or dialects.[18]

It was in 1895 that a Seventh-day Adventist called at the home of W. H. Meredith, a miner and Primitive Methodist lay-preacher. Meredith lived in Tredegar and worked as a miner at Tŷ Trist Colliery owned by the Tredegar Iron and Coal Company.[19] Within a matter of weeks Meredith decided to leave the mine and begin selling the literature of his new found faith. A year later he was called to help in the work of the Seventh-day Adventists in Cardiff. When the American evangelist J. S. Washburn arrived in Cardiff in 1896 they joined forces and held a series of meetings at what were to become known as the Park Hall Sunday Services.[20] A number of converts were baptised and joined the denomination. Washburn and his associates moved on to Swansea and there they held beach services that led to further converts. However, the group of workers were then sent to south London and it was not until 1902 that Meredith returned to hold meetings, as an evangelist, in Pontypridd. A year later the first Seventh-day Adventist Church was established in a house in West Street.[21]

During the last decade of the nineteenth century the number of converts in Britain and Ireland had so increased that it was thought necessary to provide structured church governance. At a conference in Leeds in 1902 leaders were appointed for the south and north of England, Ireland, Scotland and Wales. A. F. Ballenger, an American, was sent to Wales but remained for just two years before moving on to Ireland.[22] Upon Ballenger's move, Meredith was appointed as the Superintendent of the Seventh-day Adventists in Wales,[23] and this was to be the first of many administrative posts over the next twenty-eight years. In 1926 he became the first Briton to be appointed President of the British Union Conference of Seventh-day Adventists.[24]

Between 1900 and 1910 the Seventh-day Adventist denomination became firmly established in Wales. It was a period that saw a remarkable rise in the spirituality of the Welsh people, especially during the Evan Roberts Revival of 1904, which had an impact on all denominations.[25] Adventist literature sales were to reach an all time high between 1903 and 1905. By July 1902, 15,000 copies of *Present Truth* and 4,000 copies of *Good Health* were sold door to door,[26] while by the end of the first decade 150,000 items of literature were being sold each year.[27] Converts were also formed into congregations that met in fourteen places by the end of 1910.[28]

Services began for the first time in north Wales in 1909 at Rhosllanerchrugog, near Wrexham.[29] In 1911 the counties of Hereford and Shropshire were added to what was called the Welsh Mission, because the main rail route between north and south Wales ran through these counties. Apart from a period of ten years after the First World War, the administrative territory has since remained the same.

First World War conscription, which began in 1916, proved a problem for the largely pacifistic Seventh-day Adventists of Wales. Within a few weeks of the introduction of conscription many Adventists joined non-combatant battalions, but many of them suffered for their beliefs.[30] Between 1916 and 1919 many Adventist young men who refused conscription found themselves in prison including a group from Wales and the Border Counties who were confined in Dartmoor.[31] What came out of this experience was an understanding with the British Government, concerning Adventists and pacifism that has remained in place since that time.[32]

The organisational capabilities of the denomination in Britain improved following the purchase of Stanborough Park, north of Watford, in 1906. In the Park they were able to build a headquarters for their missionary work in the British Isles. Moreover, on the Park they established a college, printing press, health food factory and a sanatorium, and from the end of the First World War these establishments were to attract large numbers of Welsh workers. Many were drawn towards it from economic necessity,[33] but the vast majority saw it as an opportunity to work for the cause. College graduates often went overseas as missionaries and only a few returned to minister in Wales. The stream of converts leaving Wales was to be a continuous drain on the denomination's ability to maintain a steady membership in the country.[34]

One of the early converts in Newport, W. E. Read, after leading the denomination in Europe, went to the World Headquarters in Washington. He became Editor of a magazine for Jews called the *Israelite*,[35] and Chairman of the Biblical Research Committee of the General Conference. A later Chairman of this committee was H. W. Lowe who was President of the Welsh Mission between 1928 and 1932, while another Welsh convert, Gilbert Lewis of Caerphilly, translated the New Testament for the British and Foreign Bible Society into Kisi.[36] He went as a missionary to East Africa and died in South Africa in 1948. Likewise, Arthur Carscallen, a Canadian missionary, worked in north Monmouthshire in the first decade of the twentieth century and helped to establish a church in Blaenafon.[37] He soon left Wales for East Africa where he wrote the first grammar textbook in the Luo language, before going to South America to write a similar textbook for the 'Davis Indians'.[38]

Two ministers left Wales in 1935 for East and West Africa respectively. Matthew Murdoch was a minister in both south and north Wales, and worked in Kenya and South Africa as a pioneer missionary. Today the area in which he worked has one of the largest concentrations of Adventists in the World.[39] Tom Fielding left his work as a minister in Shrewsbury and Wellington in 1935 to establish a church and school in Kumasi, Ghana.[40] In that area today there are twenty-eight Seventh-day Adventist schools and an Adventist university. Both ministers did, however, retire to Wales.

Further expansion took place during the inter-war years in Wales. One of the best evangelists in Wales during this period was A. F. Bird. who was the minister at Newport between 1926 and 1929 and then established the Seventh-day Adventist church in Rhyl and later in Shrewsbury.[41] His untimely death at the age of forty-two was attributed to the treatment he had received in the First World War. His legacy was the quality of the converts in the places where he had ministered. No other evangelist was to have the same effect in the Welsh Mission until the period following the Second World War, when public meetings were held all over Wales in an attempt to gain new converts. Fifty-one public meetings were held between 1945 and 1960, with a further thirty-five between 1960 and 1970.[42] In 1970 a team from the United States headed by Richard Barron held a successful series in Cardiff and a large number were added to the south Wales churches.[43]

After 1970 public evangelism declined and converts came into the denomination through either friends or family. Membership throughout Wales and the border counties was at its peak with just over 600 in 1963 but by 2003 this had declined to 460. It has remained a fairly stable, though a very small group, in Wales but its membership in the world today is increasing at a rapid rate. However, a membership growth of seven per cent was recorded in Britain between 1994 and 2004.[44] The denomination works in 203 countries with approximately 25,000,000 people associated with the denomination around the world. Large memberships of over a

million are to be found in Brazil, the Philippines and North America. There are
large memberships in West and East Africa (5 million), and large numbers in the
other countries of South America. In Europe, the largest membership is in Romania
(67,393 c.2008). The Seventh-day Adventists have 7,597 schools and colleges with
111 universities, colleges, seminaries and training schools.[45] In Britain, ministers are
trained at Newbold College, Bracknell which is an Associate Institute of the Open
University. The college offers degree courses accredited by the Open University as
well as by the University of Wales and Andrews University (USA).

The Seventh-day Adventist Church has a congregational form of church government at the local level, and has jurisdiction over admitting and removing members
from fellowship in the Church. The denomination then has a representative government with each church sending a spokesperson to a Conference to determine the
future conduct of the administration in their area. In Wales, a conference is held
every three years where an executive committee is chosen to administer the work in
Wales and the English border counties.[46] This committee calls, relocates and can dis-
miss ministers, and is also responsible for the collection of tithes to cover the salaries
of these ministers. Around seventy-two per cent of Seventh-day Adventists pay tithe
into this central fund which keeps the Church financially viable.

Seventh-day Adventists have thereby operated in Wales since 1885, yet, in its early
years, many of its prominent members left the country to work for the Church in many
parts of the world. Today, however, the trend is reversing and there is a steady flow of
Adventists coming into Wales. There are certainly signs that Adventists will continue
to be involved with the spiritual life of Wales in the future, just as they were in the past.

Notes

1. J. S. White, *Bible Adventism* (fac. repr. Nashville, 1972), p. 12.
2. Richard W. Schwarz and Floyd Greenleaf, *Light Bearers: A History of the Seventh-day Adventist Church* (Nampa, Idaho, 1995), pp. 56–7.
3. The belief that immortality is given to the whole being at the Second Advent of Christ, they deny that the soul can be a separate entity from the body.
4. Le Roy. E. Froom, *The Conditionalist Faith of our Fathers: The Conflict of the Ages over the Nature and Destiny of Man* (2 vols. Washington D.C., 1965–6), II (*From Repression and Obscurity to Restoration*), pp. 305–13.
5. Following the teachings of the Baptist, William Miller, many had expected the return of Christ in 1843 or 1844. When Christ did not appear in 1844 the group were convinced that a new phase in His work in Heaven had began and that he is now sitting in Judgement. These ideas developed six months after what was called 'The Disappointment' of October 1844.
6. Le Roy. E. Froom, *Prophetic Faith of Our Fathers. The Historical Development of Prophetic Interpretation* (4 vols. Washington D.C., 1954), IV, p. 1025.
7. Schwarz and Greenleaf, *Light Bearers*, pp. 20–2.
8. Review and Herald Publishing Association, *The Seventh-day Adventist Bible Commentary Series* (12 vols. Hagerstown, MD, 1953–), X: *Seventh-day Adventist Encyclopaedia* (1996), Art. General Conference, p. 584.
9. G. Carson, *Cornflake Crusade* (New York, 1957).
10. Le Roy. E. Froom, *Movement of Destiny* (Washington D.C., 1971), p. 160.

11. Ministerial Association of Seventh-day Adventists, *Seventh-day Adventists Believe: A Biblical Exposition of 27 Fundamental Doctrines* (Washington D.C., 1988). See also Mike Stickland, *An Inside Look at Seventh-day Adventists* (Watford, 1997). A booklet was also published in the Welsh Language.

12. Schwarz and Greenleaf, *Light Bearers*, pp. 141–2.

13. B. L. Whitney, in *Review and Herald*, 3 November 1885, 682–3.

14. A. A. Johns, in *Present Truth*, 6 May 1886, 71.

15. This was first published at Grimsby in 1884 and ought not to be confused with the American magazine that had a short life. A complete bound collection of the British *Present Truth* is available at the British Library Newspaper (and periodicals) Collections, London.

16. *Missionary Worker*, Special Edition, 25 July 1924, 9.

17. H. Dunton et al (eds), *Heirs of the Reformation: The Story of Seventh-day Adventists in Europe* (Grantham, 1997), pp. 41–3.

18. Obituary, *Review and Herald*, 117, 50 (12 December 1940), 20, 22.

19. W. H. Meredith, in *Missionary Worker*, 18 July 1906, 116. W. H. Meredith, 'Pages from a Minister's Diary', ed. B. P. Phillips. This is an unpublished manuscript held at Newbold College Archives (n.d.) Meredith had written this diary for publication but omitted names of people and places. Names of people and places have now been included because of their importance to Seventh-day Adventist Church history.

20. The Park Hall was used by many Christian Organizations for Sunday Services before and after Washburn.

21. *Kelly's Directory for South Wales* (Cardiff, 1901) describes Pontypridd as a market town with fifteen Welsh chapels and nineteen English chapels to serve a population of 20,000. The house still stands today.

22. A. F. Ballenger, in *Missionary Worker*, 24 February 1902, 154.

23. *Missionary Worker*, Special Edition, 26 July 1924. Seventh-Day Adventist Church, *The Story of Seventh-Day Adventists in the British Isles 1902–1992: Special Souvenir of the Messenger* (1992), p. 6.

24. W. W. Armstrong, in *Messenger*, 57, 18 (5 September 1952).

25. Details of this revival are provided in B. R. Jones, *An Instrument of Revival: The Complete Life of Evan Roberts, 1878–1951* (South Plainfield, NJ, 1995).

26. *Missionary Worker*, July 1902, 139.

27. Ibid., 1909, 80; 1910, 12.

28. Ibid., 1909, 165.

29. Ibid., 100.

30. A clandestine newspaper was published during the First World War called the *Tribunal*. On 4 April 1918 it published an account of the treatment of a Seventh-day Adventist in a camp in France. Twelve signatures were given at the end of the article. The Bodleian Library at Oxford carries copies of this newspaper.

31. D. S. Porter in 'A Century of Adventism in the British Isles', Special Issue of the *Messenger* (1974), 16–18.

32. From the First World War onwards, members have actively sought to do work of 'national importance' whenever a conflict arises. Due to the general attitude in the armed forces, members in Britain usually object to military service, but in other countries different attitudes prevail and so the denomination will not pontificate, but leave it up to individual conscience.

33. Meredith, in *Missionary Worker*, 21 December 1923, 6. Before the introduction of the five day week, Adventists were often discriminated against and were sacked if they would not work during the time of their weekly Sabbath (from sunset Friday to sunset on Saturday). Seventh-day Adventists are strict Sabbath keepers but not legalists. They believe that all the Ten Commandments are a part of the Moral Law and as such are a guide in behaviour for the Christian.

34. H. W. Lowe, in *Missionary Worker*, 29 January 1932, 6. Between 1928 and 1932, seventy-one transferred their membership to other parts of Britain and in 1931 ten went as students to the Missionary Training College.

35. This magazine is now called *Shabbat Shalom* and is a twenty-eight page Jewish-Christian dialogue journal issued three times each year and is published by the *Review and Herald*, Hagerstown, Maryland.
36. M. C. Murdoch, 'Obituary', in *Messenger*, 18 November 1949.
37. *Missionary Worker*, 25 October, 1905, 172: W. Halliday, in *Missionary Worker*, 28 May 1906, 36–7. Carscallen left for Africa in 1906 having spent over a year in Blaenafon.
38. *Seventh-day Adventist Commentary Series*, 10 (1996), 300.
39. General Conference, 146th Annual Statistical Report (31 December 2008) states that there were 15,921,408 members. See http://www.adventistarchives.org/docs/ASR/ASR2008.pdf#view=fit (accessed March 2010), p. 2.
40. By December 208 the membership in Ghana stood at 346,682. Ibid., p. 36.
41. From 1929 to 1930 Bird held meetings in Rhyl and established a Church there. See *Missionary Worker*, 18 April 1930, 2.
42. Several Welsh Seventh-day Adventists have made a contribution singularly and as a group to social projects. Some were and still are influential in the fight against drug addiction and alcoholism. One member of the denomination, Harold Baker of Newport, was a leading figure in the setting up of homes for alcoholics in Newport, Cardiff and Bridgend. See *Messenger*, Obituary, 11 February 2005, 15.
43. *Messenger*, 75, 19 (11 September 1970), 1–2. Thirty-six were baptised.
44. *Quadrant*, May 2004. This is produced in Britain by the Christian Research Association.
45. Statistics are taken from the General Conference Statistic Office for 2003 and 2008. See *141st and 146th Annual Statistical Report* (2003, 2008): http://www.adventistarchives.org/docs/ASR/ASR2003. pdf#view=fit;http://www.adventist.org/world_church/facts_and_figures/index.html.en; www.advent-istarchives.org/docs/ASR/ASR2008.pdf (accessed May 2010). Between 2002 and 2003 there was an increase of over 1,000 in the number of schools recorded, with an annual enrolment of over 1.2 million students. Furthermore, Seventh-day Adventist hospitals and clinics treated over fourteen million patients in 2003 and 14,997,107 in 2008. See *146th Annual Statistical Report*.
46. The chairman and secretary/treasurer are elected at a Conference Session held every five years by representatives from across the British Isles.

CHAPTER 14

THE CHURCH OF JESUS CHRIST OF THE LATTER-DAY SAINTS (MORMONS)

Ronald D. Dennis

The first branch of The Church of Jesus Christ of Latter-day Saints (LDS) in Wales was established in Overton, Flintshire. On 30 October 1840 the thirty-two converts who were baptized (by immersion) by Henry Royle and Frederick Cook were an extension of the proselytizing effort that had begun in Preston three years earlier under the leadership of Heber C. Kimball, a missionary sent by Joseph Smith from America.[1] Elder Kimball proclaimed that the primitive gospel had been restored to the earth through the Prophet Joseph Smith in 1830 and that this Christian religion accepted as the word of God not only the Bible but also the Book of Mormon, a book that Joseph Smith had translated into English from ancient records.[2] The message of a 'restored' gospel was received remarkably well in England, and the Church's numbers there increased rapidly. In late 1842 William Henshaw, a missionary from Cornwall, arrived in Merthyr Tydfil and preached the message of 'Mormonism' in English to his fellow workers in the mines. On 19 February 1843 he baptized the first-fruits of his mission, William R. Davis, his wife, and their two sons. At Henshaw's invitation Davis also began to proselytize in both English and Welsh, thus apparently becoming the first to teach the tenets of the Latter-day Saints in the ancient Celtic tongue.[3]

By the end of 1843 William Henshaw had organized two branches of the Church – one in Penydarren with fifty baptized members and another in Rhymni with twenty-nine. Two years later there were nearly 500 Latter-day Saints in South Wales, an increase that alarmed the ministers of other faiths whose congregations were losing parishioners to the new religion.[4] The Rev. W. R. Davies, a Baptist minister in Dowlais, began to publish articles against the Latter-day Saints in various religious periodicals, urging people to call them by their proper name which he declared to be the 'Latter-day Satanist'.[5] To turn public opinion against them the Rev. Davies even went so far as to accuse them of baptizing in the nude,[6] something as abhorrent to the Saints[7] then as to any other Christians. For five years until his death in 1849, Davies would be the most vociferous opponent of those whom he viewed as satanic intruders.

In December 1845 a replacement for William Henshaw arrived in Merthyr Tydfil, the feisty and irrepressible Captain Dan Jones, originally from Flintshire. Jones had lived in America for a few years where he operated a steamboat on the Mississippi River. After hearing the numerous negative reports about Mormonism he decided to gain firsthand information. One result was his own conversion in January 1843, and another was a personal friendship with the Prophet Joseph Smith.[8] On 26 June 1844, the evening before Joseph Smith and his brother Hyrum were murdered by an angry mob, Dan Jones was with Smith in the gaol at Carthage, Illinois.[9] Significantly, just hours before his death, Smith prophesied that Dan Jones would survive the present danger and return to his native Wales to preach to his compatriots.[10]

Strangely enough, the prophecy was fulfilled and Dan Jones arrived in north Wales at the end of 1844 where he began his missionary endeavours among members of his family and acquaintances of his youth. During 1845, his first year in Wales, his success was modest, yielding only a handful of converts. The following year was a different story, however, as he took over the reins from William Henshaw in Merthyr Tydfil. From among the already baptized members there Dan Jones called a dozen or so missionaries to assist in spreading the word. He asked some to take their families to new locations and find employment where they would inform neighbours and workmates about their new religion. Others he asked to leave their families and travel to other parts of Wales to serve for varying lengths of time. Dan Jones himself travelled extensively throughout the country, often preaching to large crowds.[11] The result of this flurry of missionary activity was a surprising 100 per cent growth rate in 1846 as another 500 converts were recruited.[12] As Latter-day Saint numbers increased so also did the opposition. Angry ministers used their pulpits and the various religious periodicals to warn the people of the 'dangers of Mormonism' to their salvation. Some of those who dared to investigate the doctrines of Mormonism were publicly disciplined by their ministers. Rees Price, a member of the Rev. W. R. Davies's congregation in Dowlais, wrote of his efforts to determine the truth or error of Mormonism:

> While engaged in this careful search, in obedience to the scripture that says, 'Prove all things, hold fast that which is good', news of it reached the ears of Mr. Davies, namely that I was inclined toward a judgment and in danger of joining with the Saints; because of this I was publicly disciplined, under the accusation that I had neglected my meeting attendance; but in reality, I say, that I was diligently searching for the truth.[13]

Dan Jones published pamphlets to counter the continual attacks of his enemies. He also wrote rebuttals to the misinformation and accusations that appeared in the periodicals. But only rarely did the hostile editors grant any space for these defences. Jones wryly observed that the various sects and denominations throughout Wales should be grateful to Mormonism for its beneficent effect, as it caused them to make peace with each other and unite their forces to combat a common foe. Jones stated that the only press in Wales that would publish Mormon materials was one in Rhydybont, near Llanybydder, whose proprietor was Dan Jones's older brother, the Rev. John Jones, Llangollen. This press was promptly dubbed the 'prostitute press' by the Rev. Jones's religious colleagues for being so mercenary as to give birth to such 'monstrous' materials.[14] His response was simple and direct: 'Our work in publishing their books proves nothing more than our press is iron, and its owner is a free craftsman.'[15] In July 1846, Dan Jones published the first issue of *Prophwyd y Jubili* (Prophet of the Jubilee), a periodical he founded to defend Mormon beliefs. He exulted:

> Is everyone allowed to put out his magazine but us? Is the press locked against us? Is that the freedom of Wales in the nineteenth century? Have the month-lies been locked? We shall open our own monthly, then. Has the press been polluted by libelling us? We shall cleanse it by defending ourselves, then.[16]

Prophwyd y Jubili appeared every month for the next two-and-a-half years. In January 1849 its name was changed to *Udgorn Seion* (Zion's Trumpet), and the periodical continued until April 1862.

One of the most highly educated converts to the Latter-day Saints in Wales was a young typesetter from Carmarthen by the name of John S. Davis. Having completed his apprenticeship, Davis was in the employ of the Rev. John Jones, Llangollen, at the press in Rhydybont when the Rev. Jones began to print Mormon materials. As Davis set the type for Dan Jones's pamphlets he became convinced the writings were of the true religion. Following upon Dan Jones's departure from Wales two-and-a-half years later, Davis would become the editor of *Udgorn Seion* and the director of all Latter-day Saint printing in Wales. Another stalwart convert was William Howells, a draper and a lay Baptist minister in Aberdare. He had never conversed with a Mormon missionary before he acquired a forty-page pamphlet published by Dan Jones in 1847.[17] Upon reading the pamphlet Howells was convinced of the truth-fulness of its message. He walked from Aberdare to Merthyr Tydfil to converse with the pamphlet's author, and was baptized that same day. During the next year Howells was instrumental in the conversion of nearly one hundred of his former parishioners and family members to the LDS Church.[18]

Several ordained nonconformist ministers converted to Mormonism during the mid-nineteenth century in Wales. One of these was the Rev. David Bevan Jones, also known as Dewi Elfed Jones, the minister of the Baptist Gwawr Chapel in Aberdare. In 1851 he was attracted to the message of the Latter-day Saints when he learned that they practiced the laying on of hands for the gift of the Holy Ghost.[19] Following his baptism Jones was confirmed a member of the Church of Jesus Christ of Latter-day Saints by the laying on of hands in his own chapel. At the end of the ceremony the former minister ceremoniously turned over the keys of his chapel to the Mormon leaders and declared that it was then theirs to use for Mormon services. Litigation later decided that the chapel still belonged to the Baptists, and it was returned to them.[20]

The number of converts increased steadily. If 1846 was a good year for Mormonism in Wales, 1847 was twice as good with over 1,000 convert baptisms. And over 1,700 converts were brought into the fold in 1848. With such rapid growth came even more intense opposition, so intense that Dan Jones considered his life to be in danger, especially when it became known that he was preparing to take a group of over 300 Welsh Mormon converts to America. On the eve of their departure Jones was protected by bodyguards because of the numerous threats.[21] This first group of Welsh Mormon emigrants left 'Babylon' for their 'Zion'[22] in America in February 1849 on board the *Buena Vista*. Four months earlier a curious prophecy about the emigrants had appeared in *Seren Gomer* (Star of Gomer), a Baptist periodical. One writer, who called himself 'Anti-humbug,' predicted:

> After receiving enough money to get a ship or ships to voyage to California, their Chief-president will sail them to Cuba, or some place like it, and will sell them as slaves, every jack one of them. It will serve them right for having such little respect for the book of Christ and giving it up for the books of Mormon [*sic*].[23]

As the emigrants passed Cuba on their voyage they laughingly remembered this prediction.

Following the seven-week journey from Liverpool, they arrived in New Orleans where they boarded the steamboat *Constitution* to continue up the Mississippi River to St Louis. There they hired another vessel, the *Highland Mary*, to carry them along the Missouri River to Council Bluffs, Iowa. The cholera epidemic then raging in that area exacted a heavy toll on the immigrants, leaving hardly a family untouched by the vicious disease.[24] Worries that such news would discourage co-religionists in Wales from emigrating were unfounded, however, as the Merthyr Tydfil area was afflicted with its own cholera epidemic. Thus, there was no more safety in remaining in Wales than in leaving. Of the approximately 330 Welsh Mormon emigrants in 1849, only 84 would make the thousand-mile journey from Council Bluffs to Utah in covered wagons that year.[25]

The Latter-day Saints that Dan Jones left in Wales at his departure continued to increase in strength and number under the leadership of President William Phillips, Jones's successor.[26] Phillips assigned one of his counsellors, Abel Evans, to supervise the missionary effort in north Wales where he brought in a sizeable number of faithful converts.[27] The new president kept his other counsellor, the youthful John S. Davis, in Merthyr Tydfil as editor of the periodical. Davis also published an assortment of pamphlets on a press he had brought from Carmarthen.[28] In January 1849 the Church consisted of nearly 4,000 members organized into twenty-eight branches and five districts throughout Wales. The number of members would increase to its high point of over 5,000 by 1852, and the number of branches would eventually reach over one hundred. But growth was continually undermined by groups of varying sizes who sailed to America to gather with their fellow Saints in the Rocky Mountains. The largest of these was a group of over 500 Welsh Mormons who journeyed on the *S. Curling* from Liverpool to Boston in 1856. Their leader was Dan Jones who had returned to Wales on his second mission in 1852. Most of the large group pulled their meagre belongings in handcarts as they walked across the plains to Utah.[29]

Welsh Mormon converts came primarily from the labouring classes with many colliers and puddlers among them. However, virtually all walks of life were represented on the records of the ships that carried them to America. There were blacksmiths, butchers, carpenters, clerks, engineers, farmers, locksmiths, masons, plasterers, saddlers, schoolmasters, schoolteachers, shoemakers, tailors, wheelwrights, and whitesmiths. The stonemasons from north Wales were greatly appreciated in their new land and were the master masons of three of the four nineteenth-century temples built in Utah. Elias Morris, a stonemason from Abergele, established a construction company in Salt Lake City and became one of the wealthiest men in the Church at that time.[30] Furthermore, a choir begun in 1849, under the direction of John Parry from Newmarket, Flintshire, evolved into what is now the Mormon Tabernacle Choir. The nucleus of the original choir consisted mainly of Welsh singers, and even today well over half of the choir's members have Welsh ancestry.

Only about half of the approximately 10,000 Welsh converts to Mormonism during the nineteenth century ever made the journey to America. Age, illness, death, poverty, discouragement, and abandonment of belief were among the reasons for this failure to obey the 'call to Zion.' The proselytizing effort has continued uninterrupted except for war times to the present day, but from about 1860 to 1960 the numbers were few and the progress was slow. The exciting times from the mid-1840s to the end of the following decade have not since been equalled. Missionaries from the 1860s to the end of the century managed to bring a few new converts into the Church, but their main evangelising effort was to offer encouragement and assistance in getting long-term faithful members on the ships to America. Many of the emigrant converts returned to Wales as missionaries years later to the surprise of friends and family who often did not recognize them after years of separation. And when the sons of the emigrants went to Wales to serve missions their distant relatives were disappointed that they could not converse with them in Welsh. Yet, some Latter-day Saint converts in Wales today have pioneer ancestry. One pioneer was Moses Jones, who from his conversion in 1862 wished to join the main body of the Saints in Utah. His wife, Ann, however, did not share his enthusiasm for leaving Wales. After seven years of unsuccessfully trying to persuade Ann to change her mind Moses decided to go on ahead by himself, and prepare the way for his wife and their six children. From America he sent money on several occasions to his family in Wales for them to journey to Utah, but none of his children nor his wife ever emigrated. In 1932, three of their great grandchildren were baptized in Merthyr Tydfil, and now nearly 200 of their descendants are active Latter-day Saints.[31]

Two other pioneers were James and Ann Pitman who emigrated in 1877. Their married daughter Ellen, however, remained in Wales with her husband Thomas Biggs. They continued faithful in the Church and gave their children a Mormon upbringing. Some of the Biggs children emigrated and some remained in Wales. One who remained was their daughter Naomi who married William Forward, also a Latter-day Saint.[32] As the Forwards and the Biggses remained in Wales and taught their children in the Mormon faith, there are Mormons in Wales today who are sixth-generation members of the Church. There are over 7,000 Latter-day Saints in Wales today, most of them in south Wales. Meeting-houses (chapels) have been built in Merthyr Tydfil, Pontypridd, Cwmbrân, Cardiff, Swansea, Llanelli, Newcastle Emlyn, Rhyl, Wrexham, and Gaerwen. There are twenty-four congregations in various parts of

Wales, and Americans continue to be sent to proselytize in the country. But now it is not uncommon for the native-born Welsh to be sent to proselytize in America. One is left to ponder what the status of the Latter-day Saints in Wales would be now had the early converts not been instructed to leave their country to gather with the main body of the Church.

Notes

1. *The Latter-day Saints' Millennial Star*, November 1840, p. 192. See also R. D. Dennis, 'The Welsh and the Gospel', in V. Ben Bloxham, James R. Moss and Larry C. Porter (eds), *Truth Will Prevail: The Rise of the Church of Jesus Christ of Latter-day Saints in the British Isles, 1837–1987* (Cambridge, 1987), pp. 236–8.
2. 'Elder' is an office in the priesthood of The Church of Jesus Christ of Latter-day Saints and a title given to all male missionaries.
3. My conclusion that Davis was the first to preach Mormonism in the Welsh tongue is based on research over the years in which I have tried to determine this very issue.
4. *The Latter-day Saints' Millennial Star*, X, 253 (Issue 16, 15 August 1848).
5. *Y Bedyddiwr* (The Baptist), March 1844, 99–100.
6. *Y Tyst* (The Witness), September 1847, 199–201.
7. Followers of Christ in New Testament times referred to themselves as 'Saints' (see 1 Cor. 1:2; Rom. 1:7; Acts 9:13, 32, 41). Latter-day Saints imitate this practice.
8. Dan Jones, *Hanes Saint y Dyddiau Diweddaf* (History of the Latter-day Saints) (Rhydybont, 1847), pp. 60–1.
9. Joseph Smith and his brother Hyrum had been summoned a few days before to Carthage, Illinois, to appear before a magistrate to answer the charge of destroying the press of *The Nauvoo Expositor*. The real motive behind the arrest was to get Joseph and Hyrum away from Nauvoo where they were to be killed. Thus a number of their friends accompanied them to the town of Carthage to offer protection from the mob. They spent the first night at the Hamilton Hotel in Carthage, but not feeling safe they elected to relocate to the small jail where six or seven of their friends remained with them. One of these was Captain Dan Jones, Joseph Smith's business partner as a co-owner of the steamboat, 'Maid of Iowa'.
10. Historical Department of The Church of Jesus Christ of Latter-day Saints, Letter of Dan Jones to Thomas Bullock, 20 January 1855. See Brigham H. Roberts, *A Comprehensive History of the Church of Jesus Christ of Latter-day Saints* (Provo, Utah, 1965), p. 265.
11. From its beginning The Church of Jesus Christ of Latter-day Saints has had a lay clergy.
12. *The Latter-day Saints' Millennial Star*, 1 January 1847, p. 107.
13. *Prophwyd y Jubili* (Prophet of the Jubilee), September 1848, p. 132. An English translation of the entire periodical has been published. See R. D. Dennis, *Prophet of the Jubilee* (Provo, Utah, 1997).
14. *Seren Gomer* (Star of Gomer), December 1847, 375.
15. *Y Golygydd* (The Editor), January 1846, wrapper, 2.
16. *Prophwyd y Jubili*, July 1846, wrapper, 2.
17. *Adolygiad ar ddarlithoedd y Parch. E. Roberts* (*Review of the lectures of the Rev. E. Roberts.* Merthyr Tydfil, 1847). This pamphlet has been translated into English and has been published with numerous other nineteenth-century Welsh Mormon pamphlets in R. D. Dennis, *Defending the Faith: Early Welsh Missionary Publications* (Provo, Utah, 2003).
18. R. D. Dennis, 'William Howells: First Missionary to France', in Donald Q. Cannon and David J. Whittaker (eds), *Supporting Saints: Stories of Nineteenth-Century Mormons* (Salt Lake City, 1985), pp. 43–81.
19. The Rev. David Bevan Jones was baptized on 27 April 1851 by President William Phillips, the leader of The Church of Jesus Christ of Latter-day Saints in Wales.

20. See D. L. Davies, 'From a Seion of Lands to the Land of Zion: The Life of David Bevan Jones', in Richard L. Jensen and Malcom R. Thorp (eds), *Mormons in Early Victorian Britain* (Salt Lake City, Utah, 1989), pp. 118–41.
21. *Udgorn Seion* (Zion's Trumpet) March 1849, 57. This publication contained the 'Last greeting of the emigrating Saints to California' signed by twenty-five of the men who left on the *Buena Vista* under the leadership of Captain Dan Jones. The first signature was that of Thomas Jeremy, probably the author of the 'Last greeting', and clearly part of this document showed the unease felt by the Mormon missionaries and the need for bodyguards for Dan Jones: 'The rage of our fellow nation was so great toward us before our departure from Wales that we could not enjoy our civil rights in hardly any place; and it is abundantly true that the life of our dear brother Capt. Jones was in such danger that his house was attacked almost every night for weeks before his leaving Merthyr, so that his godly life was not safe in sleeping except between guards from among his brethren; and there were scoundrels so inhuman, who had been paid to kill him as he left, that he had to leave secretly the day before.' An earlier comment from Job Rowland, one of the twenty-five signers of the 'Last greeting' similarly observed that 'as soon as the Saints came to these areas our teachers, especially Mr. W. R. Davies, began to persecute them and hate them, saying all manner of evil against them. Mr. Davies said one time in our house that his desire was to do the same with the elders as was done to Joseph Smith, that is to kill them'. See *Udgorn Seion*, 55–8; *Prophwyd y Jubili*, December 1848, 187. An English translation of the 1849 volume of *Udgorn Seion* has been published. See R. D. Dennis, *Zion's Trumpet, 1849 Welsh Mormon Periodical* (Provo, Utah, 2001).
22. Latter-day Saints in Britain longed to be with the main body of the Saints in America and often referred to Britain as 'Babylon' and the place of gathering as 'Zion'.
23. *Seren Gomer*, October 1848, 305.
24. Over sixty-five members of this first group died of cholera before reaching Council Bluffs. See R. D. Dennis, *The Call of Zion: The Story of the First Welsh Mormon Emigration* (Provo, Utah, 1987).
25. Ibid., p. 56.
26. For English translations of William Phillips's writings that appeared in *Udgorn Seion* (Zion's Trumpet) see the website at http://welshmormonhistory.org.
27. See R. D. Dennis, *Indefatigable Veteran: History and Biography of Abel Evans, a Welsh Mormon Elder* (Provo, Utah, 1994). This biography is also on the aforementioned website in its entirety.
28. For discussions of all the items published by Dan Jones and John S. Davis see R. D. Dennis, *Welsh Mormon Writings from 1844 to 1862: A Historical Bibliography* (Provo, Utah, 1988).
29. For further details about the handcart companies see LeRoy R. Hafen, *Handcarts to Zion: The Story of a Unique Western Migration, 1856–1860* (Glendale, California, 1960).
30. Henry W. Edwards, *Integrity, Craftsmanship, Quality: The Story of Elias Morris and Sons Company, Established 1862* (Privately published, Salt Lake City, Utah, n.d.).
31. The author has met a number of the descendants of Moses Jones who are currently active Church members. At Professor Dennis' request one of these descendants, Alan Davies of Merthyr Tydfil, counted the number of his relatives who were descended from Moses Jones. In the early 1990s Davies suggested that the figure was approximately 160 at that time.
32. This information was extracted from personal correspondence with David Forward of Cardiff, a fourth-generation member of the Church through the Biggses and the Forwards. He supplied copies of his research showing those who emigrated and those who stayed. His family line comes from those members who stayed in Wales but remained active in the Church.

CHAPTER 15

JEHOVAH'S WITNESSES

Russell Grigg

'Oh, my dear, I know just how you feel. I'm a Jehovah's Witness.' A pensioner's reaction to Juliet Peck, after she said she was a local Conservative candidate.[1]

The vast majority of homes in Wales have been visited by Jehovah's Witnesses. They are well known and often disliked for their evangelising, objection to blood transfusions, non-celebration of Christmas and birthdays, and withdrawal of children from school assemblies. The distinctive Witness beliefs and practices have long been criticised, particularly by mainstream churches, 'cult' watchers and disgruntled ex-members.[2] Yet, the considerable growth among Witnesses has been seen as one of the major religious landmarks of the modern period.[3] The British Witnesses have expanded from less than two hundred core members in 1900, reaching 6,000 in 1926, 23,080 by 1951 and an average 'publisher' figure of 126,580 in 2008.[4] In 2009, around 10,000 of these gathered at the Millennium Stadium, Cardiff, for one of thirty conventions throughout Britain.[5] Since the 1950s, this expansion has occurred while membership among the churches and chapels has generally declined.[6] However, there is a remarkable shortage of academic material on the history of Jehovah's Witnesses in Britain and, aside from a recent entry in the *Encyclopaedia of Wales*, they are largely absent from the history of Wales.[7] The purpose of this chapter is to begin to address this void by outlining the development of Witness activity in Wales.

The origins of the movement whose followers came to be known as Jehovah's Witnesses are most closely associated with Charles Taze Russell (1852–1916), a wealthy draper from Pittsburgh, Pennsylvania.[8] Russell, from Scots-Irish descent, became dissatisfied with certain teachings within his Presbyterian upbringing, notably the doctrines of the Trinity, the immortality of the soul and hellfire. In 1870 he formed a group of Bible Students and, partly influenced by Adventist teachings, became convinced that Christ's return was imminent (though invisible). From 1879 he began to publish *Zion's Watch Tower and Herald of Christ's Presence* (which developed into today's *Watchtower* magazine). Through this channel, Russell kept watch on current events and interpreted Biblical chronology particularly relating to the 'last days'. From an initial circulation of 6,000 copies, by 2009 publication has exceeded 37 million per issue, appearing semi-monthly in 150 languages. In 1881 Russell formed Zion's Watch Tower Tract Society and it is the governing body of 'the Society', as Witnesses call it, which directs their global activity.

Russell invested much of his personal fortune and energy into expanding the Bible Students into an international body of Christians.[9] In 1881 two of his associates first visited Britain with the intention of printing and distributing 300,000 copies of Russell's *Food for Thinking Christians*.[10] The campaign was confined to London, northern England and Scotland. The first congregation was established in Glasgow (1882) and by 1900 there were nine in England and Scotland, under the direction of a branch office based in London. In Wales, the earliest groups can be traced to around 1910. In Fishguard (Pembrokeshire) a student who worked as a steward on the boats to Ireland distributed tracts in his spare time which caught the interest of Catherine Davies, William Baker and his wife, Elizabeth. These formed a small study group.[11] The Bakers' granddaughter, Beatrice Merrick, recalls that Catherine Davies

> would travel by herself to Pembroke Dock, Milford Haven, Neyland and Haverfordwest with a suitcase full of books and would leave the case at the railway station, fill her bag, and return again and again until all the books had been placed. This was done almost every Saturday.[12]

The first congregation was established by miners from Clydach (Swansea) in 1911. Thomas John Thomas had read Russell's *Divine Plan of the Ages* after it had been distributed by William Evans from Sharon, Pennsylvania, while on holiday in Wales.[13] In February 1911, the Clydach and District branch of the International Bible Students Association was established with seven founding members.[14] These proved to be particularly zealous by undertaking weekly witnessing campaigns in the neighbourhood. Typically, it was reported on 2 October 1912 that ten students each distributed 4,000 leaflets travelling by foot to a separate village.[15] Their efforts soon bore fruit, and by 1914 several classes were established in the region – at Morriston, Abercrave, Ystalyfera and in the centre of Swansea.

Bible Students from Wales were reported to be among the 800 or so who gathered from all parts of Britain for a convention in Glasgow in 1911.[16] Around this time Sarah Ferrie was one of the early Glasgow students who displayed remarkable zeal and commitment. She travelled to south Wales, living in and out of hotels as she worked as a professional 'colporteur' in disseminating literature.[17] While women, known as 'sisters', were not permitted to become elders or deacons, the beginnings of several congregations in Wales were the result of the zealous activity of females serving as full-time evangelisers. In north Wales, the Students relied upon colporteurs to disseminate information from well-established congregations in Liverpool and Chester. From such efforts, classes were formed in Oswestry in 1920 and Wrexham by 1936.[18] Table 1 shows the Welsh attendances at the annual Memorial meetings, although classes with fewer than twenty were unrecorded. This may account for the absence of recorded classes in areas such as Pembrokeshire.

Parallel to the efforts of individual preachers, the Bible Students utilised the local press to publish Russell's sermons and advertise their meetings. By 1916, around

Table 1: Attendances of Bible Students at memorial meetings in the 1920s[21]

Congregation	1920	1922	1924	1926	1927
Abersychan			24		
Beaufort				20	
Cardiff		49			
Clydach	41				
Colwyn Bay			20		
Dowlais		26			
Llanelli		26			
Llantrisant					23
Newport				22	
Oswestry					
Penarth		25	25	28	27
Pontypool				26	

600 provincial papers were carrying his commentaries on the Scriptures and world events.[19] *The Western Mail* was among the Welsh press which reported upon Russell's visits to Wales. In 1911, he addressed crowds at Newport, Swansea and Cardiff. At the Albert Hall in Swansea he offered Biblical evidence to refute Purgatory and eternal torture. Russell was reported to have established 'a large following in Cardiff' – 2,000 turned out to hear his address on the 'Great Hereafter.'[20] However, such interest far exceeded the handful of active workers based in south Wales. In 1913 Russell was informed that the brethren were working hard in scattered parts of Wales to spread 'the Truth', a term still used by the Witnesses to describe their collection of beliefs.

The organisation and content of the early meetings was largely left to individual congregations, although guidance was provided in the *Watchtower*. Elders were elected on a six-monthly basis and were supported by deacons, both of whom were unpaid. At Clydach, the basic weekly programme was for a Bible study meeting to be held on a Wednesday evening, followed by two Sunday meetings: the afternoon 'Testimony' gathering involved individuals speaking about their faith while a public talk was delivered in the evening. Welsh and English-medium talks were also held in different localities according to interest.[22] To reduce expenses, some meetings were held in the open air on mountain sides rather than in hired halls.[23] Once a year a speaker was invited to deliver a special Memorial talk to commemorate the death of Jesus and this remains the most significant meeting for Witnesses.

One of the foundation principles of the Bible Students was that 'no collections' were taken in their meetings. Full-time ministers (later known as pioneers) were supported by small allowances from London and a percentage of the literature's selling price.[24] Running costs were met from voluntary contributions, and in cases of particular need through gifts and loans. Hence the Bakers, who owned a shop in Fishguard, provided boots free of charge to several itinerant ministers while the Clydach elders decided to pay members' burial expenses. In June 1914, in order to pay the rent for a public showing of Russell's film-strip 'Photo Drama of Creation', the Clydach congregation was asked 'to put on a slip of paper the amount of money he or she hopes to contribute to this work and place it in a box set for the purpose'.[25]

The high level of commitment in becoming a Bible Student had its price. Many wives who did not share the same faith as their husbands found it difficult to accept their prolonged absence in meetings and the ministry.[26] Alys Grenfell, for instance, attributed the drifting apart of her parents to the time when her father joined the Swansea Bible Students in 1923 (albeit temporarily), leaving her mother at home.[27] Others accepted the message but found it difficult to break free from communal ties. Bessie Thomas from Llanelli remembered that while living in Gresford (Clwyd) her Church of England father read and agreed with Russell's *Studies in the Scriptures* in the 1920s, but it was not until 1934 that he finally decided to give up his social links to the Church.[28]

In line with their understanding of 'being no part of the world', Witnesses remain politically neutral. Historically this has brought them into conflict with governments. The focus for the Bible Students was the establishment of God's heavenly kingdom and they interpreted current affairs, such as the industrial unrest in south Wales (and internationally) during 1911, as a sign of 'the last days' which preceded the setting up of God's kingdom. The Students anticipated that Satan would be cast from heaven in 1914 marking the beginning of Christ's heavenly reign – Russell and his followers expected to enter heaven.[29] However the failure of a cosmic rupture left many Bible Students disappointed and disillusioned, despite upbeat comments from the *Watchtower*. Further internal setbacks followed between 1916 and 1918. Most significantly the death of Russell in 1916 and the subsequent election of Joseph Rutherford (1869–1942) as President of the Watch Tower Society resulted in widespread disaffection among Students.[30] In Wales, William Williams, who had formed the Llanelli congregation, left to establish an Apostolic church while it seems that only Daniel Morgan of twenty-three Pontarddulais (Swansea) Students remained loyal following receipt of anti-Rutherford literature.[31]

Many Bible Students also faced ongoing trials as conscientious objectors during World War One. They objected on scriptural grounds, although their neutrality in respect of wars meant that they were neither pacifists nor patriots. They had opportunities to explain their stance before tribunals, largely made up of patriotic local councillors, set up under the terms of the 1916 Military Services Act. Initially the tribunals had the option of granting absolute exemption or of sending conscientious objectors to Non Combatant Corps, such as those stationed at Kinmel Park, Abergele (Clwyd), which held many Bible Students from Lancashire and Cheshire. Shortly thereafter they refused military orders and received their court martial as a result. Later the opportunity arose for these to do work of 'national importance'. Many of the Students willingly accepted their placement at work centres although conditions were poor.[32] Elizabeth Houghton recalled providing meals to Students held at the Llanddeusant (Carmarthenshire) camp, where they were allowed out to attend meetings in Clydach provided they walked twenty-two miles each way, for there were restrictions on the use of public transport.[33] Among these was Alfred Pryce Hughes, who was well known as a travelling overseer throughout Wales and later assumed responsibility as the Presiding Minister for Britain.[34]

By September 1916, 264 Bible Students had applied for exemption from military service.[35] The majority was assigned to work of national importance, although forty were imprisoned. In 1917 Joseph Williams from Burry Port (son of William Williams) was detained in Wormwood Scrubs and then Wakefield work centre.[36] He was among nearly 600 conscientious objectors who were assigned such tasks as weaving, building, sewing mailbags, boot-making and growing vegetables.[37] Herbert Senior, a Student from Leeds, recalled in the early 1970s:

> One evening a young brother named Joe Williams from Llanelly . . . came to me and said Bro Senior, I have taken this stand because of what my parents taught me, but not a definite decision of my own. I said, do you mean you wish to now Consecrate – the word we used in those days for Dedicate – your life to God? He said Yes I do. I knew him and his parents for I stayed in their home when the Photo-Drama went to Llanelly. After a little talk with him I said alright, come along to my cell and we will kneel down and I will pray to our Heavenly Father first and tell him how you feel about it, and then you just give yourself in prayer.[38]

Unlike the Second World War, Students were not widely known and did not attract the same degree of hostility they experienced twenty-five years later.[39] One exception involved eight Bible Students, placed in the Non Combatant Corps against their will, who were subsequently deported to France. In early June 1916 they refused to unload Army supplies from a quayside and were charged with refusing to obey their superior officer in the face of the enemy. They were tried by Field General Court-Martial for disobedience, and sentenced to death by being shot. However, after a long pause it was made clear that the sentence was commuted to ten years penal servitude. Shortly after this episode, the Government made the Home Office Scheme available to conscientious objectors and most Bible Students found this acceptable. Whether the whole episode was a bluff tactic used by the army to unsettle and break the Students is difficult to say. Ellsworth-Jones suggests that Prime Minister Asquith had already made (unofficial) guarantees as to their safety prior to the episode. In any event, their sentence was commuted to ten years penal servitude.[40]

Following the war a Benevolent Fund was established in 1919 to provide material support for families in need. The Society organised relief parcels of food and clothing as well as money and furnishings for the unemployed living in the mining communities of south Wales during the Depression. During the 1920s and 1930s, important organisational and doctrinal changes occurred. In 1920 Rutherford published *Millions Now Living Will Never Die* in eleven languages including Welsh.[41] It attracted widespread interest, partly because Rutherford suggested that 1925 would be the time when the 'ills of humankind shall begin to be treated with divine remedy'.[42] Students were instructed to 'advertise, advertise, advertise the King and his kingdom' and a hard-hitting message was delivered to the churches, businesses and the general public.[43] Bold preaching initiatives were introduced, including street witnessing and the use of portable phonographs. Joyce Powell was among a nucleus of Students who held regular parades outside the Catholic church in Burry Port (Carmarthenshire) despite heckling from nuns.[44] Other parties marched through the streets of Swansea and Cardiff denouncing 'Christendom', a term applied to the collective mainstream churches. McKibbin attributes the inter-war expansion of the Witnesses to the high degree of congregational participation, an unpaid leadership, and a strong evangelical spirit.[45]

In 1931 the name 'Jehovah's Witnesses' (Isaiah 43: 10–12) was adopted to further glorify God's name and avoid confusion with other Bible Students involved in the earlier succession. The Witnesses moved more sharply away from mainstream Church customs and teachings. For example, after 1928 Christmas was no longer celebrated because of its pagan associations and the symbol of the cross ceased to be used in literature. After 1935, the Witnesses came to believe that many faithful ones could qualify for eternal life on a restored earthly paradise, in addition to a small 'anointed' class of 144,000 who would rule with Christ in heaven.

Rutherford's presidency has been seen as a period of growing centralisation and standardisation of policy and practice. For instance, concern over abuses in the election of congregational elders resulted in a change in 1938 when elders were appointed centrally rather than at a local level. Rutherford's emphasis on individuals striving to meet quotas in carrying out 'field service', largely door-to-door preaching, was not universally welcomed in the congregations. However, a hard core of enthusiastic ministers endeavoured to make use of the latest technological equipment – portable phonographs and sound recordings – while travelling around Wales.[46] Zanoah Cain, for example, trundled a transcription machine into Wrexham town centre where he would at first play a piece of classical music to attract a crowd before replacing the record with a discourse from Joseph Rutherford.[47]

The Witnesses were the first religious group to be persecuted during World War Two for their neutral position and their courage has attracted international recognition.[48] From the government's viewpoint, the Witnesses were seen as a seditious sect and a potential cloak for fifth-columnists.[49] The *Watchtower* and accompanying magazine *Consolation* were banned in November 1942.[50] In September 1941, despite the restrictions of transport and rationing, 10,000 Witnesses from all parts of Britain gathered in Leicester for a convention. Among these was Beatrice Merrick (neé Baker), from Fishguard, who recalled the tactics of the army who sought to break up the tents in which the Witnesses were accommodated.

Denied official recognition as ministers of religion, many Witnesses in Wales were imprisoned for their beliefs and their experiences deserves separate research. By the end of the war, 1,249 male and 344 female Students had been incarcerated. Many of these were 'absolutists' who refused to compromise and faced a pattern of arrest, trial, detention and abuse through the war.[51] The usual procedure was to imprison females for a month while the men were held for three months, but were often detained again under the 'Cat and Mouse' regulations.[52] Eighteen-year-old Iris Radford, from a sheltered upbringing, served her month in Cardiff prison and found mixing with prostitutes and the prospect of being inspected for venereal disease frightening.[53] In north Wales, three female Witnesses were among the first cases brought before the northern tribunal in 1942. They agreed to undertake non-combatant service.[54]

The Watchtower Society provided guidelines for those appearing before the tribunals, beginning with 'never evade or sidestep a question'.[55] Len Merrick recalls the tactics used by Tribunal members who insisted that he only answered their questions, such as 'David was a man of war, wasn't he?' rather than discuss matters openly. In March 1944, he was sent to Swansea prison for three months hard labour. However, he did not think his spell in prison was unduly harsh:

> It wasn't too bad. I remember the brown suit, which meant that you were a Young Prisoner rather than a hardened criminal. As first offenders, we were kept apart and exercised in different circles. I scrubbed concrete floors and did farm work on the Gower where I met other religious people, such as Born Again Christians, and we discussed our faiths. The meals were dried bread, cheese and marmalade. Some wardens were cheeky and nasty, saying things like 'I'll get you lot shot', while others were good-tempered.[56]

In 1944 the Central Board for Conscientious Objectors expressed concern at the repeated prosecution of Witnesses and appealed to the Archbishop of Canterbury to bring their case before the Minster of Labour.[57] Despite the opposition, Witnesses endeavoured to meet together as best they could. Peter Lane, who lived in a pioneer home in Swansea, recalls being struck by a brick thrown from an angry crowd during 1942 and duly hospitalised.[58] Post-war national conscription brought added pressures with the continued refusal of the Home Office to accept that pioneers were ministers of religion.

Under the direction of Nathan Knorr (1905–77), appointed President in 1942, increasing emphasis was placed on ministerial education and training. To this end, numerous theocratic schools were established for both 'rank-and-file' congregational members and full-time evangelisers. Consequently, witnessing became more standardised and focused on studying the Bible with individuals rather than placing literature. Those Witnesses with favourable circumstances were encouraged to move into new territories such as Anglesey, the Rhondda valleys, and south-east Wales. During 1948, for instance, Mabel Miller and her partner took up the call and were not untypical in living frugally in a caravan, from which they travelled around Abergavenny on bicycles, spending on average 175 hours per month spreading the word. The experience of Douglas Jones, who recalled preaching in the Holyhead district during the 1950s, was not unusual: 'At the time everyone was chapel or church, so we were very insignificant, having no meeting place or any status in the community. We were regarded as odd but tolerated.'[59]

Sociologists, such as Beckford and Holden, have explored the reasons why people join the Witnesses.[60] Historically, the early letters written to America from British Students revealed dissatisfaction with doctrines held by the churches, and concerns over perceived falling moral standards.[61] Many of those who left Welsh chapels to become Witnesses found their former co-worshippers turned sharply against them. When Phyllis Morgan, from Cross Hands (Carmarthenshire), left her Independent chapel to become a Witness she recalled the heartache of losing a baby in 1955 and being told that there would be nowhere to bury her daughter. The opening of a council-run cemetery in Llannon at the time was seen as an answer to a prayer and her daughter became the first burial in the cemetery.[62]

Until the 1960s, Witnesses met in rented private rooms, clubs, public halls, schools and other buildings. The Wrexham congregation met at thirty–nine different locations before it had its own meeting place (kingdom hall) in 1968. Quick-build kingdom halls started to appear from the early 1980s to meet expansion needs, and were usually erected over the course of a weekend by voluntary effort.[63] Many Witnesses believed that the world would end in 1975, a date calculated to be 6,000 years after the creation of Adam.[64] One estimate suggests that in the years that immediately followed, up to a million left the organisation.[65] What sceptics regarded as one of a series of failed prophecies, the organisation pronounced as a test of faith. Evidently many passed. In 1980 there were about 5,600 Witnesses in Wales meeting in seventy-two congregations. By 2000, numbers had risen to around 8,000 and eighty-five congregations.[66]

The reasons why the Witnesses have persevered are varied, and include not only their steadfast faith but also a supporting social network.[67] This enables the Witnesses to devote spare time to preaching activities. On average, each congregational member in Britain spends about eight hours a month in the door-to-door ministry.[68] Full-time evangelisers are expected to devote sixty hours each month proselytising. Many have done so for decades, as was the case of Reginald Wilson who, since the 1960s, had devoted the best part of forty years preaching on foot through the Gwendraeth valleys (Carmarthenshire). These individuals have made an important contribution to the setting up and sustaining of congregations throughout Wales, particularly between 1950 and 1970.[69] The simplicity of 'the Truth' has often appealed to new recruits, who claim that they are able to place their previous experiences and everyday anxieties into a new context following discussions with Witnesses.[70] High expectations, in terms of commitment and adherence to a strict moral code, have stood in contrast to the perceived liberal values that have increasingly influenced the mainstream churches. Nonetheless the prohibitive standards relating to sexual relations outside marriage, blood transfusions, annual celebrations (notably Christmas, Easter, birthdays and national festivals) and involvement in political affairs, inevitably means that recruitment is limited.

A specific factor in explaining the growth in parts of Wales, particularly Cardiganshire, Carmarthenshire and Caernarfonshire, has been the effect of providing more Welsh-medium literature and meetings. Welsh-medium congregations operate in Caernarfon and Bangor. Bi-annual Welsh assemblies are also held in mid Wales with average attendances of around 250, though a significantly higher number of Witnesses are bilingual speakers who decide to attend English-medium congregations. This has partly alleviated the commonly-held perception that Witnesses are an American (English) religion. At the same time, the global, multicultural dimension features strongly in Witness publications. Witnesses in urban centres such as Swansea have learnt Chinese and other foreign languages in order to communicate with newly-arrived families. The Witnesses have also benefited from civil liberties to preach and convert new members.[71]

Historically, as this admittedly sympathetic overview has shown, the most self-defining characteristic of the Witnesses in Wales and beyond has been their determination to share with others their beliefs. George Carey, former Archbishop of

Canterbury, recognised the significance of this when he called upon regular church worshippers to follow the Jehovah's Witnesses' example of door-knocking: 'There will, of course, be many disappointments when you door-knock, but there will be unexpected joys, too.'[72]

Notes

1. *Observer*, 27 December 1998.
2. J. A. Beckford, 'The Mass Media and New Religious Movements', in B. Wilson and J. Cresswell (eds), *New Religious Movements: Challenge and Response* (London, 1999), p. 105. For a critical view from an ex-Witness see A. Rogerson, *Millions Now Living Will Never Die. A Study of the Jehovah's Witnesses* (London, 1969). See also the popular critique by W. Martin, *The Kingdom of the Cults* (Minneapolis, 1985) and A. Wills, *A People for His Name: A History of Jehovah's Witnesses and an Evaluation* (2nd edn. London, 2007). More balanced and recent accounts are provided by G. Chryssides, *Exploring New Religions* (London, 1999), pp. 94–107; D. V. Barrett, *The New Believers* (London, 2001), pp. 185–92.
3. T. Thomas (ed.), *The British: Their Religious Beliefs and Practices 800–1986* (London, 1988), p. 183. See also P. Badman, 'Religious Pluralism in Britain', in S. Gilley and W. J. Sheils (eds), *A History of Religion in Britain* (Oxford, 1994), p. 492.
4. See A. H. Halsey (ed.), *Trends in British Society Since 1900* (London, 1972), p. 432. 'Publisher' is a term used by Witnesses to describe fellow believers who publicise God's kingdom, largely (but not solely) by knocking on people's doors. The 2008 figure is drawn from Watchtower Bible and Tract Society (WBTS), *2009 Year Book of Jehovah's Witnesses* (New York, 2009), p. 32. For current officials statistics see: http://www.watchtower.org/.
5. L. Jones, 'Jehovah's Witnesses prepare for their annual Cardiff convention', *South Wales Echo*, 30 June 2009.
6. P. Brierley, 'Religion', in A. H. Halsey and J. Webb (eds), *Twentieth-Century British Social Trends* (London, 2000), pp. 650–74. See also C. G. Brown, *The Death of Christian Britain: Understanding Secularisation 1800–2000* (London, 2001); S. Bruce, *Religion in the Modern World: From Cathedrals to Cults* (Oxford, 2003).
7. J. Davies, N. Jenkins, M. Bairnes and P. Lynch (eds), *Encyclopaedia of Wales* (Cardiff, 2008), p. 412. The religion's official account of its activities in Britain can be found in WBTS, *1973 Year Book of Jehovah's Witnesses* (New York, 1973); for its global activities, see: WBTS, *Jehovah's Witnesses. Proclaimers of God's Kingdom* (New York, 1993). See also A. O. Hudson, *Bible Students in Britain. The Story of a Hundred Years* (Hounslow, 1989).
8. See D. Horowitz, *Pastor Charles Taze Russell: An Early American Christian Zionist* (New York, 1986); A sympathetic account is provided by A. H. MacMillan, *Faith on the March* (Englewood Cliffs, 1957). See also C. F. Redeker, *Pastor C. T. Russell; Messenger of Millennial Hope – Distinguished Founder of the Bible Students and His Enduring Legacy* (Temple City, CA., 2006). The full-text is available on-line at: http://www.archive.org/details/PastorC.t. RussellMessengerOfMillennialHope (accessed April 2010); and R. Hollister, *Meet our British Brethren* (London, 1957), available at: http://www.heraldmag.org/olb/ (accessed April 2010).
9. During his lifetime, Russell travelled an estimated million miles and delivered 30,000 sermons, before dying on a train in Texas during a preaching tour in 1916. B. Moynahan, *The Faith. A History of Christianity* (London, 2003), p. 626.
10. *Food for Thinking Christians* can be viewed at http://www.strictlygenteel.co.uk/food1881/1881_Food_For_Thinking_Christians.pdf (accessed November 2009). See also C. R. Wah, 'An Introduction to Research and Analysis of Jehovah's Witnesses: A View from the Watchtower', *Review of Religious Research*, 43, 2 (2001), 161–74.
11. Notes to the author from Beatrice Merrick, September 2002.
12. Interview with Beatrice Merrick, 16 September 2002.

13. C. T. Russell, *Divine Plan of the Ages: A Vindication of the Divine Character and Government* (New York, 1891); reprinted by Dawn Bible Students Association (1955). See http://www.dawnbible.com/ (accessed April 2010). Examples of Russell's works can be viewed at http://www.strictlygenteel.co.uk/index.html (accessed November 2009).

14. Minutes of the Clydach and District Branch of the International Bible Students Association (hereafter Minutes), 12 February 1911. I am indebted to Ceri Evans for this and other Clydach sources.

15. Minutes, 2 October 1912.

16. *Watchtower*, 1 December 1911.

17. M. Edgar, *The Memoirs of Aunt Sarah* (Glasgow, 1918), p. 32.

18. I am grateful to Peter Curtis for this information; letter to author, 16 October 2002.

19. Hollister, *Meet our British Brethren*. Local newspapers printed selected sermons from *Studies in the Scriptures*, of which five million copies were reported to have been circulated by 1911. See *Llanelly Mercury*, 6 July 1911. For examples of sermons see *Llanelly Mercury*, 10 August 1911, 7 September 1911, 9 November 1911; *Mumbles Press*, 6 July 1911, 28 September 1911, 5 October 1911.

20. *Western Mail*, 10 November 1911. *South Wales Evening Post*, 11 November 1911. The Cardiff congregation grew from a handful in 1923 to about 30 in 1940, increasing to 80 in 1952. I am grateful to Arthur Taylor for this information.

21. Information supplied by Gary Perkins, based on returns to *Watchtower* magazine in the 1920s.

22. For examples, see advertisements in *Llanelly Mercury*, 30 November 1916 and 14 December 1916.

23. Hudson, *Bible Students in Britain*; *Zion's Watchtower*, 1 February 1914.

24. Since 1990 all literature has been offered, to those who show a genuine interest, without charge. WBTS, *Jehovah's Witnesses. Proclaimers of God's Kingdom* (New York, 1993), p. 350.

25. Minutes, 14 June 1914.

26. For a modern-day discussion of this topic, see A. Holden, 'Doing Tolerance: How Jehovah's Witnesses Live with Unbelieving Relatives', published by the Department of Sociology, Lancaster University, Lancaster, at http://www.lancs.ac.uk/fass/sociology/papers/holden-doing-tolerance.pdf (accessed April 2010).

27. J. Grenfell-Hill (ed.), *Growing Up in Wales 1895–1939* (Llandysul, 1996), p. 112.

28. Interview with Bessie Thomas, 14 November 2002.

29. G. Chryssides, *Historical Dictionary of Jehovah's Witnesses* (Lanham, Maryland, 2008), p. 2. See also *Llanelly Mercury*, 6 August 1914, and M. Cole, *Jehovah's Witnesses; The New World Society* (London, 1956), pp. 66–7.

30. Since 1917, the Bible Study Movement has acted independently of the Witnesses. See http://www.biblestudents.net/ (accessed April 2010).

31. Informal discussions with Ceri Evans.

32. J. W. Graham, *Conscription and Conscience. A History, 1916–1919* (London, 1922).

33. 'Life story of Elizabeth Houghton', unpublished manuscript supplied by Beatrice Merrick.

34. *Watchtower*, 1 April 1963.

35. WBTS, *Year Book of Jehovah's Witnesses* (New York, 1973), p. 98.

36. Williams, born in 1898, was also registered as a conscientious objector in World War Two. See *Llanelly Mercury*, 10 December 1942.

37. *Hansard*, 30 November 1917, vol. 88, cc.459–60. See also http://www.forthesakeofthekingdom.co.uk/ (accessed April 2010).

38. 'Recollections of Herbert Senior', unpublished paper (n.d.). I am grateful to Gary Perkins for this source and other advice on conscientious objectors in World War One.

39. J. Rae, *Conscience and Politics* (London, 1970), p. 75. While imprisoned, Students continued to keep out of political discussions. See D. Boulton, *Objection Overruled* (London, 1967), p. 215.

40. See W. Ellsworth-Jones, *We Will Not Fight: The Untold Story of the First World War's Conscientious Objectors* (London, 2008).

41. ISBA, *Miliynau'n Awr Yn Fyw Ni Fyddant Feirw Byth!* (London, 1920).

42. *Watchtower*, 15 April 1920. See also J. Penton, *Apocalypse Delayed. The Story of the Jehovah's Witnesses* (Toronto, 1985).

43. *Watchtower*, 1 November 1922.

44. Interview with Joyce Powell, 20 October 2002.
45. R. McKibbin, *Classes and Culture: England 1918–1951* (Oxford, 1998), p. 274.
46. J. Beckford, *The Trumpet of Prophecy* (Oxford, 1975), p. 30.
47. *Watchtower*, 1 August 2001.
48. See H. Hesse (ed.), *Persecution and Resistance of Jehovah's Witnesses During the Nazi-Regime 1933–1945* (Chicago, 2001); C. King, 'The Case of the Third Reich', in E. Barker (ed.), *New Religious Movements: A Perspective for Understanding Society* (New York, 1982), pp. 125–39. Between 1933 and 1945, 1,490 Witnesses died as a result of National Socialist persecution. See J. S. Wrobel, 'Jehovah's Witnesses in National Socialist Concentration Camps, 1933–45', in *Religion, State and Society*, 34, 2 (June 2006), 89–125.
49. J. M. Swift, *Jehovah's Witnesses: A Brief Account of the History, Beliefs and Methods of a Strange and Widespread Organization* (London, 1956), p. 9. See also *The Times*, 28 August 1942.
50. ISBA, *To All Lovers of Freedom: WARNING* (London, 1942), available at: http://www.strictlygenteel. co.uk/tracts/warning.html (accessed November 2009).
51. G. J. DeGroot, *Blighty. British Society in the Era of the Great War* (London, 1996).
52. For examples, see *Carmarthen Journal*, 30 August 1940 and 4 October 1940. Also *Tenby Observer*, 21 August 1942. See also IBSA, *Jehovah's Witnesses: Their Position* (London, 1942), available at: http://www.strictlygenteel.co.uk/tracts/jehovahswitnessesposition.html (accessed November 2009).
53. F. Goodall, *A Question of Conscience* (Stroud, 1997), p. 114. See also L. Verrill-Rhys and D. Beddoe (eds), *Parachutes and Petticoats* (Dinas Powys, 1992), pp. 121–3.
54. *North Wales Chronicle*, 28 August 1942. The first female conscientious objector in World War Two was twenty-one year old Witness Hilda Henshall-Brown from Manchester, who refused to take up nursing when she was registered with her age group for national service to the puzzlement of officials. See A. Marwick, *The Home Front* (London, 1976), p. 127
55. National Archives (NA), DPP2/957.
56. Interview with Len Merrick, 17 September 2002. See also West Glamorgan Archive Service. D/D PRO/ HMP 1/25. Registers of Swansea Prison, 1 January 1944 – 22 March 1947.
57. R. Barker, *Conscience, Government and* War (London, 1982), pp. 106–7.
58. Interview with Peter Lane, 17 December 2002.
59. Information supplied by Douglas Jones, November 2002.
60. Beckford, *Trumpet of Prophecy*; A. Holden, *Jehovah's Witnesses* (London, 2002).
61. Examples of these letters appear on the Bible Students website: http://www.biblestudents.net/ (accessed April 2010).
62. Interview with Phyllis Morgan, 10 September 2002.
63. In May 1984, the first quick-build hall outside America was erected at Dolgellau. For details of quick-build projects, see *Sunday Telegraph: Weekend Magazine*, 21 July 1990, 47–50.
64. *Awake*, 8 October 1968. The Society declared that it would not be surprised if God intervened in 1975 and that 'we are living in the final few years of this time of the end'. See *Watchtower*, 15 March 1980.
65. See A. Holden, 'Cavorting with the Devil: Jehovah's Witnesses who abandon their faith', available at: http://www.lancs.ac.uk/fass/sociology/papers/holden-cavorting-with-the-devil.pdf (accessed November 2009).
66. P. Brierley (ed.), *UK Christian Handbook, 1998–1999* (London, 2000), p. 10.3.
67. J. F. Zygmunt, 'Prophetic Failure and Chiliastic Identity', in J. R. Stone (ed.), *Expecting Armageddon* (London, 2000), pp. 65–86.
68. *Our Kingdom Ministry* (London, April 2005), p. 2.
69. A good example is the Caerffili congregation, whose origins can be traced to two full-time pioneers in the late-1930s. By the 1950s, 19 attended meetings, rising to 80 in 1978. Information supplied by Steve Edwards, letter to the author dated 2 December 2002.
70. Holden, *Jehovah's Witnesses*, p. 55.
71. See R. Stark and I. R. Iannaccone, 'Why the Jehovah's Witnesses Grow So Rapidly: A Theoretical Application', *Journal of Contemporary Religion*, 12, 2 (1997), 133–57.
72. *Daily Telegraph*, 1 January 1999.

CHAPTER 16

EVANGELICALISM

David Ceri Jones

Despite not having any churches bearing the name evangelical until the middle of the twentieth century, evangelical religion has been the dominant expression of Christianity in Wales since at least the eighteenth century. This chapter will concentrate, in the main, on the late-nineteenth and twentieth centuries when a combination of circumstances, most especially the challenge of modernity, created a more sharply drawn evangelical identity, and in the end self-identifying evangelical congregations and networks of churches. The earliest known use of the term evangelical in Welsh has been traced to 1632 when Rowland Vaughan used it in his translation of Lewis Bayly's devotional manual, *Practice of Piety* (1611).[1] Evangelical expressions of Christianity, using the term in its strictest sense, as relating to the evangel, or gospel, have been present in Wales since the Reformation, but Evangelicalism, with a capital 'E' if you like, was a product of the international religious revivals of the mid-eighteenth century, revivals which not only affected Wales, but many other parts of the British Atlantic world as well.[2] Evangelicalism, according to the now classic definition of David Bebbington, is a popular protestant movement characterised by four hallmarks: a stress on the centrality of the Bible, the necessity of personal conversion, the atoning power of the cross of Christ and the necessity of faith in action, especially in evangelism and good works.[3] Evangelical religion was primarily a religion of the heart that, while not intrinsically anti-intellectual, stressed the experiential and practical consequences of Christian faith, reflexive of its emergence in the age of the Enlightenment.[4]

Many of the other chapters in this book take a denominational approach to Wales' religious history which is, of course, unavoidable. However, the four distinctives of evangelical religion stretched across the denominations creating bonds of identity across other theological and institutional divides. While denominational differences and identities certainly ran deep in Wales, particularly by the later half of the nineteenth century, the areas which evangelicals agreed on often far outstripped those areas in which there were deeply held differences. Welsh Christianity did not only and not always run along partisan denominational lines, something that the historiography has not always adequately reflected. The mid-eighteenth century evangelical revival was genuinely inter-denominational; in England it initially drew in Anglicans, in Scotland it was Presbyterians, while in the American colonies it was Congregationalists and slightly later Baptists who took up the challenge of evangelical renewal. In Wales, the early evangelicals were almost all Anglicans, and Methodism, synonymous with Evangelicalism at this stage, started life as a renewal movement that was deeply rooted within the established church. Both Howel Harris and Daniel Rowland, despite unjust treatment and plenty of opportunities to do otherwise, remained faithful and loyal members of the Church of England, Harris even claiming at one point that God had called him 'to live and die in the communion of the established church'.[5]

They reasoned that while the doctrinal standards of the Church of England remained sound there was always the possibility that it could be reformed and revived. Their chosen means for bringing about this renewal were a combination of community revivals and the close pastoral supervision of those who professed faith as a result of them. Conscious that in many parts of Wales the Church had proven unable to make much of an impact because of its organisational limitations,[6] Harris and Rowland preached passionate evangelistic sermons, frequently out of doors, by means of which many experienced a new birth and were brought to an educated and personal acceptance of the Protestant faith for the first time. Those who experienced an evangelical conversion in a Methodist setting were then organised into small cell groups of between ten and twenty members. Meeting wherever and whenever was convenient, usually in the Welsh language, these groups became discipleship schools where new converts met together to be taught, to study, pray, sing, confess their faults, and come under spiritual discipline, in what were in essence mini churches within the Church of England.[7] Within about fifteen years almost 450 of these societies had been established in south and west Wales, with somewhere in the region of 10–12,000 members in total, a not inconsiderable achievement given the difficulties which earlier generations of Protestants had encountered in Wales.[8] In a sense this early phase of renewal was something of a false dawn.[9] The pioneering work of Harris and Rowland were soon overshadowed by the dismissal of Harris from the Methodist movement in 1750; it was not until a fresh outbreak of religious revival at Llangeitho in 1762[10] that the momentum was regained once more and Evangelicalism began on its phase of most impressive growth and greatest influence.

R. Tudur Jones has called the first half of the nineteenth century the high noon of Welsh Evangelicalism.[11] It was in this period that the spirit of the evangelical revival spilled over from its Methodist birthplace. The long-postponed secession of the Calvinistic Methodists from the Church of England in 1811 made this cross-fertilization far easier of course, but the transformation of the older dissenting denominations by a conversionist, outward-looking, evangelical spirituality had been, in reality, underway long before that.[12] The inspiration for this transformation was the wave upon wave of religious revivals that followed in the wake of the 1762 Llangeitho awakening. It has been calculated that in the century following 1762, Wales experienced at least fifteen national religious revivals, as well as countless smaller-scale local awakenings.[13] They were led by a cadre of extremely gifted preachers and evangelists who emerged following the deaths of Howel Harris, Daniel Rowland and William Williams. The Baptists could boast the charismatic Christmas Evans, the Calvinistic Methodists, Thomas Charles and John Elias, and the Independents,

William Williams of Wern.[14] Many of these individuals have not received the serious historical and biographical study they deserve; they were, as Richard Carwardine has commented, the folk heroes[15] of Welsh society in a period when Wales' religious communities were some of the few institutions that enabled it to carve out a distinct identity. The revivals which they superintended, especially those which swept many parts of Wales in the 1820s and 1830s, brought a regular influx of new people into all of the nonconformist denominations, as generation after generation, appropriated the evangelical message for themselves. These new converts could be easily accommodated in new chapel buildings which were built quickly, cheaply and conveniently, without any need for recourse to the cumbersome legislative process that hampered the ability of the Anglicans to respond to the challenge that the nonconformists presented, particularly in the rapidly growing urban and industrial communities of south Wales by the early decades of the nineteenth century.[16]

But this was also a period of what John Wolffe has called the expansion of Evangelicalism,[17] an expansion not in numerical terms alone, but also in terms of ambition and scope. It was the age when evangelicals were at the forefront of the major social movements of the day, most famously the abolition of the slave trade. In Wales it was educational provision that captured the imagination of nonconformist leaders as Thomas Charles' Sunday Schools picked up on the earlier achievements of Griffith Jones' circulating schools, teaching pupils of all ages the basic skills of literacy and numeracy.[18] It was to be a level of literacy that was soon to fuel the growth of an impressive print culture as the various denominations began publishing periodicals containing a mixture of journalistic reporting and theological discussion and debate.[19] But this was also the age of an awakening missionary interest among Welsh evangelicals. John Davies had been one of the first Welsh overseas missionaries, sailing for Tahiti with the backing of the London Missionary Society in 1801[20] and Thomas Charles had founded the British and Foreign Bible Society in 1804.[21] Both events stimulated interest in overseas mission in Wales, and inspired a steady stream of Welsh men and women to take the gospel to distant shores.

By the early nineteenth century evangelical religion had begun to make significant inroads into both north and south Wales. Precise figures for this growth are startling; in 1815 it was estimated that the Independents alone could boast 257 congregations;[22] while the Baptists had increased their membership six-fold from 1,601 in 1760 to 9,232 in 1800.[23] Such patterns of growth can be multiplied across all the Welsh denominations. By the time of the first national religious census in 1851, over three-quarters of the population of the country could be comfortably accommodated within a place of worship in Wales, and the overwhelming majority of the church-going population preferred to attend a nonconformist chapel over the local parish church.[24] But these figures really tell only half the story, and do not reflect the cultural hegemony that evangelical nonconformity had come to exert by this time. The infamous report of the Education Commissioners in 1847, the notorious 'Blue Books', which accused the Welsh of being ignorant, lazy and immoral, laying the blame for this squarely at the door of the Welsh language and nonconformity, forced the nonconformists out of their religious ghettoes and into the public sphere. What emerged in the decades between 1830 and 1870 was a culture in which nonconformity and Welshness became increasingly closely intertwined, some even arguing that the working class Welshman, unlike his English counterpart, was more naturally predisposed towards religious belief.[25] Biblicism, strict Sabbatarianism, temperance, hymn-singing and the like became key emblems of Welshness,[26] fusing seamlessly with the badges of nationhood that had been created by the Romanic revival at the end of the eighteenth and the early years of the nineteenth century.[27] It was little wonder that Christmas Evans could write that:

> Perhaps there has never been such a nation as the Welsh who have been won over so widely to the hearing of the gospel. Meeting-houses have been erected in each corner of the land and the majority of the common people, nearly all of them, crowd in to listen.[28]

The real high point of this evangelical hegemony came in 1859 when a national religious revival swept over much of Wales, once more bringing tens of thousands of fresh new converts into the churches.[29] But this revival was freighted with ironic significance since this was also the year of the publication of Charles Darwin's *Origin of Species* (1859), an event that for many proved critical, albeit in the medium to longer term, in challenging the legitimacy of many of the theological assumptions that underpinned Evangelicalism.[30] Although religious revivals remained a feature of later nineteenth century religious life in Wales, they became less frequent and probably less spontaneous, possibly because there were simply less people in need of conversion, such had been the success of the evangelicals in training each new generation in the rudiments of Christian discipleship by this point. But there was also a very definite move within nonconformity more generally in this period towards respectability and political engagement, something that undoubtedly blunted evangelistic zeal in some quarters at least.

The Liberal party's political victory in the 1868 General Election saw the close conflation of nonconformity and Liberal politics.[31] The overriding political issue for the nonconformists was the limitation of the power of the Anglican Church in Wales, which had been bolstered for generations by its control of education, marriage and burial rites, church rates and tithes, even long after it had ceased to command the allegiance of the majority of the population. The ultimate aim was the disestablishment and disendowment of the Church, but the campaign to achieve this absorbed a disproportionate amount of the energy of nonconformists in this period, and by the time the campaign had actually borne fruit in 1920, it was the nonconformists themselves who were fighting for their very survival. Accounts of the decline of nonconformity in Wales have sometimes tended to be simplistic, pinning the blame on simplistic teleological accounts of secularization, or on the influx of English-speaking incomers into Wales, or the bourgeois aspirations of the nonconformist leadership, who increasingly gravitated towards the middle classes, with the result that they became remote from the aspirations of their more working class congregations, particularly in south Wales. While these factors, amongst others, undoubtedly played their part in the decline, they do not give sufficient weight to some of the changes actually taking place within Welsh evangelical nonconformity itself. By the turn of the twentieth century theological liberalism was challenging many of the doctrines, especially regarding the deity of Christ and the authority of Scripture, which lay at the very heart of evangelical Christianity. The crisis of confidence that began to cripple the effectiveness of Welsh nonconformity by the early years of the twentieth century, was fundamentally a crisis of belief.

It is possible to argue that the late-nineteenth and early-twentieth centuries saw the gradual, but inexorable, marginalisation of evangelical opinions within Welsh nonconformity. While it would be very easy to write about this process in almost conspiratorial terms, as some evangelical historians have certainly tended to do,[32] the almost monopolistic position which evangelicals had enjoyed within most of the Welsh denominations since the beginning of the nineteenth century was slowly eroded as they firstly moved to the fringes of many of the traditional denominations, and then as the twentieth century progressed abandoned them altogether for new more purely evangelical churches. In a sense the foundation of the international Evangelical Alliance in 1846 reflected this concern as it attempted to give evangelicals, scattered across all sorts of denominations and conscious of some of the daunting challenges that confronted them, an institutional dimension to their identity.[33] In Wales the inroads made by supporters of the Oxford Movement in the 1840s and 1850s had proven sufficient to convince many evangelicals that their hegemony was under palpable threat.[34] It was no surprise, therefore, that Welsh chapels were among the most enthusiastic respondents to the Evangelical Alliance's calls for a week of prayer for unity at the beginning of each New Year throughout the second half of the nineteenth century.[35] Within the Church of England evangelicals enthusiastically supported organisations such as the Church Pastoral Aid Society, a home mission agency which had the express aim of securing the more active allegiance of the working classes to the Church.[36]

It would be a mistake to assume that Welsh evangelicalism was an ossified monolith by the middle years of the nineteenth century. There were certainly lively debates and theological shifts occurring, but these were very much within the bounds of a broad evangelical orthodoxy. Wearied by the debates about such matters as the precise extent of Christ's atonement, subjects that had preoccupied many in the early decades of the nineteenth century,[37] there was a gradual move away from Calvinism well underway. Similarly, the publication of a Welsh translation of Charles Finney's *Lectures on Revivals* (1835) in 1839[38] had subtly shifted the emphasis in evangelism towards securing public declarations of faith, what would later be called decisions for Christ. This possibly made church membership an easier commodity to come by, especially for those who regarded it as an essential badge of respectability. But it was to be the impact of the advanced theological ideas emanating from Germany that would overshadow these developments and prove to be far more damaging.

Mention has already been made of Darwinism, but the full implications of his theory of evolution, especially for the interpretation of the early chapters of *Genesis,* was not immediately realised, rather it was those influenced by the biblical criticism of the liberal theologians, that had the most far reaching consequences. Some have unfairly wished to lay the blame for this openness to new theological currents at the feet of Lewis Edwards;[39] while he remained entirely orthodox, the journal he established, *Y Traethodydd* (The Essayist), was to become one of the earliest and most influential mouthpieces for opinions which Edwards himself would surely have baulked at.[40] Initially, it was among theologians in Wales' new universities that liberal theology took root, the Victorian crisis of faith was certainly evident, if not quite so prevalent, in nonconformist Wales. The twin challenges of the outworking of the ethos of the Enlightenment and the philosophical idealism of philosophers like Hegel, gave birth to both the higher critical attitude to scripture and liberal theology.[41] But it was not until the early twentieth century, and especially following the Great War that the scepticism that had taken root in some of Wales' theological colleges and university theology departments filtered down to the man and woman in the pew, as generations of ministers emerged having had their confidence in the Bible and supernatural Christianity thoroughly undermined, if not eradicated altogether.[42]

In retrospect the religious revival led by Evan Roberts which swept through much of Wales in 1904–5 looks awfully like the last gasp of a dying nonconformist culture.[43] Whilst it garnered an impressive harvest of souls, this revival was polarising in a way that many of the previous Welsh revivals had not been. The erosion of evangelical belief, at least among the leadership of many of Wales' denominations, meant that the often unrestrained demonstrations of religious emotion that characterised the revival received a lukewarm reception. One of the eventual consequences of this process was the proliferation of independent churches in Wales as many of the converts of the revival quit the traditional denominations for churches which attempted to keep their membership doctrinally pure and keep alive the spirit of the revival. Of course, there had been churches like this in Wales before the revival. The Plymouth Brethren had their own austere Gospel Halls in many towns in Wales,[44] but the often ramshackle mission halls that now sprang up did so with the intention of maintaining a very carefully and tightly defined evangelical identity.[45]

There was also a new player on the evangelical landscape too, Pentecostalism. Born out of the Welsh revival and the 1906 Azusa Street revival in Los Angeles, California, Pentecostal denominations like Elim, the Assemblies of God and the more distinctly Welsh Apostolic Church, founded by D. P. Williams in 1916, each attempted to maintain what they regarded as the more charismatic spirituality of the New Testament Church,[46] an endeavour that had greater purchase in an era when the supernaturalism of traditional Christianity was being called into question. The kind of ecclesiastical isolation taken by many of these groups was not the path chosen by all evangelicals; many, probably the majority at this stage, chose to remain within the denominations in which they had grown up, though there was an increasing tendency to look elsewhere for spiritual sustenance, to many of the evangelical parachurch organisations which promoted a range of distinctive teachings. The most popular was the Keswick Convention, a pietistic conference for the deepening of the spiritual life, which from 1903 had its own meetings at Llandrindod Wells every summer,[47] but Keswick tended to promote an other-worldly piety that positively discouraged serious theological engagement. The early years of the twentieth century were witnessing the beginnings of a significant change in the character of Welsh evangelicalism. The days when nonconformity and evangelicalism had been more or less synonymous had all but passed, the stark choice of increasing marginalisation within predominantly liberal denominations and the lonely path of ecclesiastical separatism were to be options that increasing numbers of evangelicals were compelled to consider seriously as the twentieth century unfolded.

The increasingly liberal trajectory taken by the mainline denominations following the Great War, encapsulated in the campaign to revise the confession of faith of the Calvinistic Methodists, the *cause celebre* of the Tom Nefyn case in 1927–9,[48] and the seeming ubiquity of the social gospel,[49] were enough to provoke a conservative backlash in some quarters of the Welsh evangelical world. Fundamentalist evangelical voices seemed to congregate around R. B. Jones, the minister of a series of Baptist congregations in the Rhondda valley during the inter-war years.[50] In the pages of their magazine *Yr Efengylydd* (The Evangelist), R. B. Jones and his close associate, Nantlais Williams, a prominent Calvinistic Methodist minister from Ammanford in Carmarthenshire, laid great stress on what they thought were the fundamental building blocks of the Christian faith, particularly the inerrancy of Scripture, and trained a searchlight on anyone or anything that smacked of innovation and theological compromise. Their distrust of modernity and their often combative attitude to those with whom they disagreed mirrored the ethos of American Fundamentalism, of course, as did their very strict definitions of what counted as worldliness and sin. In the end their strand of evangelicalism became both exclusive and highly divisive, and their world-denying moral stance often produced a separation from the world and a social and cultural isolation that proved in the end to be counterproductive. However, neither Jones nor Williams were thorough-going separatists in terms of their ecclesiology; both of them preferred to work for reform and renewal within their respective denominations, although it is arguable that Jones' South Wales Bible Training Institute, which started life in the schoolroom of his chapel at Porth in 1919,[51] was a tacit admission by evangelicals that they could no longer confidently rely on the denominational theological colleges to produce sufficiently orthodox and godly minsters.[52] Their emphasis on the fundamentals of the faith also left a powerful legacy, and further loosened the ties which many evangelicals in Wales felt towards their denominations, making identities founded on exclusively evangelical, rather than broader 'mere' Christian, distinctives a greater likelihood.[53]

Anticipating conflicts that would later be fought on a larger stage were divisions which took place within the student Christian world at this time. Within the context of widespread dissatisfaction at the liberal direction being taken by the Student Christian Movement (SCM); some evangelical students at Oxford and Cambridge had already disaffiliated from it in order to uphold a more conservative theological position and preserve their doctrinal purity.[54] A similar process of distancing took place in Wales with the result that by 1923 Cardiff University had its own independent Evangelical Union. By 1930 there were similar groups at Swansea and Aberystwyth universities also,[55] all of them under the direction and leadership of the Inter-Varsity Fellowship (IVF), an umbrella organisation which had been founded in 1928 to link together all those evangelical unions which had decided to stand apart from the SCM. The generation of students who made these often sacrificial stands would form the backbone of evangelical leadership in the mid-twentieth century.

The years either side of the Second World War proved to be ones of decline and retrenchment for evangelicals in Wales. There were no leaders to take the place of R. B. Jones, the promising ministry of Martyn Lloyd-Jones in Aberafon had come to an end in 1938,[56] and his relocation to Westminster Chapel in London did not seem to auger well for his leadership of evangelicals back in Wales. While the war did not inaugurate anything like the turning back to the churches which some had hoped for and predicted, by the 1950s there was optimism in the air and an impression that there were new things occurring on the Welsh religious landscape.[57] There was a renewed sense of urgency in missions held by a new generation of evangelical students in many south Wales towns in the late-1940s and early 1950s,[58] and Billy Graham had been an early visitor to Wales, taking a number of relatively low-key missions in the Swansea area in 1946. A little later, pictures from his marathon Harringay crusade in 1955, were been beamed backed to Wales by means of the new technology of television as eager evangelicals held impromptu meetings in church halls and university common rooms anxious to take advantage of this new and seemingly gilt-edged evangelistic opportunity.[59]

It was, however, amongst a group of earnest Bangor university students that perhaps the most significant developments took place. Having had their Christian commitment intensified at a 'retreat' near Dolgellau in 1948, the group led by J. Elwyn Davies, a student at Bala-Bangor College, initially coalesced around a Welsh language magazine, *Y Cylchgrawn Efengylaidd* (The Evangelical Magazine), the first edition of which appeared in November of that same year.[60] Members of the group met regularly at the Eisteddfod, or on evangelistic campaigns, while the student members met at IVF conferences, but the activities of the group very quickly mushroomed. In 1952 the first *Cylchgrawn* conference took place and then in 1955 an English-language magazine, *the Evangelical Magazine of Wales* was established to serve the predominantly English-speaking evangelical constituency in south Wales, and it was in this year also that the *Cylchgrawn* people became more organised adopting the title the Evangelical Movement of Wales (EMW), an explicitly evangelical basis of faith and appointing Elwyn Davies as General Secretary. The core activities of the EMW were its youth camps, its commitment to evangelistic outreach, its conference and regular preaching rallies around the country, its network of fraternals for ministers, and its provision of high quality evangelical literature through both bookshops and eventually its own publishing imprint. Although the seeds of secession were present within the EMW from the beginning, at this early stage it was nothing more than a group designed to facilitate fellowship between evangelicals scattered among the various denominational groups in Wales.[61]

It was the gathering pace of the ecumenical agenda that changed the purpose and profile of the EMW. Unity discussions between the Presbyterians, Independents, Wesleyans and Baptists, the four largest Welsh denominations in Wales, during the early 1960s alarmed many evangelicals.[62] The haemorrhaging of members from most of the mainline denominations in Wales by the 1960s[63] was not quite as catastrophic among churches with a more evangelical ethos. While there was certainly decline, the networks of evangelical parachurch organisations and the tendency for evangelicals to be far more committed to the task of evangelism enabled them to maintain some degree of vibrancy, but also led them to develop a more belligerent attitude to those who did not share their theological opinions. Ever since his move to Westminster Chapel, London, Martyn Lloyd-Jones had maintained a close interest in events in Wales, and especially in the emergence of the EMW. A regular speaker at EMW events and a close confidant of Elwyn Davies, Lloyd-Jones exerted an authority that was almost papal over some evangelicals in Wales.[64] In 1966 at a meeting in London organised by the Evangelical Alliance, Lloyd-Jones issued a call to evangelicals across the denominational spectrum to leave their doctrinally mixed denominations and come together.[65] While he never specified what this coming together might involve, and certainly did not envisage a new united evangelical denomination, the ambiguity in his call did little to strengthen his case.[66] His appeal polarised English evangelicals, while some Free Church ministers heeded his call, the majority of evangelical Anglicans, led by John Stott, resisted it forcefully, and following a major conference at Keele in 1967 re-dedicated themselves to working for reform within the structures of the Church of England.[67]

It was probably in Wales that Lloyd-Jones' appeal was greeted with most enthusiasm. In the immediate aftermath a number of evangelical churches seceded from their denominations and affiliated formally to the EMW, and the EMW in turn applied for membership of the national British Evangelical Council. While many of these new independent churches were clearly relieved to be free from liberal denominational control, the lonely path of separatism was far from easy. A belligerent attitude and an often strident tone that assumed that they only remained faithful to the gospel served to increase their isolation. The pace of secessions picked up throughout the 1970s and into the 1980s[68] with the result that some within the EMW felt that there were too many churches to be adequately managed by means of the kind of loose association that the framers of the original EMW had in mind. Consequently in 1988 a new organisation called the Associating Evangelical Churches of Wales (AECW) was formed to give expression to the closer co-operation which many felt was essential for the maintenance of the evangelical witness. Thirty-five evangelical churches joined the AECW immediately, and at the time of writing there are sixty-two affiliated churches,[69] although the majority of them are concentrated in south and northeast Wales, and most of them can boast only relatively small congregations that have struggled to remain culturally relevant and engaged with the late-twentieth and early twenty-first century world in which they find themselves. While the EMW and AECW now operate alongside one another, it is very difficult to see exactly what the distinct purpose of each actually is. What had started life as a loose association of like-minded individuals who wished to give expression to their evangelical identity, has slowly evolved into a network of self-identifying evangelical churches, a quasi-denomination at the very least.

While secession from the mainline denominations was the only option for some evangelicals in Wales, for others that option has not proved as attractive. Among the ranks of evangelicals from nonconformist backgrounds, there were plenty who, while they had been sympathetic to the aims and ethos of the EMW up until 1967, found the separatist line taken thereafter unpalatable. They remained in their denominations but tended to plough a pretty lonely furrow, having often been ostracised by old friends in the EMW they were also viewed with suspicion by those within their denominations who did not appreciate their evangelical convictions. The only group of non-separatist evangelicals to take a more positive and concerted attitude towards engagement with their parent denomination was to be found in the Church in Wales. Under the direction of John Stott a small group of evangelical Anglicans had been meeting together informally since 1964. They were formally organised into the Evangelical Fellowship in the Church in Wales in 1967 at a meeting held at Stott's holiday cottage at Dale in Pembrokeshire. In its first year the group could boast twenty-eight members under the leadership of Bertie Lewis, at that time a vicar in Aberaeron, but later to be rector at Aberystwyth, but it has grown significantly in line with the increase in the numbers of evangelicals within the Church in Wales. John Stott has remained a persuasive voice within the EFCW, and his combination of a strong evangelical theology and commitment to evangelical social action has powerfully marked the evangelical witness within the Church in Wales.[70] Like the original Evangelical Movement of Wales, the EFCW is primarily a means of facilitating fellowship among Anglican evangelicals by means of conferences, camps and publishing,[71] although it is possible that, as Roger Brown writes, the recognition that 'evangelicals felt they had a place within the Church in Wales and wished to contribute to it'[72] proved to be its most far-reaching impact. Unlike the EMW, there has never been much appetite for separatism within the EFCW constituency, although recent divisions within the global Anglican Communion have begun to test that resolution to the limit as some Anglican evangelicals in Wales have enthusiastically endorsed the GAFCON concord and signed up to the newly established Federation of Confessing Anglicans.[73]

In many respects the constituencies represented by both the EMW and the EFCW are largely drawn from the more conservative end of the evangelical movement. One of the most remarkable features of British evangelicalism in the last twenty-five years or so is the extent to which any broad evangelical consensus that might have existed in earlier times has been effectively shattered. Evangelical polarisation, which has gathered pace since the late-1960s, has seen the emergence of fundamentalistic and progressive wings within contemporary evangelicalism, as well as a majority of more neutral evangelicals occupying a middle ground between the two extremes.[74] There has been hardly any work done on the varieties of contemporary evangelicalism in Wales, so it is difficult to delineate with any precision the extent to which a similar process has taken place in Wales, but it is possible to hint at a few important developments. The advent of the charismatic movement in the 1960s proved to be as divisive in Wales as elsewhere, as many evangelical churches experienced splits over the new expressions of church and the new forms of worship that the movement encouraged. But it would probably be fair to say that those evangelical churches in Wales who have embraced some of the changes stimulated by the charismatic phenomenon have become the mainstream expressions of Welsh evangelicalism, while those that have proved more resistant have become socially and culturally marginalised.

Key to this development has been the emergence of a revitalised Evangelical Alliance (EA) since the mid-1980s. The EA's embracing of organisational devolution, with the formation of Evangelical Alliance Wales in 1986, has meant that it now represents the largest single body of evangelicals in Wales.[75] At the time of writing evangelicals from over twenty different denominations and well over a hundred affiliated churches have identified with the aims and ethos of the EA.[76] Yet it is in the rationale of the EA in Wales that the biggest shift in outlook among evangelicals in Wales can be seen. Where once evangelicals were wary of what they called the 'world', today they seem positively enthused by the possibility of engaging closely with the government and the media. Indeed the EA in Wales stresses that its purpose is not only to promote insular church activities and evangelism, but to represent growing numbers of evangelicals in Wales to both government bodies, especially the National Assembly of Wales, and the media.[77]

While the speed of religious decline in Wales has not really abated, with the latest census figures showing that significantly less than ten per cent of Welsh people attend church with any degree of regularity,[78] avowedly evangelical churches are the only ones that seem to have been able to put up any resistance to the seemingly inexorable march of secularisation. This is a fact observed by the sociologist Steve Bruce who has commented that it is only those religious groups, like evangelicals, with a tight belief system, that are ideologically well-equipped to cope with an increasingly secular world.[79] Recent work by Paul Chambers on churches in Swansea seems to bear this out. His work has shown that while many churches in the city face a pretty bleak future, those evangelical churches that have been prepared to seek fresh ways of presenting their message to a post-modern and post-Christian culture have often experienced significant growth.[80] But this is a challenge that evangelicalism since its birth in the religious revivals of the mid-eighteenth century has relished, as it has adapted and re-invented itself first in response to the Enlightenment, then Romanticism and in the early twentieth century to modernism.[81] It remains to be seen whether evangelicals in Wales can grasp the opportunities presented by post-modernism and by living in a post-Christian culture and once again make the evangelical gospel relevant and transformative in very different circumstances.

Notes

1. D. Densil Morgan, 'Continuity, Novelty and Evangelicalism in Wales, *c.*1640–1850', in Michael A. G. Haykin and Kenneth J. Stewart (eds), *The Emergence of Evangelicalism: Exploring Historical Continuities* (Leicester, 2008), p. 84.
2. David Ceri Jones, *'A Glorious Work in the World': Welsh Methodism and the International Evangelical Revival, 1735–1750* (Cardiff, 2004).
3. David W. Bebbington, *Evangelicalism in Modern Britain: A History from the 1730s to the 1980s* (London, 1989), pp. 2–17. Alternatives and additions to Bebbington's quadrilateral definition have been offered in W. R. Ward, *Early Evangelicalism: A Global Intellectual History, 1670–1789* (Cambridge, 2006), p. 4; Timothy Larsen, 'Defining and Locating Evangelicalism', in Timothy Larsen and Daniel J. Treier (eds), *The Cambridge Companion to Evangelical Theology* (Cambridge, 2007), p. 1; Richard Turnbull, *Anglican and Evangelical?* (London, 2007), pp. 55–75.
4. Phyllis Mack, *Heart Religion in the British Enlightenment: Gender and Emotion in Early Methodism* (Cambridge, 2008).

5. Quoted in Geraint Tudur, *Howell Harris: From Conversion to Separation, 1735–1750* (Cardiff, 2000), p. 97.
6. Glanmor Williams, William Jacob, Nigel Yates and Frances Knight, *The Welsh Church from Reformation to Disestablishment, 1603–1920* (Cardiff, 2007), p. 168.
7. Eryn M. White, '"The World, the Flesh and the Devil" and the Early Methodist Societies of South West Wales', *Transactions of the Honourable Society of Cymmrodorion*, 3 (1997), 45–61.
8. David Ceri Jones, '"A Glorious Morn": Methodism and the Rise of Evangelicalism in Wales, 1735–62', in Mark Smith (ed.), *British Evangelical Identities: Past and Present. Volume 1: Aspects of the History and Sociology of Evangelicalism in Britain and Ireland* (Milton Keynes, 2009), pp. 110–11.
9. W. R. Ward, 'Was there a Methodist Evangelistic Strategy in the Eighteenth Century?', in Nicholas Tyacke (ed.), *England's Long Reformation, 1500–1800* (London, 1998), p. 287.
10. Eryn M. White, '"I will once more shake the heavens": the 1762 Revival in Wales', in Kate Cooper and Jeremy Gregory (eds), *Revival and Renewal in Christian History*, Studies in Church History, 44 (Woodbridge, 2008), pp. 154–63.
11. R. Tudur Jones, 'Awr anterth Efengylyddiaeth yng Nghymru, 1800–1850', in D. Densil Morgan (gol.), *Grym y Gair a Fflam y Ffydd: Ysgrifau ar Hanes Crefydd yng Nghymru* (Abertawe, 1998), pp. 285–308.
12. Bassett, *Welsh Baptists*, pp. 87–95; R. Tudur Jones, *Congregationalism in Wales* (ed. Robert Pope) (Cardiff, 2004), pp. 110–31.
13. J. Geraint Jones, *Favoured with Frequent Revivals: Revivals in Wales, 1762–1865* (Cardiff, 2001), p. 7.
14. D. Densil Morgan, *Christmas Evans a'r Ymneilltuaeth Newydd* (Llandysul, 1991), D. E. Jenkins, *Life of Rev Thomas Charles, BA of Bala* (3 vols. Denbigh, 1908); Jones, *Congregationalism in Wales*, pp. 120, 138–9.
15. Richard Carwardine, 'The Welsh Evangelical Community and "Finney's Revival"', *Journal of Ecclesiastical History*, 29, 4 (October, 1978), 467.
16. E. T. Davies, *Religion and Society in the Nineteenth Century* (Llandybïe, 1981), pp. 51–2.
17. John Wolffe, *The Expansion of Evangelicalism: The Age of Wilberforce, More, Chalmers and Finney* (Leicester, 2006).
18. Eryn M. White, 'Popular Schooling and the Welsh Language, 1650–1800', in Geraint H. Jenkins (ed.), *The Welsh Language before the Industrial Revolution* (Cardiff, 1997), pp. 337–9.
19. See Huw Walters, 'The Welsh Language and the Periodical Press', in Geraint H. Jenkins (ed.), *The Welsh Language and its Social Domains, 1801–1911* (Cardiff, 2000), pp. 349–78.
20. Gerald H. Anderson, *Biographical Dictionary of Christian Missions* (Grand Rapids, MI, 1999), p. 171.
21. 'Introduction: Two Hundred Years of the British and Foreign Bible Society', Stephen K. Batalden, Kathleen Cann and John Dean (eds), *Sowing the Word: The Cultural Impact of the British and Foreign Bible Society, 1804–2004* (Sheffield, 2004), pp. 1–2.
22. Jones, *Congregationalism in Wales*, p. 149.
23. Bassett, *Welsh Baptists*, p. 93.
24. Ieuan Gwynedd Jones, 'Denominationalism in Caernarfonshire', in idem., *Explorations and Explanations: Essays in the Social History of Victorian Wales* (Llandysul, 1981), p. 21.
25. W. P. Griffith, '"Preaching Second to No Other under the Sun": Edwards Matthews, the Nonconformist Pulpit and Welsh Identity during the Mid-Nineteenth Century', in Robert Pope (ed.), *Religion and National Identity: Wales and Scotland, c.1700–2000* (Cardiff, 2001), pp. 64–5.
26. David Hempton, *Religion and Political Culture in Britain and Ireland: From the Glorious Revolution to the Decline of Empire* (Cambridge, 1996), pp. 56–7.
27. Prys Morgan, *The Eighteenth Century Welsh Renaissance* (Llandybïe, 1981).
28. Quoted in D. Densil Morgan, 'Christmas Evans (1766–1838) and the Birth of Nonconformist Wales', *Baptist Quarterly*, XXXIV, 3 (July, 1991), 122.
29. Dyfed Wyn Roberts, 'Dylanwad diwygiadaeth Charles Finney ar ddiwygiad 1858–60 yng Nghymru', unpublished University of Wales, Bangor, Ph.D. thesis, 2005; Eifion Evans, *Revival Comes to Wales: The Story of the 1859 in Wales* (Bridgend, 1986).

30. Martin Wellings, *Evangelicals Embattled: Responses of Evangelicals in the Church of England to Ritualism, Darwinism and Theological Liberalism, 1890–1930* (Carlisle, 2003), ch. 5.
31. See Kenneth O. Morgan, *Wales in British Politics, 1868–1922* (Cardiff, 1980), ch. 1.
32. This line of argument has been given a new lease of life in Gwyn Davies' populist *A Light in the Land: Christianity in Wales, 200–2000* (Bridgend, 2002), pp. 94–100.
33. Ian Randall & David Hilborn, *One Body in Christ: The History and Significance of the Evangelical Alliance* (Carlisle, 2001), especially ch. 2.
34. Peter Freeman, 'The Response of Welsh Nonconformity to the Oxford Movement', *Welsh History Review*, 20, 3 (June, 2001), 442.
35. R. Tudur Jones, *Faith and the Crisis of a Nation: Wales, 1890–1914* (ed. Robert Pope) (Cardiff, 2004), p. 48.
36. Roger L. Brown, *Evangelicals in the Church in Wales* (Welshpool, 2007), ch. 4.
37. Owen Thomas, *The Atonement Controversy in Welsh Theological Literature and Debate, 1707–1841* (trans. John Aaron) (Edinburgh, 2002).
38. Charles Finney, *Darlithiau ar Adfywiadau Crefyddol* (trans, E. Griffiths), (Abertawe, 1839).
39. D. Densil Morgan, 'Lewis Edwards (1808–87)', *Welsh Journal of Religious History*, 3 (2008), 27–8.
40. Jones, *Faith and the Crisis of a Nation*, p. 222.
41. See Mark D. Chapman, 'Protestantism and Liberalism', in Alister E. McGrath and Darren C. Marks (eds), *The Blackwell Companion to Protestantism* (Oxford, 2004), pp. 322–32.
42. This process is traced in detail in Jones, *Faith and the Crisis of a Nation*, chs. 9 and 10.
43. Eifion Evans, *The Welsh Revival of 1904* (Bridgend, 1969); Jones, *Faith and the Crisis of a Nation*, chs. 12–14; Robert Pope, 'Demythologising the Evan Roberts Revival, 1904–5', *Journal of Ecclesiastical History*, 57, 3 (July, 2006), 515–34.
44. Tim Grass, *Gathering to his Name: The Story of the Open Brethren in Britain and Ireland* (Milton Keynes, 2006), passim.
45. Very little work has been done on these churches. For an indication of their extent see Brynmor Pierce Jones, *How Lovely are Thy Dwellings* (Newport, 1999).
46. Allan Anderson, *An Introduction to Pentecostalism: Global Charismatic Christianity* (Cambridge, 2004), pp. 91–6.
47. Brynmor Pierce Jones, *The Spiritual History of Keswick in Wales, 1903–1983* (Cwmbran, 1989).
48. D. Densil Morgan, *The Span of the Cross: Christian Religion and Society in Wales, 1914–2000* (Cardiff, 1999), pp. 122–30.
49. Robert Pope, *Seeking God's Kingdom: The Nonconformist Social Gospel in Wales, 1909–39* (Cardiff, 1999).
50. See Noel Gibbard, *R. B. Jones: Gospel Ministry in Turbulent Times* (Bridgend, 1999).
51. Noel Gibbard, *Taught to Serve: The History of Barry and Bryntirion Colleges* (Bridgend, 1996), ch. 1.
52. For the context see Virginia Lieson Brereton, *Training God's Army: The American Bible School, 1880–1940* (Bloomington IN, 1990).
53. David W. Bebbington, 'Baptists and Fundamentalists in Inter-War Britain', in Keith Robbins (ed.), *Protestant Evangelicalism: Britain, Ireland, Germany and America, c.1750–c.1950: Essays in Honour of W. R. Ward* (Oxford, 1990), p. 326.
54. David Goodhew, 'The Rise of the Cambridge Inter-Collegiate Christian Union, 1910–71', *Journal of Ecclesiastical History*, 54, 1 (Winter, 2003), 62–88.
55. Geraint D. Fielder, *'Excuse Me, Mr Davies – Hallelujah!': Evangelical Student Witness in Wales, 1923–1983* (Bridgend, 1983), chs. 2 and 3.
56. See Iain H. Murray, *David Martyn Lloyd-Jones: The first forty years, 1899–1939* (Edinburgh, 1982).
57. Callum G. Brown, *Religion and Society in Twentieth-Century Britain* (London, 2006), pp. 201–2.
58. Fielder, *'Excuse Me, Mr Davies – Hallelujah!'*, ch. 6.
59. Ibid., pp. 101, 183.
60. Noel Gibbard, *The First Fifty Years: The History of the Evangelical Movement of Wales, 1948–98* (Bridgend, 2002), pp. 28–30.
61. J. Elwyn Davies, *Striving Together: The Evangelical Movement of Wales – Its Principles and Aims* (Bridgend, 1984), pp. 5–6.

62. Noel A. Davies, *A History of Ecumenism in Wales, 1956–1990* (Cardiff, 2008), p. 10; Morgan, *Span of the Cross*, pp. 243–4.
63. C. G. Brown, *The Death of Christian Britain: Understanding Secularisation, 1800–2000* (London, 2001).
64. Gaius Davies, *Genius, Grief and Grace* (Fearn, 2001), pp. 370–2.
65. Iain H. Murray, *David Martyn Lloyd-Jones: The Fight of Faith, 1939–81* (Edinburgh, 1990), ch. 25; John F. Brencher, *Martyn Lloyd-Jones (1899–1981) and Twentieth-Century Evangelicalism* (Carlisle, 2002), ch. 5.
66. See Martyn Lloyd-Jones, 'Evangelical Unity: An Appeal', in idem., *Knowing the Times: Addresses Delivered on Various Occasions, 1942–1977* (Edinburgh, 1989), ch. 13.
67. Bebbington, *Evangelicalism*, pp. 249–50.
68. Gibbard, *The First Fifty Years*, ch. 5.
69. http://www.aecw.org.uk/aecw/churches.php (accessed September 2009).
70. Timothy Dudley Smith, *John Stott: the making of a leader* (Leicester, 1999), pp. 444–7.
71. See http://www.efcw.org.uk/about.htm (accessed September 2009).
72. Brown, *Evangelicals in the Church in Wales*, p. 272.
73. http://www.efcw.org.uk/Bwletinajk.htm (accessed September 2009).
74. This process has been outlined most effectively in Rob Warner, *Reinventing English Evangelicalism, 1966–2001: A Theological and Sociological Study* (Milton Keynes, 2007).
75. http://www.eauk.org/wales/history/history-of-the-evangelical-alliance-in-wales.cfm. (accessed September 2009).
76. http://www.eauk.org/wales/welshchurches/organisations.cfm (accessed September 2009).
77. http://www.eauk.org/wales/index.cfm (accessed October 2009).
78. Joanna R. Southworth, 'Religion in the 2001 Census for England and Wales', *Population, Space and Place*, 11, 2 (2005), 75–88.
79. Steve Bruce, *Firm in the Faith* (Aldershot, 1984), p. 92.
80. See Paul Chambers, *Religion, Secularization and Social Change in Wales: Congregational Studies in a Post-Christian Society* (Cardiff, 2005).
81. This is the broad thesis presented by David Bebbington in his *Evangelicalism in Modern Britain*.

CHAPTER 17

JUDAISM

Lavinia Cohn-Sherbok

The history of the Jewish community in Wales follows the pattern of almost all small Jewish communities in both the United Kingdom and the United States.[1] From the early eighteenth century onwards, small numbers of Jews began to settle in Welsh towns and villages.[2] In the second half of the nineteenth century numbers increased considerably, particularly after the pogroms of the 1880s which caused many Eastern European Jews to flee the Russian and Austro-Hungarian empires and to find new homes in Western Europe and the United States. They established themselves in the big cities and in smaller provincial towns where they set up small businesses and made their livings as traders and pawnbrokers.[3] This has been further discussed by David Morris who has commented that:

> As in the rest of the country, Jewish employment patterns in Wales were domi-
> nated by the commercial and artisan trades – such as hawking, shop keeping,
> tailoring and cabinet making – which Jews had traditionally occupied in cen-
> tral and Eastern Europe.[4]

These immigrants were ambitious for their children, and valued education highly. Indeed, second and third generation children were encouraged to study at university and then seek employment as professionals. Opportunities were greater in the bigger cities, and by the middle of the twentieth century small-town, provincial Jewry was in decline everywhere. Today, both in the United Kingdom and the United States, the Jewish community is as rich and powerful as it has ever been, and yet its num-bers are in sharp decline, while Jewry has become almost entirely centred in major urban conurbations.[5] Moreover, Cardiff does not have a large Jewish population, as Jews predominantly live in London, apart from sizeable communities in or near to Manchester, Leeds, Newcastle and Glasgow.[6]

Despite the decline in numbers outside London, the Jewish community in Cardiff has a population of 941 (c.2004),[7] while there are 170 Jews living in Swansea (c.2004),[8] another 39 in Newport[9] and a relatively small Jewish population living along the north coast of Wales.[10] There are also a dozen or so households scat-tered throughout the rest of the country. Thus, Welsh Jewry comprises a very small percentage of the 250,000 Jews who live in the United Kingdom, and an even smaller proportion of the population of Wales. Given their limited numbers the Welsh Jews do possess a rich history, and in the early twentieth century Cardiff, in particular, was an important centre of Jewry. This community has been distinguished by its lawyers, doctors, professors, writers, musicians, politicians, businessmen and even athletes. There have also been a number of nationally-known rabbis and ministers from Wales.[11] At one stage, when British Jewry decided that the time had come to set up a traditional *yeshivah* (rabbinical academy) and were discussing which town would be most suitable, Llanelli was a serious contender.[12]

In historical terms, the Jews are comparative newcomers to Wales. In any event, no Jews were permitted to live anywhere in Britain in the middle ages after they had been expelled by Edward I in 1290. There is no record of any early mediaeval community, although individual Jews are mentioned in relevant documents from Caerleon and Chepstow.[13] It was not until the mid-eighteenth century that the first Jews began to settle in Wales, and their chosen destination was Swansea. The earliest Jewish immigrant whose name is known was David Michael, who in 1749 arrived from Germany with two other immigrants.[14] Land was purchased for a Jewish cemetery in 1768 and in 1780 the first synagogue was opened.[15] In 1818 this was replaced by a new building in Waterloo Street. These immigrants increasingly became prominent in their localities. For example, Ludwig Mond, a German Jew, opened a nickel works in Clydach in the Swansea valley, which would later develop into ICI,[16] while in 1848 Michael John Michael was elected as mayor of Swansea. By 1850 there were well over a hundred Jews in the city, and a new synagogue was erected in Goat Street which could accommodate 228 people.[17] A separate Jewish congregation (Prince of Wales Minyan/*Beth Hamidrash*) was established in 1896 after a series of heated exchanges between elders at the Goat Street synagogue.[18] Despite this schism the numbers of Jews increased to around one thousand by the time of the First World War, largely as a result of immigration from Russia.[19] Sadly, the old synagogue in Goat Street was destroyed in an air-raid in 1941, but the community was still strong enough to build another, this time in the Ffynone district. Despite a further influx of refugees in the 1930s from Nazi Germany the decline continued. By 1969 the Jewish population was reduced to 418. In recent years there have been discussions about selling up and moving to smaller premises, but after some vandalism in 2002 it was decided to redecorate and reconsecrate the old building. Today, there are roughly forty active members of the synagogue.[20]

Jews settled in Cardiff in small numbers from *c*.1787 onwards,[21] but the present community was founded in 1840, and the following year Lord Bute provided a plot of ground at Highfield for a Jewish cemetery.[22] By 1852 the congregation numbered thirteen members and was led by an auctioneer, Mark Marks, and a synagogue was erected in the East Terrace area of the city in 1858. It was a small beginning, but by the end of the nineteenth century, the growing wealth of the city ensured that Cardiff had overtaken Swansea as the main Jewish centre in Wales. In 1895 it was even visited by the founder of Zionism, Theodor Herzl, who came to discuss his plans for the Jewish state with Colonel A. E. W. Goldsmid, a prominent resident, who saw himself as the original model for George Eliot's *Daniel Deronda*.[23] Despite some divisions in the Jewish community,[24] their numbers continued to grow throughout the first half of the twentieth century. A second

Orthodox synagogue was established and a Reform congregation was founded in 1948. In these years it was possible to lead a full Jewish life: there were several *kosher* butchers; a *mikveh* (ritual bath); facilities for Jewish education; a branch of the Jewish youth organisation (*Maccabi*); a home for retired members; and a burial society.[25] Many of these institutions still exist, but the numbers have shrunk considerably. David Morris has recorded that there was even a Jewish rugby team, the Riverside Harlequins. This was a team formed in the 1920s

> in a room at the rear of Mrs Driscoll's sweet shop in Tudor Road, and consisted of all Jewish boys with the exception of two ... They competed in the Cardiff Ex-schoolboys' league, and created a local record by going through two seasons undefeated, also winning the Abe Hauser knock-out competition.[26]

By 1968 the Jewish population had nevertheless declined to approximately 3,500, and today it is not much more than a quarter of that figure. There is no kosher butcher and meat has to be transported from Manchester, the new millennium stadium was built on the old ritual bath site, and there are only two synagogues (one Orthodox, one Reform). On the positive side, however, there are plans for the Orthodox synagogue to be rebuilt and enlarged; the old-age home is flourishing and the community produces an excellent magazine which won the Jewish Community Magazine of the Year award in 1996 and 1997.[27]

Relatively speaking, Cardiff is a success story, but other towns and villages where Jews have settled have not fared so well. By the end of the nineteenth century there were several established Jewish communities along the south coast and valleys of south Wales. As Wales attracted economic migrants from all over the British Isles to work in the mines, the iron and steelworks and on the docks, Jewish people also settled there. Most of them did not work directly in these booming industries, although there were a few Jewish miners and, in Cardiff, there was some involvement with the shipping business. In general, however, they set up small enterprises to serve the new communities. In comparison with other ethnic groups involved in the service industry today in Wales, the Jews in the late-nineteenth century provided a fairly lucrative and essential role.[28] They were also prominent as itinerant peddlers, and were to be seen hawking their wares from village to village in the mining communities. They were involved in the clothing trade, particularly as 'credit drapers', which meant that working people, who were paid weekly, could purchase their clothes by regular instalments. In particular, they dominated the important pawnbroking trade in certain areas. For example, in Tredegar in Monmouthshire three-quarters of Jews involved in commercial activity in this town were described as pawnbrokers.[29]

Other areas too had a small but visible Jewish population. A synagogue was established in Victoria Street, Merthyr Tydfil in 1848 and a larger one in 1876,[30] and there were others in Tonypandy, Tredegar, Porthcawl, Pontypridd, Llanelli and Aberdare.[31] From these villages and mining towns, Jewish communities spread to Newport where, in 1859, Abraham Isaacs, Jacob Druiff, Isaac Isaacs, S. Fogotson, Joseph Isaacs, Meyer Manoy, H. Woolf and Jacob Kaufman met to organise the

Newport Hebrew congregation.[32] The first Jewish burial in the town took place in 1861, the first Jewish wedding was conducted in 1866, and in 1869 a new synagogue in Francis Street was opened. In 1871 it was consecrated by the Chief Rabbi, Dr Herman Adler.[33] Even though the synagogue was closed and sold in 1997, the Newport community still survives in a smaller building, and has an enrolled congregation of thirty-nine members. In contrast, the Jewish valley communities have long since disappeared as most were not viable by the mid-1940s. The Tredegar synagogue closed in 1955, followed by those at Aberdare, Brynmawr, Llanelli and Pontypridd. The Merthyr Tydfil community finally sold its buildings in the 1980s.[34] Yet the influence of these once-vibrant groups is still to be felt. Grahame Davies' recent anthology was inspired by a visit to the Merthyr Jewish cemetery. In this study he commented:

> In the hills of the Brecon Beacons, on the steep slope of Cefn Cilsanws mountain, there stands a small cemetery. Thousands of motorists pass it every day ... But if you were to stop the car, and make your way to this little mountainside resting place, you would soon find that this is part of a Wales very different to the one most people know. The names – Rosenburg, Schwartz, Sherman, Lipman; the inscriptions in the unfamiliar outline of Hebrew; the little stones placed on the headstones ... All these things tell of how the Jews, a people with a unique calling, played out part of the drama of their destiny in the land of another small people – the Welsh.[35]

He was inspired to write a Welsh elegiac poem which was published (in translation) in the *Cardiff Jewish Journal*.[36] This was very well-received, and further evidence of nostalgia for these old communities is to be found in the success of the 1999 film, *Solomon and Gaenor*.[37] This told the story of a doomed romance between the son of an Orthodox Jewish draper and the daughter of a chapel-going mining family set against the background of early twentieth-century south Wales. It was a vehicle for two well-known Welsh actors, Ioan Gruffudd and Nia Roberts, along with the redoubtable Maureen Lipman who was cast as the Jewish mother. The dialogue switches between Welsh, Yiddish and English, and the film was nominated for an Oscar in the Best Foreign-Language category. It provides a fascinating glimpse of two rich cultures existing side-by-side less than a hundred years ago.

There were also Jewish communities along the north Wales coast, and synagogues were established at Rhyl, Colwyn Bay, Bangor and Llandudno. These were somewhat different from the south Wales congregations because they were not entirely composed of Ashkenazi (Eastern European) Jews. After the First World War, a small number of Sephardim (Oriental Jews), who were refugees from the disintegrating Ottoman Empire, relocated to north Wales. There they joined their co-religionists in setting up Jewish communities at Rhyl and Llandudno, but unfortunately these declined and the synagogues at Rhyl, Colwyn Bay and Bangor were closed during the 1970s. Although the Jewish-owned Wartski jewellery emporium, which used to trade in Llandudno High Street is long gone, the company still promotes its Welsh origins in advertising hordings for its London store in Bond Street. Despite the decline in the Jewish community the congregation has nevertheless survived, and for a time numbers were swelled by regular summer visitors. Regrettably, in more recent times, very few Jews seem to travel to the north Wales coast for their holidays, and the synagogue has only a small, elderly congregation.[38] At its peak the Jewish community of Wales was supporting eighteen synagogues and its total population was probably more than 10,000 strong. Most were refugees, or the children of refugees, who had fled from the anti-Semitic pogroms of Eastern Europe. Historians of the community have tended to emphasize the continued existence of anti-Semitism when the Jews arrived in south Wales.[39]

The riots of 1911 have been described as a 'pogrom' or 'semi-pogrom', but if they are compared to the attacks on 1,300 Jewish houses and businesses in Kishinev in 1903, when forty-nine Jews were murdered and more than 500 were injured, it is clear that the Welsh riots were not on the same scale as the events in Moldova. Geoffrey Alderman has nevertheless observed that 'anti-Semitism in south Wales was spreading and had a long history'.[40] This impression is also perpetuated at a popular level. In *Solomon and Gaenor*, which is set against the background of the 1911 riots, Solomon's father and mother are seen boarding up their shop, while the filmscript noted that:

Rezl (the mother) reaches behind the brick and pulls out the leather pouch with the money in it. She looks at it curiously, then stuffs it into the pocket of her coat. She catches her husband's eye at the window. They understand one another. They have been here before. Old fears are being aroused, and old training utilised.[41]

The same attitude is explored by modern historians who have remarked that the Jewish community can be classified alongside other immigrant groups as subjects of suspicion and prejudice.[42] Neil Evans has stated that

the momentous social changes of the nineteenth and early twentieth centuries were frequently punctuated by anti-immigrant riots, ranging from the first serious attack on the Irish in 1826 to anti-Jewish and anti-Chinese riots in 1911 and the assault on black newcomers in 1919.[43]

Even though he subsequently admits that 'Jews were so well integrated that they shared the central experiences of the majority of the population', Evans also stresses that 'politically it took Jews a long time to arrive, with Cardiff getting its first Jewish councillor in 1928 and its first Jewish Lord Mayor in 1987'.[44] In the same volume, Paul Chambers observed that 'petty prejudice and intolerance were part of the daily experience of these Jewish communities', and, not surprisingly, 'in the long term Judaism did not flourish in Wales'.[45]

Lists can be drawn up of possible anti-Semitic incidents, including the so-called 'Jewess-Abduction Case' of 1869. An eighteen-year-old Jewish girl, Esther Lyons, ran away from her family on 23 March 1868. She was sheltered at first by a Baptist minister, the Rev. Nathaniel Thomas of the Tredegarville Tabernacle in Cardiff, and subsequently in London. Her father, Barnett Lyons, claimed that she had been kidnapped and brainwashed into accepting Christianity. The matter went to court and the Lyons family won their case, although the verdict was subsequently reversed on appeal. Despite suggestions in the accounts of modern historians that there was a strong tradition of Baptist anti-Semitism and conversionism, the facts are that Esther Lyons was unhappy at home and that she left voluntarily. In addition, the popular newspapers of the time, which reported the incident, were highly critical of Thomas' behaviour and generally supported the actions of the Jewish parents.[46]

The Tredegar riots of 1911 were more complicated. A gang of about 200 young men, supposedly singing Welsh hymns, attacked Jewish shops in Tredegar. Then, over the next few nights, Jewish shops were attacked in other south Wales mining towns and the police and infantry were called upon to restore order. Damage to Jewish property was said to amount to £16,000, but there were no Jewish injuries. This is the generally accepted version of the events. It is argued that the riots were symptomatic of deeply-rooted anti-Semitism, that they were organised in advance, that neither the Welsh political authorities nor the Christian religious leaders were disturbed by the events, and that the whole episode was marginalised by the Anglo-Jewish London establishment which chose not to draw unnecessary attention to this 'incident'.[47] W. D. Rubinstein has questioned all of these assumptions, and argues that there is far more evidence of philo-Semitism than anti-Semitism in Wales during the early decades of the twentieth century. He demonstrates that there is no evidence of premeditation. Furthermore, there had been looting of non-Jewish shops in 1910 and in 1911 there were sporadic incidents of vandalism against gentile property.[48] Rubinstein concedes that 'the initial phases of the August 1911 rioting were aimed exclusively, or almost exclusively, at Jewish shopkeepers', and he points out that 'contemporary observers were in unanimous agreement that Jewish shopkeepers were targeted for economic reasons and that no more generalized anti-Semitic feelings existed'.[49] He argues that, if anything, the London-based Jewish sources exaggerated the resemblance of the riots to a Russian pogrom: 'in part this was done for sensationalist purposes; in part, because of fears by the very same "anglicized Jews" that it could indeed "happen here"'.[50]

Whatever the truth of this matter, there is no doubt that there have been a few unpleasant incidents over the years. There have been examples of the petty expulsion of members from social clubs in the 1930s and 1950s on account of their religion,[51] and there was anti-semitic activity in 1947 when the Jews were trying to establish a Jewish state. In this year graffiti was daubed on Jewish property in Cardiff and the back door of the Cardiff *Jewish Chronicle* correspondent was painted with the message 'Jews … Good Old Hitler.' During the same period, a young man was arrested in Swansea. He had announced that he was on his way to kill Abe Freedman, the Chairman of Swansea Town Football Club.[52] Occasionally, graves have been desecrated, while the National Front and other extremist organisations have maintained their anti-Semitic propaganda. Moreover, the South Glamorgan Racial Equality Council reported in the 1980s that a shot had been fired at buildings owned by Jews (as well as several at those owned by Asians).[53] In 2002, vandals attacked the Swansea synagogue. They drew swastikas on the wall, destroyed a Torah scroll and attempted to burn the building down. No-one was arrested on that occasion and it is not known whether the perpetrators were committed anti-Semites or disaffected adolescents.[54] While these incidents were all individually very distressing, the Welsh are largely tolerant of the Jewish population and abjure such racist behaviour.

More distasteful, and arguably more serious, was the intellectual anti-Semitism which crept into the Welsh nationalist movement of the early twentieth century. Saunders Lewis (1893–1985), one of the founders of Plaid Cymru, a hero of the Penyberth arson protest and the inspirer of *Cymdeithas yr Iaith* (the Welsh Language Society), was in sympathy with the conservative, hierarchical, neo-Catholic views of such English writers as Hilaire Belloc, T. S. Eliot and G. K. Chesterton. Through the 1920s until the mid-1940s, he also shared their anti-Semitism. In his 1939 poem 'Y Dilyw' ('The Deluge'), which was based on his experience of the depression in Wales, he wrote:

Then, on Olympus, in Wall Street, nineteen hundred and twenty-nine
Busy at their immortal scientific task of guiding the profits of fate,
The gods, with their feet in the Aubusson carpets,
And their Hebrew noses in the quarter's statistics,
Decided that the time had come to make credit scarce.[55]

Sadly, Saunders Lewis was not alone. O. M. Edwards (1858–1920), the founder of the magazine, *Cymru,* and the children's journal, *Cymru'r Plant,* a chief inspector of schools in Wales and a devoted promoter of the Welsh language, wrote racist passages about European Jews in his travelogue of 1889, *O'r Bala i Genefa* (From Bala to Geneva). This contains such commentaries as,

I knew then that it was possible to see what one sees every day on this Continent can also happen in Wales – a Jewish wolf falling on his prey in the darkest hour ... I asked Frau Nebel at suppertime if there were many Jews in Heidelberg. She looked at me in shock, and said there were enough of them wherever there was blood to be sucked ... They (the Jews) look on the property of all the uncircumcised as lawful prey of the children of promise; the gentile's property ... belongs to the Jew on the same condition that the fish of the sea belong to him ... The Jew does not talk of holiness and religion – perhaps he does not understand what they are any more – but about gold jewellery and gems and fine clothes.[56]

It must be stressed that this kind of prejudice did not survive the Holocaust. When *O'r Bala i Genefa* was reissued after Edwards's death, the offensive passages were all removed. Similarly, Lewis unequivocally condemned Nazism and anti-Semitism from the mid-1940s onwards. But in view of this history it is not surprising that few Welsh Jews take much interest in Welsh nationalism. There have been Welsh Jews who have served as Members of Parliament for both the Labour Party (Leo Abse) and for the Conservatives (Michael Howard), but none for Plaid Cymru. Two generations of the Janner family also sat in the House of Lords. It has not passed unnoticed that, even in today's multi-cultural, multi-religious Wales, Urdd Gobaith Cymru (the

Welsh children's patriotic association) still contains a declaration of allegiance to Christ in its mission statement.[57] Despite the modern Plaid's pacifist, environmentalist and internationalist platform, Jews are instinctively uncomfortable with any form of nationalism. Too often in the past they have been its victims. Despite the views of historians, sociologists and literary critics, Welsh anti-Semitism has been limited. Wales was never a Russia or a Poland. What has been the subject of far less study is the success of the Jews, both individually and as a community. In general they have settled well into Welsh society, and Wales has been a good home for them. As Hal Weitzman and David Weitzman stress,

> In the grand historical sweep of Jewish wanderings, this Welsh interlude will surely be reckoned among Anglo-Jewry's happiest periods and will have earned a secure place within its collective experience.[58]

Why did the Jews in Wales assimilate so well? Perhaps it is because in many ways they are very like the Welsh themselves, not least in their shared recourse to the Promised Land and the sacred language. In his studies of the Welsh and their landscape, Dorian Llywelyn has shown how the Welsh have identified their country as a holy land and their nation as a sacred people.[59] These are not unfamiliar ideas for Jews. Both are small nations with a long history of oppression, but both have maintained their language against all the odds. In view of this, it is not surprising that some writers have sought to understand the Welsh in Biblical terms as one of the lost tribes. The foundation of the State of Israel in 1948 was inevitably interpreted by some as a wake-up call to Wales. For example, Harri Webb (1920–1994) contrasts the original abject state of the Jews: 'Listen, Wales. Here was a people whom even you could afford to despise' with the successful, victorious Israelis: 'The mountains are red with their blood, The deserts are green with their seed. Listen, Wales.'[60] It is a matter of pride to many of the Welsh that David Lloyd George was one of the prime movers behind the Balfour Declaration (1917) which pledged the support of the British government for the creation of a Jewish state. The Welsh map is dotted with familiar biblical place-names (Horeb, Bethlehem, Nazareth, Sion and Nebo), and both nations share many of the same surnames (Jacob, Benjamin, Samuels, Moses, Isaacs and Nathan) too. Indeed, in Jan Morris' satirical *Our First Leader*, Wales is occupied by Hitler in the Second World War. After Llewellyn Parry-Morris, the Welsh leader of the new puppet state, pays Hitler a formal visit, Hitler's reaction is predictable, 'Scum of course', he said to Goebbels, 'anybody can see he's a neo-Hebrew shit, but he amuses me'.[61] There are more fundamental similarities. As a very broad generalization, both groups are more interested in sound than in vision. It can also be suggested that music is more important than art or architecture. 'Thank the Lord we are a musical nation' was expressed by Dylan Thomas's minister of Llaraggub, but the sentiment could be echoed by any rabbi. For both peoples there is the same respect for education and the same desire for their children to attain 'professional' status. There is supposedly the same clannishness, the same reverence for the family matriarch, and the same fierce loyalty to extended family. In her commentary on the Welsh, Jan Morris could equally be referring to the Jews. They have, according to Morris, survived as a nation chiefly by cunning and reserve. If they are more anxious than most to please, if their hospitality is deservedly proverbial, still in dealing with outsiders of any kind they are seldom uninhibited. They play for time, they fence, they scout out the situation, they do not commit themselves. Those sweet smiles are truly sweet, but they are well under control. It is a performance that greets you, polished and long-practised, played on a deceptively cosy stage ... It is the outward sign of a social order that is essentially communal ... In successively smaller and tighter formations the Welsh are ranked, ready for all comers.[62]

Paradoxically, the reassurance Jews have been given in Wales has contributed to their gradual decline. As they have been welcomed and appreciated, it has been all too easy to fall in love across the religious divide. In a small country, with a small Jewish community and a less-than-adequate Jewish infrastructure, it is unlikely that the children, and still less the grandchildren, of mixed marriages will identify themselves as Jews. As more Jews intermarry, the greater the imperative for their co-religionists to move to larger Jewish centres. Here they have a greater choice of potential Jewish marriage partners as well as further educational and professional opportunities. For the dedicated Zionist, there is also the call to remove to Israel.

The numerical decline of the Jewish community in Wales simply reflects a similar diminution in all British and American provincial communities. Welsh Jews have not left because they have been threatened with persecution or even by persistent anti-Semitism. The decline in numbers reflects both the desire for greater opportunities elsewhere and general assimilation in areas where they presently reside. In his 1999 study on the Jews in Wales, David Morris has charted the decline of Welsh Jewry between 1930 and 1996 as well as the impact of secularism.[63] For example, he has observed that the Merthyr Jewish population peaked at 400 in 1919, dropped to 198 by the 1950s and disappeared altogether by the late-1970s. Similarly, as shown elsewhere in this study, Newport Jewry declined from 250 in 1914 to 50 in 1985. Swansea has seen an equally quick decline, while the north Wales Jewry disappeared rapidly.[64] Even in Cardiff, where the Jewish population increased up until the late-1950s, there has been a steady decline.[65] Nonetheless, there has been a significant Jewish presence in Wales which was remarkably successful both in sustaining a recognisable Jewish lifestyle and in being accepted and respected by the Welsh people. In this context, the work of Dannie Abse clearly shows how Jews and the Welsh have learned to co-exist. Born in Cardiff, Abse was a member of a distinguished Jewish family. One brother became a psychiatrist; another was the long-serving member of Parliament for Pontypool, and Dannie himself became a doctor and is one of the best-known Welsh poets writing in English. In his fictionalised memoirs, Abse described what it was like growing up as a Jewish boy in the Cardiff of the 1930s:

> 'You don't believe in Christmas, do you?' Sidney said to me.
> 'What's it like to be Jewish?' asked Philip.
> 'S all right', I said.
> 'What's the difference?' demanded Philip.
> 'They put 'ats on when they pray, we takes them off', Sidney said ...

Later the same day, the household was visited by Abse's unsuccessful Uncle Isidore:

> Uncle Isidore wasn't exactly an Uncle. Nobody knew his exact relationship to the family; but my parents called him 'Uncle' and my cousins called him 'Uncle', and my uncles called him 'Uncle'. He came round to our house once a week, to collect his half a crown and to eat a bit of supper ... The door slammed and I was left in the house alone with Uncle Isidore ... Philip was silly asking me what it was like to be Jewish ...

> > 'Uncle?' I asked,
> > 'Well?'
> > 'What's it like to be Jewish all your life?' I asked.
> > 'S all right', he said, and for a moment we smiled at one another.[66]

Notes

1. For details of Jewish communities and settlement patterns see Cecil Roth, *The Rise of Provincial Jewry* (London, 1950); L. P. Gartner, *The Jewish Immigrant in England, 1870–1914* (London, 1960); Stephen Brook, *The Club: Jews in Modern Britain* (London, 1989); V. D. Lipman, *History of the Jews in Britain Since 1858* (Leicester, 1990); Todd M. Endelman, *Radical Assimilation in English Jewish History, 1656–1945* (Indiana, 1990); Geoffrey Alderman, *Modern British Jewry* (Oxford, 1992); Norman Cantor, *The Sacred Chain: A History of the Jews* (London, 1995); W. D. Rubinstein, *A History of the Jews in the English-Speaking World: Great Britain* (London, 1996); Elliott Abrams, *Faith or Fear: How Jews can Survive in a Christian America* (New York, 1997).
2. For examples see David Morris, 'The History of the Welsh Jewish Communities, 1750 to the Present', unpublished University of Wales, Ph.D. thesis, 1999, pp. 12–13.
3. General occupational structures in England are provided in Harold Pollins, *Economic History of the Jews in England* (London, 1982); J. Buckman, *Immigrants and the Class Struggle: The Jewish Immigrants in Leeds, 1880–1914* (Manchester, 1983).
4. Morris does nevertheless acknowledge the loss of important records which hampers a fuller investigation. See Morris, 'History of the Welsh Jewish Communities', pp. 4, 7–8.
5. For a personal account of this process, particularly focussing upon Denver, Colorado, see Dan and Lavinia Cohn-Sherbok, *The American Jew: The Community Patriarch* (London, 1994), pp. 180–5.
6. Morris, 'History of the Welsh Jewish Communities', p. 5. Jewish communities in London and developments in provincial Jewry are discussed in C. Russell and H. Lewis, *The Jew in London* (London, 1900); Bill Williams, *The Making of Manchester Jewry, 1740–1875* (Manchester, 1976); K. E. Collins, *Second City Jewry: The Jews of Glasgow in the Age of Expansion, 1790–1919* (Glasgow, 1990).
7. Stephen W. Massil (ed.), *The Jewish Year Book* (London, 2005). The Jewish population in the city halved between 1945 and 1990, from 2, 500 (*c.*1946) to 1,400 (*c.*1990). See http://www.jewishgen. org/jcr-uk/Community/Cardiff.htm (accessed May 2010), and citing the Jewish Year Books for 1947 and 1991.
8. Massil (ed.), *The Jewish Year Book* (2005). As the statistics from the Year Books indicate the Jewish population in Swansea has fluctuated from the first settlement in *c.*1731. In 1895 there were 300 Jews in Swansea, increasing to 1,000 by 1935 and declining thereafter: 500 (*c.*1946) and 245 (*c.*1990). See http://www.jewishgen.org/jcr-uk/community/swansea.htm, and citing the Jewish Year Books for 1896, 1936, 1947 and 1991. An accessible study of the Jewish population in Swansea is provided in Neville Saunders, *Swansea Hebrew Congregation, 1730–1980* (Swansea, 1980). See also Leonard

Mars, 'Cooperation and Conflict between Veteran and Immigrant Jews in Swansea, 1895–1915', in Peter Gee and John Fulton (eds), *Religion and Power, Decline and Growth: Sociological Analyses of religion in Britain, Poland and the Americas* (London, 1991), pp. 115–30; Harold Pollins, 'The Swansea Jewish Community – The First Century', *Jewish Journal of Sociology*, 50, 1–2 (2009), 35–9.

9. Massil (ed.), *The Jewish Year Book* (2005). As with the other Jewish communities, Newport has witnessed a steady decline in the Jewish population from 250 (*c.*1934) to 180 (*c.*1945) and 110 (*c.*1990). See http://www.jewishgen.org/jcr-uk/community/newp/index.htm (accessed May 2010), and citing the Jewish Year Books for 1935, 1946 and 1991.

10. The main focus for Jews in north Wales is the Llandudno and Colwyn Bay Hebrew Congregation. For details of Jewish communities and synagogues previously located in Bangor, Rhyl and Wrexham see http://www. jewishgen.org/jcr-uk/wales.htm (accessed May 2010).

11. For general details, see Graham Davies (ed.), *The Chosen People: Wales and the Jews* (Bridgend, 2002). For a comprehensive analysis of the Jewish population in Wales see Morris, 'History of the Welsh Jewish communities'.

12. In the event, the privilege went to Gateshead in the north east of England. As Hal and David Weitzman remark in their recent study, 'how different this essay might have been had the decision gone the other way'. See H. Weitzman and D. Weitzman, 'The Jews in Wales', in *The Jewish Year Book* (London, 2000), pp. 24–31.

13. See 'Wales', in *Encyclopaedia Judaica* (16 vols. Jerusalem, 1971–2), XVI (1972), pp. 250–1.

14. Saunders, *Swansea Hebrew Congregation*, p. 29.

15. Morris suggests that this may have been in the 1770s and located in Wind Street at the back of Michael's house. See Morris, 'History of the Welsh Jewish Communities', p. 13.

16. Ibid., p. 18.

17. Saunders, *Swansea Hebrew Congregation*, pp. 31, 35.

18. Ursula Henriques (ed.), *The Jews of South Wales: Historical Studies* (Cardiff, 1993), pp. 101, 103.

19. Morris, 'History of the Welsh Jewish communities', p. 45, and citing the *Jewish Year Book* for 1914.

20. For further details of the history of the Swansea congregation see 'Swansea', in *Encyclopaedia Judaica*, XV, pp. 544–5; Bernard Goldblum, 'Swansea', unpublished papers presented to the Jewish Historical Society Conference, 1975. I am also indebted to Mr Sherman of Swansea for providing information about the present-day community.

21. Ursula Henriques has noted the presence of Michael Marks, a slop-seller, and Levi Marks, a watchmaker, in Cardiff in 1813. See Henriques (ed.), *Jews of South Wales*, p. 11.

22. Ibid., p. 12.

23. M. Lowenthal (ed.), *The Diaries of Theodor Herzl* (New York, 1956), pp. 78, 82–3. For details of Zionists in Wales see Henriques (ed.), *Jews of South Wales*, pp. 36–7; Morris, 'History of the Welsh Jewish Communities', pp. 54–5.

24. This is discussed in Morris, 'History of the Welsh Jewish Communities', pp. 53–4.

25. For other Jewish social activities see ibid., pp. 56–7.

26. Ibid., p. 55, and citing *Cajex*, 1, 4 (July, 1951), 38.

27. For the history of the Jews of Cardiff, see M. Dennis in *Cajex: Magazine of the Association of Jewish ex-Servicemen and Women, Cardiff*, 1–5 (1950–5). See also Ursula Henriques, 'The Jewish Community of Cardiff, 1813–1914', *Welsh History Review*, 14, 2 (1988), 269–300; Morris, 'History of the Welsh Jewish Communities', passim.

28. Henriques (ed.), *Jews of South Wales*, passim; Morris, 'History of the Welsh Jewish Communities', p. 19.

29. A discussion of commercial activities from Home Office files, including pawnbroking, tailoring, haberdashery and female employment, is provided in Morris, 'History of the Welsh Jewish Communities', pp. 46–50.

30. Henriques (ed.), *Jews of South Wales*, pp. 47, 56.

31. Ibid., p. 47; Morris, 'History of the Welsh Jewish Communities', pp. 57–68.

32. *Cajex*, 9, 2 (June 1959), 26–7, and also cited in Morris, 'History of the Welsh Jewish Communities', p. 14.

33. Israel Rocker, 'As One Door Shuts', *Bimah: The Platform of Welsh Jewry* (September, 1997), 7–9. Further information on the Jewish community of Newport has been generously provided by Avram Davidson of that city.

34. In a recent *South Wales Echo* report the former Grade II listed synagogue it was suggested was going to be turned into a number of apartments. See Jackie Bow, 'Merthyr synagogue in Thomastown set to be turned into flats', *South Wales Echo*, 18 November 2009.

35. Davies, *Chosen People*, p. 9.

36. For examples see *Cardiff Jewish Journal*.

37. *Solomon and Geanor* (dir. Paul Morrison, 1999), and discussed in Davies, *Chosen People*, p. 7.

38. I am indebted to B. Hyman of Llandudno Junction for this information. The Jewish communities in north Wales are also discussed in Morris, 'History of the Welsh Jewish Communities', pp. 68–77.

39. For example, see W. D. Rubinstein, 'The Anti-Jewish Riots of 1911 in South Wales: A Re-examination', *Welsh History Review*, 18, 4 (December, 1997), 667–99; Geoffrey Alderman, 'The Anti-Jewish Riots of August 1911 in South Wales: A Response', *Welsh History Review*, 20, 3 (June, 2001), 565–71; Anthony Glaser, 'The Tredegar Riots of August 1911', in Henriques (ed.), *Jews of South Wales*, pp. 151–76; Colin Holmes, 'The Tredegar Riots of 1911: Anti-Jewish Disturbances in South Wales', *Welsh History Review*, 11 (1982), 214–25; Geoffrey Alderman, 'The Jew as Scapegoat? The Settlement and Reception of Jews in South Wales Before 1914', *Transactions of the Jewish Historical Society of England Transactions*, XXVI (1979), 62–70.

40. Alderman, 'Jew as Scapegoat', 65.

41. Quoted in Davies, *Chosen People*, pp. 176–7.

42. Charlotte Williams, Neil Evans and Paul O'Leary (eds), *A Tolerant Nation: Exploring Ethnic Diversity in Wales* (Cardiff, 2003).

43. Neil Evans, 'Immigrants and Minorities in Wales', in Williams, Evans and O'Leary (eds), *A Tolerant Nation*, p. 19.

44. Ibid., p. 20.

45. Paul Chambers, 'Religious Diversity in Wales', in Williams, Evans and O'Leary (eds), *A Tolerant Nation*, p. 126.

46. For details of this case see Ursula Henriques, 'Lyons versus Thomas: The Jewess Abduction Case 1867–68', in Henriques (ed.), *Jews of South Wales*, pp. 131–6; Morris, 'History of the Welsh Jewish Communities', pp. 96–9.

47. See Geoffrey Alderman, 'The Anti-Jewish Riots of August 1911 in South Wales', *Welsh History Review*, 6, 2 (1972), 190–200; Holmes, 'Tredegar Riots of 1911', 214–25. It should be pointed out, however, that in the late–nineteenth century there was considerable sympathy for the Jewish victims of the Russian pogroms, but also significant intolerance in the twentieth century. See Morris, 'History of the Welsh Jewish Communities', ch. 5.

48. Rubinstein, 'Anti-Jewish Riots of 1911', pp. 670–2, 685.

49. Ibid., 689.

50. Ibid., 692.

51. Morris, 'History of the Welsh Jewish Communities', p. 145.

52. Weitzman and Weitzman, 'Jews in Wales', p. 27.

53. *South Glamorgan Racial Equality Council Annual Report, 1986–7* (Cardiff, 1987), p. 24.

54. For details of this attack see Marie Woolf, 'Burnt scrolls, broken windows and vicious graffiti: a synagogue is desecrated again', *Independent*, 13 July 2002.

55. This English translation of the poem is extracted from Davies, *Chosen People*, p. 166.

56. The translation is provided in ibid., pp. 158–65.

57. There is considerable pressure for this to change. When I spoke to an officer of the Urdd, he said that it was very much under discussion and 'it is a very sensitive issue'.

58. Weitzman and Weitzman, 'Jews in Wales', p. 31.

59. Dorian Llywelyn, *Sacred Place, Chosen People: Land and National Identity in Welsh Spirituality* (Cardiff, 1999), passim.

60. Harri Webb, 'Israel', in *Harri Webb. Collected Poems*, ed. Meic Stevens (Llandysul, 1995), pp. 91–2.

61. Jan Morris, *Our First Leader* (Llandysul, 2000), p. 90.

62. Jan Morris, *The Matter of Wales* (London, 1984), p. 21.
63. Morris, 'History of the Welsh Jewish Communities', chs. 6–7.
64. Ibid., pp. 152–4.
65. In 1985 it was estimated that the Jewish population was close to 1,700. Ibid., p. 154.
66. Dannie Abse, *Ash on a Young Man's Sleeve* (London, 1954).

CHAPTER 18

ISLAM

Muzafar Jilani

ALLAH-U AKBAR
Allah is the greatest.
ALLAH-U AKBAR
Allah is the greatest
ASHHADU ANLA ILAHA
I bear witness that there is no
ILLALLAH
deity but Allah.

ALLAH-U AKBAR
Allah is the greatest.
ALLAH-U AKBAR
Allah is the greatest.
ASHHADU ANLA ILAHA
I bear witness that there is no
ILLALLAH
deity but Allah.

ASHHADU ANNA MUHAMMADAR RASULULLAH
I bear witness that Muhammad is the Messenger of Allah.
ASHHADU ANNA MUHAMMADAR RASULULLAH
I bear witness that Muhammad is the Messenger of Allah.

HAYYA ALAS SALAH
Come to prayer.
HAYYA ALAL FALAH
Come to your Good.
ALLAHU AKBAR
Allah is the greatest.

HAYYA ALAS SALAH
Come to prayer.
HAYYA ALAL FALAH
Come to your Good.
ALLAHU AKBAR
Allah is the greatest.

LA ILAHA ILLALLAH
Here is no deity but Allah

The call to prayer (Adhan) of the Muslims, heard five times every day in Mosques and homes all over twenty-first-century Wales, is a sure sign of the presence of Islam in Wales. Yet, how did Islam come to Wales and what effect is it having on the Wales of today and of the future? These questions are the essence of this chapter. In order to appreciate how and why Islam and Muslims affect the country or community in which they live, it is important to understand what Islam is about.

What is Islam?

Islam is the call to the true and pure worship of Allah.[1] Islam is the acceptance of, and obedience to, the teachings of Allah, as revealed through his last prophet and messenger, Muhammad (saw).[2] It is a religion which confirms and renews the basic doctrine brought by the earlier prophets such as Noah, Abraham, Moses and Jesus.[3] For Muslims, it is the final message revealed to mankind, not only a religious doctrine but a complete social and economic system. It is a way of life; and one that, as the fastest growing world religion, is becoming increasingly common and accepted in modern Wales. Linguistically, the word Islam is an Arabic word derived from two words: Ikhlas, which in English means 'purity of faith', and Istislam, which means 'total obedience or submission to Allah'. Therefore, Islam is purity of faith along with a total submission to Allah. According to Muslims, this message is the same message brought by all the prophets of Allah since the time of Adam. Muslims believe in and respect all these previous prophets and understand that Allah (SWT)[4] sent them and the prophet Muhammad (saw) with the same message of Islam. The laws and regulations of each time were different and have since been modified. Confirmations and abrogations were made until the final and complete religion was revealed to the prophet Muhammad (saw) as preserved in the Holy Qur'an[5] and in the Hadeeth.[6] Allah (SWT) asserts in the Qur'an, 'This day, I have perfected your religion for you, completed My Favour upon you, and have chosen for you Islam as your religion'.[7]

The basic Islamic beliefs are six in number: belief in Allah, the angels, His books, the prophets and messengers of Allah, the day of judgement, and Al-Qadr (predestination). The first, belief in Allah, means to believe in the one true God, unique and incomparable, whose Lordship knows no bounds, who has no son or partner and who alone deserves to be worshipped. Part of this belief is also in the many names and attributes of Allah, that are his alone, and through which Muslims can gain an understanding and appreciation of their Lord. Examples of these are Ar-Rahman (The Merciful), Al-Adl (The Just), and Al-Razaq (The Provider). The second belief is in the existence of angels as a creation of Allah and in the specifically named angels, such as Jibreel,[8] and the roles they play. The third belief is that books were revealed to the prophets such as the Taurat (Torah) and The Injeel (Gospel), and the last revelation of the Holy Qur'an being revealed to Muhammad (saw). The fourth belief is in the prophets and messengers from Adam to Muhammad (saw), all of whom were human beings without the divine qualities of Allah. The fifth belief is in the day of judgement, a day when all of mankind will be resurrected and judged before their Lord. The sixth and final of the core beliefs is in Al-Qadr, the belief in predestination. This does not mean that mankind is devoid of freewill and, as such, absolved of responsibilities. Humans have been given freewill, as opposed to all other living elements of the physical world. These all follow the laws of the universe: the laws of the Creator. This makes the entire physical world, other than mankind, necessarily submissive to Allah and, therefore, in a state of Islam. Although mankind is free to choose right or wrong, the belief in Al-Qadr, still includes four elements: Allah knows everything; Allah has recorded all that has happened and all that will happen; Whatever Allah wills to happen, will happen. Whatever He wills not to happen, does not happen; Allah is the Creator of everything. Although this is philosophically contradictory, it is believed by Muslims on the basis of mukhalafa – absolute difference – human logic cannot apply to God. Along with the six core beliefs, are the more widely known five pillars of Islam. These are the basic duties of a Muslim. Again, these have been present in some form throughout the history of revealed religion. Although indicated in the Qur'an, the details are conveyed via hadeeth – the records of the statements and actions of Muhammad. For example, the Qur'an urges believers to 'keep up prayer' but it was Muhammad who gave the information on how this was to be carried out.[9]

The first pillar is the Shahadah, or the Confession of Faith 'Lailaha IllaAllah Muhammadur Rasoola Allah' (There is none worthy of worship except Allah and Muhammad is the messenger of Allah). This statement could have equally well been applied at the time of Moses as: 'There is none worthy of worship except Allah and Moses is messenger of Allah', or at the time of Jesus as, 'There is none worthy of worship except Allah and Jesus is the messenger of Allah.' It is a simple formula which encompasses the religion of Islam and as such, if said with conviction and understanding by an individual, would allow them to enter Islam.[10]

The second pillar is Salat, which means prayer. This is to be performed five times daily. Although each prayer is not necessarily more than a few minutes long, it is a direct link between the worshipper and his creator, Allah. It serves as a source of comfort and as a reminder for Muslims throughout the day. The third pillar is Zakat, or support of the needy. The word Zakat means both purification and growth. It is a two and a half per cent tax on a Muslim's wealth that is distributed amongst certain categories of the needy. Zakat is considered a purification of one's wealth and is compulsory on all wealth above a small, fixed, basic amount that has been held for a full lunar year. It is considered that the needy are not only deserving but also have a right to this Zakat. Fasting in the month of Ramadhan is the fourth and one of the most well known pillars of Islam. Again, this is a continuation of the theme of fasting revealed to all previous prophets. Muslims fast from daybreak to dusk every day for the complete month of Ramadhan (twenty-nine or thirty days). The medical and physical benefits of fasting are recognised, but it is the spiritual element of purification and worship that is most sought after by the believer. The fifth and final pillar is one of pilgrimage to Makkah, called Hajj. It is a once in a lifetime obligation upon all who have the means to complete it. The Ka'aba in Makkah, towards which all Muslims pray, is the original house of worship built by Abraham and his son Ismail.[11]

So, Islam is a religion whose fundamental focus is the worship of Allah, but seclusion or withdrawal from society is not approved of. Human beings are placed on this earth so that they can form their characters, and this can only be done through involvement in the world. Muhammad is seen by Muslims as 'the perfect person' whose example should be followed, and he married, had children, and led the community as a teacher, in battle and as a statesman. According to Muslim traditions, he would also help with work both inside the house and out, and he visited the sick and needy and was a friend for all the children.[12]

Worship of Allah through prayer is obligatory, but simply living as Allah intended is also seen as a form of worship. It is through this second aspect that a Muslim would play his or her part in the building of an ideal society. For instance, marriage and family are central in Islam, and it is seen as a religious duty to marry and have children. In the Shari'a, the Islamic law code, the rights of both husbands and wives, of children, parents and the wider family are clearly outlined, as are the rights of neighbours, whether Muslim or not. Muslims are encouraged to help each other at all times, physically and financially. Both the traveller and the guest have rights, as do non-Muslims who live in a Muslim state. The intention to build a better community and society should extend from the greatest act to the very smallest, such as removing an obstacle from the path of another, or even in the encouragement to smile.[13]

Unfortunately, two stereotypes have emerged, the Muslim as terrorist and the Muslim woman as oppressed female. In fact, the vast majority of Muslims oppose terrorism and the position of women in Islam is often misunderstood. The position of women in Islam should be one of respect and equality, and not one of subjugation and oppression. Her rights as a wife and mother are recognised. Her role in the raising and education of children, and in thus forming future societies is emphasised. The Muslim woman is considered precious and an individual in her own right, who is protected and valued. It is perhaps due to this clarity and equality afforded to Muslim women that educated western women are turning to Islam in far greater numbers than western men.[14] The Muslim ideal is that the individual and community will not emulate any particular nation,[15] or culture, other than that of Islam. Yet, paradoxically, it is probably due to this that many Muslims are finding a welcoming base in Wales, a country whose value system and history of nonconformity allows it to see beyond the stereotypes and begin to appreciate a true picture of Islam.

Muslims in Wales

The history of Islam in Wales is relatively short and there are only a few studies which offer some insights into this religious community.[16] Indeed, those books which cover the history of Islam in Europe do not mention its arrival in Wales.[17] The very first Muslims to arrive in Wales in any numbers were Yemeni seamen who came to Britain after the opening of the Suez Canal in 1869. The intention was to come to Britain for work, but many of them settled in and around the docks area of Butetown, Cardiff, where they married and raised families.[18] As loyal subjects many of them took part in the First World War. Yet in the post-war years there was a considerable animosity towards Muslim young men as it was felt by demobbed British soldiers that the Muslim men were taking their jobs.[19] Indeed, between 7 and 9 June 1919 rioting occurred in Barry, Cardiff and Newport. In Bute Street doors and windows of Muslim-owned properties were smashed.[20] Ibrahim Ismaa'il, a Somaili seaman, provided a fairly graphic description of events. As a young man he witnessed the attack upon a Warsangeli's house in Millicent Street:

the fight started at about 7.30 p.m. and lasted a fairly long time. Seven or eight Warsangeli defended the house and most of them got badly wounded. Some of the white people also received wounds. In the end, the whites took possession of the first floor, soaked it with paraffin oil and set it alight. The Somalis managed to keep up the fight until the police arrived. One of them was left for dead in the front room and was later carried to the hospital where he recovered; some escaped through a neighbouring house and came to tell us the story of what had happened, the others gave themselves up to the police, and we did not see them for a long time.[21]

Further events show the ferocity of the violence, including lynch mobs who allegedly attacked Mahomet Abdullah, a young Arab. Abdullah died later in hospital from a fractured skull after defending an Arab restaurant in Bute Street.[22] For other emigrant people the future was equally bleak as two hundred faced repatriation.[23] *John Bull*, a weekly paper, took up the plight of these people and in 1919 stated, 'These coloured Britons had all done first-class war work ... yet they were treated worse than repatriated enemy aliens.'[24] Nevertheless they remained committed to serving British interests and fought again in the Second World War. Regrettably hundreds of them were drowned when convoys were sunk.[25]

There were some changes in the composition of the Muslim community in Britain as a result of the arrival in 1936 of Sheikh Abdullah Ali al-Hakimi.[26] In 1938 he told a *Western Mail* reporter that there were 5,000 Muslims in Cardiff and expressed his desire to found a mosque in the city.[27] The next substantial arrival into Wales, particularly Cardiff, was that of Somalis in the mid-twentieth century. These Muslims, like the Yemenis, also settled in and around the docks area of Cardiff.[28] At the time there were no mosques in Cardiff, and so the local Muslim community prayed in the front rooms of their houses. They then started to buy houses for use as places of prayer, and eventually converted shops and churches to mosques. The first purpose-built mosque in Cardiff, the Noor-ul-Islam, was erected in 1944 at Maria Street, Butetown, at a cost of £7,000,[29] and the following year Cardiff staged Britain's first ever Muslim conference.[30] From 1949 to the departure of al-Hakimi in August 1952 there were, however, some disputes between the followers of the two Muslim communities resident in Cardiff led by al-Hakimi and Sheikh Hassan Ismail.[31]

A second mosque, the Islamic Centre and Allawi Zawiya, was erected below Loudon Street in 1967 and was run by Sheikh Saeed Hassan Ismail.[32] The first Centre nevertheless proved too small, and in 1980 it was then knocked down and the current mosque, which stands at Alice Street was built in its place. The Conaught Road mosque was built in 1976 and the Broadway mosque between 1979 and 1980. Currently, there are twenty-three mosques in Cardiff.[33] There are also mosques throughout Wales, notably in Aberdare, Barry, Bridgend, Carmarthen, Haverfordwest, Llanelli, Newport, Swansea, and in a number of towns in north Wales such as Bangor, Llandudno and Wrexham.[34] Wherever the Muslim population have settled, then, they have either built mosques or converted houses, churches or other similar properties into mosques. A recent addition is the Berea

Masjid (mosque) in Blaina. This is the first mosque to be established in the south Wales valleys. The building previously was a chapel called Berea Chapel.

Between the early 1950s and early 1960s there was an influx of people from the Indian sub-continent, including Muslims from Pakistan, India and Bangladesh. Although the original Muslims, Yemenis and Somalis, were mainly manual workers, the occupation of Muslims from the Indian sub-continent was varied and consisted of professionals such as doctors, engineers, accountants, teachers and businessmen, large and small. These businessmen might own a corner shop, or a supermarket, or factories or similar large businesses. The 2001 census recorded 22,000 Muslims in Wales, a proportionately low number compared to Britain in general – with Muslims in Wales numbering 0.7 per cent of the population compared to 3.1 per cent in England.[35] Nevertheless, Islam in modern-day Wales is freely practised and the identity of Muslims, particularly in bigger cities and towns, is visibly maintained. The majority of Muslims in Wales live around the Cardiff, Newport and Swansea areas, but there is also considerable growth in north Wales. In larger towns and cities it is now quite acceptable to see the *Hijab* (headscarf and outergarment) worn by Muslim women, and it is not a strange sight to find a lone Muslim praying, in a motorway service area car park or other places. However, it is true to say that it is still unusual to see a woman in Hijab in a rural Welsh village.

Muslims, it seems, are quietly contributing to the everyday social fabric of Welsh society. For example, many of the so-called 'Indian' restaurants are run by Bangladeshi Muslims, such as the Spice Merchant Restaurant in Cardiff Bay as are many take-away businesses. Likewise, hospitals up and down the country have significant proportions of doctors and nurses who are Muslims. There are also many teachers and professionals in other disciplines. Many immigrant Muslims nevertheless remember the difficulties they faced in all aspects of life in the early years of their move to Wales, from issues such as where to get the right kind of food, to where to bury their dead. These difficulties have been addressed through organisations and associations that tackle issues which affect the local Muslim community, as well as to address wider areas of the relationship with the host community. In Cardiff, the Association of Muslim Professionals (AMP) was formed in 1996. The AMP was 'an alliance of people, united by a shared belief and vision, striving together for the common good in an organised, disciplined and responsible manner'. The AMP observed that there was the 'need to channel the wealth of expertise, experience and professionalism of Muslims for the betterment of the Muslim community in particular and society in general'. The documented aims of the AMP also stated that 'Muslims perceive Islam as a thought, a hope, a vision, a concern and a way of life that aims to nurture human qualities and build a just and civilised society in the world.'[36] As previously stated, Islam encourages active participation in social life, and the AMP stresses that Muslims should not become 'complacent or indifferent to social ills. They should not let societies move towards ruin and social disintegration, since this is not an attitude of responsible and caring people; rather, Muslims must work actively for reform, improvement, development, growth and progress.'[37]

Understanding and appreciation of Islam has been helped by the inclusion in school curricula of the study of certain aspects of the religion. In other educational institutions, such as the principal Welsh Universities, there are Islamic societies that help increase the awareness of Islam. At the University of Wales, Trinity St David's, there is presently an active Centre for Islamic Studies which has attracted many students.[38] One notable student of Islam was Abu Ameenah Bilal Phillips who was awarded his doctorate from Lampeter University in 1994 and is currently a lecturer of Arabic and Islamic Studies at the American University in Dubai and Ajman University in Ajman. Coming from a Christian background he was born in Jamaica and brought up in Canada, he is now well-known and respected in the Islamic world. He has written many books on various aspects of Islam, and translated and explained chapters from the Qur'an. He also lectures regularly throughout the world.[39] Another institution for Islamic Studies in Wales is the European Institute of Human Sciences, situated near Llanybydder. This is a residential institution, run by Dr Meshandari. It was established on 1 November 1999 and is one of two such institutes in Europe, the other being in Paris.[40]

Since devolution there have been other developments, particularly the establishment of a Muslim Council of Wales, which is affiliated to the Muslim Council of Great Britain, while the AMP is similarly affiliated to the British Council of Wales. Illustrative of the acceptance of Islam in Wales was the holding of a fast breaking ceremony, by Dafydd Elis-Thomas, the speaker of the Welsh Assembly, in the month of Ramadhan in 2002. Approximately fifty Muslims from many walks of life were invited to this ceremony, where they were met by various ministers.[41] Such activities obviously break down the race barriers and are welcome additions to multi-faith Wales. This event became the first of many such fast-breaking ceremonies.

Culture versus Islam

The concept of Ummah, that is, the Islamic Nation, does not entertain the notion of different Muslim nationalities, such as Arab Muslim, Indian Muslim, Pakistani Muslim, Welsh Muslim, etc. In theory, if you are a Muslim, you are a Muslim, and one Muslim is a brother or sister to another Muslim. There are, however, cultural differences and these have sometimes caused conflicts. Interestingly, many of these conflicts are inter-generational. The impact of 9/11 and other related issues, pushed many young Muslims into a re-assessment of their faith, and they often discovered that what they had been taught was Islamic was, in fact, simply cultural.[42] Being a Muslim does not necessarily equip a person with the full knowledge of Islam and their parents and grandparents had simply transferred their own cultural understading of Islam to Wales. For example, in Newport the majority of Muslims have come from the Mirpur area of Pakistan. They have maintained strong links with their homeland, both Islamically and culturally. These links are weakening as Welsh Muslims develop their own identity. This is particularly seen in institutions such as universities, where Muslims find their religious, rather than cultural, identity more influential when making social choices. This will hopefully be stimulated by new educational developments in Wales. In May 2005 the *Western Mail* reported that a new Centre for the Study of Islam in the UK (CSI-UK) was being established at

Cardiff University along with a new MA/Diploma course in 'Islam in Contemporary Britain'. The official launch of the Centre was held in November 2005. According to the organiser of the degree programme, Dr Sophie Gilliat-Ray, the Centre intends to reflect multi-cultural multi-faith Wales. She has observed that:

> Some of the research is showing now that some of the most dynamic imams in Britain are forging strong alliances with Christian clergy who understand Islam. If you have Christian clergy understanding something about the Muslim community, it's much easier to form relationships and create dialogues and trust across communities.[43]

But how have individual people in Wales responded to Islam?

Islam in Wales – The Human Perspective

In order to convey an understanding of what it means to be a Muslim in Wales, how Muslims live their lives and contribute to society in Wales, and how they interact with the indigenous population of Wales, the author has included summary profiles of three Muslims and one non-Muslim in Wales.

1. The Imaam

An Imaam is a religious leader who, apart from leading the prayers, may be involved in teaching, solemnising marriages, and being an arbitrator in disputes, which could also include marital disputes. Sheikh Saeed Ismail, is the Imaam of the Islamic Centre in Cardiff, and is a second generation Yemeni, born in 1930 at South Shields.[44] His father was killed in the Second World War, when he drowned in one of the convoys at sea. As an orphan,[45] he was introduced to the then Imaam of the Islamic Centre in Cardiff on his visit to South Shields. With his mother's permission, the Imaan took Sheik Saeed to Cardiff in 1940 and he stayed in Cardiff with Sheik Hassan Ismail from the age of ten to sixteen. After this he went to Yemen to study Islam, before returning to Cardiff in 1950. Before he was chosen to succeed Sheik Hassan Ismail as Imaam, who had retired and returned to Yemen, Sheik Saeed Ismail had worked as a welder in South Shields. He is married with three children, two sons and a daughter. Apart from working as a welder, he dedicated his life towards serving Islam by being the Imaam of the mosque and mouth-piece of the Islamic community in Cardiff. On many occasions he has given interviews on television on various Islamic issues and in the community in which he lives.[46] He has attended various schools in Wales to advise them on Islamic history and culture, and welcomes and instructs people on organised visits to the mosque. As the Imaam he was involved in mainstream mosque activities, including solemnising marriages, teaching children Islamic education, and lecturing at various functions including 'dawah' work (invitation to Islam). He stresses the need for understanding and acceptance, 'I hope people will understand and know our values. Once we get that across, it will be a peaceful place.'[47] Sheik Saeed has close links with various Muslim communities in and around Cardiff and the south Wales valleys and he attends regularly religious functions where he participates and educates. It is clear that Sheik Saeed, although now retired, has contributed considerably to the society in which he has lived, and conveyed the message of Islam to both Muslims and non-Muslims alike. This he still continues to do.

2. The Professional

S. K. is a successful accountant and has his own accountancy business. He is also Chief Executive of The Ethnic Business Support Programme (EBSP). This is a joint venture with the Welsh Development Agency, to encourage people from the ethnic community to start businesses in Wales. It is not limited to Muslims.[48] He came to Wales in 1972 to study accountancy and then remained to gain practical business experience. Success as an accountant followed and in 1985 he started his own practice. When he first came to Cardiff, there were only two mosques, but between 1976 and 1980 he witnessed a rapid growth in the Muslim population as demonstrated by the building of a new mosque at Conaught Road, quickly followed by a further one at Severn Road. Yet another mosque was built between 1979 and 1980 at Broadway. Apart from his practice as an accountant, S. K. is very active in Islamic matters. He was involved in the purchase of Dar-ul-Isra Mosque and became a Trustee. The mosque previously was a Presbyterian Church, and after it was purchased in the 1970s it was converted to a mosque. It is now an active centre for Islamic activities. Kidwai has also been involved in the creation of the South Wales Islamic Educational Trust which was the body to open the first Islamic School in Wales called, Tayibah School, in 1995.[49] He was also the founding member and first secretary of the Association of Muslim Professionals which started in 1996–7.[50] At present, he is actively involved in the Muslim Council for Wales, helping to strengthen its affiliation with the Muslim Council for Great Britain as its secretary.

S. K'S help in developing links with the Interfaith Council for Wales started in October 2001 at the invitation of the Welsh Assembly. This council brings politicians and religious leaders together to discuss various issues concerning the community. He has been instrumental in developing strong links between the Association of Muslim Professionals and Universities, the Welsh Assembly, hospital authorities, social services departments, the public prosecution department and the South Wales Police. Indeed, in January 2003, along with the Right Rev. Dr Barry Morgan, Archbishop of Wales, he called for calm over the issue of asylum seekers. He stated:

> I am concerned that some individuals have sought to use this issue to inflame anti-Islamic rhetoric, which might lead to a repeat of the kinds of appalling incidents seen following the events of September 11th 2001 ... We call on politicians and journalists to act responsibly and to do nothing which might encourage lawless action, and to do all they can to support good community and cross-cultural relations throughout Wales.[51]

These links have been very much appreciated by all these bodies who are keen to learn about the needs of the Muslim community and to understand how best to serve the Muslim community in Wales.

Married with children, S. K. serves the community as a Muslim, as a husband, as a father, as a professional, taking every opportunity that might come his way in developing links and understanding between the Muslim community and other communities in Wales.

3. The Revert

J. K. was always interested in other religions. She was originally a Catholic, born in Wales. Her mother was Welsh, her father an Irishman. She was brought up in Ebbw Vale, where even in the early 1970s there were only four Muslims in total, as far as she can remember. Her early education was in a Catholic school, but in secondary school she met other Christians and at the time, everyone was horrified at learning that one of the students was an atheist. She went to a Catholic College and studied Divinity. Here she was taught by nuns and consequently took it all for granted and did not question Christian beliefs. She wrote a thesis on the subject of 'God's call to man', where she traced certain prophets and looked into their history, from Abraham to Jesus.[52] She was, however, always interested in other religions and attended a class on comparative religion run by a Church of England Canon, where she met her now husband, a Muslim, who also attended the classes.

J. K. feels that Islam complemented Christianity, and she saw this as having 'added' another chapter to her experiences. She gradually accepted more Islamic practices such as praying, giving Zakat, fasting and she has also gone to the Hajj pilgrimage. She states that, 'I am happy that I am on the right path. I see Islam more as community religion and I see how the rules of Islam help communities.' She went on to say, 'Everything we have lost over the years, Islam has kept.' However, she feels it is not an easy thing to practice, 'In a place like this [Wales] … You are different.'[53] Her family did not quickly acknowledge her conversion to Islam, but they have gradually accepted her religious convictions. Before going on Hajj pilgrimage, J. K. went to Saudi Arabia and visited Madinah-Al-Munawarah, where she attended classes and religious gatherings for new Muslims and found it extremely helpful. J K is a housewife and part-time teaching assistant. She is married to a GP and has two adult children. She contributes as a Muslim, as a wife, as a mother, and as a teacher to the Welsh community.

4. The Non-Muslim

P. A. is a married man in his mid-forties, who is a practising Christian and has changed his views about Islam and Muslims over the years. He is a senior psychiatric nurse. Born and brought up in Llanelli Hill he went to Nantyglo School in Blaenau Gwent, where he had no contact with anyone else except the local Welsh community. He did not even have any contact with someone of a different colour. After training as a nurse and moving to Pontypool, he started to have contact with Muslims. His first contact was as a student nurse with Muslim doctors, and started to learn more about Islam after one of his family members married a Muslim man. He accepts that Islam offers the same values as Christianity, although he does see a major difference between the two faiths, notably over the crucifixion and the resurrection. For P. A., Muslims follow strict rules which guide them throughout their lives, and he compares this to Christianity where the rules have become weakened or diluted with the growth in secularism. He has, in the past, considered Islam a violent religion, mainly because of what he had heard from various sources about Islam. However, he has now come to realise that there are heretics and violent people in all religions and Islam is no exception.[54]

As can be seen, the history of Islam in Wales is a developing one. Muslims continue to contribute to many aspects of Welsh society through the all encompassing message of Islam. In return, the Welsh people have accepted Islam among the diverse range of religions in the country. The events of 9/11 and the London bombings of 7/7 did strain the relationships developed over decades between Muslims and the population of Wales. It has to be said, however, that the hostility felt by Muslims in Wales was much less in comparison to the situation in the rest of the United Kingdom. In the first few weeks following 9/11 there were some signs of hostility towards Muslims in Wales, particularly in Cardiff because of the higher concentration of Muslims. This, however, from various media reports, was limited to some acts of spitting at Muslim women wearing the hijab (head dress or veil), verbal aggression in the form of abusive language and some manhandling. The Association of Muslim Professionals was quick to arrange a meeting with the South Wales Police at County Hall, Cardiff. This meeting was open to the public and helped to reassure the Muslim population at a very difficult time. Greater understanding of Islam with acceptance of the fact that Islam is a religion of peace which denounces the use of unjust violence, will, in time, help to develop trust and improve relationships between the Muslim community in Wales and the rest of the Welsh people. The developing history of Islam in Wales will no doubt influence and be influenced by its setting. The launch of the Islamic Cultural Year 2006 in Wales, as in the rest of the UK, was sponsored in Wales by the Muslim Council of Wales and the National Museum of Wales. Such events no doubt will help to inform and educate the general public about Islam, and provide another chapter in the rich history of Islam in Wales.

Notes

1. Allah is the Arabic word for God. It is, however, specific to the one true God, the Creator of the Universe, a unique word which is not accurately substituted by the word God, which has both plural (Gods) and female (Goddess) forms. An individual who responds to this call is a Muslim (from the actual participle of the word Islam). For a wider study of the nature and history of Islam as well as the current problems the Muslim community faces in Britain see Philip Lewis, *Islamic Britain: religion, politics and identity* (London, 1994); Emory C. Bogle, *Islam, Origin and belief* (Austin, Texas, 1998); David Norcliffe, *Islam: Faith and Practice* (Brighton, 1999); Anne Geldart, *Islam* (Oxford, 1999); Jonathan Bloom and Sheila Blair, *Islam: A Thousand Years of Faith and Power* (New Haven and London, 2002); Homayun Ansari, *The Infidel Within: Muslims in Britain Since 1800* (London, 2004); Tahir Abbas (ed.), *Muslim Britain: Communities Under Pressure* (London, 2005); Tariq Modood, *Multicultural Politics: Racism, Ethnicity and Muslims in Britain* (Edinburgh, 2005);

Peter Hopkins and Richard Gale (eds), *Muslims in Britain: Race, Place and Identities* (Edinburgh, 2008). For two unpublished studies see also Gary R. Bunt, 'Formative Contacts Between Britain and Islam, and Their Repercussions for Contemporary British Muslim Communities', unpublished University of Durham, MA thesis, 1992; Gary R. Bunt, 'Decision Making and Idjtihad in Islamic Environments: A Comparative Study of Pakistan, Malaysia, Singapore and the United Kingdom', unpublished University of Wales, Ph.D. thesis, 1997.

2. 'Salla Llaahu Alayhiwa sallam', a phrase said after mention of the prophet Muhammad's (saw) name. Approximately translates as, 'Allah's peace and praise be on him.'

3. Muslims respect and revere Jesus as a prophet of Allah. They believe in the Virgin birth, but deny the Christian concept of the Trinity. They do not believe that Jesus was crucified, rather that he was raised up to Allah, his likeness put onto another man who was then crucified by the enemies of Jesus.

4. 'Subhaanahoo Wa Ta'aalaa', often uttered after the mention of Allah's name. Translated as, 'He is exalted above weakness and indignity.'

5. Muslims believe that the Holy Qur'an is the only one of the revealed books to have been preserved in its original form. They also believe that it is a miracle of the Qur'an that no single word has been changed in over 1,400 years, though the recent discovery of early Qur'ans at Sana in the Yemen with different wordings is bringing this into question . In ch. 15, verse 9, of the Holy Qur'an, Allah says, 'Verily it is We who have sent down this Qur'an and surely, We will guard it (from corruption).'

6. A reliably transmitted statement of the prophet Muhammad (saw), i.e. his sayings, deeds and approval, etc. Collectively these form the Sunnah (what the prophet Muhammad (saw), said or approved of). This is the second sacred source after the Holy Qur'an.

7. Qur'an, ch. 5, verse 3.

8. Arabic name for the Angel Gabriel, who has always been charged with transmitting Allah's message to His prophets.

9. For details of the Five Pillars of Islam see Bukhari, ch. 2, Hadeeth 7; John L. Esposito (ed.), *The Oxford Dictionary of Islam* (Oxford, 2003) and Oxford Islamic Studies Online: http://www.oxfordIs-lamicstudies.com/article/opr/t125/e1859?_ hi=32&_pos=3 (accessed March 2010).

10. Islam has no concept of Baptism or Christening. It holds that every child is born a Muslim and it is their parents who bring them up as Jews, Christians, etc. Thus anyone who turns to Islam having been brought up in another way is termed 'a revert' to Islam, rather than 'a convert'. See Rasheed, Asra, *A Simple Call to the Worship of One God* (Ipswich, 1994).

11. Bukhari, ch. 2, Hadeeth 7.

12. Malek' Mowatta' #531.

13. Al Tirmidhi #1956.

14. *The Times*, 16 November 2003. For a recent study of Muslim women see Aisha Bewley, *Islam: The Empowering of Women* (London, 1999).

15. Whilst the concept of nationalism goes against the teachings of Islam which holds all Muslims, wherever they are, to be part of the same Ummah (community), there is an increasing sense of nationalism in many Muslim countries.

16. For details see Kenneth S. Little, *Negroes in Britain: A Study of Racial Relations in English Society* (Revised edn. London, 1972); Patricia Aithie, *The Burning Ashes of Time: From Steamer Point to Tiger Bay on the Trail of Seafaring Arabs* (Bridgend, 2004); Fred Halliday, *Britain's First Muslims. Portrait of an Arab Community* (London, 2010), pp. 17–24; http://www.bbc.co.uk/religion/religions/islam/history/uk_1.shtml (accessed April 2010). Personal insights are also recorded in this chapter.

17. For example, *Encyclopaedia Britannica*.

18. Halliday, *Britain's First Muslims*, pp. 4, 17–19.

19. For details of this period see Neil Evans, '"Regulating the Reserve": Arabs, Blacks and the Local State in Cardiff, 1919–1945', *Immigrants and Minorities*, 4, 2 (1985), 68–115.

20. Details of race riots in Wales in 1919 are provided in Neil Evans, 'The South Wales Race Riots of 1919', *Llafur: The Journal of the Society for the Study of Labour History*, 3, 1 (Spring 1980), 5–29; Peter Fryer, *Staying Power. The History of Black People in Britain* (London, 1984), 303–10. An additional study has been made by Jacqueline Jenkinson, 'The 1919 Riots', in P. Panayi (ed.), *Racial Violence in Britain in the Nineteenth and Twentieth Centuries* (revised edn. London and New York,

1996), 92–111; Halliday, *Britain's First Muslims*, pp. 24–7 and citing the reports from the *Western Mail*, 12 June 1919, 13 June 1919.

21. Richard Pankhurst, 'An Early Somali Autobiography', *Africa* (Rome), XXVII (1977), 373–4, and cited in Fryer, *Staying Power*, 306.
22. Fryer, *Staying Power*, 307. The details of other victims are provided in Halliday, *Britain's First Muslims*, pp. 25–6.
23. Halliday, *Britain's First Muslims*, p. 27.
24. *John Bull*, XXVI, 687 (2 August 1919), and cited in Fryer, *Staying Power*, 307.
25. I am grateful to Sheikh Saeed for providing some of these details.
26. For details of his life and influence in Britain see Halliday, *Britain's First Muslims*, pp. 27–39.
27. Ibid., p. 31, and citing the *Western Mail*, 6 May 1938. See also Appendix 1 of Halliday's study (pp. 146–51) whereby he provides correspondence relating to the efforts to erect mosques in Cardiff and South Shields in the north-east of England, c.1938–9.
28. Fred Halliday has noted that there were approximately 1,500 Yemenis and 1,000 Somalis in Cardiff during the Second World War and offers some explanations for the post-war decline in new settlers. See Halliday, *Britain's First Muslims*, pp. 21–4. There were also sporadic bouts of racism towards these settlers from the 1930s onwards. See Marika Sherwood, 'Racism and Resistance: Cardiff in the 1930s and 1940s', *Llafur. Journal of the Society for the Study of Welsh Labour History*, 5, 4 (1991), 51–70.
29. Earlier references to religious activities were recounted in Roy Saunders, 'Islam's faithful at prayer in a Cardiff mosque. The foreign seamen in the city's dockland', *Western Mail*, 20 March 1934, p. 7. For details of the raising of funds for the mosque see Halliday, *Britain's First Muslims*, p. 31. The mosque was, however, bombed during World War Two (c.1940). See http://www.ww2talk.com/forum/great-britain/23451-germans-bombed-our-mosque-butetown-cardiff.html (accessed April 2010). It had been rebuilt by the summer of 1943 and was opened by the Saudi Arabian Minister on 16 July. See *The Times*, 1 July 1943.
30. http://www.bbc.co.uk/wales/religion/sites/timeline/pages/religion_in_wales_15.shtml (accessed April 2010).
31. In his study of Britain's Muslim communities, Fred Halliday provides some details concerning these disputes. See Halliday, *Britain's First Muslims*, pp. 31–6.
32. This period and some of the people in this community are discussed in ibid., pp. 39–44. These brief biographical insights include Hajj Salih Hassan al-Udhaini who presented a Welsh flag to King Feisal of Saudi Arabia in 1966 while on his way to Mecca, and Abdullah Mohammed, a rugby player, who stated 'I am the first Arab to play at Cardiff Arms Park'.
33. http://www.scribd.com/doc/8603715/UK-Mosque-Database (accessed April 2010).
34. Most are recorded in ibid.
35. UK Census 29 April 2001. See http://www.statistics.gov.uk/census/
36. From the AMP the Muslim Council of Wales was established. For further details see Paul Chambers, 'Islam in Wales', *Planet: The Welsh Internationalist*, 168 (December–January, 2004), 49–53, 'Secularization, Wales and Islam', *Journal for Contemporary Religion*, 21, 3 (2006), 325–40. See also http://www.muslimcouncil wales.org/ (accessed March 2010).
37. Constitutional Documentation and Stated Aims of Association of Muslim Professionals.
38. Recent changes in Higher Education in Wales has led to the formation of the University of Wales, Trinity Saint David, and the creation of the School of Theology, Religious Studies and Islamic Studies.
39. For details of his work and publications see http://www.bilalphilips.com/ (accessed April 2010).
40. Details are provided at http://www.eihs.org.uk/ (accessed April 2010).
41. The author of this chapter was invited and agreed to attend this annual event.
42. Knowledge gained by author from attending various informal meetings and gatherings in south Wales where these feelings/issues were raised by the Muslims who attended.
43. Jenny Rees, 'Course is first to study Muslim society in modern Britain', *Western Mail*, 19 May 2005.
44. The history of the Yemeni migrant population is discussed in Richard I. Lawless, *From Ta'izz to Tyneside. An Arab Community in the North-East of England During the Early Twentieth Century* (Exeter, 1995); Halliday, *Britain's First Muslims*, passim.

45. In Islam, an orphan is someone whose <u>father</u> has died.
46. For example, he was interviewed by the BBC Radio Wales for the documentary series 'Bay People – an oral history of settlers in Cardiff's Tiger Bay' (aired 21 and 28 October 2001).
47. M. M. Jilani interview with Sheik Saeed Ismail, March 2003.
48. For details see http://www.ebsp.org/ (accessed April 2010).
49. M. M. Jilani interview with S. K., March 2003.
50. Details from the personal experience of the author as he was part of the founding committee.
51. The Church in Wales press release, 21 January 2003.
52. Due to anonymity a reference to this text cannot be cited.
53. M. M. Jilani interview with J. K., March 2003.
54. M. M. Jilani interview with P. A., March 2003.

CHAPTER 19

SIKHISM

Shinder Thandi

There are estimated to be around twenty-two million Sikhs worldwide, and the vast majority of them live in the state of Punjab in India. Although estimates vary, there are approximately 1.5 million Sikhs scattered across the globe outside India. Punjab was one of the last territories to come under formal British colonial rule in 1849. Major socio-economic changes, displacement and internal migratory movements occurred during this British colonial period, which ended with the bloody partition of the old Punjab Province into a geographically larger West Punjab (now in Pakistan) and a smaller East Punjab, in India. East Punjab was partitioned further in 1966 creating the new states of Punjab and Haryana, and with some areas transferred to Himachel Pradesh. The vast majority of the Sikh population in Britain have their roots in the present Indian Punjab, which currently has a sixty-five percent Sikh majority. According to folklore, the first Sikh to live in Britain was Maharajah Dalip Singh, the exiled young son and heir to Maharajah Ranjit Singh, the first and only Sikh to establish a kingdom ruled by a Sikh in Punjab. Dalip Singh later acquired the Elveden Estate in Norfolk and his main place of residence is now one of the many popular tourist places promoted by Sikh organisations that want to highlight and strengthen the long (and some may say 'romanticised') history of Anglo-Sikh relations, including with the Prince of Wales and the Royal Regiment. During the colonial period there was a small Sikh presence in Britain, especially in the port cities of London and Cardiff, but the main period of migration started in the 1950s.[1]

According to the 2001 Census, of the three main South Asian religions represented in Britain, people of the Sikh faith ranked third at 336,000, behind Hindus (559,000) and then Muslims (1.6m).[2] This relatively small number of British Sikhs, even allowing for errors and omissions in response to the first ever question on religion in British census history, came as a surprise to a number of people especially to those within the Sikh community who had estimated the Sikh community to be at least around 500,000. In fact, one Sikh organisation, the Sikh Secretariat, had lobbied Parliament for at least the previous two years for Sikhs to be granted a separate ethnic category in the British census, partly on the basis of their numerical strength, which they claimed stood at 700,000![3] Compared with estimates derived from the 1991 census, then, there appears to have been hardly any net growth in the Sikh population over the past decade. This raises a number of pertinent and interesting questions about the demographic dynamics of the community, and processes of assimilation and non-assimilation, especially among the second and third generations. Was it now possible to think, given that the first generation of migrants who came mainly in the 1950s are fast disappearing, that second-generation migrants or child migrants had adjusted their family size to the British norm or do not wish to be identified as Sikhs? And given that fresh migration had basically been eliminated through successive immigration controls, had the Sikh community reached a plateau, and will it now decline numerically over the next few decades? These are some of the issues that are now beginning to dawn on Sikhs in the new millennium and these provide a good starting point to examine the Sikh presence in Britain in general, and Wales in particular, and assess their migration and religious experiences over the past fifty years.

This chapter is divided into four sections. The first section provides a very basic introduction to Sikh beliefs and practices. Due to the word constraint, only the bare essentials of the Sikh religion are covered. The second and third sections trace Sikh migration experience in England and Wales and the final section raises some contemporary issues facing British Sikhs today.

Brief introduction to Sikhism

Sikhism is recognized as the fifth largest religion in the world. It is a very distinct faith from other major religions of South Asia such as Hinduism and Islam, and is the only indigenous religion of Punjab. In order to understand the Sikhs in Wales it is necessary to start with their religious roots. A brief description of Sikhism is also necessary to explain the basic tenets of the faith and how these tenets have, over time, helped to define Sikhs as a distinct people and community. This discussion will also enable the reader to differentiate Sikhs from other people from the Indian sub-continent.

For Sikhs, Sikh *dharam* ('way of life') or *Khalsa Panth* ('path of the pure ones') is an original revealed religion based on the *Shabad* (Word) of the Gurus, founded by the first Guru, Guru Nanak. Guru Nanak (1469–1539) was born in Punjab in a place called Talwandi (now known as Nankana Sahib, in Pakistan) and after his divine call to spread the *Guru Shabad*, he travelled extensively in India and as far west as central Asia, spreading the message of peace, brotherhood and love and worship of one God (V*ahiguru*, literally meaning God is great or glorious), who is formless, omnipotent and omnipresent. For Nanak, Vahiguru is the Absolute Being; the eternal truth, immortal and beyond fear and enmity; the creator, the preserver and destroyer.[4] Guru Nanak argued intensely with those who preached and with those who engaged in the worship of idols and images, and he exposed their hypocrisy and external ritualism. For Nanak, inner meditation, contemplation and devotion were the true path to *mukti* (liberation of human spirit from rebirth). Guru Nanak chose to settle down in Kartarpur (now in Pakistan) where he founded a community of people who came from different social backgrounds, and who later became known as the *Sikhs* (disciples or learners). In fact, it was the great attraction of egalitarianism and the emphasis on humanism in Guru Nanak's teaching which led many to become *Nanak-panthis* (followers of Nanak). These followers were clearly rejecting and moving away from the social exclusion and hierarchical relations legitimised by the Hindu Brahmanical system. Guru Nanak's strong rejection of a caste-based social order and gender inequalities were especially important in attracting a large and growing following. This aspect was aptly captured in Guru Nanak's introduction of *Langar* (communal kitchen) in which all took part on an equal basis.

Guru Nanak's philosophy emphasises that everything that exists in the natural and physical world and all change within it, only happens through God's will (*hukam*). The goal and purpose in life should be to seek its creator and to merge with God, breaking the cycle of birth and death. As the human form is the highest form of life on this earth and since human beings are uniquely conscious of their actions and reactions, human life and form is therefore the ideal carnation when the cycle of transmigration can potentially be broken. *Karam* (human actions and their consequences) determines whether a human being will achieve union with God. Inability to have union with God leads to a repetition of the cycle of rebirth, which may mean rebirth into lower forms of life than human. Thus, the purpose of life is to achieve liberation (*mukti*) of the human spirit from the bonds of transmigration. Human beings face many barriers towards this path of *mukti*. The false lure of *maya* (an illusory drive for material possessions) can result in *haumai* (self-centredness), *kam* (lust), *karodh* (anger), *lobh* (greed), *moh* (worldly obsession for material possessions) and *hankar* (pride). All of these deviations act as a barrier to union with God and need to be overcome. Guru Nanak reiterated that a true path towards overcoming these barriers is to develop *santokh* (contentment), *dhan* (charity), *daya* (kindness and compassion), *parsanta* (happiness), and *nimarta* (humility). One of Guru Nanak's enduring guiding principles for truthful living remains *nam japo, kirat karo, wandh shako*, that is, remember the name of God, engage in honest labour and share your earnings for *sarbat da bhalla* (welfare of all).[5]

Guru Nanak was succeeded by nine further Gurus over a period of about two centuries, who continued to pass the *jyot* (spiritual light) from one to the other. These Gurus continued to spread Guru Nanak's message. They composed and consolidated the growing corpus of devotional hymns and their contribution forms the largest collection in Sikh scripture. The Guruships end with the tenth and last Guru Gobind Singh who, in 1708, bestowed eternal Guruship in the *Guru Granth Sahib*, the Sikh scripture revealing the *bani* or Guru Shabad.[6] The Guru Granth Sahib (hereafter GGS) thereafter becomes the eternal Guru of the Sikhs and the sole basis for spiritual authority. There was also one other significant act performed by Guru Gobind Singh a few years earlier. In 1699, in Anandpur, on the special occasion of Vaisakhi, the annual harvest festival and where there was an unusually large gathering, the Guru performed the *Khande-di-Pahul* (acceptance of *amrit*, the sweetened nectar of everlasting life) ceremony, which initiated the *panj pyares* (the five beloved) into the *Khalsa Panth*, later followed by many others. This was the most important act in the history of institutionalisation of the Sikh faith. Through this ceremony, which has continued to be a regular occurrence around *Vaisakhi* time among Sikhs wherever they live, the Guru had bestowed temporal authority in the *Khalsa Panth*. Sikhs who had taken *Khande-di-Pahul* had made a conscious commitment to observe a strict code of behaviour (later refined and now known as the *Rehat Maryada*) and to wear and respect the significance of the 5 Ks (*kesh*, uncut hair; *kanga*, a small comb, *kara*, a steel bangle or bracelet; *kirpan*, a small ceremonial sword and *kachcha*, underwear).[7] Sikhs now had a distinct and outwardly visible identity, which would clearly differentiate them from others.

The schematic chart (fig.1) traces core phases in the evolution of Sikh belief and practice. It is useful to begin the narrative by highlighting the earlier influences on Sikh religious belief (as reflected in the Sant Tradition in North India) and on Guru Nanak's own life and thought. This is also necessary because their contribution is greatly acknowledged by the Gurus themselves who included their devotional hymns in the compilation of the *Adi Granth* (the first or original Book) and retained them in the definitive version of the GGS. It is also worth emphasizing that all of the five *Sants* included in this first box hailed from lowly caste backgrounds and drew on followers principally from these communities, including Muslim *Sufis*. From among these five, the devotional hymns of Kabir are given the most predominant space in the SGGS.[8]

It is useful to divide the main period of formation of Sikh religious belief system into two main phases. The first, starting with the founder Guru Nanak and ending with Guru Arjan around the turn of the seventeenth century, is a period during which most of the devotional scripture (hymns) was being composed and this period

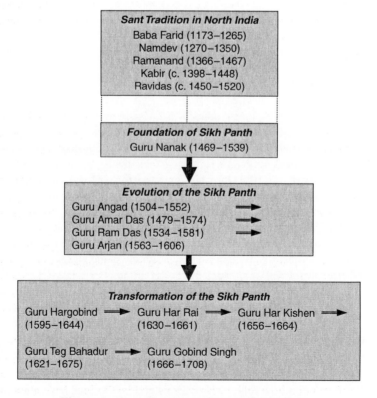

Figure 1: Core Developments in Sikh Religion

ends with their compilation into the Adi Granth, the first 'original' version of what was later to become the Guru Granth Sahib, by Guru Arjan himself in 1604. This is a period of relative peace and calm and of religious pluralism and tolerance in Punjab. At this time, the Sikh community, although still small, was beginning to be noticed and gathered followers, especially from among the agricultural and nomadic tribes such as the *Jats*. The second phase, starting symbolically with the martyrdom of Guru Arjan in 1606, witnessed a marked transformation of the Sikh community, from one which was relatively passive and pacifist, to one which was becoming increasingly militant and militarised, in the face of relentless oppression and growing religious intolerance among successive Moghul rulers. This period closes with the martyrdom of Guru Tegh Bahadur (under Emperor Aurangzeb's rule) and the initiation by Guru Gobind Singh of the militant Sikh order, *Sant-Sipai* (Saint-Soldier) or Khalsa Sikhs, who would defend the right to practice one's own religion by upholding the principle of religious freedom and welfare of all humanity (*sarbat da bhalla*). By the end of this period, Khalsa identity had been fully consolidated: the Sikhs had a distinct religious belief system, a distinct scripture, distinct religious institutions and a distinct language.[9] Table 1 below provides a brief summary of the major landmarks in the emergence of Sikh religious beliefs, practices and institutions during the Gurus' period. Subsequent developments in Sikh history are merely attempts to refine, uphold and strengthen these beliefs and symbols of Sikh religion in the face of rapid socio-economic change, internal and external interferences, and global migratory movements of Sikhs.

Sikh Presence in Britain

According to the 2001 census there are a total of 336,000 Sikhs in Britain, comprising about 0.6 per cent of the country's total population.[10] An overwhelming majority of the Sikhs live in the two largest urban conurbations in England, Greater London and the Midlands. Being one of the oldest communities from South Asia, there has emerged over time a sizable literature on the period of Sikh settlement, evolution of the community and specific issues confronting the community, at both national and local levels.[11] However, much of this literature is now rather dated and there still exists no authoritative assessment of the struggles and collective achievements of the Sikh community despite its diverse character. If anything, much of the ethnographic literature on the Sikhs tends to present a very negative and distorted picture, with more emphasis placed on processes creating various forms of differentiation and disjunctions within the community, rather than on their collective achievements in the face of tremendous social and cultural constraints.[12]

Literature in the 1980s further reinforced these representations with the additional backdrop of the difficult political situation faced by Sikhs in their homeland.[13] This overall orientation by researchers has meant that there is a dearth of literature focusing on how Sikh organisations and institutions have attempted to deal with issues of maintaining Sikh religious tradition and transmitting Sikh

Table 1: Landmark Developments in Sikh Institutions and Identity

Name	Age	Age at Guruship and relationship to preceding Guru	Number of children	Name of town founded	Significant contribution to Sikh Belief and Identity
Guru Nanak	70	38, founder	2	Kartarpur	Egalitarianism, gender equality, religious tolerance, honest labour, sharing (early forms of *langar* - community kitchen) and devotion through meditation (*bhakti* or *naam simran*)
Guru Angad	48	35, a follower, formerly known as Bhai Lehna	3	Khadur	*Gurmukhi* (Panjabi) script and Grammar
Guru Amardas	95	73, a follower	4	Goindval	*Sewa*, (selfless service of community), extension of *langar*; (community kitchen)
Guru Ramdas	47	40, son-in-law, formely known as Bhai Jetha	3	Ramdaspur (Amritsar)	Special *Lavan* (hymns) for *Anand Karaj* (Wedding) ceremony, *Kirtan* and *Katha*, (devotional singing and preaching), eradication of *sati* (Hindu belief in widow immolation on her husband's funeral pyre)
Guru Arjan	43	18, youngest son	1	Kartarpur, Tarn Taran, Sri Hargobindpur	Compilation of *Adi Granth*, Harmandir Sahib (Golden Temple at Amritsar), *daswandh* (sharing of one-tenth of earning)
Guru Hargobind	49	11, only son	6	Kiratpur	*Akal Takhat* (Seat of temporal power), *Miri Piri* (Temporal and Spiritual power), *Nishan Sahib* (Sikh Flag)
Guru Har Rai	31	14, grandson	2	–	Promotion of hospitals and animal welfare
Guru Harkishen	8	5, younger son	–	–	Promotion of schools and education
Guru Tegh Bahadur	54	43, grand-uncle	1	Anandpur	*Jiwanmukt* (*sacrificing life or living for others*)
Guru Gobind Singh	42	9, only son	4	Paunta, Damdama	*Amrit* (Khalsa Identity), *Sant-Sipai*, (Scholar-Soldier), Martyrdom and Sacrifice

culture and heritage to the younger generations. There are, for instance, hardly any studies which focus on the critical role of the *gurdwara(s)* (literally, a place or home of God), community language teachers, *gurmat* camps (week-long or week-end retreats focusing on transmission of Sikh religious tradition), and visiting religious preachers and musicians in both nurturing the faithful and imparting knowledge to younger generations. There is also hardly any literature which provides critical analysis of the various protracted legal struggles Sikhs have both won and lost in protecting their religious rights and symbols in a hostile environment and against a predominantly euro-centric legal system.[14] Thus, there are hardly any academic accounts of Sikh struggles on their right to wear a Turban, keep a beard, wear a *kirpan*, and other religious practices, which have been taken up in British courts and industrial tribunals. However, despite these hurdles, the Sikh community has successfully raised its economic and social profile and there is now a good representation of Sikhs in the public, business, media and music and arts domains, as well as in political participation both at the national and local levels. The community has reached the age of maturity and participates fully in celebrating its cultural and religious identity.

As already noted, the Gurus drew followers from across different social groups and particularly from among those who were either outside of, or whose position was ambiguous, in the Brahmanical hierarchical caste system. This diversity in following is also reflected in the social background of Sikhs who migrated to Britain in different periods and in different contexts. Thus, if the social background of the Sikh community in Britain today is examined, it is possible to observe *Jats* (an agricultural and nomadic social group and comprising mainly of direct migrants from central districts or *doab* of Punjab) who happen to be the largest group, *Khatris* (a merchant/trading group who are both direct and indirect migrants), *Ramgharias* (artisan groups, mainly 'twice migrants' coming mainly via East African countries), and *Bhatras* (a trading class or group who are mainly direct migrants). Two other social groups, which are worthy of mention as they both originate from Punjab and also have organic links with the Sikh community, are the *Adharmis* or *Dalits* (comprising mainly lower status groups who follow the teaching of Guru Ravidass whose hymns are included in the GGS) and *Valmikis* (a lower caste group who follow the teaching of Maharishi Valmik). There are also a small number of peripheral groups who broadly belong to the Sikh tradition but who do not accept that the spiritual authority rests solely in the GSS.[15] Given the different trajectories in their migration experience, their attempts to maintain social cohesiveness among their own community within the context of liberal and accommodating multiculturalist policies in Britain that provides public funding for cultural organisations, each one of these social groups have mobilised support through developing their own separate organisations and institutions. These are, however, often uncritically associated with the development and perpetuation of casteism among Sikhs in Britain.[16]

Sikh Presence in Wales

According to the 2001 census, there are approximately 2,000 Sikhs living in Wales and the majority of them are concentrated in the three most urbanised areas of Wales, namely Cardiff, Swansea and the Rhondda valley. Cardiff is the only place where the Sikhs could potentially be considered to be visible (at 0.3 per cent of Cardiff's population) but elsewhere they are small in number and relatively dispersed.[17] This invisibility and potential isolation brings its own problems, especially the increased exposure to racist hostility and powerlessness in achieving mainstream community support. Table 2 below provides a brief summary of numbers in the main areas of Sikh settlement in Wales.

The Sikh presence in Cardiff is one of the earliest in Britain, along with that of the community in Southall in west London. One of the major groups of Sikhs to settle in Cardiff were the Bhatra Sikhs who may still constitute the majority of Sikhs in Wales. According to one of the very rare studies on this small group of diaspora Sikhs, Paul Ghuman estimated their number alone to be around 360 in 1980, compared with the current total Sikh population in Cardiff at just over 900.[18]

The main perception that emerges from the scant literature on Bhatra Sikhs is that they are members of a low-status group, although they themselves trace their lineage to the Brahmin high caste group. According to Ghuman, in Bhatra mythology, their ancestry can be traced back to Madho Mal, a Brahmin *rishi* (holy/wise man), a singer and poet, who fell in love with and then married Kam Kundala, a dancing girl. Madhwas and Bhatras were the children of this marriage/union,[19] however the question of ancestry is far from settled. Harbans Singh's edited volume, *The Encyclopaedia of Sikhism* provides a more plausible background. According to this, the Bhatras themselves trace their origins to Baba Chang Rai of Sangl dip (modern day Sri Lanka) who was

admitted as a disciple by Guru Nanak during his journey to the South . . .[20] Changā Rai, himself a devout Sikh with a substantial following, added the

Table 2: Sikh Community in Wales

Welsh Towns and Counties	No. of Sikhs	% of the population
Cardiff	928	0.3
Neath Port Talbot	115	0.1
Swansea	153	0.1
Rhondda Cynon Taff	144	0.1
Newport	85	0.1
The Vale of Glamorgan	74	0.1
Torfaen	47	0.1
Monmouthshire	43	0.1
Total in remaining areas	426	N/A
Total in Wales	2,015	0.1

Source: NSO, Census 2001 (2003).

suffix 'Bhatra' to his name. His followers came to be known as Bhatras. Changā Bhatra established Sikh *sangats* in many parts. Since Bhatras were mostly itinerant missionaries, they did not take to settled life. Having no time to learn and practice skilled occupations, they were eventually drawn to the peddling profession. Their mobility led to the scattering of the community in several parts of the country and beyond.[21]

Due to the lack of research on this community, it is very difficult to get accurate information about their main areas of settlement in Punjab, their specific area of origin and their migration experience. Despite their obscurity and general marginalisation, they attach great pride to their integral links with the Sikh community and remember how in certain historical periods they had been patronised by the Gurus and trusted to look after the gurdwaras. Partly due to the general perception of their lower status and partly because of their historical links, the Bhatra Sikhs have remained very *pukka* (true or strong, in terms of adhering to the 5 Ks and Sikh tradition) and somewhat orthodox, but very closely-knit and very pro-active in ensuring transmission of their cultural and religious heritage to the younger generations compared with other major Sikh groups in Britain. However, despite the fact that the elder Bhatras may have isolated themselves from other Sikhs and from the wider Welsh community, they retained strong links with their relatives back home in Punjab. They took particular pride in acquiring land and property in India, which fulfilled the dual function of providing economic security for the future but also in raising their social status, similar to how the small-landowner *Jats* and the *Adharmi* (lower caste followers of Guru Ravidass) Punjabi community did later on in Britain. This, however, was not the case with the younger Bhatras. Ghuman, commenting specifically about the younger generation stated that

In Cardiff, the young up-and-coming leader wears all the Sikh identifying symbols, has his own business, acts as a liaison officer, is on the management committee of the gurdwara, and also has the basic advantage of being the son of a well-known Bhatra.[22]

It is very unfortunate that the early research on this old Sikh community has not been repeated and currently very little information is available about them, their networks and their aspirations.[23]

Bhatra Sikhs began to migrate out of Punjab as a result of the displacement caused by the partition of Punjab in 1947. However, some Bhatra families had migrated to Britain as early as the 1930s, especially to the port cities of London, Glasgow, Cardiff and Manchester, the latter two cities becoming the main areas of eventual settlement. The limited sources that are available suggest that they were the original Asian peddlers or petty traders, engaging in door to door selling of mainly small items, such as ties, handkerchiefs, socks, scarves and jewellery, drawing upon their ancestral occupations. Many were later able to upgrade to become small shopkeepers. Other types of ancestral activities they drew upon were ear-piercing and palm-reading or fortune-telling, with the latter becoming their trademark occupation in popular mythology among Punjabis in Britain.[24]

Over time, other social groups from the Sikh community began to settle in the main cities of Wales and also began establishing *gurdwaras*. However, Wales has always suffered from many locational disadvantages for migrant groups and this has prevented the development of a larger settlement pattern. The limited employment opportunities, distance from friends and relatives settled in major urban areas of Britain, and costly and inadequate availability and access to cultural commodities such as an Indian cinema or various convenient ethnic foods, meant that the Sikh community grew only very slowly. In such a relatively small community, the institution of the *gurdwara* acquires greater significance both as a spiritual and as a community centre, and over time several *gurdwaras* came into being, mainly concentrated in Cardiff. Although no reliable statistics exist, anecdotal evidence suggests that many Sikhs are self-employed as small shopkeepers, such as owners of grocery stores, newsagents or post offices, or operate as independent taxi-drivers. There is also some evidence that suggests that there has been a sizable movement of Sikh families over the past decade, especially into central and northern areas of Wales.[25] This is particularly due to rising business property prices caused by excess demand for many small businesses in the Birmingham and Black Country areas of central England, especially businesses such as petrol stations, newsagencies, post-offices and pharmacies.

Currents Issues facing the Sikh Community

In just over half a century, Sikhs in Britain have achieved enormous success economically, socially, politically and culturally. They have proved to be a very vibrant, enterprising and progressive minority community, which has led to greater visibility in the British landscape far in excess of their number in the total population. They have waged legal struggles for the recognition of their religious rights and have won most of them.[26] They have developed strong cultural organisations and have established numerous religious institutions (over 300 *gurdwaras*), which carry forward the religious and cultural traditions of Sikhism for future generations. The recent opening of the most costly and largest Sikh *gurdwara* in the world outside India, in Southall, Middlesex, in west London, is an important symbol of the accumulated achievements of the Sikh community in Britain.[27]

Despite these successes however, there are areas of concern within the Sikh community. The earlier concerns of the older generations about the problems of transmission of culture to the younger generations have not faded, although the earlier fears of 'absorption' by mainstream British culture have proved to be largely unfounded. There are also emerging challenges associated with the break-up of extended family relations, the emergence of a sizable elderly community and issues related to their social and health care, the housing and health problems associated with living in run down inner city areas, and problems associated with a rise in racial harassment, especially among small marginalized communities such as those in Wales. These are, however, challenges which face all minority communities and as is always the case, the future evolution of the minority community will mainly be determined by how these challenges are managed.

Notes

1. A 400 year history of Asians in Britain is comprehensively captured in Michael H. Fisher, Shompa Lahiri and Shinder Thandi, *A South Asian History of Britain*, (London, 2007). For the history of the settlement of Sikhs in Britain see A. W. Helweg, *Sikhs in England: The Development of a Migrant Community* (Delhi and Oxford, 1980); R. Ballard and C. Ballard, 'The Sikhs: The Development of South Asian Settlements in Britain', in J. L. Watson (ed.), *Between Two Cultures: Migrants and Minorities in Britain* (Oxford, 1977), pp. 21–56.
2. National Statistics Office (NSO), Census 2001 (2003).
3. The Sikh Secretariat is an umbrella organisation promoting the cause of several political organisations of the Sikhs, including the Sikh Federation. The first Sikh political party in the UK was established in 2003. Details of their aims and activities can be seen on their web-sites at http://www.sikh-secretariat.com and http://www.sikhfederation.com/index.htm. (accessed January 2006).
4. This is taken from the *Mūl Mantar*, which begins each section of the *Guru Granth Sahib*. In full translation the Mūl Mantar states, 'God is one, call Him the Eternal Truth, He is the Supreme Creator, He knows no fear and is at enmity with none, His Being is timeless, immanent, beyond birth or death, self-existent: He is autogenous, attainable through the grace of the Guru', For a full translation and elaboration see the entry in Harbans Singh (ed.), *The Encyclopaedia of Sikhism* (4 vols. 2nd edn. Patiala, 2002), III, pp.139–42.
5. The concepts of *sewa* (selfless service) and *sarbat da bhalla* (welfare of all humanity) are recurring themes in Sikh scripture and underline the daily actions and social practices of the Sikhs.
6. Since this period mainstream Sikhs do not believe in any living Guru, and the *Guru Granth Sahib* has been accepted as their timeless Guru. The composition of the Guru Granth Sahib occurred over different periods starting with the original compilation by Guru Arjan. The current canonical version, the definitive scripture, contains 5,817 shabads set in thirty-one rags and runs to 1,430 pages. For a comprehensive historical account of the making of Sikh scripture see Gurinder Singh Mann, *The Making of Sikh Scripture* (New York, 2001); Pashaura Singh, *The Guru Granth Sahib: Canon, Meaning and Authority* (Delhi, 2000).
7. After taking *Khande-di-pahul* or *amrit*, the Khalsa or *Amritdhari* Sikh male or female is required to wear the five articles of faith - the 5 Ks – to distinguish them from other Sikhs who have not yet made or maintained their commitment to the faith. Each of the 5 Ks signifies both a religious and symbolic allegiance. *Kesh* (uncut hair) shows respect for the sanctity of all bodily hair and not only towards hair on the head. Sikhs, mainly males, tie up and cover up their hair with a Turban, the most outwardly distinctive sign of Sikh identity. *Kangha* (a small comb) is usually kept with the tied head of hair and signifies the importance of both cleanliness and an orderly approach to spirituality. *Kara* (steel bracelet) is worn to remind oneself of the universality of God and as a symbol of universal brotherhood. *Kirpan* (a small ceremonial sword) acts as a reminder for Sikhs to uphold the right to dignity and self-respect. It also symbolises the readiness to fight in defence of the weak and the oppressed. *Kachcha* (underwear shorts) serve the dual purpose of allowing agility of movement in time of warfare as well as modesty and moral restraint. An important point to emphasise about the 5 Ks is that not only do they have a moral and a practical dimension, they also carry the spiritual message of obeying the *hukum* (will of God) and Gurus' teachings. For an illuminating discussion on the significance of the meaning of amrit for defining Sikh identity see Pashaura Singh, 'Sikh Identity in the Light of History', in P. Singh and N. Gerald Barrier (eds), *Sikhism and History* (Delhi and Oxford, 2004).
8. For a recent, concise and excellent introduction to this period, major personalities and inclusion of their hymns in the Guru Granth Sahib see Pashaura Singh, *The Bhagats of the Guru Granth Sahib: Sikh Self-Definition and the Bhagat Bani* (Delhi and Oxford, 2003).
9. For an excellent, short and clear introduction see Gurinder Singh Mann, *Sikhism* (New York, 2003).
10. NSO, 2001 Census.
11. According to much of this literature, the period of mass migration starts in the 1950s (a period of acute labour shortage in post-war Britain) with male migration. Over time, both as a response to changing immigration controls and the desire of Sikhs of settle down permanently in their newly adopted country, their families join them. Further migration, although highly regulated, and especially the

arrival of Asians due to their expulsion from East African countries, increased the number of Sikhs in Britain. For details of Sikh migration see Ballard and Ballard, 'The Sikhs: The Development of South Asian Settlements in Britain'; N. Gerald Barrier and Verne A. Dusenbery (eds), *The Sikh Diaspora: Migration and the Experience Beyond Punjab* (Delhi, 1989); Darshan Singh Tatla, *The Sikh Diaspora: The Search for Statehood* (London, 1999).

12. For an essay on this theme see Roger Ballard, 'Differentiation and the Disjunction amongst Sikhs in Britain', in Barrier and Dusenbery (eds), *Sikh Diaspora*, pp. 200–32.

13. This is not altogether surprising as the 1980s was a difficult decade for the Sikh community given the rise of militancy and the Khalistan movement in Punjab. This created tensions among the Sikh community and led to factional fighting, leading to the impression of a divided community. Matters came to a head in June 1984 when the Indian army (in so called Operation Bluestar) invaded and destroyed the Akal Takht located within the Golden Temple complex in Amritsar, with the purpose of flushing out armed Sikh militants led by Sant Bhindranwale. He had waged a struggle against the injustices perpetrated against the Sikhs by the central government. For a full account of the impact of Punjab politics on the British Sikh community and their responses see Tatla, *Sikh Diaspora*. Also see S. S. Thandi, 'The Punjabi Diaspora in the UK and the Punjab crisis', in Pashaura Singh and N. Gerald Barrier (eds), *The Transmission of Sikh Heritage in the Diaspora* (New Delhi, 1996), pp. 227–50.

14. One of the earliest accounts of a Sikh struggle over religious symbols is given in David Beetham, *Transport and Turbans: A Comparative Study of a Migrant Community* (London, 1970).

15. Subsequent to the ending of *guruguddi* (heirs for the Guru's position) by Guru Gobind Singh in 1699, there have emerged a number of dissident movements within the wider Sikh movement who claim their descendency either from the Gurus' family and relatives or from the various followers (*Babas*) in the nineteenth century. The more notable of these movements are the *Namdhari*, *Nirankari* and *Nanaksar* movements. These all have separate religious institutions in Britain. For information about these institutions and a short profile of these communities see P. Weller (ed.), *Religions in the U.K: A Multi-Faith Directory* (Derby, 1997).

16. All the Gurus came from the Khatri or merchant social background but the Gurus were totally opposed to the caste system and showed their abhorrence to this in their devotional hymns and in daily practice, for example in promoting communal eating as in serving *langar*. The notions of purity/impurity associated with the Hindu caste system have no relevance within the Sikh belief system. Sikhs, for instance, use the name *Singh* (literally, lion) for males and *Kaur* (literally, princess) for females, to underline the social equality between individuals. Every *gurdwara* today welcomes the entry of Sikh or non-Sikh of any social background but naturally *gurdwara* managements have tended to be representative of their main *'sangat'* (congregation). The literal translation of the north Indian term 'jāt' or 'zāt' as 'caste' is problematic when applied within the context of the Sikh belief and value system, and this ambiguousness is reflected in the debate about the existence of casteism within the Sikh community. For example see Sewa Singh Kalsi, 'The Sikhs and Caste: The Development of Ramgarhia Identity in Britain', in P. Singh and N. Gerald Barrier (eds), *Sikh Identity: Continuity and Change* (Delhi, 1999).

17. NSO, Census 2001.

18. P. A. S. Ghuman acknowledges that his own focus on the Bhatra Sikhs was accidental as his original intention was to study the Sikh community in south-east Wales as a whole. It was only when he realized that Bhatra Sikhs had control over the Cardiff *gurdwara* that he re-oriented his focus towards the Bhatras. See P. A. S. Ghuman, 'Bhatra Sikhs in Cardiff: Family and Kinship Organization', *New Community*, 8, 3 (1980), 308–16.

19. Extrcated from Ghuman 'Bhatra Sikhs in Cardiff', 313.

20. His name figures in the old text as Haqiqat Rāh Mukām Rāje Shivanābh Ki.

21. Quoted in Harbans Singh, (ed.), *The Encyclopaedia of Sikhism* (4 vols. 2nd edn. Patiala, 2002), I, pp. 350–1.

22. Quoted in Ghuman 'Bhatra Sikhs in Cardiff', 313.

23. Besides Ghuman's research and a research note in response to Ghuman's article by E. M. Nesbitt there has been no subsequent focused research on the Bhatra Sikhs. One reason for that may be due, as one of my informants confessed, to the fact that this early research painted a very negative and distorted portrait of the Bhatra Sikh community and since this time they have been very suspicious

of outside researchers and are very reluctant to cooperate and confide in them. See E. M. Nesbitt, 'A Note on Bhatra Sikhs', *New Community*, 9, 1 (1981), 70–2.

24. These popular perceptions and negative connotations still continue, partly a result of ignorance about the socio-economic background of the community. For a flavour of the debate see http://www.punjabi. net/talk/messages/1/41026.html?1069988002 (accessed January 2006). Bhatra organisations themselves are also trying to correct stereotypes and distortions. For example, see http://www.freewebs. com/bhatline/getitright.htm (accessed March 2010).

25. There is no research into this migration although anecdotal evidence drawn from conversations with Asian market traders and tourists from the Midlands who frequent the region indicates that Indian population in general and Sikhs in particular have grown in number over the past decade or so.

26. In July 2008, a 14 year old girl of mixed Welsh and Sikh origin, Sarika-Watkins Singh, from Cwmbach, south Wales, won her High Court discrimination case against Aberdare Girls' School for excluding her in November 2007 for wearing her *kara* (steel bangle) which the school deemed as breaking its 'no jewellery' rule. Sarika's argument, upheld by the judges, was that the kara was an important symbol of her Sikh faith. For further details of the ruling see Anthea Lipsett, 'Sikh schoolgirl wins bangle court case', *Guardian*, 29 July 2008.

27. History of the construction of gurdwaras in Britain goes back to the earlier part of this century. The very first gurdwara is alleged to be the Shepherd's Bush Gurdwara. The *Khalsa Jatha* (a band of Khalsa Sikhs) was instrumental in initiating this development. The Jatha was formed in 1908 to promote religious and social activities among the Sikhs who had settled in Britain. Later in the same year it became affiliated to the Chief Khalsa Diwan, Amritsar. In 1911 the Jatha acquired a house in Putney (South London) for a period of two years. Maharaja Bhupindra Singh of Patiala performed the opening ceremony at this temporary gurdwara. In 1913, the Jatha bought the lease, again with the help of a financial donation from the Maharaja, of 79 Sinclair Road, Shepherd's Bush, London. This site has popularly become known as the first official gurdwara in Britain and the Khalsa Jatha remained there for the next sixty-three years. The official opening ceremony of the Sri Guru Singh Sabha gurdwara in Southall, Middlesex, was on 30 March (2003) and was preceded by a *'Nagar Kirtan'* (procession) of about 50,000 Sikhs towards the new building in an atmosphere 'of both celebration and reverence'. The Southall Sikh community is one of the oldest Sikh communities in Britain and it was very apt that this opening of the new gurdwara building (one among over 300 others in Britain) should have coincided with the annual *Vaisakhi* festival marking the birth of the Khalsa in 1699. The new architect-designed building cost £17.5 million and took nearly three years to complete. It is the largest in Europe, with facilities that can cater for up to 3,000 people. The building exemplifies the vision of the new twenty-first century gurdwara: a large air-conditioned hall for the *sangat*, a community centre, educational centre and museum, dining hall and other multi-purpose space, a total of 6,000 sq. metres. It is expected to become the main religious centre for Sikhs in Britain and Europe. Information relating to the history of this gurdwara, its new architecture and activities is available at http://www.sgsss.org/ (accessed May 2010).

CHAPTER 20

Bahá'í Faith[1]

Vivian Bartlett

Followers of the Bahá'í religion do not see the introduction of their faith to Wales in the light of a Christian revival aimed at moving the heart and soul of a people capable of passionate devotion to God and humble service to His Will. Rather, they view their faith as the sowing of the first seeds of a new Revelation of the Divine. Far from calling itself a sect, or denomination of any of the major world faiths, the Bahá'í Faith, beginning in Persia (now Iran) in the middle of the nineteenth century, has increasingly been recognised as an independent world religion.[2] There are now over five million followers worldwide, to the extent that it constitutes the world's second most widely diffused religion.[3] It has its own sacred scriptures, divinely inspired institutions, laws and ordinances, a 'Covenant' that prevents fragmentation, and a central purpose – the unification of humanity. Its founder is Bahá'u'lláh, a name meaning 'The Glory of God' who, in volumes of writings, clearly stated that He is the 'Promised One' of all peoples and religions – the 'Father', whom Christ prophesised would come to bring mankind together as 'sheep of one fold'. Inspired by the dramatic events of Bahá'u'lláh's forty years of intense suffering and persecution and set on fire by His soul-transforming words, a handful of early Western believers were galvanised into action. Through special messages known as 'The Tablets of the Divine Plan' they were directed to scatter far and wide, and to teach all peoples that God had yet again intervened in human affairs bringing teachings relevant for a new age.[4]

The early believers successfully established Bahá'í centres in several countries. By 1923 there were enough democratically elected local Bahá'í Spiritual Assemblies in the British Isles to form the base for the establishment of the very first elected Bahá'í National Assembly of these islands. At this time there was not a single believer in Wales. In fact, Wales had to wait another two years until two American Bahá'í women, responding to the call of spreading the new message worldwide, visited Cardiff and held Wales' very first Bahá'í meeting. After addressing the Esperantist and Theosophical Societies at the Park Hotel, the *Western Mail* provided details of this significant event in their 15 November 1925 edition:

> Two women have been in Cardiff on a very interesting mission. They are Miss Martha L. Root, a Pittsburgh journalist, and Mrs Florence Schopflocher

of Montreal. They met in England by accident, both being independently engaged in a world tour for the same purpose, and came to Wales together for the weekend. Their purpose is the spreading of the knowledge of the Bahá'í religion. This is a movement which started in Persia and has spread with marvellous effect.

Its twelve basic teachings are: The oneness of mankind, independent investigation of truth, the foundation of religions is one, religion must be the cause of unity, religion must be in accord with science and reason, equality between men and women, prejudice of all kinds must be forgotten, universal peace, universal education, spiritual solution of the economic problem, a universal language, an international tribunal.

These adherents believe that their creed is the world-uniting force ... These two women have, between them, visited practically every country in the world – moved to this voluntary mission by their profound faith.[5]

Interestingly, Martha Root became known as the archetype of Bahá'í itinerant teachers, circling the globe four times during which she introduced the Bahá'í Faith to a granddaughter of Queen Victoria, Queen Marie of Romania, the first monarch to become a believer.[6]

The response from those who attended the first public address on the Bahá'í Faith in Wales is not recorded. It is known, however, that those interested were directed to obtain more information from Bahá'ís outside Wales, an indication that no Bahá'ís were yet resident in the country. At this point it may be pertinent to consider an important insight into the establishment of the Bahá'í Faith throughout the world and then return to the theme of its taking root in Wales. To gain this insight, imagine living at the genesis of say, Buddhism, Christianity or Islam. One would directly experience the social environment of that age and be aware of the types of responses of one's fellow citizens to the new Revelation. Certainly, such an experience would equip the mind with a deep, intimate understanding of the milieu in which the fresh Revelation was destined to take root. Inevitably, the very best that can be achieved today is to gather fragmentary evidence of these developments. This is not so with the birth and spread of the Bahá'í Faith as the following observation makes clear:

For the first time in history humanity has available a detailed and verifiable record of the birth of an independent religious system and of the life of its Founder. Equally accessible is the record of the response that the new faith has evoked, through the emergence of a global community which can already justly claim to represent a microcosm of the human race.[7]

It appears that the first Welsh person to declare their faith in Bahá'u'lláh was May White who lived outside Wales in Torbay.[8] May was a staunch believer who, on a number of occasions, visited Cardiff as a Bahá'í 'travel teacher'. Wales, however, had to wait seventeen years from the meeting at the Park Hotel before the first

Bahá'í was resident in the country. In 1942 Rose Jones moved to 14 Werfa St, Roath, Cardiff, from London shortly after her marriage. Rose had first heard of the Bahá'í Faith when she was a child and even attended children's classes. Although arriving in Cardiff with the blessings of the London Bahá'í community, her main reason for moving was that her husband had acquired a job in the city. It had taken nearly one hundred years from the inception of the Bahá'í Era in 1844 for the new Revelation to gain a foothold in Wales. Moreover, several national plans under the direction of Shoghi Effendi, the great grandson of Bahá'u'lláh and the appointed Guardian of the Bahá'í Faith, had secured an increasing number of Bahá'í centres throughout the world. At their 1944 Annual Convention, the Bahá'ís of Great Britain, inspired by the success of the American campaign to spread the new Revelation, resolved to ask the Guardian for their own national plan. The request was granted but it came as a huge shock to find that within six years they were expected to expand from five established local Spiritual Assemblies to nineteen spread over England, Wales, Scotland, Northern Ireland and Éire.[9]

The Guardian of the Bahá'í Faith, informed and directed by the Tablets of the Divine Plan, stimulated the expansion of the Bahá'í community through his inspirational messages. He called for 'travelling teachers' to promote the faith throughout the British Isles and overseas, and also urged believers to become 'pioneers' – uproot themselves from their homes, settle in a 'goal locality' (either at home or abroad), and build a local Spiritual Assembly. The Guardian emphasised that it was premature for large Bahá'í communities to develop at the expense of areas which had no easy access to the new God-given message. Filled with an unquenchable faith many Bahá'ís dispersed to all parts of the world and laid the foundations of the Bahá'í administration. Their focus was to establish a nine-member, democratically-elected local Spiritual Assembly that would ensure the growth of the Bahá'í community in its locality and administer its affairs. Consequently, the Bahá'í community has grown without any priests or clergy and without the related congregational/minister of religion model commonly thought necessary in many belief systems. To assist this process, Bahá'í Spiritual Assemblies were established in all parts of the British Isles, including Wales. Thus, in 1948 the first Assembly was established in Cardiff, where believers were encouraged to 'disperse, to settle, to persevere, and to appeal more directly and effectively to the masses who are waiting for this Divine Message'.[10]

The first pioneer in Cardiff was Joan Giddings. She originally lived in Bradford and was the wife of a ship's captain, but as she required medical attention she chose to move to Cardiff in the hope that there she could receive the necessary treatment. Joan joined Rose Jones at her home in Roath, and on 21 April 1947 the first Bahá'í meeting of resident believers in Wales was held. No sooner had these two intrepid women began to organise their teaching activities than a message was received from the Guardian requiring them to provide a Spiritual Assembly in Cardiff within the year, rather than in the three year period as they had expected. Very soon more pioneers began to move into the city, and the Guardian was delighted and full of deep admiration for the spirit they manifested. He commented on 'the services you render and the determination with which you are initiating the great historic teaching enterprise in Wales'.[11] The Bahá'í Faith was proclaimed to a growing number of Cardiff citizens, and 'firesides' were arranged, where travel teachers supported the work of the resident group in their homes. In 1947 the Park Hotel was again chosen as the venue for a public meeting, twenty-two years after the first one in Wales. Twelve people attended, including Suzanne Solomon, a young Viennese nurse, who some months later joined the Bahá'í community and became the very first person in Wales to declare her faith in Bahá'u'lláh.[12] During this period the Rev. Gwyn Daniels, a kindly disposed Welsh clergyman, presented to the Cardiff Bahá'ís a Welsh trans-lation of a 'Unity Prayer' of Bahá'u'lláh. This is the first recorded translation into Welsh of any work of Bahá'u'lláh.[13] It has since been recited in hundreds of places throughout the world.

Although teaching activities were quickly developed and more public meetings were held at Cardiff's Royal, Queen St, Park, and Angel Hotels, and also the City Hall, the required number of nine believers to form Wales' first Assembly had not been achieved. It was only the arrival of three more pioneers on 21 April 1948 which secured the Assembly.[14] Over the next ten years the Cardiff Bahá'ís worked with devotion and energy to teach their faith and maintain their Assembly membership of nine. Great interest was aroused, but results were limited as adherents who followed the writings of Bahá'u'lláh were not allowed to aggressively proselytise in order to quickly gain new adherents. Yet, during these testing times, the Bahá'ís in Cardiff increased their faith as they promoted Bahá'u'lláh as the Lord of the Age. Inspired by the vision promised by Bahá'u'lláh that 'soon will all that dwell on earth be enlisted under these banners',[15] and comforted by His exhortation, 'Grieve thou not at men's failure to apprehend the Truth. Ere long thou shalt find them turning towards God, the Lord of all mankind',[16] they persevered in their chosen mission. Supported by a constant flow of pioneers into Cardiff to replace those who, for compelling reasons, had to move out, the Assembly was maintained for a decade. Added to the unrespon-siveness of the local population to the news that Bahá'u'lláh was 'Christ returned in the Glory of the Father', further tests of faith and endurance accompanied virtually every pioneer in Cardiff. For example, it is recorded that one pioneer was forced to spend every winter evening in the railway station waiting room because 'his landlady would not allow him a fire in his bed-sitting room'.[17]

Despite these setbacks, the Cardiff Assembly eventually became secure with a number of new believers. The first indigenous Welsh adherent was David Lewis, a Cardiff architect, who enrolled in the Bahá'í Faith in 1956. David learned about the Bahá'í Faith from his wife, Audrey, who was dying of cancer in a Cardiff hospital. Prior to her illness, Audrey had been introduced to the Bahá'í Faith by her specialist, Dr Miller, a Bahá'í who had given up a lucrative practice in Liverpool to promote the faith in Cardiff and maintain the local Assembly. Just before she died, Audrey called on her husband to embrace the Baha'i Faith as she had done. After Audrey's death, extension teaching was undertaken with the overall objective of establishing Bahá'í Assemblies in all the major urban centres in Wales. Pontypridd's first Bahá'í in 1959 was Beatrice Newman, a Baptist deaconess. Others soon followed, and the Pontypridd Spiritual Assembly was elected in 1961 consisting of nine Welsh believers. This was an important development as Pontypridd was the first place in the British Isles to be established without a single pioneer moving in and whose membership was entirely composed of indigenous believers.[18] Eric Kent, a lay-preacher of a Pentecostal Church in Merthyr, and eager to spread the Gospel of Christ's imminent return, moved into Caerffili (Caerphilly) with his wife to start evangelising. A few years later in 1958, Eric wholeheartedly accepted Bahá'u'lláh as the 'Promised One' referred to by Christ.[19] This led to further developments as some members became travelling teachers and pioneers within Wales and overseas. Working with Bahá'í helpers from outside Wales, more Assemblies were established in south, north and mid-Wales according to well-defined plans. Swansea, for example, was chosen as the next urban centre for the Bahá'ís, and in 1966 their first Spiritual Assembly was formed. This was quickly followed by the formation of the Aberystwyth, Newport and Bangor Assemblies. By the early 1980s there were fourteen local Spiritual Assemblies in Wales. Since this date, although there has been a decrease in this number because of geographical boundary changes, over seventy places in Wales have resident Bahá'ís working to establish an Assembly. Following the decision in 1997 of the international governing body of the Bahá'í community, the Universal House of Justice, to 'formalise a new element of Bahá'í administration' – Regional Bahá'í Councils, the first ever nine-member Bahá'í Council for Wales was elected in 2000.[20] The seeds of a new Revelation had thereby taken root in Wales.

Bahá'u'lláh called all humanity to become conscious that mankind is a single entity, to discard prejudice, and to recognise that religion is also a single body. Moreover, God has fulfilled His promise to manifest Himself in His 'Glory' in the person of Bahá'u'lláh. Bahá'ís believe that all the signs indicate that the people of Wales have the capacity to respond to this call. They hold that, of every nationality and culture, the Welsh people, who are looked upon as 'a talented race',[21] 'will not only respond to the (Bahá'í) Message if given the opportunity, but contribute a distinctive share of their own, when they arise in its service'.[22]

Notes

1. Much of this chapter has been drawn from an unpublished document written by Carl Card, entitled 'Our Precious Heritage – The Coming of the Faith to Wales'. Supplemental to this has been a paper entitled 'The Bahá'í Faith in Wales' written by David Lewis, believed to be the first Welsh Bahá'í resident in Wales. A great debt of gratitude is owed to these early Welsh Bahá'ís. The author was also able to call upon his memories of the growth of the Bahá'í Faith in the country since the mid-1960s, as he has been intimately involved in these developments. For further studies of the Bahá'í Faith see John Ferraby, *All Things Made New: A Comprehensive Outline of the Baha'i Faith* (London, 1957); Mary Perkins and Philip Hainsworth, *The Bahá'í Faith* (London, 1980); William S. Hatcher and J. Douglas Martin, *The Baha'i Faith: The Emerging Global Religion* (London, 1984); Peter Smith, *A Short History of the Bahá'í Faith* (Oxford, 1996); Moojan Momen, *The Bahá'í Faith: A Short Introduction* (Oxford, 1999); Wendi Momen and Moojan Momen, *Understanding the Bahá'í Faith* (Edinburgh, 2005).

2. For interesting insights into the Baha'i Faith and Eastern religions see Christopher Buck, *Paradise and Paradigm: Key Symbols in Persian Christianity and the Baha'i Faith* (Albany, N.Y., 1999); Moojan Momen, *Islam and the Bahá'í Faith* (Oxford, 2000).

3. *Britannica Yearbook* (1988) indicates that, although the Bahá'í community numbers only about five million members (numbers have increased since then), the Faith has become the most widely

diffused religion after Christianity. There are today nearly 190 Bahá'í National Assemblies throughout the globe and more than 15,000 elected Assemblies functioning at the local level. It is estimated that there are well over 2,000 nationalities and tribes represented.

4. The Tablets of the Divine Plan were revealed in 1916 and 1917 by 'Abdu'l-Bahá, the eldest son and appointed successor of Bahá'u'lláh. The Bahá'ís of the United States of America and Canada were the recipients of these remarkable documents calling on them to promote the teachings of Bahá'u'lláh throughout the world. The Tablets of the Divine Plan are provided in the Bahá'í Reference Library under the auspices of the Bahá'í International Community. See http://reference.bahai.org/en/t/ab/TAB/ (accessed May 2010). The most authoritative account of the first hundred years of Bahá'í history is that provided by Shohgi Effendi. See Shohgi Effendi, *God Passes By* (Wilmette, Illinois, 1944). Additional details are provided in Nathan Rutstein, *Teaching the Bahá'í Faith* (Oxford, 1984).
5. *Western Mail*, 15 November 1925.
6. Shoghi Effendi, *God Passes By*, p. 387.
7. The Bahá'í International Community Office of Public Information, *Bahá'u'lláh* (New York, 1991), p. 2.
8. Information from Bahá'í Records Office. May White is also mentioned in 'Our Precious Heritage' by Carl Card.
9. Shohgi Effendi, *The Unfolding Destiny of the British Bahá'í Community: The Messages from the Guardian of the Bahá'í Faith to the Bahá'ís of the British Isles* (London, 1981), p. 169. A message from the Guardian to the National Spiritual Assembly of the Bahá'ís of the British Isles, 25 May 1944.
10. Ibid., p. 174. A message from the Guardian to the National Spiritual Assembly of the Bahá'ís of the British Isles, 27 March 1945.
11. Ibid., p. 393. A message from the Guardian to the Bahá'ís of Cardiff, 1 November 1947.
12. Card, 'Our Precious Heritage', 9.
13. Ibid., 12.
14. Shoghi Effendi, *Unfolding Destiny*, p. 394. This was a message from the Guardian to the Cardiff Spiritual Assembly, 17 October 1948.
15. Shoghi Effendi, *God Passes By*, p. 182.
16. *Tablets of Bahá'u'lláh* (Haifa, nd), pp. 263–4.
17. Card, 'Our Precious Heritage', 6.
18. Ibid., 28, 32.
19. Ibid., 26–7.
20. Letter dated 30 May 1997 from the Universal House of Justice to National Spiritual Assemblies.
21. Shoghi Effendi, *Unfolding Destiny*, p. 395. A message from the Guardian to the Cardiff Spiritual Assembly, 15 February 1950.
22. Ibid., p. 396. A message from the Guardian to the Cardiff Spiritual Assembly, 30 January 1957.

CHAPTER 21

THE ECUMENICAL DIMENSION: PAST TRENDS, FUTURE PROSPECTS[1]

Noel A. Davies

For a nation with a relatively small population on a fairly small patch of earth, Wales has an incredibly complex but rich ecumenical history. This is inevitable. Denominational complexity requires a diversity of responses if it is to move (or be moved) towards a greater wholeness and unity. Moreover, the sometimes tumultuous and always ambiguous relationships with our larger and more powerful neighbour, our cultural and linguistic diversity and our political struggles, lay upon the churches, and the ecumenical movement in which they have all engaged, challenging responsibilities to respond with prophetic words and transforming actions. This chapter will examine the beginnings of this emerging movement during a century in which ecumenism has played a key role. It will evaluate some of the trends within the ecumenical movement, and the ways it has been shaped by, and has shaped, the life and witness of churches in Wales, as well as the powerful influence of the worldwide ecumenical movement on the ecumenical vision and priorities of Wales. It will conclude by exploring some of the future prospects for ecumenism in the twenty-first century.

Edinburgh 1910 and Disestablishment

Two factors played a major role in ecumenical beginnings in Wales in the twentieth century. The first was the world missionary conference in Edinburgh in 1910 which brought together representatives of the major world missionary organizations and societies (rather than churches and denominations). According to Adrian Hastings, 'Edinburgh 1910 marked with confident optimism the first step forward in what was to be in truth an ecumenical century.'[2] One of the key insights and affirmations of this groundbreaking event was that worldwide evangelization required greater unity and mutual understanding among the churches themselves. Edinburgh 1910, therefore, ensured that the search for unity would be rooted in mission and evangelism: unity and mission could not be separated without betraying their inherent theological and biblical nature. This birthplace of the modern ecumenical movement would have a significant effect within the Welsh churches as the century progressed. The other important factor was the long political and cultural struggle for the disestablishment of the Church of England within Wales and the formation of the Church in Wales in 1920. This gave Anglicanism within Wales a new sense of belonging and made possible a new sense of partnership with the nonconformist churches and denominations in Wales. During the same year, the Lambeth Conference of Anglican Bishops, echoing the 1888 Lambeth Conference's call to unity, called for a new commitment to unity – a call which captured the imagination of many nonconformist leaders in Wales who encouraged the churches to take initial steps towards greater co-operation.

New ecumenical initiatives

The consequence of these events was the formation, in 1929, of the first truly ecumenical committee in Wales, including the newly formed Church in Wales, namely, the Joint Committee for Mutual Understanding and Co-operation between the Christian Communions in Wales. The Joint Committee provided a forum for church leaders and senior officers, where common concerns of theology and practice could be aired and denominational differences explored at this early stage in ecumenical relationships in Wales. It provided a place of meeting, an open forum for debate and an instrument for initiating first steps in collaboration. Genuine ecumenical partnerships are not easily forged and these early exploratory stages were, therefore, significant. Ecumenical relationships, especially on a personal level and within the local situation, were also greatly helped through the Welsh Ecumenical Society formed in 1954 as a successor to *Urdd y Deyrnas* (literally, the Order of the Kingdom), formed in the early days of the ecumenical movement in Wales to explore contemporary questions of faith and witness in Wales, partly at least in view of attempts to face the challenge of applying the socio-political aspects of the Gospel.

The impact of world ecumenism

Another worldwide process was also at work which would, in due course, have a powerful impact in Wales. One of the consequences of the Faith and Order Movement, as well as the Life and Work Movement inaugurated at Edinburgh 1910, was a genuine desire among church leaders around the world for an ecumenical body that would embrace all the churches, bringing them together into genuine fellowship and partnership and providing an organization that would hold together Faith and Order and Life and Work, as well as issues of mission and evangelism. This was co-ordinated on a worldwide basis through the International Missionary Council, another fruit of the Edinburgh meeting in 1910. The impact of this emerging fellowship within worldwide Church, the search for peace and reconciliation and the felt need for greater integration between Faith and Order, and Life and Work, was an agreement in 1938 to establish the World Council of Churches (WCC).[3] This was delayed by the Second World War and its first constitutive Assembly was held in Amsterdam in 1948.[4]

The Council of Churches for Wales

The WCC Assembly, along with the establishment of the British Council of Churches in 1942, was the trigger for the next key development in Welsh ecumenism, namely, the transformation of the Joint Committee for Mutual Understanding and Co-operation between the Christian Communions of Wales into the Council of Churches for Wales in 1956. This marked a celebration of what had already been possible ecumenically and a promise of, and commitment to, what would be possible in the future. This was made clear in a statement made at its inaugural meeting on 24 May 1956:

> We would affirm our conviction that the unity of the Church, on which our faith and hope is set, is grounded in the unity of God and the uniqueness of His redeeming act in Jesus Christ.
>
> We, therefore, rejoice that in recent years the Ecumenical Movement has grown so rapidly ... We trust that the Council of Churches for Wales may prove an effective means whereby the Churches in Wales may bear witness together to their common allegiance to Jesus Christ and co-operate in matters requiring united action.[5]

Ecumenical developments in Wales during the latter half of the twentieth century focussed particularly on two aspects of the life and work of the Council of Churches for Wales. The first was the attempt to foster relationships and unity among the churches and denominations of Wales, locally and nationally. The second was an ecumenical approach to Christian social witness and engagement in Wales and worldwide. Other components, such as mission and evangelism and Christian Aid (the member churches' chief overseas and development agency), were also central to the recent ecumenical history of Wales. However, the story of these two central streams shows that the ecumenical movement in Wales, as it was worldwide, was more than the endeavour for Christian unity, and more than a framework for co-operating in Christian witness. Basically, the heart of the ecumenical movement is in the relationship of the two streams to each other. Joint witness can strengthen unity, and deepening unity can facilitate Christian witness. The Council of Churches for Wales was a catalyst for this process in Wales. One of the main contributions of the Council, as a small instrument within the ecumenical movement, was to raise the sights of Welsh Christians to discover the excitement and challenge of the worldwide Church.

The Council of Churches for Wales

The attitude of the denominations towards the Council varied greatly from denomination to denomination and from topic to topic. For example, discussions on the search for unity were instigated by the Council itself, as a result of the Nottingham Conference on Faith and Order in 1964, convened by the British Council of Churches. Yet this activity was owned and recognised by the churches and they were more than ready to entrust responsibility for promoting the discussions to the Council. Likewise, the Council was a means of securing the partnership of the churches and the denominations with each other during the 1984–5 dispute in the mining industry.[6] Indeed, their partnership through the Council was the chief factor in the effectiveness of that campaign.[7] In situations such as these, the Council could be seen as a body which represented the denominations. On the other hand upon issues, such as independence for Wales and campaigning against apartheid in South Africa,[8] the Council did represent the standpoint of some of the denominations but its position was unacceptable to others. To some extent, therefore, the Council was a pioneer, offering leadership to the churches and, by means of study programmes, joint activities and worship, it sought to encourage the denominations and the local churches to embrace the Council's perspective.

The Council of Churches for Wales was also primarily responsible for the growing mutual understanding and co-operation which has become such a natural element in the life of denominations and local congregations. From time to time, it is inevitable that differences of opinion create tension, but these did not often divide denominations and churches from each other. The Council played a key role in this process of fostering natural friendship and trust among the Christians of Wales. It can also be pointed out that the Council of Churches for Wales was not the only inter-church body seeking support during this period. Some of the denominations belonged to the British Council of Churches, the Conference of European Churches and the World Council of Churches, as well as worldwide denominational bodies. Each of these sought financial support through annual contributions. There was a price to pay for the change which took place in the ecumenical movement, in Wales and worldwide, from being marginal to the life and work of the denominations to being central to them, and it was no easy matter finding the financial and other resources to pay that price.

The Council and Christian Unity

The first priority of the pioneers, who were chiefly responsible for setting up the Council, was to secure an instrument enabling them to promote a 'reuniting' of the churches. In the 1950s and 1960s the denominational and ecumenical journals in Wales were full of articles encouraging (and, of course, sometimes criticising), movement towards Christian unity. These pioneers were confident that God was calling his people to unity and that the Council was a vehicle for the promotion of unity in Wales. The Council was very effective in this task during the early years, concentrating attention and energy on the goal of unity, most particularly in the wake of the Faith and Order Conferences held in Carmarthen (1963) and Nottingham (1964). The Covenant towards Visible Unity in Wales was the fruit of this activity. During the same period there were discussions between the four Welsh language nonconformist denominations in Wales and between the Church in Wales and the Methodist Church. Neither of these negotiations achieved their goal, but the efforts to promote the Covenant continued, not least through the Council itself. The Covenant discussions were launched in 1965 following the Nottingham Faith and Order conference, and the Covenant entered into formally between the Church in Wales, the Methodist Church, the Presbyterian Church of Wales, the United Reformed Church and, initially in January 1975, twelve churches within the South Wales Area of the Baptist Union of Great Britain and Ireland. Their partnership within the Covenant was founded on the following commitment:

> We now make this solemn Covenant before God and with one another, to work and pray in common obedience to our Lord Jesus Christ, so that the Holy Spirit may bring us into one visible Church, to serve together in mission to the glory of God the Father.[9]

Over the years, considerable efforts have been made to promote the covenant locally, regionally and nationally, especially through the Commission of the Covenanted Churches, established in 1976, renamed ENFYS (*Rainbow*) in 1990. Publications such as *Principles of Visible Unity in Wales* (1979),[10] *The Holy Communion* (1981),[11] *Ministry in a Uniting Church* (1986),[12] and *Baptism* (1990)[13] have played a significant role in enabling the churches to explore the challenge and opportunity of the Covenant. Despite the mutual understanding and co-operation between the Covenanted Churches increasing, nationally and locally, no specific steps towards visible unity have been possible so far. Indeed, at the time of writing there has been a thoughtful process of evaluating the future of the Covenant and, as a result, the Covenanted Churches have reaffirmed their Covenant commitment and redirection of the churches' pursuit of the Covenant's aims. In 1997, talks were inaugurated with a view to establishing a United Free Churches in Wales. But there was inadequate support for the proposals and these have now been abandoned.

Thus, after a period when Christian unity did not feature prominently on the denominational agenda, during recent years considerable attention has been paid to the search for unity. There is no doubt, however, that the inter-church climate has been very different during this period as compared with the 1950s and 1960s. The goal of unity has also changed. The majority of the denominations no longer think in terms of one visible ecclesiastical body but in terms of a pattern of partnership and collaboration which would enable churches to recognise each other as churches and to recognise and exchange ministers and members. By this means, rather than by forming one visible church, they live in unity whilst retaining their own independence. Unity in diversity and diversity in unity have become increasingly central to the search for Christian harmony. And although this is a very different vision from that of the early pioneers, the Council, in striving for fuller unity, made an important contribution to keeping the vision of Christian unity before the churches by promoting a constant engagement with the challenging issues raised by the search for unity and, perhaps more than anything, to fostering faithfulness to this fundamental call and challenge.

The deeper partnership with the Roman Catholic Church, particularly during the last decade of the Council, following the Papal visit in 1982, was an important factor in this change.[14] This partnership was a subject of joy to the majority of those who were involved in the Council of Churches for Wales. It also gave a new edge to the search for Christian unity, which is very high in the priorities of the Roman Catholic Church. This new partnership has certainly raised new and fundamental questions about the nature of the Church and its ministry, and about the content of the faith. It is also fair to note that the Roman Catholic Church has urged other denominations to take steps towards fuller union with each other which it could not itself take. But without doubt the presence of the Roman Catholic Church in the partnership of churches together[15] has made a fundamental difference. It could almost be said that the endeavour for unity had to be on a totally different plane, and that it was necessarily slower and more difficult. The Council was central to the promotion of this partnership but it may have been less effective in promoting discussion of the questions which were raised in its wake.[16]

Perhaps there is now a need for a wider vision of Christian unity than was cherished in Wales in recent times. A vision which will endeavour to seek the unity of the churches, and search for unity, harmony and justice for persons, societies, nations and humanity as a whole. According to Michael Taylor, 'here ... lies the real genius of the ecumenical movement . . . to unite a divided church, to make one a divided world, to make the many into a whole, to draw together into communities what is separate and apart'.[17] It may be that it is through developing an understanding of Christian unity rooted in this holistic vision that the challenge and excitement of the ecumenical call to twenty-first-century Christians in Wales will be found.

The Council and Public Life

The history of the Council reveals a tension between institutional Christianity and individual Christianity. Most often, this tension, within the churches and in the media, is in the form of a question: What right have the churches to interfere in politics? Much of the criticism of the Council has arisen among people who have disagreed with its particular standpoint, mostly with regard to public life in Wales or worldwide. The history of the Council's involvement with South Africa, for instance, and its backing for the World Council of Churches' Programme to Combat Racism, reveals this tension in a dramatic way. Throughout its history, the Council for Churches in Wales has been committed to making a stand for justice in Wales and across the world.[18] Indeed, it was these contentious issues which gave the Church much of its public credibility. The Council believed that Christian social witness in public affairs was central to mission and evangelism.

The Council and Theological Engagement in Wales

Another question is suggested by a review of ecumenism in Wales: to what extent did the Council and the ecumenical movement it served succeed in promoting inter-denominational theological engagement in Wales? Notable examples become apparent in the history of the Council. For example, theology had a central place in the churches' discussions in relation to covenanting for union in Wales. The essays on the nature of the Church, the ministry, the priesthood, and the sacraments[19] made an important contribution to a mutual understanding of the traditions of the churches. Likewise, the invitation to respond to the report of the World Council of Churches, *Baptism, Eucharist and Ministry*,[20] was a unique opportunity to engage in theological debate in relation to some of the fundamental doctrines of the Christian faith. In a completely different field, the Industrial Committee made a notable contribution in trying to consider the theological significance of the industrial world and the critical changes which challenged persons and communities. *Towards a Contemporary Theology of Work*[21] was a unique contribution in Wales in this debate, and it was the product of activity within the Council of Churches for Wales. In the same way, *Swords into Ploughshares*[22] and a Peace Council held in Wrexham in 1987 were attempts to weigh up the theological issues in relation to nuclear armaments, one of the most critical issues which ecumenism in Wales faced during the century.

Some argue that neither individual Christians nor the denominations of Wales have taken theology seriously during recent decades, particularly compared with periods of fierce theological debates in the past. A number of factors can be at work in a process like this: indifference towards theology as such, or (worse) indifference to the nature and content of the Christian faith, or a lack of theological discussion among Christian leaders in Wales. One of the contributions of the contemporary ecumenical movement has been to encourage consideration of the way in which Christian action in society, contemporary theology, and Welsh and worldwide developments challenge tradition, cast new light upon it and urge us to reshape this tradition for a new era. The raw material for this process is already available to the churches. The challenge now is to tackle this task together.

But there is a further question: to what extent did the Council succeed in promoting discussions on contentious theological issues which have divided the denominations? Some of these issues have already been touched upon, since the essays of the Covenant and the responses to *Baptism, Eucharist and Ministry* faced these selfsame questions, such as the nature of the Church, the nature and recognition of ministry, the meaning of the sacraments and the possibility of inter-communion. The acceptance of the Covenant by some denominations in 1974 was a sign that they had grown closer to each other with respect to these contentious topics. But there were no substantial discussions on some of the other fundamental subjects which divide Christians, such as the relationship of the Bible and tradition as sources of authority in the Church, the place of Mary, the mother of Jesus, in the scheme of salvation, and the meaning of justification by faith. These continue to be topics that demand further ecumenical enquiry and exploration.

The influence of the Council

The basic question remains: what influence did the Council and, through it, the ecumenical movement, have within Welsh church life? Some of the main influences were very remarkable. The publication in 1988 of *Y Beibl Cymraeg Newydd* (the New Welsh Bible), which was initiated and co-ordinated within the Council of Churches for Wales, was one of the historic events of the twentieth century. The forming of Inter-Church Aid and Service to Refugees (now known as Christian Aid) in 1945 and its development during almost sixty years has been one of the key ecumenical influences in Wales. Working together for Christian Aid was the beginning of local ecumenism in many communities in Wales and it has continued to be one of the most effective instruments for fostering the partnership of churches together, and their awareness of partnership with fellow-Christians all over the world.

It is likely that some developments would not have happened at all had it not been for the vision of some early ecumenical pioneers. Two noteworthy examples of this were the conferences which were held in Carmarthen in 1963 (on Faith and Order) and 1970 (on Church and Society). From the former stemmed the discussions which led to the Covenant towards Union, ecumenical studies of worship and liturgy, and the encouragement of local ecumenical experiments and projects. From the latter stemmed the increasing co-operation in the field of social responsibility in Wales and worldwide, specifically by establishing the Church and Society Department of the Council, which for the first time provided the Welsh denominations with a forum for study and action in this field. One important aspect of this activity, which preceded the development of the Church and Society Department, was Christian witness within industry. Throughout the years, the Council encouraged this creative and progressive field of Christian witness by fostering an awareness of these issues among Christians and by supporting industrial chaplaincies. This experience was later to become one of the key factors in the efforts of the Council to work for reconciliation during the coal dispute.

The Council and the worldwide ecumenical movement

The formation of the World Council of Churches in Amsterdam in 1948 was perhaps the chief stimulus for the establishment of the Council of Churches for Wales in 1956. The first WCC Assembly was a signal, three years after the Second World War, that reconciliation between Christians was possible, even after such a terrible massacre in Europe. Particularly during the early years of the WCC, worldwide conferences had a pervasive influence on ecumenical events in Wales. We need do little more than name these conferences: The Second Assembly of the World Council of Churches, Evanston, 1954; the Third Assembly in New Delhi, 1961, when a number of Orthodox Churches became member churches of the WCC and the International Missionary Council was integrated into the Council; the Montreal Faith and Order Conference, 1963, which led to the British conference in Nottingham, 1964; the Church and Society Conference, Geneva, 1966, which was the basis of the

Carmarthen Conference four years later; the Fourth Assembly in Uppsala, 1968, which was seen as an opportunity to renew the ecumenical vision and commitment in Wales using the booklet, *Uppsala and Wales*, published by the Council.[23] Representatives from Wales were present at the majority of these conferences and in subsequent conferences and assemblies. These conferences would not have had such an influence if it had not been for the early Welsh ecumenical pioneers who shared the WCC's vision and devoted themselves to rooting their challenging, worldwide vision in the soil of Wales, its culture, its social condition and its Christian life. It could be argued that the vision of these pioneers was the key which succeeded in unlocking the ecumenical developments which became a natural part of the life of the churches and denominations in the last years of the twentieth century. Moreover, when the Council of Churches for Wales became an Associate Council of the World Council of Churches in 1982, it was seen as an expression of the Council's commitment to the worldwide movement through a direct relationship, and not through the British Council of Churches as previously.

It must be recognized, of course, that the British Council of Churches has also had an important place in the ecumenical history of Wales. Three of the indigenous denominations in Wales, namely, the Church in Wales, the Presbyterian Church of Wales and the Union of Welsh Independents were members of the British Council of Churches from the early years of its existence. The British denominations which had churches in Wales were also members. As a result, it was a means of promoting ecumenical awareness in Wales in the years between 1942, when the British Council of Churches was established, and 1956, when the Council of Churches for Wales was created. But, on the other hand, one reason for establishing the Council of Churches for Wales was the feeling among many that the British Council of Churches was not able to represent the interests of Wales effectively. For example, in relation to promoting local ecumenism and fostering awareness of the wider ecumenical movement, most particularly through the medium of Welsh. As national awareness grew in Wales, the desire also increased to strengthen the Council of Churches for Wales as a national ecumenical body which was administratively independent of the British Council of Churches but which also continued to co-operate on common issues. This had the support of general secretaries of the BCC, such as Harry O. Morton and Philip Morgan.

Over the years, there was considerable international recognition. For example, Philip Potter and Emilio Castro paid visits to Wales during their time as General Secretaries of the World Council of Churches. The membership of G. O. Williams (1968–75), Meirion Lloyd Davies (1975–83), Carol Abel (1983–91) and Archbishop Barry Morgan (1998–present) of the Central Committee of the World Council of Churches have likewise been very significant. Delegations were received from the Soviet Union, Argentina and China, as well as visits by individuals from other countries, such as Desmond Tutu in 1986. During his time as General Secretary, Noel Davies visited India and Sri Lanka (1981), China and Hong Kong (1983), Argentina (1985), and South Africa and Lesotho (1986), as well as attending a number of the major meetings of the World Council of Churches and of the Conference of European Churches. These exchanges enabled a deeper awareness of the partnership of the churches with each other within the one worldwide ecumenical movement.

Future Prospects

As we turn from evaluating past trends and look towards the future, a number of themes suggest themselves. First, as we have already noted, there will need to be a re-evaluation of the search for Christian unity and union in Wales. The recent failure of the proposals for a United 'Free' Church in Wales and the recent process of evalu-ating the future of the Covenant for Union in Wales have raised with some urgency the issue of how we view the call and search for unity and union. There are those who believe that a death knell has been sounding in Wales. There are others who believe that the nature of Christian unity and union needs to be redefined. Not least in respect to partnership agreements, for example, between the Methodist Church and the United Reformed Church, and between the Methodist Church and the Church of England. What now are the goals of the search? What is to be the nature of unity? Can there be an organic or structural vision of such unity, or must it be redefined in relational and more local terms?

Next, there needs to be a re-affirmation of the ecumenical task as political engagement. In a Wales which has had limited self-government through the National Assembly Government during recent years, and which has grown in its political self-confidence, despite a high degree of political apathy within Welsh communi-ties, what are the priorities for the churches? Cytûn's Assembly Liaison Officer has contributed in very significant ways to the two-way communication between the Assembly and the churches. How should this engagement develop for the future? Should the churches' collaboration in relation to the Assembly be extended to include a broader engagement with issues raised locally, regionally and nationally (and internationally)? What is the nature of the churches' 'prophetic' task in contem-porary Wales, and how do ecumenical instruments forge partnerships that contribute to this task? How can the churches of Britain and Ireland draw further on the insights and perspectives gained through the processes of political engagement within the nations through Churches Together in Britain and Ireland, the successor body to the British Council of Churches?

Third, there are challenges around identity and unity. These two issues converge around the current WCC Faith and Order Programme, Ethnic Identity, National Identity and the Unity of the Church, which has held two of its key international consultations in Wales (in 1997 and 2003). How do issues of identity, notably culture, language, tra-dition, political and socio-economic relationships, moral/ethical principles etc., affect the understanding of our unity? How can diversity and unity be understood, not only in ecclesiastical terms but also in social and communal terms? There are key issues here that need to be addressed from a Welsh perspective, within our multilingual, multiethnic and multifaith society. Fourth, there is a need to redefine ecumenism in a global and pluralist environment. In his unpublished address at the inaugural meet-ing of the Welsh National Centre for Ecumenical Studies in January 2001, Professor Michael Taylor highlighted the need to explore the nature and understanding of the ecumenical vision in the light of growing globalization and the increasingly plural nature of Western society. The current world situation presses this need upon us with great urgency. The recently established Inter-Faith Forum for Wales, initiated by the Welsh Assembly Government, will be an important catalyst in this process.

Finally, there has been a fundamental change in the nature of the ecumenical partnership that is bound to have an effect on ecumenism in the coming years. In 1990, following the Inter-Church Process on 'the nature and purpose of the Church in the light of its calling in and for the world', Cytûn: Churches Together in Wales was set up as a successor to the Council of Churches in Wales. At the heart of this commitment was the role of Cytûn not so much in undertaking the ecumenical task on behalf of the churches and denominations, but rather as an enabler of the churches' engagement as partners in their ecumenical enterprise. Cytûn facilitates this commitment, but the nature and pace of this task is firmly rooted within the churches themselves. Unless the churches and denominations have a common will to foster this enterprise in the future, the ecumenical process will falter.

In a powerful meditation on Biblical images of the house (*oikos*) and its relationship to the earth and the whole of humanity (*oikoumene*), given at the Sixth Assembly of the WCC in Vancouver in 1983, Philip Potter, WCC General Secretary at the time, said:

> It is this image and understanding of the living house which has motivated the ecumenical movement ... (It is) the means by which the churches which form the house, the *oikos* of God, are seeking so to live and witness before all the peoples that the whole *oikoumene* may become the *oikos* (house) of God.[24]

There has been a tendency in Wales to think of the ecumenical movement in terms of church unity alone, and to judge it on the basis of different attitudes towards that unity. The images which are the derivation of the word 'ecumenical' demonstrate that this is too narrow an understanding. The quest for Christian unity and the witness of the churches to reconciliation, justice and peace are not two separate aspects but rather elements of the same ecumenical endeavour. The Council of Churches for Wales was a means for building this house in Wales. Over the years it has been necessary to extend and adapt it. By 1990 it was felt necessary to rebuild it, and so Cytûn was formed. But the intention throughout this period was to make the ecumenical instruments in Wales more effective tools for the building of this 'house' for the Christian family in Wales and more effective signs of the reconciliation, unity and renewal which is possible for the people and nation of Wales through the Gospel. This chapter has been a very brief attempt to evaluate the story of this 'house', its success and its failure. The story has been told in the belief that the ecumenical movement has been a vehicle of renewal, through the Holy Spirit, not only in the churches but, at its best, in local communities and in the nation, and that, in the words of the basis of the Council of Churches for Wales, 'to the glory of God, Father, Son and Holy Spirit'.

Notes

1. This chapter focuses especially on the contribution to ecumenical growth and development of the Council of Churches for Wales, as the main agent of the ecumenical movement within Wales during most of the latter half of the twentieth century. Thanks are expressed to Marcus Wells for initially

translating the original Welsh text into English. For a more comprehensive account of ecumenism in Wales in the twentieth century see Noel A. Davies, 'The History and Development of the Council of Churches for Wales, 1956–1990', unpublished University of Wales, Bangor, Ph.D. thesis, 1997. The thesis formed the basis of a Welsh-language account of the history of the Council of Churches for Wales, see Noel A. Davies, *Un er mwyn y Byd: Agweddau ar Hanes Cyngor Eglwysi Cymru* (Swansea, 1998) and his *The History of Ecumenism in Wales, 1956–90* (Cardiff, 2008). The final paragraphs of this article closely reflect the 'Concluding Reflections' as they appear in that volume.

2. Adrian Hastings, *A History of English Christianity* (London, 1987), p. 87.
3. W. A. Visser 't Hooft, 'The Genesis of the World Council of Churches', in Ruth Rouse and Stephen. T. Neill (eds), *A History of the Ecumenical Movement, 1517–1948* (2 vols. 3rd edn. Geneva, 1986), I, pp. 697–724.
4. *The First Assembly of the World Council of Churches: The Official Report* (Geneva, 1949).
5. Minutes of the first meeting of the Council, 24 May 1956, now in the National Library of Wales, Aberystwyth, within the Council of Churches for Wales Collection.
6. D. Densil Morgan, *The Span of the Cross: Christian Religion and Society in Wales, 1914–2000* (Cardiff, 1999), p. 269ff.
7. Davies, *Un er mwyn y* Byd, pp. 105–16.
8. Ibid., pp. 119–37.
9. For example, see *Covenant towards Union in Wales* (Bangor, 1971), Part 1, p. 14.
10. Commission of the Covenanted Churches, *Principles of Visible Unity in Wales* (Bangor, 1979).
11. Commission of the Covenanted Churches, *The Holy Communion* (Swansea, 1981).
12. Commission of the Covenanted Churches, *Gweinidogaeth mewn Eglwys yn uno: O Gydnabod i Gymodi/Ministry in a Uniting Church: From Recognition to Reconciliation: Ministry in a Uniting Church* (Swansea, 1986).
13. Commission of the Covenanted Churches, *Baptism* (Swansea, 1986).
14. For a comprehensive survey of Roman Catholic attitudes to ecumenism up to the 1960s, see Trystan Owain Hughes, *Winds of Change: The Roman Catholic Church and Society in Wales, 1916–62* (Cardiff, 1999), pp. 110ff, 189ff, 225ff.
15. The Roman Catholic Church had not been a member of the Council of Churches for Wales in its early years, but is now a full member of Cytûn and of the ecumenical instrument in England and Scotland and at British and Irish level.
16. For a review of the growing ecumenical engagement of the Roman Catholic Church within Wales in the period following the Second Vatican Council, see Davies, *Un er mwyn y Byd*, pp. 58–75.
17. Taylor, *Not Angels but Agencies* (Geneva, 1995) p. 167.
18. Davies, *We Intend to Stay Together*, pp. 12–17.
19. Commission of the Covenanted Churches, *Covenant towards Union in Wales* (Bangor, 1971), Parts I and II.
20. World Council of Churches, *Baptism, Eucharist and Ministry*, Faith and Order Paper No. 110 (Geneva, 1982).
21. Paul H. Ballard, *Towards a Contemporary Theology of Work* (Cardiff, 1982).
22. *Swords into Ploughshares: An Ecumenical Study Pack* (Swansea, 1986).
23. World Council of Churches, *Uppsala and Wales* (Bangor, 1969).
24. David Gill (ed.), *Gathered for Life: The Official Report of the Sixth Assembly of the World Council of Churches* (Geneva, 1983), p. 193.

NOTES ON CONTRIBUTORS

Richard C. Allen is Reader in Early Modern Cultural History and Head of History at the University of Wales, Newport. He has published widely on many aspects of Quakerism in Wales and elsewhere, and on migration and identity. His most recent works are *Quaker Communities in Early Modern Wales: from resistance to respectability* (Cardiff, 2007) and the co-edited *Irelands of the Mind: memory and identity in modern Irish culture* (Newcastle, 2008) and *Faith of our Fathers: popular culture and belief in post-Reformation England, Ireland and Wales* (Newcastle, 2009). He is currently writing a study of Quaker migration entitled, *Transatlantic Connections: Welsh Quaker emigrants and Colonial Pennsylvania*, as well as co-authoring, *Quaker Networks and Moral Reform in the North East of England* (Manchester, 2013).

Vivian Bartlett became a member of the Bahá'í Faith in 1966 in Cardiff and served on several national Bahá'í committees, including the Welsh Teaching Committee until 1976. As an Auxiliary Board Member for Wales from 1977 until 1999 he had an educational and pastoral role in the community. Between 1999 and 2004 he served on the Bahá'í Training Institute for Wales and then on the first elected Bahá'í Council for Wales. He was a Bahá'í representative on the first Interfaith Council for Wales established in 2003 and was a member until 2008. He has written and travelled extensively lecturing on the Bahá'í Faith; his book *Finding the Real You* was published in 1986. In 2000, the Swindon Young People's Empowerment Programme (SYEP) for vulnerable young people, of which he is a co-founder, was piloted and is presently ongoing (2010) in an increasing number of primary and secondary schools. Now a retired secondary school teacher, he is writing about the innovative work of helping young people become aware of their spiritual dimension.

Noel A. Davies is a minister of the Union of Welsh Independents and Director of the Welsh National Centre for Ecumenical Studies at Trinity College, Carmarthen, where he is a part-time lecturer in the School of Theology and Religious Studies. He has previously taught at Cardiff University and the Open University. From 1977 until 1990 he was General Secretary of the Council of Churches for Wales and the Commission of the Covenanted Churches and from 1990 to 1998 was General Secretary of Cytûn: Churches Together in Wales. From 2005 until 2009 he was Co-ordinator of Training for the Welsh Congregational College and the Union of Welsh Independents. He has published widely, including *The History of*

Ecumenism in Wales, 1956–90 (Cardiff, 2008); (with Martin Conway), the SCM Canterbury Press core text and reader on *World Christianity in the 20th Century* (London, 2008).

Ronald D. Dennis is Professor Emeritus of Portuguese and Welsh at Brigham Young University, Provo, Utah. His four decades of research into the history of the Church of Jesus Christ of Latter-day Saints in Wales during the nineteenth century have resulted in a number of publications. His current project is to publish facsimile translations of the nine extant volumes of *Udgorn Seion (Zion 's Trumpet)* from 1850–57. Digitized versions of his publications can be accessed through his website at http://welshmormonhistory.org.

Lieutenant-Colonel Jenty Fairbank is a Salvation Army officer, whose career in the Movement spanned thirty-seven years, during which she saw service in pastoral work in the UK, in Zimbabwe as a college of education lecturer, and at the Army's International Headquarters as Press Officer and Director of Information Services. For almost fifteen years she was Archivist and Director of the International Heritage Centre, before becoming Editor-in-Chief and Publishing Secretary for the UK, from which position she retired in the year 2000. She is the author of the children's book, *William and Catherine Booth: God's Soldiers* (London, 1974), and *Booth's Boots: the beginnings of Salvation Army social work* (London, 1983). Her poetry has appeared in several published collections, and numerous articles and book reviews by her have appeared in publications both within and beyond The Salvation Army. She has travelled widely on the international scene, lecturing on Salvation Army history. Since retiring she has edited *There's a Boy Here . . .* (London, 2002), the autobiography of General John Gowans, *and For Such A Time: the story of the young Florence Booth* (London, 2007).

Russell Grigg is Senior Lecturer in the Faculty of Education in Trinity College, Carmarthen. Most of his professional time is concerned with teacher-training. He provides in-service training courses for teachers and inspects primary schools in England and Wales. His research interest lies in nineteenth-century education in Wales. To this end, he has written books and articles on teacher-training, reformatory schools and the education of destitute children. He has been a Jehovah's Witnesses for twenty years.

John R. Morgan-Guy is Lecturer in Theology and Church History at University of Wales, Lampeter, and in 2010 a Visiting Fellow at the Centre for Methodism and Church History, Oxford Brookes University. He has published numerous papers on the ecclesiastical history and the visual culture of Wales. He is currently a co-editor of *The Oxford Handbook to the British Sermon 1689–1901*, to be published by Oxford University Press, and of *Biblical Imagery from Wales*, to be published by Sheffield Phoenix Press. Recent publications include 'Arthur, Harri Tudur and the Iconography of Loyalty in Wales', in Steven Gunn and Linda Monckton (eds), *Arthur Tudor, Prince of Wales. Life, death and commemoration* (Woodbridge, 2009), and '"Tinkers and other vermin": Methodists and the Established Church in Wales, 1735–1800', in Dyfed Wyn Roberts (ed.), *Revival, Renewal and the Holy Spirit.*

Studies in evangelical history and thought (Milton Keynes, 2009). He also contributed the chapter on 'Religion and Belief, 1660–1800' to volume three of the *Gwent County History* (Cardiff, 2009).

Guto Prys ap Gwynfor is a minister in three Independent churches at Llandysul, Llangeler and Cynwyl Elfed. Having started his ministry at Pencader and Alltwalis in 1977, he was appointed the Professor of Church History at the Memorial College Aberystwyth in 1980. He taught at Aberystwyth whilst caring for Independent churches at Talybont and Borth, then Lampeter, Parcyrhos, Ffaldybrenin and Esgairdawe until 1989. He was accepted as a missionary with CWM, and served in Guyana, South America. In 1991 he returned to Wales as a minister in Clydach and Tŷ Croes. He was appointed as the editor of *Y Tyst*, the weekly newspaper of the Welsh Independents in 1994 until the end of 1999. He moved to his present home in 1998. He has written many articles for different journals and books and at present he is the President of the Union of Welsh Independents and the chairperson of the Fellowship of Reconciliation in Wales.

Trystan Owain Hughes is the Anglican Chaplain to, and a lecturer at, Cardiff University, Wales. He attained a Masters in Applied Theology from Oxford University and a Ph.D. in twentieth-century church history from Bangor University. He is widely published in both church history and theology, including his books *Winds of Change: the Roman Catholic Church and society in Wales 1916–62* (Cardiff, 1999) and *Finding Hope and Meaning in Suffering* (London, 2010) and various articles in refereed journals (including two in the *Journal of Ecclesiastical History*, 2000 and 2001). While working as a research fellow in Bangor University, as an Associate Lecturer for the Open University, and then as Head of Theology in Trinity University College, Carmarthen, he gave papers at numerous international conferences, including at Sydney, Chicago, Philadelphia, Edinburgh, and Dublin. He was also Director of the Welsh National Centre for Ecumenical Studies from 2001 to 2004, and is presently a member of the Church in Wales Governing Body and the theological commission that assists the bench of Welsh Anglican bishops.

Muzafar Jilani, F.R.C. Psych. is a consultant Psychiatrist having worked in this capacity since 1977 when he first came to Wales. He trained as psychiatrist in Hull and Birmingham, having obtained his basic medical degree (M.B; B.S) in Srinagar Kashmir where he was born. He arrived in the U.K. in September 1968. He has been Secretary and then Chairman of Welsh Psychiatric Society. He is a Fellow of the Royal College of Psychiatrists. He is a Medical Member on the Mental Health Tribunal for Wales. He is founder member and Chairman of Imaan Islamic Society and a part-time Imam. He is member of Association of Muslim Professionals and has been its chairman. He regularly gives talks to school children in primary and secondary schools on Islam and topics related to psychiatry/psychology.

David Ceri Jones is a Lecturer in History at Aberystwyth University. He is the author of *A Glorious Work in the World: Welsh Methodism and the International Evangelical Revival, 1735–50* (Cardiff, 2004). He has also written widely on the

Enlightenment and Romanticism, particularly in a Welsh context. He is one of the editors of *The Correspondence of Iolo Morganwg* (3 vols. Cardiff, 2007). He has recently completed a history of Calvinistic Methodism in England and Wales during the eighteenth century and is also an ordinoid in the Church in Wales.

Euros Lloyd completed his MPhil thesis on 'Datblygiad Undodiaeth yn y Smotyn Du' ('The development of Unitarianism in the Black Spot'). He has contributed an article on Unitarianism in *Ceredigion*, XV, 4 (2008). His work on Unitarianism has also been published in the Unitarian periodical *Yr Ymofynydd*.

D. Hugh Matthews is a retired Baptist minister. Educated in the University of North Wales and Bangor Baptist College, he also undertook postgraduate studies in Spurgeon's College, London. Ordained to the ministry in three small churches in Lampeter in 1961, he was called to pastor Castle Street Welsh Baptist Church in London in 1968. In 1985 he returned to Wales, to teach in Cardiff Baptist College and the University School of Theology. He became Principal of the Baptist College in 1990, retiring in 2001. Between 1978 and 2009 he was editor of the Welsh-language *Transactions of the Baptist Historical Society*, contributing many articles to the publication. He has written several books – mostly in Welsh and most relating to the New Testament.

Brian Phillips was born in Hengoed, Glamorgan in 1935. He left school at fifteen to begin engineering training with Mechanical and Electrical Engineers Department of British Rail, attending the then Glamorgan Technical College at Treforest. He undertook nurse training during national service and returned to work for Renold Ltd, Transmission Engineers. As a Lay-preacher in the Seventh Day Adventists Denomination he conducted services in many parts of South Wales and on Sundays preached in the Chapels and Churches of other denominations. In 1981 he returned to full-time education and graduated with a BA (Hons) degree in Humanities at the Polytechnic of Wales. In 1993 he was awarded a Ph. D. by the University of Glamorgan. He has been a Minister of Religion since 1989 and has served as an observer for Seventh Day Adventists on the Council of Cytûn. He was asked to serve as President of the Welsh Mission of Seventh Day Adventists in the year 2000 and stepped down from that role in 2006.

Robert Pope is Reader in Contemporary and Applied Theology and Head of the School of Theology and Religious Studies at Bangor University. He is the author of a number of books and articles on recent Welsh Nonconformist history and on the interface between theology and culture. He is a member of the Center of Theological Inquiry, Princeton, New Jersey, USA and a minister of the United Reformed Church.

Lavinia Cohn-Sherbok was Principal of West Heath School in Kent and is the author of three novels and several books in the field of Judaism. These include the revised edition of *Who's Who in Jewish History* (London, 2001); and several joint-authored and edited publications (with Dan Cohn-Sherbok), notably *What Do You Do When Your Parents Live Forever?: a practical guide to caring for the elderly*

(Ropley, 2007); *An Encyclopedia of Judaism and Christianity* (London, 2004); *Judaism: a short reader* (Oxford, 2001); *Judaism: a short history* (Oxford, 1994); and *Jewish and Christian Mysticism: an introduction* (New York, 1994).

Shinder S. Thandi is currently Head of the Department of Economics, Finance and Accounting at Coventry University and has teaching interests in areas of development economics and international business in the Asian Pacific. He has published widely on Indian and Punjabi Sikh migration and settlement in the UK and on different dimensions of Indian and Punjabi diaspora-homeland relations. He is founder editor of the *Journal of Punjab Studies* and has co-edited two books: *Punjabi Identity in a Global Context* (edited with Pritam Singh, OUP, 1999) and *People on the Move: Punjabi colonial and post colonial migration* (edited with Ian Talbot, OUP, 2004). He is co-author (with Michael Fisher and Shompa Lahiri) of a recently published book entitled *A South Asian History of Britain: four centuries of peoples from the Indian sub-continent* (Greenwood Press, 2007). His most recent work is on *The Sikh Diaspora: from struggles to celebration*.

Eryn White is a Senior Lecturer in the Department of History and Welsh History at Aberystwyth University. Her research concentrates on aspects of religion and culture in eighteenth-century Wales. She is the author of *'Praidd Bach y Bugail Mawr'*: *seiadau Methodistaidd de-orllewin Cymru* 1737–50 (Llandysul, 1995), *The Welsh Bible* (Stroud, 2007), and co-author of *Calendar of the Trevecka Letters* (Aberystwyth, 2003). She also serves on the editorial board of the *Studies in Welsh History* published by the University of Wales Press.

INDEX

World Council of Churches 251, 252, 254, 255, 256–7
World Pentecostal Fellowship 140
worship:
    charismatic 141–2, 196
    Independent 31
    in Islam 218
    Moravian 112 n. 21
    Quaker 57
    and singing 43
Wright, Richard 117–18
Wroth, William (1575/6–c.1641) 5, 27, 55
Wynne, John, bishop of St Asaph 23 n. 27

Wynne, R. O. F. 72
Wynne, Thomas (1627–1691) 56

Y Cylch Catholig 73, 76
Y Cylchgrawn Efengyllaidd 194
Y Faner (newspaper) 73–4
Y Traethodydd (The Essayist) 85, 192
Y Wesle bach (The Minor Wesleyans) 97–8
Yr Eurgrawn 96, 100

zakat 217
Zinzendorf, Count Nicholas von 107–8